Secondary School
Curriculum Improvement

J. Lloyd Trump
*National Association of
Secondary School Principals*

Delmas F. Miller
West Virginia University

Secondary School Curriculum Improvement

Challenges, Humanism, Accountability

SECOND EDITION

Allyn and Bacon, Inc., Boston

*To Martha Magill Trump
Burley Connor Miller*

Library of Congress Catalog Card Number: 72-87657

Contents

Preface

Turmoil has always affected schools, especially in countries like the United States where the public speaks freely and school people invite opinions. Teachers and principals are expected to have ideas about the curriculum. They also encourage their pupils to participate in curriculum development.

Some writers today apparently believe schools are facing disaster. Sometimes they propose alternatives to schools. Students say the curriculum is not relevant. We think basic changes are necessary; however, we see no reason for panic. We want to help people to make wise choices.

These reasons are why this book focuses on curriculum practitioners. Its targets include teachers in middle schools and junior and senior high schools who keep the curriculum in motion as they seek constantly to develop the maximum potential of each individual pupil, no matter how different his maximum may be from the others. The principals and supervisors who help those teachers constitute an equally significant audience—so do persons who work in state education departments and others who teach and study in universities.

Our aim is to provide materials that will stimulate college and university students and educational practitioners to examine their own thinking about the curriculum and to develop plans to transfer their ideas into school programs that they can accept and manage. The thrust is forward rather than at the current scene.

To set the record straight, we indicate what the book is *not*. We have not made a compilation either of various philosophies of curriculum or of current practices in schools, although references are made at times to both of these topics. We have not assembled extensive references on philosophical statements, descriptions of practices, or reports of research. Anyone interested in such a bibliography may utilize such guides as *Education Index,* the *Encyclopedia of Educational Research,* and the various issues of the *Review of Educational Research,* all of which are found in most education libraries.

We take relatively strong positions on many issues. We believe deeply in these points of view or we would not express them. In fact, that is why we have written this book. We believe that readers also need to establish their own defensible positions—that is our goal for you.

This second edition reflects the increasing rapidity of curriculum change. Increasingly educators recognize the necessity of improving simultaneously all aspects of the school program. Curriculum is more than content. Where teaching and learning occur, the variety of strategies, the evaluation methods, the differentiated staffs that produce changed roles of teachers and learners, and how a school uses time, spaces, numbers in pupil and teacher groups, and money all effect educational quality. Innovations in one area are nullified by failures to change other program aspects because all are interdependent.

Humanistic efforts call for the same global concept of curriculum improvement. The same is true when persons try to hold others accountable for relating financial input to product output in the area of education. This second edition places even more emphasis on those relationships.

The content in parts I, IV, V, and VI represents further development of ideas expressed by J. Lloyd Trump in the book, *Focus on Change—Guide to Better Schools,* published by Rand McNally & Co. in 1960. Articles by the same author on similar topics also have appeared in a number of educational journals, including the following: *American School Board Journal, Bulletin of the American Library Association, The Bulletin of the National Association of Secondary School Principals, California Journal of Secondary Education, The Clearing House, Education, The Education Digest, Educational Forum, Educational Screen and Audio-Visual Guide, The High School Journal of Health, Physical Education and Recreation, The Journal of the National Education Association, Journal of Secondary Education, Michigan Education Journal, Music Educators Journal, NABTA Bulletin, NAEB Journal, North Central Association Quarterly, Pennsylvania University Schoolmen's Week Proceedings, The Phi Delta Kappan, PTA Magazine, Science Teacher, Social Education,* and *Visual Education.*

This revision of *Secondary School Curriculum Improvement*

reflects further developments of the ideas in the foregoing publications. A Model Schools Project, sometimes called Schools of Tomorrow—involving a considerable number of schools—also provides some ideas that are included.

We emphasize ever more than previously the concepts of individualizing learning, humanizing schools, and improving accountability. This second edition also updates many developments in the curriculum content areas.

JLT

DFM

PART I

Challenges and Some
Alternative Responses

CHAPTER 1

What Do You Believe Now?

How will you cope with the critics of your school's program? How would you change schools? How will you make the schools more humane? How will you make schools more accountable for what the program does to pupils and teachers?

Many questions affecting curriculum development divide professional workers in schools and universities. Parents, board of education members, and persons outside the schools also discuss these matters. Research findings are available to help resolve some of the issues, but others require more investigation. However, with or without evidence (but we hope with thoughtful consideration), every middle, junior high, and senior high school staff and the clientele they serve will resolve each issue one way or another—and you may have a part in the decision.

Are schools too permissive or too rigid in the learning environments they provide for pupils and teachers? Should the curriculum resolve such conflicts in society as whether to preserve the environment or enhance technology and economic growth; preserve the older mores or go along with the new freedoms in sexuality, dress, and conduct; stress cooperation more and competition less; and many other issues? What is the relative importance of sensory experiences in schools and conceptual knowledge? Have affective learnings in the curriculum been neglected by an overemphasis on cognitive and skills developments?

What do you believe now? This chapter lists and explains ten issues that are among those which will be discussed more fully in later chapters. At the end of each explanation you are asked to make a decision. After you have read and considered the subsequent material, you may change your mind. Answering the questions now, however, will help you to understand the nature of the secondary school curriculum better. Regardless of your present situation—student, teacher, administrator, supervisor, or someone outside the immediate professional field of education—your opinion is important, because you, along with other experts, will help to formulate the curriculum.

So, we ask you to think carefully about the ten issues that follow. Of course, you may add others if you wish. At the end of the chapter you can check your understanding of the nature of curriculum with the definition we provide.

SOME ISSUES IN CURRICULUM DEVELOPMENT

Who shall determine what is relevant curriculum content for secondary schools?

An increased mobility of students pushes secondary education towards a national curriculum. So does the increased use of such mass communications media as television, radio, newspapers and magazines, standard textbooks, and programed instruction. Many persons recognize the importance of common denominators in the curriculum content of all secondary students in the United States. Increasingly the question is asked, Should pupils in Bangor, Maine; Jackson, Mississippi; Portland, Oregon; or Farmer City, Illinois, be taught different facts, concepts, and skills in United States history? Curriculum programs aimed at national audiences are being developed by university professors and school teachers with foundation, commercial, and federal government support.

Other persons argue that the trend away from local curriculum development is unfortunate—that local initiative and interest are lost as national agencies and groups take over more and more responsibility for curriculum development. There is an accompanying fear of a federal department of education, national examinations, centralized control of materials, and other similar concerns.

Between the extreme positions are those who accept the advisability of a national curriculum for the basic education required for all citizens while preferring that the local school retain control over regional content and the "elective" subjects or "depth education" aspects of the curriculum wherein individual teacher and student interests and talents are manifest. Such persons point out that teaching methods and expenditures for special supplies and equipment tend to be localized. They emphasize that state governments and local districts have effectively resolved conflicts in the past.

What do you believe about this issue? (See Chapter 2 and Part II.)

Shall all pupils be expected to remain in the secondary school six years?

A three-year junior high school (grades 7, 8, and 9) followed by a three-year senior high school (grades 10, 11, and 12), or a six-year school (grades 7 through 12), constitutes the commonly accepted organization of secondary education in the United States. Because of their high ability and high motivation, some students are able to complete this program and pass examinations satisfactorily in less than six years. However, they may be kept productively busy for the six-year period through the provision of enrichment materials.

Shall there be more rapid acceleration through the schools or shall there be more enrichment of subject matter at each grade level, the amount of extra work being based on individual differences among students? Another suggested alternative is to eliminate annual promotions and to ungrade the schools so that each student may progress at his own rate of speed. (These ideas are discussed further in Chapter 22.) These decisions, of course, affect articulation with the elementary school and with the freshman year of college.

Related to this issue is the question of admitting what are now regarded as elementary-age pupils to secondary education in a "middle school." This school may include pupils formerly enrolled in the fifth grade and some advanced fourth graders. Television and other mass media produce more sophisticated and informed children. Should the new secondary school serve pupils eight or more years? How do the number of years affect the curriculum?

How shall pupils be grouped for instruction?

Most schools conduct instruction in a given subject in a self-contained classroom, with one teacher responsible for twenty-five to thirty-five students. Sometimes these classes are divided into subgroups on the basis of ability or achievement. When there is more than one section of a given subject, the entire class may be grouped on the basis of ability or past achievement. However, the issue is

5

not necessarily one of homogeneous versus heterogeneous ability or achievement grouping. Other grouping plans are also being demonstrated in schools.

Some schools vary the size and composition of pupil groups, depending on the purposes and content of instruction and the needs of individual students. The issue is whether to organize classes of twenty-five with heterogeneous or homogeneous grouping or to use a combination of independent study, large-group instruction, and small-group discussion—three terms that are discussed in chapters 18, 19, and 20, respectively.

What type of grouping do you prefer? Will it be the same for all subjects?

To what extent shall individual programing of pupils be encouraged?

As pupils mature and receive more education, the individual differences among them increase. How much of a pupil's day should be spent in classes required of everyone and how much of his day should be spent in work that is particularly interesting and appropriate for him as an individual? Are the "required-elective" system and the conventional school schedule for curriculum organization superior to a system of "basic-depth" education (see Chapter 22) and flexible scheduling (see Chapter 23)?

The present system of programing and scheduling has evolved over many years as a systematic way to measure subject credits, graduation requirements, teacher and pupil class loads, and a variety of other administrative arrangements. The system is widely accepted and understood by pupils, parents, and teachers. But what about the relationships between quantity and quality?

The issue is, Can individual differences among pupils be served adequately in a conventionally organized curriculum or are basic changes needed? The alternatives to the two extreme points of view involve the variety of rationalized changes presented in parts IV and V.

What do you believe now?

Shall the curriculum content be organized into discrete subject-matter areas or into broad fields that integrate the materials?

Curriculum developers throughout the centuries have organized human knowledge in a variety of ways. Traditionally, the secondary schools in this country have taught such subjects as English, social studies or social sciences (history, geography, civics, economics, etc.), science (botany, zoology, biology, physics, chemistry, etc.), mathematics (algebra, geometry, etc.), music, art, agriculture, auto mechanics and so on, as discrete subject-matter areas. (We use that organization of curriculum content in this book in chapters 4 through 14.) Those who favor this approach to content point out that it eases the transition from secondary school to university, since universities follow similar patterns. The vocational goals of pupils also are stated in subject-matter terms: an engineer needs to know science and mathematics in addition to other professional skills; a writer needs to specialize in English; an attorney needs basic education in the social sciences. Those who favor discrete subjects point out that integration and correlation of content occurs in the mind of the learner as he calls on what he has learned in the various subject disciplines.

Other curriculum authorities prefer to structure content according to life experiences and needs, contending that every experience requires knowledge in many subjects. For example, preparing for effective home and family living requires understandings not only in home economics, but also in mathematics, social studies, English, fine and practical arts, sciences, health and physical education, and, in fact, every other curricular area. Understanding the concept of *democracy* also requires study of many subject disciplines. Curriculum writers urge "core," "integrated," "broad fields," and other combinations of subject content.

An alternative to the two extremes might be the use of the discrete subject-matter approach in the basic education required of all pupils and the integrated subject-matter approach in the depth education programs which the school sponsors as a part of the independent study program; or you could argue a converse arrangement. ("Basic education," "depth education" and "independent study" are discussed in chapters 2 and 18.)

At the present time, what is your opinion about the organization of curriculum content?

Who shall operate programs of work experience education?

Not all youth profit from a totally academic or school-building-centered educational program. Some of these pupils drop out of school, and others stay reluctantly, with limited gains. During the 1930's, the National Youth Administration and the Civilian Conservation Corps, federally supported and operated work experience programs, apparently met the needs of large numbers of students. Many schools today engage in work programs to a limited degree (for example, in distributive education), but such efforts reach relatively few students. Both federal and state agencies emphasize *career education*. They often propose work experience programs similar in many respects to those of the 1930's. Also, more funds for vocational education are proposed. Why did these earlier programs fail to become integral parts of the curriculum for all students?

Should junior and senior high schools deal mainly with the academically oriented pupils and leave work experience programs to federal agencies or to industry? (See Chapter 14.) Another aspect of the issue concerns the acceptance of the idea of the comprehensive high school as opposed to separate academic and vocational schools. A third is whether vocational schools should be operated by federal agencies rather than by local or area administrations.

Other curriculum questions revolve around the need for such specialized courses as *business* English, *shop* mathematics, or *pre-engineering* science. Should basic education be the same for all students, work-bound or college-bound, with adaptations being made at the level of electives or depth education?

What would you decide and on what basis?

Shall more or less emphasis be placed on extraclass (co-curricular) activities?

Today's emphasis on extra homework for the regular school subjects cuts into the time pupils may give to athletics, clubs, social activities, publications, and other school activities. So do nationally televised programs. Is the need for extraclass activities diminishing? Most teachers enjoy working with students in extraclass activities, but some object to this "extra work" for a variety of reasons.

Should the school turn over these activities to various youth-serving agencies in the community? Many school people argue strongly against that solution, pointing out that the extraclass program complements the other curriculum services to students. They object to the pressures placed on pupils by persons and agencies outside the school who may not visualize the total needs of individual pupils.

An alternate solution of the problem is to recognize extraclass activities as an integral part of the curriculum. This solution requires changes in school schedules, assignment of teachers, school records and reports, and similar matters.

How would you resolve the issue? (See Chapter 15.) What activities, if any, would you add or subtract?

To what extent should schools attempt to supplement the work of parents, society in general, and social agencies?

The location of some schools produces de facto segregation of pupils along racial, religious, or national lines. Some persons argue that such a distribution affects curriculum adversely. They argue that pupils should be transferred from one area to another to create a more balanced distribution, bussing the children if necessary. Others argue that the fault is with housing regulations or social mores and the school should not do what society itself has not done.

Parents should provide sex education in the home, according to some persons. Others point effectively to parental failures along these lines and urge comprehensive sex education programs in schools. Analogous arguments are presented concerning the school's role in health education, religious education, moral training, and the like. Should the schools do what parents fail to do or do ineffectively?

Family incomes vary widely. Should schools provide free services to students who cannot afford to pay while charging others for the same provisions? Should the school serve as a social agency when economic opportunities are limited for some pupils?

What is your belief about these and similar issues? (Information on the foregoing questions occurs throughout this book, especially in parts II and III.)

Are school programs too permissive or too rigid in the learning and teaching environments they provide for students and teachers?

The terms, "open" and "closed" are used to describe schools. Students in open schools can study where they want to with no required attendance. Teachers and administrators hold them responsible for performance and passing tests and other measures of productivity. The closed environment aims to keep all students in classrooms for specified periods of time with emphasis on attendance and control. Educational progressives advocate the open school; the conservatives believe in the closed philosophy. Similar beliefs divide the students and their parents. School principals and their assistants find themselves in the middle of a hot controversy.

How would you resolve this dilemma?

How shall increased funds be spent
to improve educational quality?

Educators' professional organizations frequently argue that increased funds should be spent for higher salaries for teachers and for smaller classes. However, some persons contend that those factors alone do not produce better educational quality, so increased expenditures are also needed for technical devices, clerical services, and instruction assistants to aid teaching and learning. These persons also ask for more free time for teachers so that they may keep up to date, confer more with their professional colleagues, and perform other professional tasks. Generally speaking, schools spend much more money on buildings and less on tools than do industrial organizations.

Should financial input be related more scientifically to educational output? (Chapters 25, 28, and 30 will explore this question in more detail.) Does curriculum improvement require different criteria than schools use now in spending the funds they receive?

Who is responsible for increased accountability in the use of school funds, materials, spaces, and the time of pupils and teachers? How is the content of curriculum related to accountability? Who will determine the performance criteria that show the productivity of the institution?

What do you think? Do you have ideas about what expenditures school officials might reduce in order to have more funds for the research and development of new ideas? Are industrial development ideas appropriate for schools?

Should schools abandon the Carnegie Unit or similar
measures of learning in favor of performance based
criteria that do not involve standard time modules?

The conventional method for recording pupil progress through the school program and for graduation is to give credit for a course when a pupil spends 200 to 250 minutes per week for 18 weeks (.5 credit) or 36 weeks (1 unit), having earned at least the minimum passing grade—typically D–. The proposed alternative is to give the credit whenever a pupil passes the tests and does whatever else is required in an acceptable manner, regardless of how long he requires. The latter alternative is basic to the continuous progress or ungraded concept which individualized learning emphasizes (see Chapter 22). Yet, universities require definite numbers of units for entrance and so do many high schools in accepting pupils from other schools or for determining who receives a diploma. How might this issue be resolved?

Shall the common A, B, C, D, F system for evaluating pupil achievement be replaced by a P, F (pass, fail) system or by more comprehensive schemes that record each student's progress in completing specified segments in various sequences of learnings, describe special projects completed, and appraise other selected outcomes, especially in the affective domain?

Two basic issues actually are involved. One question is whether the school shall recognize and formalize *failure* in the final appraisal and reporting system or whether it will only report the student's progress or lack of it. The other issue is whether the school shall collect and report much more data than single letter grades, including P, F, describe. Since the reporting system influences pupil goals and parental aspirations, the issue is basic. Of course, a related issue concerns the degree to which the school's pupil evaluation system emphasizes competition among pupils vis-à-vis a pupil's competition with his own past record. All these matters are discussed in Chapter 27.

What do you believe about the grading system?

What criteria shall be used in evaluating the excellence of a given school?

The evaluative criteria typically used by accrediting associations and state education departments are being questioned by some persons. So are the values of such factors as the number of merit scholarship winners in a school, pupil performance on standardized achievement tests, the quality of the school building, and the public relations program.

Is it possible and important to measure growth in individual responsibility for learning and the quality of what students do while engaged in independent study? Or is it sufficient to use data from the usual standardized achievement tests? Having defined school goals in terms of changes in pupil behavior, can a school discover whether these changes actually have occurred? Or is possession of knowledge a sufficient test of educational outcomes? Do qualitative judgments have a place in evaluation, along with the collection of quantitative data and the professional interpretation of the data? What criteria deserve highest priorities? What is a workable scheme? (See chapters 26 and 27.)

Again, what do you believe?

Shall the present arrangements for educating youth be replaced by completely different programs and procedures or can present schools be modified to accommodate the proposals that critics are making?

Because most schools either ignore community resources or else use them only minimally or incorrectly, some writers urge "schools without walls." That arrangement calls for schools in warehouses, office buildings, or abandoned stores that serve only as headquarters while most learning is in community agencies, institutions, offices, museums, factories, and the like. The alternative is individualized, flexible scheduling and a variety of curricular changes (see chapters 23, 25, and 30).

One more example is to abolish credential requirements for teachers and principals because present preparation programs produce so many educators who oppose change and do not relate well to the people and problems in the "real world." These critics would replace principals with experts on social change drawn from industry and other fields outside of education. Similarly, lay persons would be recruited as teachers, with a preparation program completely different from the present teacher education curricula.

Are there other alternatives?

FACTORS THAT AFFECT THE CURRICULUM

Answering the foregoing questions reveals a number of factors that enter into a definition of the curriculum: content, methods, and structure. We use the term "structure" in a broad sense to include organization, configuration, facilities, resources, time, and numbers—the educational setting for teaching and learning.

The answers also point out the human dimensions in curriculum. The characteristics and needs of individual pupils are basic considerations. Equally important are the needs and characteristics of each teacher, especially the manner in which his competences are utilized.

The school principal is the key administrator in each school so far as the curriculum is concerned. Political, social, economic, and other cultural forces outside the school also influence the curriculum. Various supervisors and administrators and a host of other persons are doing research, producing materials, issuing pronouncements, raising funds, and taking political action. Vigorous statements by prestigious individuals and groups influence what teachers do. Research focuses on particular learning theories and teaching methods creating special styles in teaching and learning. Foundations, governments, corporations, and organizations provide funds to foster particular curricular ideas and special programs for the education of teachers and students. These influences and others are explored in some detail in chapters 2 and 3.

A TIME OF INNOVATION

A recent survey by the National Association of Secondary School Principals revealed numerous exemplary programs in the use of television, video-tape, data processing, telephone amplification, dial-access systems, minority studies, drug studies, use of learning packages, differentiated staffing, flexible scheduling, team teaching, independent study, use of teacher-counselors, changed grading systems, and other innovations. Today's secondary schools are especially innovative in challenging many traditional beliefs about curriculum content, methods, and structure.

Are these curricular innovations merely fads which teachers and principals follow in order to be up-to-date? Consider what often happens when a course outline is revised, or the schedule is changed, or a learning resources center is added to the curriculum. The revision may exhilarate the teachers and pupils but an evaluation after the change has operated for a period of time shows limited or no pupil gains. Curriculum restructuring requires coordinated, innovative approaches. Attempting to alter any one aspect of the curriculum—content, for instance—without varying teaching and learning methods and structure in a carefully conceived *instructional system* limits the effectiveness of the changes. All factors must change together if the maximum potential benefits are to be realized. Parts III, IV, and V of this book amplify these statements.

DEFINING CURRICULUM

The conventional way to define curriculum is to refer to the variety of instructional activities planned and provided for pupils by the local school or school system. The definition is all right; it simply lacks vigor. Curriculum is a vital, moving, complex interaction of people and things in a free-wheeling setting. It includes questions to debate, forces to rationalize, goals to illuminate, programs to activate, and outcomes to evaluate. These topics are what this book is all about.

Chapter 2 lists the authors' basic beliefs about teaching and learning. You must accept, reject, or modify these beliefs—and possibly add some others—as background for your work. Chapter 3 helps you to understand the current pressures for curriculum change.

Part II of this book helps you understand the curriculum issues and major developments in eleven secondary school subject areas. Extraclass activities and adult education are discussed in Part III. Part IV deals with education setting and Part V with evaluation. The final section, Part VI, suggests ways to organize for change, the need for different teaching roles, and how to plan and conduct experimental studies and demonstrations. Some pitfalls to be avoided are identified.

By the time you finish this book, you will have a sound, coordinated basis for secondary school curriculum improvement in your school. This broad operational plan is more likely to produce significant gains in learning for each individual pupil than would a narrow, segmented approach to change. As part of the improvement program, you will take important steps to professionalize the teaching staff and to recognize their individual differences. You will understand that secondary school curriculum improvement requires more than revising content. All aspects are interrelated.

TOPICS FOR STUDY AND DISCUSSION

1. From the fifteen issues listed in this chapter, select the one that interests you the most. Read as much material on this issue as time permits, then prepare a case on one side or the other to present to your colleagues.
2. What other educational issues affecting curriculum planning and development seem important to you? List at least one and indicate the arguments on either side.
3. Who should decide issues of curriculum development? What are the roles of teachers, school administrators, parents, and the public? What is the role of the curriculum expert? Which goals are local, state, or national concerns?

SELECTED REFERENCES

ALEXANDER, WILLIAM M., ed. "Issues in Secondary School Curriculum Improvement." In *The Changing Secondary School Curriculum—Readings*. New York: Holt, Rinehart & Winston, Inc., 1967, pp. 203–394.

Concerns the search for curriculum content; organization of staff, facilities, and time; the provisions for individual differences, and balance and diversity in secondary school curriculum.

BENT, RUDYARD K., and UNRUH, ADOLPH. "Criticisms and Issues" and "Educational Revolution." In *Secondary School Curriculum.* Lexington, Mass: D. C. Heath and Company, 1969.

Provides another statement of issues and some approaches to solving them.

BRACKENBURY, ROBERT L. "Guidelines to Help Schools Formulate and Validate Objectives." In *Rational Planning in Curriculum and Instruction.* Washington, D.C.: National Education Association, Center for the Study of Instruction, 1967, pp. 89–108.

Provides a rationale for effective analysis and evaluation of curriculum issues.

DOLL, RONALD C. "Resolving Forces in Curriculum Decision-Making." In *Curriculum Improvement: Decision-Making and Process.* Boston: Allyn and Bacon, Inc., 1964, pp. 94–116.

Summarizes historical, psychological, social, and content forces that affect curriculum and shows how decision making relates to process.

FOSHAY, ARTHUR W. "The Agenda." In *Curriculum for the 70's: An Agenda for Invention.* Washington, D.C.: National Education Association Center for the Study of Instruction, 1971.

Emphasizes student participation in curriculum plans, the subject disciplines as general education, and humaneness in education.

GOODLAD, JOHN I. "Curriculum as a Field of Study." In *School, Curriculum, and the Individual.* Waltham, Massachusetts: Blaisdell Publishing Co., 1966, pp. 27–47.

Delineates the field with special attention to decision making and conceptual systems in curriculum development.

GROSS, RONALD, and OSTERMAN, PAUL, eds. "Wanted: A Humane Education." In *High School.* New York: Simon and Schuster, 1971, pp. 108–21.

The Montgomery County, Md. Student Alliance, a group of high school students, criticizes the schools for creating fear, dishonesty, destroying eagerness to learn, and a number of other shortcomings. They have twenty-four suggestions ranging from the evaluation system through the curriculum, to the need for students on the School Board.

KIRST, MICHAEL W., and WALKER, DECKER F. "An Analysis of Curriculum Policy Making." *Review of Educational Research,* vol. 41, no.5 (December 1971), pp. 479–509.

Shows the many groups and individuals within and outside schools that shape curricula, showing how the necessity for long-range planning, the ambiguity of educational goals, and the meager knowledge of schooling occurs leaving the field wide open.

NATIONAL ASSOCIATION OF SECONDARY SCHOOL PRINCIPALS. "Humanizing the Schools." *NASSP Bulletin,* vol. 56, no. 361 (February 1972).

Articles by Fred T. Wilhems, Charles R. Keller, and J. Lloyd Trump describe general features of humanistic schools. John M. Jenkins, Loren S. Jones, and Catherine Hopper, two principals and an assistant, tell how to do it in schools. Other authors, mostly teachers, describe changes in subject areas.

POPPER, SAMUEL H. "Dysfunctions and Instability." In *The American Middle School.* Waltham, Massachusetts: Blaisdell Publishing Co., 1967, pp. 187–225.

Analyzes the differences between theory and practice in junior high schools and suggests a technique useful in resolving curriculum issues and planning improvements.

SILBERMAN, CHARLES E. *Crisis in the Classroom.* New York: Random House, 1970, pp. vii–552.

See especially, chapters 4, "Education for Docility," and 8, ". . . Reforming the High School," pp. 113–57 and 323–69. The first reference criticizes what elementary and secondary schools do to pupils; the second suggests some solutions—both documented from school situations.

CHAPTER 2

Some Beliefs We Accept

Now that you have examined some of your beliefs about the curriculum, you need to know the special biases of the authors, because this book represents a selective rather than an encyclopedic treatment of the secondary school curriculum.

You should know first of all that we both have worked to change and improve schools for many years. The terms, individualization, humanization, relevancy, accountability, better utilization of teacher competences, behavioral objectives, criterion-referenced evaluation, curriculum reform, and the like, are old ones to us. We have worked with teachers, principals, and professors in a variety of local, state, and national projects for several decades.

We do not believe that the only way to improve the curriculum is to abandon the secondary school for some alternative enterprise. Nor do we believe that changing the name of a school or the grades it includes or who controls it will insure the kinds of curriculum improvements that we urge in this volume. We regard many of the proposals and developments urged today as alternatives to schools constitute mythical changes rather than basic improvements.

We know that it is difficult and time-consuming to improve the curriculum. We have much to say along those lines in the latter part of this book. Presently one of us is working with a group of schools in a longitudinal effort that exemplifies this concept of carefully conceptualized curriculum improvement in local schools by following a model for a period of years.

We believe in the comprehensive-type secondary school with

a balanced curriculum designed to serve the widely varied interests and talents of *all* the children in the United States. We believe that similar goals should guide curriculum developments in other countries.

Conversely, we reject such ideas as the following: some curricular areas are more important than others; some methods of teaching and learning may be used constantly to the exclusion of others; some young people are more important than others; and youth in one part of the country is more important than youth in other parts.

We believe that the basic purpose of education is to develop the curiosity and creativity found in all small children. We accept the challenge to help each person discover his interests and develop his talents as effectively as possible. Of course, we recognize that people exist in a variety of social groups, so we must emphasize effective communications and relationships among individuals and groups for the maximum benefit of both. We believe that the school, as an educational institution, must not isolate itself from the families that produce the pupils or from the society in which the school exists.

We believe that nowhere in the world have so many children and youth been educated so well as in the United States. We also believe that this superiority lies in the constant search for better ways of teaching and learning. We foresee even more rapid changes in curriculum content, methodology, and the educational setting. We think that schools need to make better use of the professional talents of teachers and principals, the potential capacities of learners, the purchasing power of school monies, the resources of communities, and the findings of educational research.

SOME RECENT HISTORICAL STATEMENTS EXPRESSING BASIC TENETS

We accept the broad purposes of secondary education as expressed in several landmark statements issued at different times during the past one-half century. Such declarations share the beliefs that the secondary school is designed to serve *all* young people and that its curriculum should encompass preparation for college, for work, for civic responsibilities, for effective living at home and at school, for artistic experiences, and for coping as a well-adjusted human being with oneself and with others.

That broad concept of secondary education was expressed in 1918 by the Commission on the Reorganization of Secondary

Education in the famous *Seven Cardinal Principles of Education*.[1] Readers will recall these seven goals: health, command of fundamental processes, worthy home membership, vocation, citizenship, worthy use of leisure time, and ethical character.

Almost twenty years later, in January 1937, a Committee on the Orientation of Secondary Education, appointed by the Department of Secondary Principals of the National Education Association (later called the National Association of Secondary School Principals) and chaired by Thomas H. Briggs, issued an influential statement entitled, "Functions of Secondary Education."[2] These ten functions may be summarized as follows:

1. To provide for the integration of students by identifying the common knowledge, appreciations, ideals, attitudes, and practices needed by all.
2. To satisfy the students' important immediate and probable future needs in the areas of social and personal values.
3. To reveal the racial heritage of experience and culture so that students are challenged as individuals and groups to higher levels of responsibility and achievement.
4. To explore higher and increasingly specialized interests, aptitudes, and capacities of students.
5. To systematize knowledge previously acquired or being acquired to show wider ranges of application.
6. To establish and develop interests in the major fields of human activity.
7. To guide students into wholesome and worthwhile social relationships, to maximum personality adjustment, and to advanced studies for vocations in which they are most likely to be successful and happy.
8. To use in all courses methods that involve independent thought, research, and somewhat self-directed practice in desirable activities.
9. To increase differentiated education on the evidence of capacities, aptitudes, and interests of students while providing a balanced, general education for them.
10. To retain each student until he is ready for more independent study in some other school or direct him to work for which he seems most fit.

Less than a decade later, the NASSP published *Planning for American Youth*,[3] describing an educational program for youths of

[1] NEA Commission on the Reorganization of Secondary Education, *Cardinal Principles of Secondary Education*, U.S. Bureau of Education Bulletin 1918, no. 35, GPO, 1918.
[2] "Functions of Secondary Education," *Bulletin of the Department of Secondary School Principals*, vol. 21, no. 64 (January 1937), pp. 5–226.
[3] *Planning for American Youth* (Washington, D.C.: The National Association of Secondary School Principals, 1945), pp. 2–63.

secondary school age based upon *Education for ALL American Youth*,[4] the 1944 statement of NEA's Educational Policies Commission. The following ten imperative needs of youth were identified on the assumption that *"All* youth have certain educational needs in common. All parents can agree that the school should meet these needs, which become the modern goals of education." The ten youth needs may be summarized as follows:

1. To acquire salable skills and the understanding and attitudes of successful workers.
2. To develop good health, physical fitness, and mental health.
3. To understand and fulfill obligations in the community, state, nation, and world.
4. To learn about conditions conducive to successful family life.
5. To purchase and use goods and services wisely.
6. To understand the methods of science and the influence of science on human life.
7. To develop the capacity to appreciate beauty in literature, art, music, and nature.
8. To use leisure well.
9. To develop respect for other persons, to live and work cooperatively with others, and to grow in the moral and spiritual values of life.
10. To think rationally, to express thoughts clearly, and to read and listen with understanding.

That the main considerations guiding curriculum and school development have not changed basically is indicated in *Schools for the 60's*,[5] a publication of the NEA Center on Instruction. That volume's thirty-three recommendations emphasize such concerns as the following:

There is a need for coordinated decision making by local, state, and federal authorities toward improving the curriculum.

Not less than 1 percent of school system budgets should be allocated for research, experimentation, and innovation.

Opportunities are needed for developing the individual potentialities represented in the wide range of differences among people.

There is a common fund of knowledge, values, and skills vital to the welfare of the individual and the nation.

National problems, including controversial issues and the study of communism, should be included in the curriculum.

The curriculum should offer a comprehensive program of required studies and at the same time provide individualized programs for each student based on careful counseling.

[4] *Education for ALL American Youth* (Washington, D.C.: Educational Policies Commission, National Education Association, 1944), pp. v–421.
[5] *Schools for the 60's*, Project on Instruction, National Education Association (New York: McGraw-Hill Book Co., 1963), pp. v–146.

The vertical organization of the school should provide for the continuous progression of all learners.
The assignment of pupils to classroom groups should be based on knowledge of students and teachers and an understanding of the goals to be reached.
New instructional materials and technology should be located in appropriate spaces in the school.
New concepts of space should permit and encourage independent study, access to a variety of instructional media, and groups ranging from small seminars to multiple-class meetings.

The NEA Center on Instruction has continued urging similar ideas in a series of statements called *Schools for the 70's and Beyond*.[6] Three phrases—Individualization, Humanization, and Accountability—occur frequently in the literature.

THE HUMANE SCHOOL

The following outline characterizes the humane school that we believe treats learners and teachers as individuals, each with unique programs and responsibilities:

1. Focuses on options rather than on uniformity in developing and administering policies and practices. In other words, it does not subject each individual to group standards even though it informs him about model behaviors and procedures.
2. Devises a program for each pupil in which he can move forward with success in terms of his own talents and interests no matter how diverse they may be.
3. Makes sure that every pupil is known as a total human being, educationally, by a teacher-adviser, who helps him personally to diagnose his needs, plan his program, make and change his schedule, evaluate his results, and plan accordingly for the future. (This procedure goes far beyond the typical homeroom or the programing by school counselors or assistant principals.)
4. Creates an environment in which each teacher may make maximum utilization of his professional talents and interests, that recognizes individual differences among teachers and provides differentiated staffing help to identify better the role of the professional teacher.
5. Separates curriculum content so that each learner knows what is *essential* for everyone as distinct from the cognitive, skill, and affective behaviors that are important for those

[6] *Schools for the 70's and Beyond: A Call to Action*, NEA Center for the Study of Instruction (Washington, D.C., National Education Association, 1971), pp. iii–148.

learners with special goals in the areas of hobbies and careers. The goal here is to reduce greatly the *required* learnings so that each pupil at all ages has more time than now to develop and follow his special interests.

6. Systematically tries to interest each pupil and teacher in learning more than he thinks he wants to learn. The technique is through motivational presentations and discussions.

7. Practices accountability for pupils and teachers, realizing that such procedures show that the school *cares* as opposed to permissiveness or vagueness that indicates that it does not worry about what happens to individuals.

8. Provides a variety of places in the school and in the community where pupils may study and work under supervision so that each pupil may find learning strategies that suit him best instead of being required to learn in one classroom under only one teacher.

9. Has continuous progress arrangements so that each pupil may progress at his own pace under competent supervision with a variety of self-directing, self-motivating, and self-evaluating materials and locations.

10. Evaluates pupil progress and teacher performance on the basis of the individual's own past record rather than on a comparison with others in the same group while at the same time provides data that will help each person know what others are accomplishing.

11. Substitutes constructive reports of achievements for the threat of failure as the prime motivational device of the school. The school records the special projects that each pupil completes, no matter how small, that go beyond what the school requires of everyone.

12. Recognizes that the principal more than any one other person creates a humane environment in the school; therefore, frees him from routine managerial tasks so he can get out of the office to work with pupils and teachers to develop more humane programs and procedures for everyone.[7]

The concept of the school's accountability is discussed in detail elsewhere in this volume.

ESTABLISHING PRIORITIES FOR CURRICULUM IMPROVEMENT

As you read this book and think about curriculum improvement, you will need to select your directions carefully. Obviously, you cannot do everything at once even though you are likely to discover

[7] J. Lloyd Trump, "On Humanizing Schools—Point of View and Basic Issues," *NASSP Bulletin*, The National Association of Secondary School Principals, vol. 56, no. 361 (February 1972), pp. 9–16.

soon that one change affects other curricular aspects.   So, you will need to decide what matters most.

We devote the rest of this chapter to some priorities we believe deserve early consideration.   The order of the subsequent topics is not significant.   We repeat, you need to set your own order of priorities.   Some of the topics represent educational clichés; almost everyone writes and talks about them.   The questions are: will you do something about them? and which ones will you tackle first?

Refining curriculum content

A major overhaul is needed in the curriculum content of all subject fields.   The task includes identifying the differences between *basic materials* and those which are in the realm of *creativity* and *special interests*, for today's conventional schools often require much content that pupils neither want nor need.   Inclusion of unnecessary material causes many students to lose interest—they may rebel or become underachievers.   Even worse, they may lack the time and energy to follow their special interests and to develop their unique talents.

Required learnings.   To determine basic, or fundamental, education, teachers and curriculum experts must identify the facts, concepts, skills, and appreciations that are *essential* in our society for anyone who is educable.   Beyond that minimum, the schools should also identify the content which is *desirable* for most people, and that which is *enriching* for the specially talented.   It is possible that national groups will identify this curriculum content for all persons in the United States.   Then other groups can add materials needed by persons in a given state.   Local teachers will complete the content by adding topics regarded as essential for the local community and region.   The foundational content must be arranged logically and sequentially so that the pupils progress continuously from the time they enter the school program until they leave to go to work or to continue in a higher institution.

The required work should be held to a minimum.   The evaluative question is: what progress has been made toward identifying essential content?   For example, what facts about the history of the United States are *essential* for the "good American"?   What mathematics does the typical person—not the engineer or scientist —need?   Is memorizing the names and dates of the popes essential for proper religious behavior?

Typically, pupils should have to devote only one-half of their school time to basic learning.   The rest of the time should be used to pursue special interests, no matter how transitory, with the professional aid of an appropriate teacher. Unfortunately, most of today's curriculum planning and development projects add to the pupil's burden or required learnings rather than reducing the quantity through refinement.

Creativity and depth education. The teacher should provide extra information and make assignments that will motivate pupils to go beyond the fundamental or required content in creative ways or in greater depth. Such a program would eliminate the outmoded "required and elective" system, which often limits the breadth of experience for pupils in the upper years by keeping them away from fine and practical arts or from specialized work in mathematics or literature. The average pupil may complete the *essential* content by the time he is sixteen years of age so that his basic education beyond that occupies only 10 to 20 percent of his school time. (He always needs some time to keep up to date, refresh his memory, or correct wrong information learned earlier.) He devotes the rest of his time to creativity and depth studies in the world of work or advanced studies leading to the university.

The teacher should use content that has been developed nationally and regionally, only accepting or criticizing what the experts have done. The time and effort saved may be spent more profitably on planning how to relate local content to the essential national and regional materials.

Way to separate content. A three-way division may help teachers in a local school to solve the problem of required vis-à-vis elective content. First, as suggested earlier, the required content in all areas of human knowledge is what everyone in the society needs to know to live adequately. A second level is what a given pupil needs to know and do in order to enjoy hobbies that arise from special interests that the school had stimulated through the required content and the motivational presentations that will be described in Chapter 19. The third level aims to provide content for pupils who wish to discover options in careers.

In history, for example, teachers need to provide answers to these questions: what content is essential for everyone in order to help make effective decisions? what content is needed for pupils who become interested in a hobby of special interests in some aspects of history? what content is necessary for the pupil who plans to become a professional historian, to make his living by using or developing some aspects of history? The same questions are relevant for all areas. Even though a teacher in a local school uses a state or city curriculum, he needs to make the three-way separation available to pupils.

Motivation

The quality of a pupil's learning is related directly to the effectiveness of his motivation. Young people, like all of us, are motivated by contacts with stimulating personalities or exciting ideas. Students want to write poetry when they are in contact with a great poet or a teacher who loves poetry and knows how to stimulate the interest of other persons.

Motivation depends on the nature of the assignments and the diversity of learning experiences. It also is stimulated by placing students in situations where each can work at his own pace. Conversely, motivation is destroyed when the able student must sit in class until less able pupils catch up or are removed for remedial work. It is impaired also when a student is in a class beyond his capability and consequently is frustrated by his own comparisons with other students who are much more able and interested at the moment than he is.

Evaluation, of course, directly influences pupil motivation. How the teacher reacts to a pupil's independent study efforts is crucial. Young people who are constantly compared with others in an unfavorable manner soon lose interest.

Much of the material in Part IV of this book bears on improved motivation. We believe the importance of motivation calls for basic changes in the curriculum setting. Many practices in today's schools destroy pupil interest and produce the considerable number of reluctant learners and disinterested students who occupy such a noticeable place in the secondary classrooms of this country. On the other hand, we are not enchanted by motivation that results from a fear of failing crucial examinations such as those given in many European schools or the College Board Examinations of the United States.

Problem solving

Although it may be unrealistic to assume that a school's curriculum can be organized entirely around problems for students to solve, the excellence of instruction and learning will be influenced by the degree to which students can pick areas of the curriculum to analyze, divide those areas into meaningful parts, attack each aspect intellectually and systematically by collecting appropriate information and interpreting effectively what they discover, and then arrive at defensible solutions. Students do not have to discover everything for themselves, but the process of discovery and analysis is one to be encouraged and learned to the fullest extent possible.

The assignments which teachers provide for students should stimulate the higher mental processes. Some memorization, of course, is essential to learning, but the memorization should enable students to engage in higher mental activities rather than merely passing the next examination or participating in a discussion during the next ten minutes.

Value development

Values are learned best by practice, but they also are accumulated as pupils encounter vicarious experiences in listening, viewing, and reading. The instructional program should help pupils to relate appropriate knowledge from various fields. Habits of extensive reading, writing, and oral communication, and values that call for creative efforts, are developed systematically by the school curriculum, not by accident.

The school program speaks louder than the goals expressed in a curriculum guide. A curriculum that requires the fine arts only through grade eight says very loudly to the students that "the fine arts are unimportant in the lives of citizens." (No wonder so many homes are poorly decorated and our cities have so much ugliness in them.) A school curriculum that says to students, "This year you must care about science [or United States history] and then you can forget about it for two years [or completely]," is not developing the idea that a person should *always* keep his eyes and ears open for new developmnts or interesting ideas in all areas of human knowledge.

Individual pupil goals

Each person should strive for the following educational goals: the skills of study, the desire to study, and the state of keeping constantly up to date in all areas of human knowledge while seeking new truths and better ways of doing things. A curriculum designed to further these goals differs in many respects from the one existing in many of today's schools, where a subject is required at a given stage in a pupil's development, a grade is given and credit is extended largely on the basis of local examinations, and then the subject may be forgotten. The evaluation of pupil progress should emphasize the objectives listed above. To realize these goals, each pupil must spend relatively more time in independent study—sometimes individual and sometimes in small groups—and comparatively less time in standard-sized classes doing much the same things as the others in the class.

Individualization of instruction that aims to develop each pupil's maximum potential requires the emphasis in evaluation described in chapters 26 and 27. The school then compares the individual mainly with his own past accomplishments rather than with other pupils in the class.

Individual programing requires flexible scheduling so that a student at any given time, based on a professional decision of teachers and counselors, may spend greatly increased amounts of time working in a science laboratory, an art room, or the gymnasium or engaged in some civic, aesthetic, or work experience outside the school. Responsibility for learning is developed only as individuals have opportunities to make their own choices. Although the school should reserve the right of final decisions about a pupil's program, the aim should be to give each pupil as much responsibility as possible.

Teacher goals

The basic goal of every teacher insofar as his pupils are concerned is to become dispensable, as rapidly and as completely as possible. That purpose requires that the teacher place more responsibility on learners. It colors his assignments and his activities in ways that are described throughout this volume. The teacher's success is measured in terms of what the pupils do when the teacher is not present—what they do in the resource centers or at home at night, on Saturday, or during the summer months when classes are not in session.

A second basic goal of teachers is to become more professional. This goal requires that they go far beyond their efforts to obtain higher salaries and more elaborate teaching certificates with increased hours in their subject areas or in the professional field of education. Teachers need to discover what they must do themselves and what can be done by less costly clerks and instruction assistants. They have to understand what they must teach personally and what students can learn largely by themselves through the use of such devises as programed learning (teaching machines and teaching books), television, recordings, and films.

Professional teachers also spend considerable time keeping up to date, conferring with their professional colleagues, improving their preparation for teaching, improving evaluation of pupil progress, and meeting with individual pupils at their request. No professional teacher should be scheduled with groups of students for more than twelve or fifteen hours per week, so that he will have time for such professional activities.

A third teacher goal is for each one to do what he is most competent and most interested in doing. Today's schools largely ignore individual differences among teachers through such procedures as the self-contained or self-sufficient classroom in which one teacher is expected to perform all services for students in a given subject field or grade level. The principle of individuality is also violated by uniform salary policies, standard class loads, uniform retirement policies, and a host of other standard personnel policies. Teachers need to meet regularly in teaching teams with other teachers to plan what each may do best and to give each the privilege of doing it.

Point of view

Those who would improve the curriculum must constantly and honestly examine what they believe. We have stated our concerns so that readers may know the points of view that illuminate and influence the concepts presented throughout the rest of this book.

We are critical of many practices that exist in today's schools. We believe they reflect inconsistencies between stated purposes and procedures used to accomplish the goals. Those who study curriculum development and try to change schools translate beliefs into positive action. What results from their work, in our opinion, will be different from and better than the program that exists today.

TOPICS FOR STUDY AND DISCUSSION

1. Discuss the changes in secondary education curriculum goals that appear in statements issued during the past one-half century. What others would you add?
2. What curricular goals deserve highest priority today?
3. Consider a subject area, perhaps the one you teach. At two given ages, for example 12 and 17, what content is essential for all or most pupils?
4. Take some typical topic or unit in a subject you teach; list some hobbies or careers that would be open to pupils who learned more than the essentials required of everyone.
5. What motivational factors other than those listed in this chapter should curriculum planners consider?

6. React to the beliefs about curriculum submitted by the authors. Are there any you would reject or others you would add?

SELECTED REFERENCES

ANDERSON, ROBERT H. *Teaching in a World of Change.* New York: Harcourt Brace & World, Inc., 1966.

Presents beliefs similar in many respects to those of the authors of this book.

BEGGS, DAVID W., III. *Decatur-Lakeview High School: A Practical Application of the Trump Plan.* Englewood Cliffs, N.J.: Prentice-Hall, Inc., 1964.

Describes how one school applied the beliefs highlighted in this chapter and elsewhere in this book.

EURICH, ALVIN C., ed. *High School 1980.* New York: Pitman Publishing Corp., 1970.

Twenty-five authorities state what they believe will happen in the change process, the curriculum areas, in the utilization of persons and resources, and in evaluation.

FEYEREISEN, KATHRYN V., et al. "A Systems Approach to Curriculum Design—A New Rationale." In *Supervision and Curriculum Renewal: A Systems Approach.* New York: Appleton-Century-Crofts, 1970, pp. 130–152.

The authors urge the process of systems analysis for designing curriculum, ranging from objectives to content to methods to media to evaluation with more precise decision-making processes than schools conventionally use.

GLINES, DON E. *Creating Humane Schools.* Mankato, Minn.: Campus Publishers, 1971, pp. 1–281.

This book presents vigorous proposals for changing schools at all levels, including an extensive bibliography on innovations and ideas for changing schools at all levels.

GOODLAD, JOHN I. Parts I and IV. In *School, Curriculum, and the Individual.* Waltham, Massachusetts: Blaisdell Publishing Co., 1966, pp. 3–20 and 220–259.

Discussions of educational goals, emphasis on individual differences among learners, changes in the selection and organization of content, and better utilization of staff suggest many changes in curriculum.

GORMAN, BURTON W. *Secondary Education: The High School America Needs.* New York: Random House, 1971, pp. vii–362.

This book makes proposals for improving all aspects of secondary schools including "The High School of 1990."

OSEN, D. S. K. *Student Perceptions of Selected Innovations in*

Secondary Education. Ann Arbor, Michigan: University Microfilms, 1970.

The author's doctoral dissertation reports on the reactions of a sample of students and graduates of three California high schools to the ideas of J. Lloyd Trump as found in a considerable number of publications. The author also predicts the future impact of "The Trump Plan" in this study done at the University of Southern California under the direction of Professor William Georgiades. Includes bibliography.

OVARD, GLEN F. "Curricular Programs and Organizational Structure." In *Administration of the Changing Secondary School.* New York: The Macmillan Company, 1966, pp. 110–138.

This chapter describes a number of evolving patterns for organizing the curriculum.

THE CURRICULUM: RETROSPECT AND PROSPECT. The Seventieth Yearbook of the National Society for the Study of Education, Part I. Chicago: University of Chicago Press, 1971, pp. vii–364.

Fifteen authors cover curriculum development from the 1920's to the present, plus a look into the future.

TRUMP, J. LLOYD, and BAYNHAM, DORSEY. *Focus on Change— Guide to Better Schools.* Chicago: Rand McNally & Co., 1961.

An earlier statement that indicates some bases for the beliefs stated in this book.

————, and KARASIK, LOIS. *Focus on the Individual—A Leadership Responsibility.* Washington, D.C.: National Association of Secondary School Principals, 1965. Booklet, 33 pp., and Filmstrip, 135 frames, color with sound.

This booklet describes methods used to individualize learning and professionalize teaching.

VAN HADEN, HERBERT I., and KING, JEAN MARIE. *Innovations in Education: Their Pros and Cons.* Worthington, Ohio: Charles A. Jones Publishing Company, 1971, pp. iii–184.

Outlines significant components, advantages, difficulties and some assessments, leaders, and locations in innovations under the following categories: individualized learning, accountability, curriculum expansion and improvement, reorganization, and personnel utilization and improvement. The content relates also to parts IV, V, and VI in this volume.

CHAPTER 3

Influences on the Curriculum

As mentioned in Chapter 1, the curriculum for schools in a democracy is constantly under pressure from the changing social order. At present, these pressures are intensified by an expanding technological order and its counterpart in automation. These have resulted in a variety of forces that are influencing curricular decision making. Some label these forces as revolutionary, while others refer to them as being the basis for sweeping educational reforms. Such identification does nothing to solve the problems of the practical-minded curriculum planner.

The present period does not mark a revolt against entrenched, maladjusted learning procedures such as characterized Rousseau's revolutionary thinking in the eighteenth century or the Progressive movement in the first half of this century. The urgent need is for readjustment to unprecedented technological changes. Entrenched forces do not resist the situation, except through built-in inertia and a lack of visionary leadership for furnishing rapid adjustment to change.

Impetus for curriculum changes is coming from worried parents who believe that the schools are not doing enough for their boys and girls, and from academic scholars who are troubled by the out-dated information being given to pupils because curriculum materials have not kept pace with the vast areas of scientific and technological discoveries. Probably the most penetrating questions are raised by those who struggle with the ever-present paradox of school programs that build lofty philosophical and technical castles within the school walls and ignore the practical problems without, or the equally paradoxical situation where programs are geared to the technological exigencies of today and fail to provide answers for the accompanying social problems of tomorrow.

THE ACADEMIC DISCIPLINES

In colleges and universities academic scholars are voicing concern about the preparation of youth who enter their classrooms.   The wholesome thing about the situation is that instead of scorning their students' mis-preparation, or lack of preparation, they have set out to discover causes and share responsibility for corrective measures.   Large numbers of professional people, from kindergarten through graduate school, are bent on combining theoretical with practical solutions.   The cooperative effort involved promises to bridge the articulation gap that has existed so long between the secondary schools and colleges.

The chief concern of the scholars of the disciplines has been to prevent a lag between knowledge dealt with in the classrooms and that being developed constantly by the scientists.   They are also concerned with ability of students to apply knowledge to solve problems.

The fields of science and mathematics offer prime examples of combined efforts of educational forces to produce exciting new curriculum materials.   Academic scholars have identified the kinds of information they consider necessary for students in preparatory schools, and classroom teachers from public and private schools have drawn on experience and practical methodology to give the material functional structure.   Examples of this cooperative effort in the preparation of curriculum materials may be found in the School Mathematics Study Group, the Beberman work at Illinois, the Biological Sciences Curriculum Study, the Chem Bond and the Chem Study formulations, and the Physical Sciences Study.

Probably one of the most valuable results of this welcome invasion of the academic scholar into the curriculum field is the amount of attention being given directly to the different phases of instruction.   Emphasis is on the arrangement of materials according to the best psychological concepts of learning rather than on scope and sequence.   Terms such as "problem solving," "critical thinking," and "discriminating judgment" are part of the discussion at all levels.   The presentation of learning materials to pupils is integrated to show relationships among many areas of knowledge. Pupils are led to practical application of factual information rather than storing it for the passing of examinations. The conceptual approach has replaced the fact-by-fact approach.[1]

Academic scholars are scrutinizing many other subject-matter areas in addition to science and mathematics. New curriculum materials—including textbooks, supplementary readings, visual aids and laboratory equipment—are available for use in most of the subject-matter fields. A detailed treatment of these fields is presented in later chapters.

Concomitant to the development of materials and the changing emphasis on instructional procedures is the construction of school programs that provide for the reallotment of such variables as time, space, and personnel. These require the regrouping of pupils to facilitate learning through team teaching, independent study, and other applicable arrangements.

In spite of the optimistic view taken of the academic scholar's interest in the preparation of curriculum material, evidence is not conclusive as to whether these materials are applicable to all segments of the school population. Some teachers contend that the new materials work well with able pupils but need considerable adjustments for the others. It is possible that the arrangement of the material reflects the thinking of men like Jerome S. Bruner, who maintains that the capacity of pupils to learn difficult material has been grievously underestimated. The question is whether these men are familiar with the learning capacities of unselected pupils of elementary and secondary schools. On the other hand, it is equally possible that teachers working daily with all levels of pupils become so frustrated with pupils of low ability that they tend to underestimate the ability of the other pupils. Only research and experience will furnish the final answers here.

SCHOOL ORGANIZATION AND THE CURRICULUM

A basic concept in school organization and administration deals with the relationship between the instructional program and the organizational pattern that implements it. Good theory suggests that the instructional program be built and the organizational pattern established that best facilitate maximum results for classroom learning.[2] Unfortunately, this is not the usual procedure. Too

[1] Arthur R. King, Jr. and John A. Brownell, *The Curriculum and the Disciplines of Knowledge* (New York: John Wiley and Sons, Inc., 1966), pp. 81–95.
[2] Gail Inlow, *The Emergent in Curriculum* (New York: John Wiley and Sons, Inc., 1966), pp. 12–44.

often the organizational pattern impedes the learning progress of boys and girls. Frequently, it is a source of pressure for maintaining status quo.

The organization of the educational system needs to be modified to bring structure into harmony with new curriculum developments. At present there is a series of supposedly integrated levels—elementary, junior high, senior high, junior college, four-year college, and graduate school. But instead of interlocking, these levels have become separate segments, each seeking its own image and traditions. And to further stifle a free flow of learning, each institution is highly departmentalized within its own framework and fragments knowledge into packages of equal size and content called "courses." A prime example of this is the Carnegie unit in the senior high school.

Since learning varies with different pupils, certainly there should be flexibility and variability in programs of learning. Fortunately, there is extensive experimentation going on in this area of school organization. The traditional 6-3-3 plan is under attack. One of the most prevalent substitutes is a 4-4-4 plan.

The advocates of this plan consider it better adapted to the social, physical, and mental development of pupils. The first four years are devoted to the establishment of the so-called fundamentals, with stress on every child learning to read. There are no grade barriers; it is simply a matter of each child learning to read at his own pace. He progresses from the primary unit when he has learned to read, or when it has been established that he cannot learn to read. The next four years form the intermediate school. Here the pupil strengthens his fundamentals and widens the learning experiences necessary for the secondary school years to follow. The final four years, of course, are the senior high school.

The proponents of the 4-4-4 plan are enthusiastic about its ungraded features and the elimination of the deficiencies of the junior high school—the school that has never fulfilled its established purposes. The pivotal feature of the 4-4-4 plan is the placement of the ninth grade with the senior high school. This is where an increasing number of school authorities believe it belongs.

Space here does not permit a complete survey of the many experimental organizational patterns in progress. Flexible scheduling, variable modules of time, methods of independent study, and team teaching will be described later. The problem of articulation continues to be perplexing. Some progress may be found in areas where instructors and teachers at various levels are uniting their efforts to reshape subject matter into a better continuity for learning. Much of the new school construction also reflects an effort to meet physical needs for a better flow of learning.

THE DROPOUT PROBLEM

There must be times when those responsible for planning the curriculum despair at the seemingly impossible task they face in providing experiences for all youth that will be purposeful, valuable, and even attractive. Frequently, any maladjustment of the young is assigned to the inadequacies of the school curriculum. One researcher, after making an exhaustive study of school marriages, concluded that the best way to reduce the incidence of these events was to provide a challenging secondary school program. Another, in commenting on the problems of motivation, suggested that the only way intellectual activities could compete with athletic, social, and extraclass activities was to have a curriculum that could capture the excitement of doing, exploring, and creating.

Pressure centers on the school for a solution to the dropout problem, and justly so. School dropouts are generally associated with curriculum maladjustment. A common consensus is that if the school meets the needs of all pupils and learning is made attractive, the dropout rate will be reduced greatly. Evidence is cited to the fact that the dropout has normal intelligence, is not a delinquent, and comes from a lower-class environment, frequently a slum school.

The typical dropout is around sixteen years old. Tension, suspicion, and strain mark his relations with his teachers and his fellow pupils. His attendance is poor, and he is frequently retarded by as much as two years. His parents are not interested in education, and he is often victimized by a home that has little respect for learning. He does not participate in extraclass activities and is sometimes put in an awkward position because he does not have the money necessary to be a participant. Apathy and frustration toward the whole school program are his trade marks.

Roots of the problem may be centered in society, but the school is an agent of society and is its most potent force for the correction of ills. The task calls for an all-out effort on the part of the school, with coordinated help from the various social agencies. A permanent goal of the school must be to provide each pupil with experience best suited for him as an individual and for his expected needs as a future citizen. The most urgent and most difficult need is to help the pupil see the concrete value of what he is learning and how it relates to real-life situations.

Effective guidance programs can be of real value in dealing with educationally maladjusted pupils. Identity can be established through testing and counseling. Solutions can be sought to the real or imaginary inequities felt by the pupil in the classroom and

the extraclass activity area.   Part-time jobs or work-school cooperative programs can give financial aid.   If a pupil can acquire a
sense of "belonging," his desire to stay in school can be greatly
enhanced.

Many solutions have been offered to meet the underprivileged aspects of the pupil dropout.   Vocational education is usually
suggested to prevent the pupil from leaving school without skills or
promise of useful employment.   The issue of vocational education
is discussed further in Chapter 14.   Sufficient to ask here, Who is
going to determine job skills in an automated society?

Other solutions center around "compensatory service" ideas.
Culturally deprived youth may attend cultural events.   Preschool
children may enroll in Headstart classes.   Work-study programs
and job corps programs feature "make-work" opportunities for
youth to have desirable experiences and earn money.   Robert J.
Havighurst's "moral equivalent of work" is associated with most of
such programs.   Whether the "compensatory service" idea will aid
the dropout problem is still a matter of conjecture.

The foregoing discussion has sought to identify the dropout
problem and associate it with the pressures that affect curriculum
planning.   The fact remains, however, that the final answer to the
problem lies with the classroom teacher.   The best planned curriculum will be impotent if it is not implemented by visionary teachers
loaded with the talent and energy to make learning meaningful for
all pupils.   In the final analysis, the teacher is the curriculum, and
there have never been enough good teachers to go around.

SOCIETAL PRESSURES

Societal pressures on the school curriculum are all associated directly or indirectly with the scientific and technological developments of the age and the resulting automation of much of man's
activities.   This has come with great rapidity; uncertainty and
confusion accompany it.   The agricultural revolution and the industrial revolution each took centuries for full manifestation, but
the scientific and technological revolution has matured almost
within a decade.

The social order surrounding the schools is casting its rever-
berating problems—mobile populations, unemployment, poverty,
delinquency, and changing home conditions—into the laps of curriculum planners.[3]   Many of the ills of modern society are attrib-

[3] Robert Smith, "Educating Youth in a Revolutionary Society," *Educational Leadership* (January 1966), pp. 279–284.

uted to the collapse of stable home life.   The decline of a strong kinship system in an urban society has left the family rootless, mobile, and small.   Directed activity of government agencies and planning commissions has replaced family centered living.   Social action, once face-to-face and personal, has now become indirect and bureaucratic.   The resulting imperfections are congestion, disorganization, and delinquency.   While these conditions are not prevalent throughout the country, they are found in large segments of urban populations and must be recognized as affecting many school programs.

In this country any extensive mobility of population is certain to create racial and ethnic problems.   The mass exodus of blacks from the South to urban centers in the North and the invasion of suburbia by various ethnic groups have created social problems of great magnitude.   Combined with all of this, of course, was the decision of the Supreme Court to integrate the public schools.   Educational planners must resist pressure from those who believe that racial and ethnic understanding can be effected by instructional processes; they must develop organizational practices that provide equal status of membership in groups.

Supreme Court decisions have done much to clarify religious issues in the schools.   Bible readings and prayers have been invalidated, but religious holiday celebrations, released time, and transportation of parochial pupils remain administrative problems that involve conflict and often constitute curriculum pressure.

One of the most stultifying factors in curriculum development is the infliction of regulations by state legislative and regulatory bodies.   These are the avenues by which special interest groups such as patriotic, civic, or labor organizations can influence the instruction materials of the classroom.   In some states it is a law that communism must be studied; in others, certain units of history are required.   In one state, the harmful effects of alcohol are supposed to be taught in five different subject-matter areas and the principal of the school is subject to a fine for failure to do so.   Obviously, there is no effort to enforce the law, but it is typical of how pressures through legislative enactments can clutter up curriculum objectives.

Influence of lay citizens

Historically, the construction of the curriculum has been centered at the local level.   A main objective has been to involve as many people as possible.   Membership of curriculum committees has consisted of pupils, teachers, lay citizens, and school administrators as well as curriculum specialists.   It has been a grassroots theory of complete communication.   Recent events have effected a change in both emphasis and direction.

The influence of lay citizens tends to shift the curriculum from a purely local emphasis.   This is due to the mobility of population resulting from automation and technological factors.   A new manufacturing plant will enter a community.   With it will come a host of technical and managerial workers bringing with them, from many parts of the country, ideas on how schools should be operated.   It is fortunate when the entrenched ideas of the local community do not clash with those of the newcomers.   These new residents are young, vigorous, and deeply interested in the welfare of their children.   They bring with them ideas for desirable educational innovations, and if local leaders can successfully integrate these ideas, local programs of instruction may be improved greatly.

The involvement of lay citizens has backfired to some extent.   Citizen groups have been infiltrated by extremists and vested interest groups.   In many instances, these groups have become pressure agencies for their own ideas rather than for the welfare of boys and girls.   This may be the fault of educational leaders who have failed to instruct these groups in proper educational thinking.   Where lay groups are asked to participate in curriculum planning, they should be carefully oriented and their role defined.   Involvement is desirable, but the role of each participating group ought to be mutually understood.

STATE AND FEDERAL GOVERNMENT

Probably the greatest factor in the change from a purely locally conceived curriculum is the stepped-up activity of state and national governments in the field of education.   Even the most ardent critic of federal aid to education will have to admit that it is now an accomplished fact.   It may have come through the back door, but it is here to stay, and the federal government has elected to channel a large part of its efforts through state departments of education.   Debate may go on over federal aid and resulting federal control, but it is purely an academic question.   Participants in federal aid know that purse strings have built-in control factors.   Financial responsibility is necessary, otherwise irresponsible spending, wanton waste, and even graft may result.

The role of the United States Office of Education in the development of new curricula is very much in evidence.   The activity of the U.S. Office had been primarily a consultative one, but with the passage of the National Defense Education Act of 1958, it began to disburse funds, and its influence in curriculum making was established. The interest of the national government in research phases of education has a certain amount of respectable antiquity. A historical survey of such interest would include the creation of the Smithsonian Institution in 1877, the passage of the Morrill Act for land grant colleges in 1862, the creation of the National Academy of Science in 1863, and the creation of the United States Office of Education in 1867. Historical precedents for federal aid in the vocational education field include the Smith-Hughes Act in 1917, the George-Dean Act in 1936, the George-Barden Act in 1946, and the Vocational Education Act of 1963.

The entrance of the national government into curriculum making on a broad base came under Title III of the National Defense Education Act, which provided financial assistance for strengthening subject-matter areas in science, mathematics, and modern foreign languages. Subsequently, this activity was broadened to include English and social studies. Financial assistance has been used in a variety of ways to improve instruction in these fields. The general pattern includes an examination of existing curricula, design and development of new curricula, testing and refinement of curricula in practical situations, and the production and distribution of new curricular materials.

The most sweeping of all federal aid to education was in the Elementary and Secondary Education Act of 1965. Financial assistance from this act had far-reaching effects on curriculum making. It provided for the allocation of large sums of money to the various states for programs of instruction and instructional materials. Emphasis was placed on new programs and innovative procedures for teaching. This was truly federal aided curriculum construction. Although it was under the supervision of the various state departments of education, to label it anything less than a form of governmental pressure would be misleading.

Court decisions in California, Minnesota, Texas, and other states concerning the inequalities of the property tax as a support for public education is certain to rearrange the financial structure with resulting pressures on curriculum decisions according to the flow of monetary aid. Whether the property tax is state administered or the federal government devises other means of replacing it, local responsibility and authority for what boys and girls are taught in the classroom is bound to diminish. This will increase the responsibility of local educators for seeing that state and federal participation in building curricula does not result in the stifling of imaginative programs and the bringing about of monotonous conformity. One of the redeeming features of federal funding has been the requirement that new programs must show innovative processes and adequate provisions for evaluation. This has not always been true in state funding.

THE ACCOUNTABILITY SYNDROME

The accountability syndrome is certain to influence curriculum decisions for some time to come. Causes for emphasis on accountability may be traced to the ever-increasing demand for educational dollars. The federal government has poured billions of dollars into the educational mix, and negotiated teachers' contracts continue to call for ever-increasing financial obligations on local school boards. As demands increase and inflated dollars shrink, educational constituencies become more concerned over value received. Congressmen, tax payers, school board members, and school patrons all ask the same question: what are we getting for our money?

Educational leaders have been ready to assure the public that increased support for education means better schools. Teacher organizations have promised better educational results from better pay. There is a growing concern on the part of the public that educational results do not match educational promises. Either better educational programs have not been forthcoming, or educational leaders have not been able to identify results in a satisfactory manner.

Manifestations of the accountability syndrome may be found in such movements as national assessment, performance contracts, differentiated staffing, and so-called taxpayer revolts. Those who originally opposed national assessment on the basis that results would provide for an unwholesome comparison of various school systems are now demanding national assessment data to prove their schools better than those of their neighbors. Bills are being introduced into state legislatures to make provisions for state assessments, and soon local assessment will be in vogue.

The popularity of performance contracting is further evidence of a desire on the part of school boards and school officials to prove to the public the extent of their educational accomplishments. Sponsors of performance contracting, mostly private business concerns, are willing to guarantee learning successes for boys and girls. They operate mostly in the subject-matter areas of mathematics and language arts where controllable procedures can produce measurable results. Educators are critical of such methods claiming they could follow the same procedures and produce the same results but point to the undesirability of such "force feeding" methods and the possible lack of any permanent benefits.

Differentiated staffing is an interesting educational development. The fact that the profession is willing to take a new look at it is evidence that it has an accountability aspect.   Differentiated staffing is a plan whereby different teachers do different jobs and get different rates of pay.   Critics of differentiated staffing call it camouflaged merit pay, but general acceptance of it by teacher organizations gives credence to the idea that the demand for better educational results will lead to compensatory acknowledgement for those who produce better educational results.   Curriculum experts advocate differentiated staffing for other reasons.   They hold the best learning results will be secured when the members of the educational team are differentiated according to talent, temperament, and training.[4]

One of the problems that continues to plague educational planners is the lack of reliable evaluative criteria.   School boards act as policy-making bodies, professional administrators do the implementing, and the general public passes judgment on the effectiveness of the product.   There is no agency, however, that has responsibility for encompassing an assessment function in any meaningful way.   School patrons may vote down a bond issue, but no one really knows what the negative vote means.   Seldom do the people have ways of communicating their concerns in such a manner as to insure improvement in the school curriculum.

Theoretically, education has a conceptual flaw.   There is no aspect of the system that regularly generates effective data, nor is there anything in the concept that requires the system to pay any attention to the feedback if it should appear.   The secondary school curriculum is particularly vulnerable to this phenomenon.[5]   In a period when the critics are demanding proof of results and educational leaders have no effective way of showing results, the discovery of effective evaluative criteria must be a high priority on the curriculum planner's agenda.   Perhaps with the development of sophisticated systems analysis and computerized data, pertinent assessment may become a reality.

THE PRESSURE FOR CLAIRVOYANCE

In every period of curriculum study and development those responsible for the process are tormented by the uncertainty of their ability to evaluate the needs of the future.   The philosophic seers of education haunt the practical-minded curriculum builder with demands of proof that what the pupils are learning today will be applicable

[4] Sterling G. Callahan, *Successful Teaching in Secondary Schools* (New York: Scott Foresman and Company, 1971), pp. 56–68.
[5] Robert C. McKean, *Principles and Methods in Secondary Education* (Columbus, Ohio: Charles E. Merrill Publishing Co., 1971), pp. 186–192.

in their world of tomorrow. This might be labeled the pressure for clairvoyance.

At present, this pressure for prediction involves the two searching questions which follow. The first question is certainly not a new one, and the second is rooted in the necessity for balance in curriculum matters.

Are scientific and technological values being stressed at the expense of social and moral values?

The question of relative values is always present in planning the school curriculum. It is posed in many different forms—Are the values realistic? Are they consistent? Are they applicable? Are they in balance? Thoughtful critics of today's curriculum ask whether the pupil, engulfed in the mastery of the ever-increasing scientific and technological knowledge, has the opportunity to develop discriminating judgment of social and moral values. This is a question of balanced emphasis. In a larger sense it raises the question of whether man will be able to live in the automated technological world he is building.

Emphasis in today's curriculum is on the development of problem-solving ability for scientific and technical pursuits. Individual competition is stressed in a myriad of ways through competition for scholarships, academic groupings, and prizes for the intellectual elite. Too little attention is given to balancing these experiences with activities that enable youths to think in terms of social solutions and moral obligations. There is no question but that scientific and technical pursuits are necessary, but they are not enough in a world troubled with social inequalities. The unsolved problems of today and tomorrow are related to social behavior.

Adult leaders are forced to make decisions concerning the welfare of mankind in a world of thermonuclear capabilities, expanding global populations, rapid technological evolution and unprecedented leisure. This calls for ability and experience quite different from the scientific thinking that created such conditions. It calls for discriminating powers in areas of social values where the search for answers is both frustrating and confusing.

Are the experiences of the pupils within the school consistent with the experiences they face outside the school?

Educators training youth for the future must establish some form of reference for beliefs and expectations. What is at stake is the standard of values of mankind. A regrettable mistake in the past

has been to make the assumption that school life, neatly compart-
mentalized into Carnegie units of subject matter and supplemented
with the "socializing" effect of extraclass activities, inherently provides discriminating powers for social decision making.   This assumption ignores both the violent clashes between peoples, classes,
and races outside the school and youth's awareness of these clashes.
Educators who foster such bland curriculum experiences fail to
understand the intensive search of youth for a cause.   The whole
panorama of youth in "protest" ought to make clear to educational
leaders how hungry youth is for opportunities to participate in
serious decision making in the realm of social problems.

The schools are charged with the task of preparing youth
for "life," and, paradoxically, youth finds little in his educational
experiences that is either applicable or germane.   He is part of a
world of work, war, race tension, sex exploitation, economic
affluency, economic distress, and organized protests against the
social order.   These are not bookish things and are not related to
any basic set of facts.   They raise questions in the minds of pupils
for which they find only limited answers in the classroom.   The
question might be asked: when will the curriculum contain honest
courses on sex, anthropology, history, psychology, and religion?
When will international affairs, race prejudice, poverty, and egocentric amusement activities be given equal importance with the
areas of problem solving that are of a scientific and technological
nature?

The choice confronting modern education is not necessarily
one between humanism and liberal arts on one hand and science
and technology on the other.   It is more a problem of the balance
of relative values.   It is senseless to debate the importance of one
against the other.   They are both supplementary and complementary.   The plain fact is that both the social and scientific transition
being experienced will make a chaotic world unless better communication is established between the proponents of human values
and the new mechanistic forces.

A survey of emerging social problems reveals a whole new
concept of work and the jobs involved, materialistic efficiency resulting in forced leisure, and millions of human beings—formerly
nameless, silent, and oppressed—entering the mainstream of civilization and demanding the fruits of an abundant life.   These problems are complex and solutions are difficult.   They are social in
nature and call for the highest type of curriculum soothsaying.
They point to the need of youths for experiences that enable them
to be aware of their social environment and to be flexible and imaginative in dealing with it.   The past is only a prologue, not a pattern, and yesterday's dying echo must not determine tomorrow's
theme.

TOPICS FOR STUDY AND DISCUSSION

1. Is there an answer to the age-old question of whether the schools should prepare youth to change society or merely to make satisfactory adjustment to societal conditions?
2. Statistics show that the 6-3-3 plan of school organization is the most popular in the nation. Why are school officials experimenting with a 4-4-4 plan?
3. The title of a recent address by a school administrator at a national convention was, "The Solution to the Dropout Problem." Hypothetically, what would be the substance of his address?
4. What is the role of the school in the great moral issues of society?
5. The opponents of federal aid to education has consistently contended that federal control of education is a certain concomitant of federal aid. Is there evidence in the present federal aid programs that this fear is justified?
6. What would be the merits of a national curriculum for education?
7. Analyze the school's responsibility for the maintenance of balance between the pressures of a technological age and the maladjustment it may cause in the social order.
8. What dangers are inherent in statutory regulations of subject matter to be contained in public school curriculums? What authority should be vested with this power?
9. What will be the total affect of the accountability syndrome on the public school curriculum?
10. There is general agreement that effective evaluation of the educational product is necessary. Why has so little progress been made in this direction?

SELECTED REFERENCES

ALEXANDER, WILLIAM M., and SAYLER, J. GALEN. *The High School: Today and Tomorrow.* New York: Holt, Rinehart and Winston, Inc., 1971.

   Through the efforts of two well-known authorities in the secondary school curriculum field, all facets of modern high schools are analyzed. The book has a very challenging overview of secondary schools of the future and points to the principal who must be an innovator of new curricula, techniques, organizations, and administrative practices.

ANDERSON, VERNON E. *Principles and Procedures of Curriculum Improvement.* New York: The Ronald Press Company, 1965.

This is a good coverage of procedures to be used in curriculum improvement dealing with human development and learning, culture, democratic ideals and values. It discusses approaches to pupils of various learning levels and includes a good treatment of creative research in curriculum development.

BRUNER, JEROME E. *The Relevance of Education.* New York: W. W. Norton and Co., 1971.

Bruner proposes that the era of subject-matter reorganization is completed for the time being. He advocates the next step is to make practical application of new materials to problem-solving situations related to social and environmental needs. As the title suggests, he devotes a great deal of time to the relevance of curriculum materials to youthful needs.

DOLL, RONALD C. *Curriculum Improvement: Decision-Making and Process.* Boston: Allyn and Bacon, Inc., 1970.

This book is a good treatment of decision making in curriculum. Processes for curriculum improvement are outlined. The various subject-matter areas are related to inherent problems contained therein. Curriculum evaluation is discussed.

HANSEN, JOHN H., and HEARN, ARTHUR C. *The Middle School Program.* Chicago: Rand-McNally and Co., 1971.

Typical of many authors writing on the middle school, Hansen and Hearn dwell on the failures of the junior high school as a basis for establishing middle schools. They propose the middle school for its freshness, innovation, and adaptability. They recommend it as an institution for meeting the needs and potential of youngsters from 10 to 14. They point to the opportunities for variations of all kinds, including nongradedness and individualized instruction.

HASS, GLEN, and WILES, KIMBALL. *Readings in Curriculum.* Boston: Allyn and Bacon, Inc., 1965.

This book contains the contributions of eighty carefully selected authorities in the field of curriculum. The various treatments include the subject-matter fields, social forces involved, the nature of learning, and the attainment of knowledge. Recent research findings are analyzed.

HAVIGHURST, ROBERT J., and NEUGARTEN, BERNICE L. *Society and Education.* 3rd ed. Boston: Allyn and Bacon, Inc., 1966.

This volume deals with the relation of the school to major social problems. Special attention is given to the problems of urban areas. The relation of education to the social structure of the nation is evaluated. The disadvantaged pupil is identified in relation to the social structure.

HOOVER, KENNETH H. *Readings on Learning and Teaching in the Secondary Schools.* Boston: Allyn and Bacon, Inc., 1971.

This book of readings includes a clear and comprehensive treatment of current instructional developments. It would make a good source book for principal and staff in curriculum planning sessions. Material is gathered from provocative addresses, lectures, and essays.

NEAGLEY, ROSS L. *Handbook for Effective Curriculum Development.* Englewood Cliffs, N.J.: Prentice-Hall, Inc., 1967.

This book discusses various issues on the national, state, and local level, and it identifies and predicts curriculum changes.

TANNER, DANIEL. *Secondary Curriculum: Theory and Development.* New York: Macmillan Company, 1971.

This is a comprehensive book explaining all aspects of secondary education including philosophic principles, analysis, and evaluations of curriculum processes. Major types of curricula in current practice are discussed along with various experimental programs.

VAN TIL, WILLIAM. *Curriculum: Quest for Relevance.* Boston: Houghton Mifflin Co., 1971.

This volume points to the fact that the struggle among forces in American society for curriculum change grows sharper. Road blocks in the quest for relevance are identified as follows: present curriculum patterns fail to illuminate social realities, meet individual needs, or develop humane values; the integration of knowledge in subject-matter areas is lacking; and no socially oriented proposals for humanizing education gather momentum.

WILSON, CRAIG L. *The Open Access Curriculum.* Boston: Allyn and Bacon, Inc., 1971.

Pupil needs are the center of this treatise concerning the curriculum. Open access deals with the availability of educational opportunities for all students. Greater emphasis is put on the philosophical principles of curriculum development than on the how to do. Material is especially pertinent to problems of relevance for pupils of urban areas.

PART II

Issues and Action in the Subject Areas

CHAPTER 4

Business and
Distributive Education

THE CHANGING SCENE

The touring motorist ordered the station attendant to "fill her up."
The attendant wiped the windshield, checked the oil and water,
and filled the tank. He then accepted the customer's credit card
and prepared his bill. In due time, the motorist received his
monthly statement and returned a check for payment. The entire
transaction was convenient, swift, and accurate. It marked a
routine business transaction.

Of total insignificance to the motorist was the fact that no
further human recording, calculation, or billing was necessary
from the time of the purchase of the gasoline until the arrival of
the monthly statement. However, the transaction was of great
significance to the business education teacher of the local school
system. It illustrated the impact of automation on business procedures and posed problems for those in charge of the preparation of
business education pupils.

The situation described above raises the question of what
type of training the office worker of the future will need. One of
the most pressing demands in the field of business education is the
determination of what will constitute adequate preparation for the
new types of positions available in a business world of magnetic
tapes, punch cards, and almost human mechanical computers. It
may be predicted safely that the reduction of size and cost of com-

49

puters will make it possible for even small businesses to have them as standard equipment.

A universal programing language is on the horizon. Problems will be translated into machine language, and the average office worker will be able to use a computer to solve his problems. Many solutions will be in progress simultaneously, since the computer will be receiving problems from several office stations. Possibilities of computers are almost unlimited. With prodigious memories running into millions of words (symbols), operational speeds of hundreds of millions of digits a second, and random interrogation ability, computers can do the work of an entire office or even an entire business.

There is no doubt the human secretary will still be needed, and there will be plenty of work for her to do. She will still be a buffer for her boss, and her chief task will be to act as an intermediary for reports going to or coming from a computer. The condensing and summarizing of information will be part of her task, so she will need a thorough knowledge of data processing.

There is ample evidence that all business positions will require higher level skills than ever before. The exact nature of these skills, however, is yet to be ascertained.

DUAL OBJECTIVES NEEDED

Business education programs in the comprehensive school need flexibility and variety. In this era of transition it may be necessary to have dual objectives: to plan programs to meet the yet unforeseeable impact of automation and, at the same time, to revitalize and upgrade the present curriculum for immediate needs. Perhaps it may be possible to synthesize these objectives as the program unfolds. Since the future is always enticing, it may be interesting to analyze first what may be in the offing.

Typewriting is closely associated with data processing, and since part of the data processing procedure involves the making of punch cards and magnetic tapes, the teaching of typewriting will include experiences beyond the regularly accepted objectives of today. Companies building typewriters are now offering multiple purpose machines that soon will be necessary equipment in business education departments of schools. The teaching of typewriting for business and personal use will be supplemented by many additional uses.

Bookkeeping and accounting may soon find that consolidated files have made much of the present accounting system obsolete. Business will be file oriented, with whole new groups of materials to be filed.   Included will be integrated data processing and electronic data processing media.   There will be whole new vistas of punched card files and punched tape files.

An example of the filing processes may be found in consolidated file methods that eliminate an accounting department on an accounts receivable or payable basis.   All information about a customer will be filed together, including accounts receivable, all data on accounts, goods ordered, credit ratings, and other pertinent information.   The preparatory training of pupils for work in such business will have to be greatly reshaped.

Increased office automation will also affect the teaching of shorthand.   Subject-matter and teaching procedures will not be greatly affected, but there will be many changes in vocabulary and a decreased demand for personal dictation.   The portable dictating machine is becoming standard equipment in many offices.   As has been mentioned before, the personal secretary will still be needed, but her functions as a stenographer will continually diminish.

The total impact of automation on the business education curriculum is difficult to predict.   Attention probably should be turned to the present needs for adjustment and improvement.

For the past several years, business education has had dual objectives reaching into the general education field and the vocational education field.   Most of the emphasis has been on the skill subject aspects desirable for vocational purposes.   But even business leaders are now contending that general education objectives should receive far greater consideration.

These objectives can be achieved through stress on basic economic concepts, a clear understanding of how business works, and the need for consumer knowledge necessary to use the goods and services of business efficiently.   Every pupil, regardless of what his vocational pursuits may be, must have basic business fundamentals to handle his personal financial affairs, banking services, and tax matters.   He must also have an intelligent understanding of the free enterprise system.   An intensive minimum skill program in typing is basic for all pupils and especially important for the college bound.   In some instances a streamlined, job-directed course in shorthand for part-time employment of terminal and college bound students is advisable.   Business education leaders advocate that every pupil have a basic course in business education at either the ninth or tenth grade level and that it be possible for any pupil to elect business education courses on the eleventh and twelfth grade levels.   Since area vocational schools have business education programs in the thirteenth and fourteenth years, they afford an opportunity for delayed specialization by students who did not elect to pursue a full business education program in the previous four years.

RESHAPING PRESENT CURRICULUM

One of the best statements as to what direction the curriculum in business education should take may be found in a statement by the Policies Commission for Business and Economic Education. It is entitled "This We Believe About Business Education in the Secondary Schools" and includes:

(1)   Every secondary school should provide opportunities for students to prepare for careers in business.
(2)   The time devoted to preparation for business occupations should depend upon the student's abilities, interests, and personal qualities.
(3)   The sequence of learning experiences should be planned so that the student will achieve his highest occupational competency upon completion of his program.
(4)   On-the-job experience through cooperative education should be an integral part of the student's program.
(5)   Opportunities must be provided for secondary students to develop an understanding of how the business system operates.
(6)   Requirements relating to the development of personal and social economic competencies should be reciprocally recognized by the respective departments of the school ————.

Turning now briefly to the curriculum needs of the business education program of the immediate future, one finds subject-matter content an issue for debate.

Revisions in shorthand

Shorthand courses emphasizing theory in a long, drawn-out procedure are being questioned. There is a tendency to place ever-increasing emphasis on the ability to produce useful transcript. This, of course, means giving more attention to the practical application of shorthand. The simplification of shorthand has been in progress for some time. Major systems of shorthand are being revised in this direction.

There are five major systems of shorthand in this country. Each system has its advantages and disadvantages. It is not a question of which system is best, but rather a question of which system meets the school's objectives best. Are these objectives slanted toward personal use, stenographic use, executive secretarial use, or court reporting? A well-developed shorthand curriculum in a comprehensive school ought to provide shorthand for vocational use and personal use as well as a special accelerated program.

The accelerated program should be for capable pupils who need a program condensed into one year for use in post-school education. Many of these pupils are college bound and will use their shorthand for note-taking at lectures and seminars. Part of them will earn needed financial assistance doing secretarial work for campus personnel where a high degree of business efficiency is not necessary.

Personal use shorthand, frequently called notehand, emphasizes special techniques for converting expressed ideas into capsule statements. It translates original meaning rather than original words, emphasizing the ability to get the gist of remarks rather than taking them verbatim. This is a one-semester course and should enroll both boys and girls.

There will be a continued need for a two-year vocational program, but it must be adjusted to meet changing conditions. Such a program no longer attracts the brightest pupils; they are usually in the accelerated or the personal use courses. Therefore recognition must be given to the need for more pupil help in spelling, punctuation, and proofreading. There is an advantage, however, to such homogeneous grouping. It results in a smaller spread of learning activities and calls for more intensive, direct teaching.

Those planning the shorthand phase of the business education curriculum must concern themselves with the proper selection of students, adequate theory presentation, proper motivation for maximizing skill-building efforts, provisions for individual rates of learning, and full utilization of multimedia for facilitating learning. Skill building and the fusion of shorthand, typewriting, and English usage ability must receive continual stress.[1]

An innovation in the teaching of shorthand and transcription in many secondary schools is the introduction of machine shorthand. While mechanized shorthand may be confined to large urban and suburban schools for some time to come, there is ample reason for business education planners to investigate the feasibility of such processes in all secondary schools. The shorthand machine is fairly inexpensive and is light and compact to handle. It does require, however, additional space in a business education department and a separate system of instruction. The installation and use of shorthand machines by business offices is necessary to give any validity for shorthand machine instruction in the schools. It is problematical how rapidly this will happen.

[1] Mark Langemo, "Focus on the Secretarial Program," *Business Education Forum* (October 1970), pp. 11–12.

Bookkeeping: a question of survival

Serious questions are being raised in the bookkeeping field. There is need for reshaping objectives and reorienting areas of emphasis in teaching the subject. Much of the present teaching perpetuates business forms and business activities that are obsolescent. Extensive streamlining is necessary to acquaint students with modern business situations. The accounting operations of so many business corporations are tailored especially for their particular activities that only minimum essentials have much value for positions with these corporations.[2] Most of the training is obtained on the job or at a special school provided by the particular business organization. A certain measure of rethinking on the semantics of bookkeeping is also in order. Many of the everyday English words used in bookkeeping in a technical sense do not retain their usual meaning. The need is for simplification and the reduction of obscurity.

Whether bookkeeping remains in the business education curriculum is a moot question. Strong defenders of the subject would have all business education pupils have an elementary course. They point to its basic values for vocational pursuits in the business world,[3] citing the need for a basic understanding of business operations such as combination journals, handling cash, use of business papers as source information, and concepts of depreciation and bad debts. They also point out that bookkeeping is a good preparation for advanced study in accounting, since it provides an understanding of maintenance of records and develops the ability to organize quantitative data.

These proponents of the basic values of bookkeeping further enhance the position of the subject in the business education curriculum by listing the factors good teachers can emphasize to relate bookkeeping to economic literacy. These include (1) private enterprise in a market oriented economy, (2) calculation of the role of profits in a capitalistic economy, (3) productive costs—fixed, variable, average, and marginal, and (4) such general business activities as withholding taxes, controlled inflation, marketing stocks and bonds, etc.

Boosters of bookkeeping also point to the personal use value of the subject. They contend that bookkeeping helps meet general education objectives by teaching future citizens to keep records,

[2] Donald R. Coffman, "Constant Change in Today's Bookkeeping," *The Journal of Business Education* (December 1965), pp. 98–100.
[3] Lewis E. Wall, "The Bookkeeping and Accounting Program," *Business Education Forum* (December 1971), pp. 11–12.

plan family budgets, prepare tax returns, reconcile bank statements, and understand financial statements.

The teaching of bookkeeping offers many opportunities for modernization of instruction as advocated in chapters 17 to 25 of this book. Good processes in the teaching of bookkeeping place emphasis on individualized learning. The use of "practice sets" has many of the characteristics of modern simulation procedures. Curriculum planners for all business education programs have excellent opportunities for providing individualized instruction through the use of: pacing, differentiated assignments, independent study, programed materials, small-group instruction, simulation experiences, and gaming device activities.

New approach in typing

In the teaching of typing, the time-honored procedure of having pupils develop speeds measured in so many words a minute with minimum errors is being looked on askance. It is advocated that a pupil's typing ability be measured in terms of his ability to do functional production work. Speed and accuracy remain relatively important, but the multiple uses made in variations of the typewriter call for additional skills.

In addition to necessary skills in typing, pupils should attain facilities for greater practical service. Basic knowledge in reading, spelling, punctuation, and proofreading should be concomitant learnings. Time for perfecting these fundamentals may be attained by reducing the time spent on practicing such infrequently-used typing needs as legal documents, bills of lading, and quantities of invoices, statements, receipts, etc. Emphasis should not be on training pupils for initial positions, but rather on preparation of secretaries to presidents of important businesses. This necessitates a thorough understanding of the basic skills of communication.

Typewriting was the first subject in the business education field to be suggested as being valuable for personal use. There is now general acceptance among curriculum planners of the dual role of typing instruction for vocational pursuits and personal use. The more enthusiastic advocates of the value of typing instruction suggest that one year of the subject be required of all pupils. They would retain the second year for those planning vocations requiring additional typing ability.

New directions in typing instruction point to intrinsic values that can be built into good teaching of the subject. Studies of elementary school children reveal that typing has a favorable effect upon general academic achievement, causes improvement in word skills and English mechanics, and stimulates certain types of creativity. The question is raised as to why secondary school typing cannot achieve the same ends if they are stressed as objectives.[4] Creativity takes the form of self-expression in typing accomplishments. Instead of teaching six rigid business forms, the instructor teaches only one, and the pupil is encouraged to concentrate on the organization of thought, the division of paragraphs, and the proper grammatical structure. Much of this kind of typing is done from direct dictation or rough draft forms.

The accomplished typist is frequently called on to type from the rough draft of a letter that has not been edited. This requires acute concentration and discrimination. The pupil must learn to make necessary corrections without changing the meaning. In such activities, the pupil is required to think as he types. This raises the typist from the level of a mechanical reactor to that of an intelligent participant. This process requires experience in what might be called "think and type" situations.

Any change of objectives or emphasis does not lessen the need for stressing skills. Since typing is basically a skill subject, it will continue to require from one-third to one-half of a pupil's instruction time to insure both competence and confidence. New approaches to teaching the subject will make typing classes more stimulating and afford the pupils greater breadth of learning.

Distributive education

Distributive education is in the family of vocational education subjects that are supported by federal aid to education. It came into being with the George-Dean Act of 1936 and was greatly strengthened by the George-Barden Act of 1946. It also shares in the greatly increased support furnished by the Vocational Education Act of 1963.

Distributive education is vocational in nature because it involves supervised training on the job. The typical program has the pupils in the classroom for part of the day and in regular distributive merchandising jobs for the remainder of the day. Salaries are given to pupils for their merchandising work. Federal monies are furnished to supplement the salary of the distributive education coordinator (the teacher in charge of a distributive education program) and furnish certain other fringe benefits for his program.

The coordinator's duties go beyond classroom teaching to pupil counseling, job placement, and program salesmanship. Dis-

[4] Louise E. Wheeler, "Apply Psychology to Production Typewriting," *Business Education Forum* (November 1971), pp. 18–20.

tributive education classroom work includes receiving, selling, merchandising, sales promotion, and control.   The related classroom program usually involves required general education classes such as English and social studies and commercial subjects such as salesmanship and commercial law.   Frequently, typing and bookkeeping are background requirements.

The on-the-job training is designated as the cooperative phase of distributive education.   On-the-job activities provide pupils with practical experience and enhance their respect for what they learn in school.   They become familiar with job opportunities, job requirements, salary scales, business procedures, and the exacting requirements of the business world.   In many cases the money they earn enables them to stay in school.   Dropouts among distributive education pupils are very low.   A concomitant factor that may accrue to a secondary school that sponsors a distributive education program results from the better relations established with businessmen.   The distributive education coordinator becomes familiar with the needs of the business community, and he is in a position to interpret educational problems to the business community.

Although distributive education is a comparatively recent subject in the secondary school curriculum, its leadership is constantly seeking new ways to organize classes, new methods of instruction, and new ways of utilizing staff resources to achieve more effective and vital programs.   This is in keeping with an age of continual change.

Distributive education leaders recognize that an improved and widely expanded distributive education program can make a definite contribution to the solution of many social, economic, and educational problems of a community.   Programs of distributive education are associated with problems of dropouts, teen-age unemployment, and changing patterns of the distribution of commercial products.

New teaching methods.   In the area of teaching methods, distributive education coordinators are experimenting with team teaching and programed instruction.   Where programs involve more than one teaching coordinator, the team idea is feasible.   Even when there is only one coordinator, enlistment can be made of other faculty members in the related fields, such as English and social studies.

Such enlistment is probably a good practice, since it involves the distributive education program with other divisions of the school.   Too often, vocational education programs suffer from isolation from other school activities.   Sometimes pupils are reluctant to enter vocational education programs for this reason.   It is reasonable to assume that values associated with team teaching in other classes will be present when it is used in distributive education classes. This same assumption may be made with the use of programed instruction, although experimentation to date offers no conclusive evidence.

One of the most successful teaching activities associated with distributive education programs is the sales laboratory. Here, the distributive education coordinator can demonstrate the tenets of modern merchandising, such as self-service and centralized check-out, in a learning by doing fashion. Instruction is more realistic in this environment, and vocational competency is obtained with greater ease. A well-organized sales laboratory enables students to make direct application of classroom theories under directly supervised instruction. The equipment and facilities in a sales laboratory may include cash registers, showcases, display stands, display windows, marking machines, wrapping counters, gummed tape machines, and other merchandising paraphernalia.

THE ISSUES IN BUSINESS EDUCATION

Curriculum problems in the field of business education involve at least three critical issues. The solving of these issues, discussed earlier in this chapter, will have an important impact on the type of business education pupils will receive. Issue one raises the question of the importance of general education and the amount of time that should be devoted to it in the business education program. It asks whether emphasis on general education will sacrifice time which should be devoted to the facets of business education generally considered important. It poses the interesting thesis that business education may be considered a necessary part of general education in the future. Decisions on this issue will determine the shaping of the vocational aspects of the curriculum that are equally beneficial to the college-bound and to the terminal student. It will also determine the amount of business education needed by a citizen to make wise economic decisions, manage his own business affairs successfully, and vote intelligently on economic and business problems.

The second issue concerns the expansion and adjustment needed to provide for the rapid development in automation. Business education programs in many schools now include training on punch card machines, sorters, and some of the more complicated data processing machines. These processes are changing so rapidly that innovations made in school programs involving automation may be obsolete before they are installed.   This issue will continue to complicate the vocational aspects of business education.

The third issue is related to the teaching of skills in the present program of business education.   The question is raised as to how much the teaching of these skills may be accelerated.   The squeeze on business subjects by a broadened general education program and the necessity for meeting automation needs may require special attention to the development of business skills at a much more rapid rate.   There is encouraging evidence that the time needed to teach these skills can be reduced and that the kinds of skills needed can be adjusted to provide for more economical use of training time.

The needs of the business office of the future will require two types of workers as a result of technological advancements in both data processing and communication processing.   One group of workers will be needed in large numbers to collect, register, and copy information, and a second group of more selective workers will be needed for operating the total information system.   This calls for critical decisions on the part of curriculum planners for business education programs.

TOPICS FOR STUDY AND DISCUSSION

1. Contrast the business education curriculum content that was satisfactory for the secondary schools in 1950 with what will be needed in 1980.
2. Evaluate the relative functions of business education subjects as to their vocational aspects and their general education aspects.
3. A 1919 report of a committee on business education criticized bookkeeping as unrealistic in relation to actual job opportunities in the business world. Why does the subject continue to be fairly well entrenched in business education curriculums?
4. Why is distributive education usually associated with the business education curriculum of the secondary school? Is there a commonalty of educational objectives?
5. Analyze the possibility of business education curriculums of the future being orientated along the lines of general education rather than vocational education.
6. Evaluate the place of business education's furnishing saleable skills for students in meeting objectives for career education.
7. Project the need for human skills in the world of business machines.
8. Prepare a paper for a business education program that includes an on-the-job training requirement.

SELECTED REFERENCES

BULLS, DERRELL W. "Innovations in Business Education." *Bulletin of the National Association of Secondary Principals* (November 1969), pp. 88–97.

This is a series of two articles that describe two innovations in business education teaching. One deals with mobile simulation in office education and the other with office practice and the computer.

DRISKA, ROBERT S. "Focus on the Secretarial Program." *Business Education Forum* (October 1971), p. 15.

The entire October 1971 issue is devoted to the latest developments in the teaching of shorthand. Succeeding issues of *Business Education Forum* do the same thing for typewriting (November 1971) and bookkeeping (December 1971).

EVANS, GEORGE W., JR. "Meeting Employer Needs in Business Data Processing." *Business Education Forum* (December 1971), pp. 43–45.

This article includes a good description of employer needs in data processing. It presents a good listing of objectives for secondary school programs in preparing students for future employment in offices using data processing.

EYSTER, ELVIN S. "New Directions in Business Education." *American Vocational Journal* (September 1965), pp. 18–19.

This article indicates trends in business education and predicts general business and economic education as an integral part of general education for all pupils.

HALL, J. CURTIS. "What Kinds of Basic Business Education and for Whom." *Business Education Forum* (March 1965), pp. 3–5.

This article advocates basic business education for all pupils, recognizing different abilities and different levels of achievement. It points to authorities in the several business education fields who advocate this.

HIGGINBOTHAM, LOUIS. "Curriculum Revision in Business Education at the Secondary School Level." *National Business Education Quarterly* (May 1960), pp. 18–23.

This article discusses the objectives for business education subjects in the secondary school curriculum and asks several pertinent questions concerning the validity of present practices.

NATIONAL BUSINESS EDUCATION ASSOCIATION. *The Emerging Content and Structure of Business Education.* Eighth Yearbook, 1970.

This yearbook discusses the changing factors affecting business education and suggests ways of improving the curriculum

on all levels.   Current programs are described with special attention to government-sponsored and business-sponsored programs.

SELDEN, WILLIAM.   "Business Education."   *Yearbook, National
Society for the Study of Education,* 1965, pp. 118–126.

This article emphasizes the fact that there is a place in the
vocational-business program for the varied needs of all pupils—
the above average, the average, and the marginal.   Pupils who
are the most readily evaluated are the graduates of the business
education curriculum.

CHAPTER 5

English Language Arts

A prevailing custom in school systems is to shift the blame for learning difficulties from one level to another, particularly in the field of English. College teachers complain of the poor preparation their students received in the secondary schools. High school teachers contend they have to spend too much time teaching things that ought to have been mastered in the elementary grades. This leaves only the parents and the elementary school teachers to blame when some youths use their native tongue improperly.

Learning difficulties associated with the teaching of English present one of the enigmas of present-day education. More pupils are enrolled continuously in classes of English than in any other subject, yet learning results are far less effective than they should be. The amount of English instruction in the secondary schools is graphically demonstrated by an enrollment of 92.9 percent of all pupils as compared to 68 percent in the social studies and 55 percent in mathematics.[1] According to the number enrolled and the amount of time spent in instruction, pupils should show greatest proficiency in language, literature, and composition.

The widespread criticism of the teaching of English, from both lay and professional people, is probably not justified. It has taken more than 100 years to eradicate illiteracy in this country. During that time, thirty thousand high schools, one hundred thou-

---

[1] Nathan S. Blount, "Summary of Investigations Relating to the English Language Arts in Secondary Education," *English Journal* (May 1971), pp. 633–640.

sand elementary schools, and twelve thousand colleges have been erected, and over thirty million youths from all levels of society have been educated. They have come from the linguistically privileged and the linguistically underprivileged, including many children with accents, dialects, and faulty native structural expressions. Significantly, they have included the entire range of learning abilities, and, even so, the goal of total literacy has almost been achieved. Some authorities contend that it is too much to expect a high degree of proficiency in all of the literate efforts of the total population. Others, however, are critical of the failure of secondary school graduates to master oral and written expression.

The English language is a living thing and as such is constantly in a state of flux. Although the change is evolutionary and very often imperceptible, it becomes obvious over an extended period of time. Ironically, the teaching of English has changed relatively little over the past fifty years. College entrance requirements had a tremendous impact on the study of English for the first half of the twentieth century. As a result, the English program was limited to the study of a few selected classics and the perfection of the mechanics of language. Endless hours were spent reading and analyzing a single work of literature and memorizing grammatical nomenclature and usage.

It might be argued that the high school English curriculum has made at least two radical changes in half a century. The "activity" or "experience-centered" programs of the thirties and forties, and the communication theory of semantics of the early fifties were reactions to the traditional program. But basically these changes were superficial, since the teaching of English grammar and composition continued to be patterned after Latin. Even today, in many schools, students begin their study of English grammar by learning an almost identical list of parts of speech.

The prevailing mood in education is for change, and the field of English Language Arts is no exception. With the rise of the so-called "new sciences" and "new math" comes what is sometimes referred to as the "new language arts" or the "new English." These terms are rather imprecise. Traditionally the goal of language instruction has been to standardize the language of students, to purify it of non-standard or non-grammatical patterns of speech and writing. Such a goal ignores the fact that the mark of an educated man is his ability to accommodate himself to a variety of situations, including linguistic ones. It is important that an educated man can speak not only good English, but that he can shift easily and comfortably among various levels and varieties of English. The uneducated man is handicapped by the fact that he speaks a non-standard dialect, and he is often confused in communicable situations.

The trend in recent years has been away from approaching language atomistically and in terms of frequency of individual errors, to an exploration of various grammatical structures in other linguistic units to see how they work, to see what alternatives exist for any of them, and to see in what ways they go together. Rather than concentrating on avoiding what is bad and trying to stamp it out, the concern is for alternative acceptable possibilities. The pace of change remains evolutionary, involving new ways of analyzing the language and new ways of teaching it. The new approaches to teaching are actually based upon the analysis of the language itself. Broad change is probably far off, since many experimental programs are being tried, rejected, and argued within academic communities. Anyone looking for something more or less unified, much less monolithic, in the "new English" is doomed to disappointment. Routes for reform and redirection in English are so far spread that the only certainty for the time being appears to be greater diversity. One thing is certain. Reforms are needed. Until a consensus emerges, however, curriculum planners will have to pick and choose from what they consider the best of the innovations.

IMPORTANT ISSUES

The complexity of contemporary life calls for the framing of directions, the writing of reports, and the articulation of ideas, even in the routine activities of earning a living. The rapid development of scientific and industrial practices increases greatly the need for improved power of communication. Industrial firms find it necessary to hire expensive rewrite experts in order to bring clarity to the reports of their research engineers. Schools of law and medicine frequently decry their students' ineptness in writing and speaking. The task of English teachers needs identification, dimension, and direction. Resolution of the following fundamental issues is of major importance for school curriculum study projects in the English language arts field.

What disposition shall be made of the teaching of grammar?

There are wide differences of opinion concerning the value of teaching grammar.[2] Some teachers and administrators have an almost mystic faith in what the study of grammar can do for every pupil,

[2] Robert Crews, "Linguistic versus a Traditional Grammar Program," *Educational Leadership* (November 1971), pp. 145–149.

while others see little value in such study. Some teachers contend that they would not emphasize grammar if it were not for the insistence of their principals. The principals in turn, blame the teachers for undue emphasis on the subject.

Much of the controversy is based on opinions and feelings rather than on scientific research. But the research that has been done negates the value of grammar in the improvement of English expression. It repeatedly shows only a tenuous connection between the study of grammar and effectiveness in writing, speaking, or reading.

Furthermore, much of the grammar available in the firmly entrenched textbooks and workbooks is a doubly inadequate description of the structure of English. It is inadequate, first, in that it regards our living language as a monolithic structure, immutable either in time or conditions of usage. More importantly, it is inadequate in its failure to appreciate that the structure of English does not correspond, except in a very general way, with the structure of Latin. As taught in our present-day schools, traditional English grammar is based on seventeenth and eighteenth century upper-class usage, expressed in the concepts and terms of Latin.

While many scholars have contributed to this traditional view of English grammar, the one man who probably had the greatest influence, both in England and America, was the eighteenth-century clergyman Robert Lowth. He had little knowledge of the history and structure of English, and only a conventional understanding of the Latin model into which he twisted his native tongue. Nevertheless, Lowth and his fellow grammarians freely prescribed rules for English and condemned any deviation from those rules. This concept of absolute right and wrong forms is the basis for the traditional, or prescriptive, approach to the teaching of grammar. Disciples of this school contend that pupils should strive for a thorough mastery of the rules, arbitrary though they may be and that usage is based entirely on conformity to norms of correctness.

Controversy over the teaching of grammar is caused by scholars who are sharply opposed to a blind faith in unvariable forms of teaching the subject. Curriculum planners should evaluate traditional grammar as it is taught in the schools in order to assess emerging changes offered by advocates of the new grammar. In the beginning the traditional study of grammar dealt with parsing sentences and memorization of rules to identify parts of speech and to correct false syntax. In parsing sentences pupils were asked to take each word, identify its part of speech, and relate it to applicable categories. It was necessary to memorize rules of grammar so that the pupil could prove the correctness of his choice of words when the occasion demanded or, more accurately, when the teacher demanded. The rules were supposed to insure the pupil against possibilities of false syntax. An early modification of tra ditional grammar came with the placing of emphasis on parts o sentences as well as parts of speech. Thus attention now is giver to subjects, predicates, objects, and modifiers, each of which i: encompassed by grammatical rules. Emphasis is placed on the study of sentence structure and sentence analysis.

A revolutionary approach to the teaching of grammar wa: espoused by advocates of structural linguistics. Probably the mosl important force in the new movement was the publication of Noan Chomsky's monograph, *Syntactic Structures*.[3] The central theme ol structuralism relates to language as a system in which each separate part is related to all other parts, a sort of grand gestalt. A system of language is discovered by selecting a part and establishing its relationship to all other parts.

Structuralism has peculiarities of its own. The structural- ists insist that speech is the real language. Consideration of mean- ing should be avoided until phonology, morphology, and syntax have been disposed of, which means in practice that meaning is given little attention, or that it is dealt with covertly. In spite of certain limitations, structuralism is attractive because it offers in- sight into the nature of linguistic systems, into the way language is put together.

Modern linguists advocate a structural approach to gram- mar teaching by which usage determines correctness of form.[4] They view usage in English as distinct from grammatical structure. They see spoken language as the primary source of grammatical data for written language. If a great number of people use a certain structure in oral communication, it becomes acceptable usage. These scholars suggest that language be viewed as a psychological, historical, and sociological phenomenon rather than a corrupt descendent of a more perfect parent.

The structural linguistic approach to the teaching of gram- mar offers exciting vistas for teachers who are discouraged with the futility of teaching grammar in the traditional manner. Op- posing forces, of course, say that although usage is a powerful fac- tor in linguistic change it is not an adequate criterion in itself for acceptance or rejection of such change. These forces hold that for the sake of logical consistency certain rules must be maintained and any change creates more problems than it solves.

It is apparent that the threshold of a counter revolution in the teaching of grammar has been reached.[5] The term "new

---

[3] Noam Chomsky, *Syntactic Structures* (Hague, Netherlands: Mouton, 1957).
[4] Charles C. Fries, *Teaching of English* (Ann Arbor, Michigan: George Wohr Publishing Company, 1962), pp. 102–121.
[5] Dwight L. Burton and John S. Simmons, *Teaching English in Today's High School* (New York: Holt, Rinehart and Winston, 1970), pp. 28–54.

grammar" is appearing with increasing frequency. Perhaps greater accuracy would dictate the identity of several "new grammars." An outmoded and incorrect grammar is being replaced by new grammars that actually describe the structure of English as a unique language.[6] The linguist refers to the step beyond structural grammar as generative transformational grammar. It deals with complex structures. It identifies rules governing transformations which users of a language have habitually followed without consciously recognizing them as rules.

A generative grammar is a set of rules that describe the structure of every normal sentence in a language, and these rules dictate automatically which sentences are normal. Structural grammar is occupied with the question of *how* one knows the structure of a given sentence. What are the signals, word order, function words, endings, and so forth that convey grammatical meaning and indicate structure? In generative grammar there is no such concern. Instead of worrying over how the structure of a language is determined, the generative grammarian will expend his energies in stating as explicitly as possible what the structure is. To do this the generative grammarian uses quasi-algebraic formulas, instead of everyday language in stating rules. He would contend that everyday language is often ambiguous. Quasi-mathematical statements force the grammarian to be explicit, and the identification of sentences as being normal must be explicit. It should be pointed out that the use of such abstract symbolism is often confusing and distressing to many English teachers. It is probably necessary to trust the generative grammarian as to the necessity of such procedures.

While it is not too difficult to describe generative grammar, transformational grammar presents quite a different problem. A grammar can be generative without being transformational, and at least theoretically the reverse is true. The problem in describing transformational grammar is it can be a great many things—some of them quite different from the other. For example, consider four sentences: "To rise early is healthful," "Rising early is healthful," "It is healthful to rise early," and "For one to rise early is healthful." These four sentences can be thought of as superficial variations of the same underlying, abstract structure. The underlying or "deep" structure shared by all four sentences cannot be pronounced, only represented by symbols. These symbols represent what the four sentences have in common and the interconnection of the ideas "rising," "early," and "healthful." This deep structure has a relationship to the superficial or "surface" structure of each of the four distinct sentences, and that relationship can be described as

---

[6] Doris V. Gunderson, "Research in the Teaching of English," *English Journal* (September 1971), pp. 792–796.

a transformation or change in the structure as focus is moved from one stratum of the grammar to another. A grammar using descriptions of this sort is transformational. In effect, transformational grammar describes certain relationships between sentences as though they were changes in the sentences.

Generative transformational grammar has much to offer, but it is still very much in the formative stage. Basic and far-reaching changes are constantly being made. Those who pioneer in introducing transformational grammar into their English classes today must be prepared to find it obsolete tomorrow. Even now disturbing rumbles can be heard in the grammatical stratosphere by those proclaiming the merits of stratificational grammar.

New linguistic theories and new revolutions in grammar are likely to keep turning up for some time to come. Curriculum makers in the field of English cannot sit back and hope the whole thing will go away. The new grammars promise to describe the workings of the English language accurately, and they have a direct application in teaching pupils how to write English sentences. Perhaps a breakthrough is imminent in the teaching of the most difficult of all skills—that of teaching boys and girls to write well.

General acceptance and implementation of the newer approaches to the teaching of grammar will be related closely to the training of knowledgeable teachers. It will be necessary in many instances to reeducate teachers in the actual linguistic structure of the language.

Is there adequate scope and sequence in the English language arts program?

The issue of scope and sequence in the English language arts field is regarded from many different points of view. There are those who contend that English has no subject matter of its own; the skills of communication should be taught as they are needed in other subjects. Others contend that English does possess subject matter, which should be divided and presented logically. A third group recognizes the presence of subject matter, but not in an orderly form. This group holds that sequence in subject-matter order must follow the growth and development pattern of the pupils.

English lacks the logical, clear sequence that is found in other subjects. To the pupils it must appear that they go from English to English to English without being able to tell one grade from another—same grammar, same drills, and same theme topics. Their theme assignments include "My Pets" and "How I Spent My Vacation," and they are asked to write their autobiographies at least seven or eight times. Too often curriculums are a collection of unrelated trivial activities showing a lack of unity and purposeful rationale.

From a survey of curriculum activities in the field of English language arts three identifiable patterns are developing which offer a solution to the problem of scope and sequence. They represent three organizational efforts for the establishment of unity and rationale. The first is an older theory based on the traditional division of English language arts into written composition, language study, and literature. Units of subject matter from each of these divisions are allocated to the various grade levels according to the logical development of the content.

The second curriculum pattern has been labeled the "sequential steps curriculum." Here the psychological rather than the logical is stressed. Each grade level includes material on the structure of the English language, writing effective prose, and reading literary forms, with subject matter developed sequentially, according to the learning levels of the pupils. For example, in one curriculum, the steps in the development of literary sensitivity include the simple enjoyment of a story, appreciation of seeing one's own experience mirrored in literature, projection of oneself into another world, understanding of symbolism, and sensitivity to patterns of literary style.

A third plan for establishing orderly sequence in English is based on the use of thematic units. This approach appears to be gaining in general acceptance, particularly in the middle grades of the secondary school. It involves the selection of subject matter according to an established theme, concept, idea, or human experience. Usually, thematic units stress humanistic values, such as man and his relation to deity or man and his relation to his fellow man. They are arranged according to the learning abilities of the pupils, and sequence can be established through the number of units to be presented and the order in which they are presented.

Whatever approach is taken, it should be noted that pupils become bored studying the same literary selections in as many as three successive years. An example of an overworked poem is "The Rhyme of the Ancient Mariner," which is used in the ninth grade as a good sea story, in the tenth as a literary ballad, and in the twelfth as an allegory of the spiritual regeneration of man.

What are the valuable dimensions in the teaching of literature?

The value of literature in the English language arts program needs neither identification nor justification. Some people, however, charge that school authorities do not recognize this value. They contend that literature is relegated to the background, while emphasis is placed on the more practical aspects of the language arts program. Others, of course, admit a reasonable amount of time is spent in studying literature and the time is justified by the ultimate contribution it makes to the education of the pupil. The issue appears to be concerned with the utilitarian value of the subject.

It is nonsensical to argue that literature is useful in the usual sense of the word. As a vital part of the humanities, its value must be measured in other dimensions—development, humanism, and form. The first dimension relates to the development of human values, such as aesthetic experiences with language provided by words themselves. Rhythm, refrain, repetition, and incantation are fundamental needs of the human organism. Literature also extends the experiences of human beings beyond their limited worlds. It serves as an escape function, helping the individual to escape from the confines of the moment. Further values are found in the types of experiences described. The reader is enabled to enlarge his own experiences greatly by living vicariously the experiences of fictional characters.[7] Literature can be of special value to an individual in his search for identity. As he learns to understand human nature and the complexities of the human character he learns to understand himself.

The contact that literature makes with the culture of a society it describes gives it a humanistic dimension.[8] This does not come through memorization of book titles, authors, or memory gems, but rather from an understanding of man's struggle with his environment. Literature explains the unexplainable; it probes the mystic and unknown. It shows the ideas and conflicts that have engaged man over the centuries. It gives an imaginative explanation for all phenomena. In the elementary school, subject matter deals with fairly tales, fantasies, legends, and folklore. In the upper grades it deals with man and his contemporary concerns. The topics are heroes, animals, and strange happenings. In the secondary school the pupil is introduced to the major modes of man. This is usually done through thematic units on such topics as the comic mode, the romantic mode, the psychological introspective mode, and the ironic mode.

Through the dimension of form, the artistry of writing comes into focus. Poetry is an example of an art form that lends itself to the entire gamut of human emotion and literary expression. The drama, the essay, the short story, and the novel are all literary forms that give the writer great breadth of communication. As

[7] Mary Elizabeth Fowler, *Teaching Language Composition and Literature* (New York: McGraw-Hill Book Company, 1965), p. 219.
[8] Dwight L. Burton, *Literature Study in the High Schools* (New York: Holt, Rinehart & Winston, Inc., 1964), p. 11.

the pupil learns to read and understand many literary forms he lengthens his avenues for understanding the humanities. Emphasis is on how to understand, interpret, and judge what is read, and on reaching an increasing awareness of literature as a means of understanding.

It is more important to utilize pupil purposes and pupil needs in the study of literature than it is to debate the selection of subject matter. Less emphasis should be given to the fetish that there are "must" selections for pupils to read. Increasingly, teachers are turning to worthwhile contemporary writing that gives pupils an understanding of the modern world. This does not mean that older literature must be abandoned, but that the approaches to it must be reevaluated in order to use it more advantageously. The field of classical literature can contribute significantly to the culture of the educated person, but some of it is far beyond the comprehension of many pupils. Forcing them to read it will turn them against literature.

As curriculum emphasis on science and mathematics appears to be leveling off, the academic pendulum is swinging toward the humanities. Certain advocates of the humanities are proposing the idea of combining the study of literature with the study of art and the study of music. The argument is made that such a combination helps pupils understand the interrelationships between these art forms. It is contended that each of these fields is closely interwoven with the cultural heritage of mankind and that each field spans the gap between this cultural heritage and the dramatic social problems of the day. Each field is a reflection of the joys and sorrows of all ages. Advocates of combining the three fields point to the perfect affinity of music, art, and literature as expressions of mankind.

Opponents of the humanities combination contend that teachers are not sufficiently versed in the subject-matter content of music, art, and literature to give any degree of depth to such study and that such an arrangement under the banner of the humanities would tend to divorce literature from the field of English. To remove literature from the field of English would remove one of its most exciting components and rob students of needed ideas for writing and speaking.

What is a proper balance of emphasis in the communication arts?

To determine a proper balance of emphasis, administrators must ask, What constitutes a field? What is the relative importance of the various divisions of subject matter? and What emphasis shall be given to activities within the divisions of the subject matter? They must also consider individual differences of learning and patterns of growth.   Even if curriculum planners make the proper decisions in all these matters, a good balance of learning experiences for the pupil will depend on the skills of the teacher.

The language arts field normally involves the communication skills: listening, reading, speaking, and writing.   Recognition of the proper function of each is a basic objective for each pupil. These are the avenues of thought that lead to an awareness of personal importance and power.

Listening.   Although listening has only recently been recognized as a communication skill, its proponents contend it is the medium through which a large part of communication is achieved.   Indeed, it is reasonable to estimate that listening activities take 45 percent of the total time involved in communication, a percentage which will probably increase as mass media of communication involving listening activities develop.   Those urging increased emphasis of listening skills maintain that pupils must be taught to listen effectively and critically.[9]   Hearing, they hold, is a more or less passive process, while listening is an active, attentive skill which contributes to the development of good thinking habits and good reading skills.

Reading.   There are wide differences of opinion concerning the proper place of reading skills in the language arts program.   Value is not in question, but rather the amount of time to be devoted to the development of such skills.   This is an especially pertinent issue in the secondary schools, where more and more pupils have reading deficiencies and an ever-increasing amount of time must be devoted to remedial reading.   Certainly it cannot be assumed that this is the sole function of the English teacher, but realistically he will be expected to guide the activity, since reading is normally a language arts skill.   Attention to developmental reading skills is another obligation of the secondary school.   Improvement in speed, understanding, and appreciation is desirable for all pupils, and, here again, while this is the responsibility of all teachers, the leadership role is assigned to the English teacher.

A reading specialist is desirable for both remedial reading and developmental reading.   New techniques stress reading by structures rather than by words or parts of words.   English is a syntactic language rather than a morphological language; therefore the study of groups of words and their relationships is more valu-

[9] J. N. Hook, *The Teaching of High School English* (New York: The Ronald Press Company, 1965), pp. 402–421.

able than the study of changing forms of groups of words. A very important concomitant factor here is the relationship of reading skills to the development of writing skills involving syntactic structure.

A main objective in a secondary school reading program should be to help pupils become proficient in the use of various approaches to reading. There is a tendency to confuse "reading rates" with "reading ability." Too much attention is given to measuring increased reading rates. The accomplished reader does not have a single rate; he commands and uses a variety of rates. A pupil must become as skillful as possible in using different approaches in his reading, and he needs good judgment in selecting that approach or combination of approaches compatible with his purposes for reading.

Future curriculum decisions in the teaching of reading in secondary schools may be influenced by experimental programs now in progress in the elementary schools. One such program, known as the *Augmented Roman Method* or the *Initial Teaching Alphabet,* represents the twenty-six letters of the alphabet by forty speech sounds. The Initial Teaching Alphabet uses forty-three characters designed in such a way that a letter represents just one sound and both uppercase and lowercase letters have only one form. The teacher is free within this system to use either the whole word or the phonetic approach.

Another intriguing method in the developmental stage is the *Language Experience Approach,* which combines reading and other communication skills. Through words and pictures, pupils share ideas from their own experiences and interests. The teacher records each pupil's stories and the pupil reads his stories aloud to the class. During the process, the teacher calls attention to letter formation, relationship of beginning sounds to symbols used, capitalization, punctuation, and sentence meaning.

Speaking. It can be estimated that about one-third of all verbal communication is devoted to speaking. Since speech habits are started in early childhood and involve the total experiences of the pupil, the English teacher shares with the parents the responsibility for the education of the pupil in verbal communication. Unfortunately, however, if the speech patterns are poor, the English teacher is assigned most of the blame. The task of the English teacher is complicated by the necessity of dealing with the technicalities of correct usage, substandard speech patterns, slang, jargon, colloquial expressions, and many different dialects.

The major problems in the teaching of good oral communication are those of motivation and practical application. The use of oral drills or formalized public speaking activities are of negligible value in the improvement of speech patterns.   There is general agreement among language arts authorities that pupils must be stimulated to improve their oral communication skills through needs associated with realistic experiences.

Oral communication is a good tool for development of thought processes, because gradual formation of concepts follows the talking over and putting together of ideas.   There is a high correlation between a pupil's ability to communicate orally and his success in learning to read.   Greater emphasis should be placed on the oral aspect of language in an effort to build linguistic power and ease in speaking, reading, and writing.   A concerted effort should be made to interrelate the different areas of the language program through basic oral communication.   It is here the decisions of proper emphasis must be made.

Writing.   Although a small percentage of a person's time is spent in writing, this phase of the communication skills looms large in importance because the impressions are enduring.   As has been mentioned before, framing directions, writing reports, conducting business and personal correspondence, and general articulation of ideas through the written word are all done in strategic areas where appropriate form is of major significance.   The importance of written communication and the difficulty of teaching it complicate the amount of emphasis that should be placed on it.   There are those who contend it is one of the most important activities in the curriculum, in spite of the fact that it occupies so little of one's time.   Others consider the teaching of writing skills the most difficult of all teaching activities, and the more pessimistic say the teaching of lucid, accurate, effective composition to most pupils is hopeless.   If this is true it means that students of limited ability will be unable to master these skills.   Over-emphasis will lead only to dissatisfaction and boredom.   Another consideration in the teaching of writing might be raised by the contention of certain critics that the extensive use of objective testing and the lack of time for checking papers prevent pupils from reaching experiences in written composition.

All the answers regarding the teaching of writing are not available yet; however, certain ground rules are emerging from the newer programs of English composition, which emphasize the fact that what pupils do before they write is more important than what they do when they write.   Before every piece of written work, the teacher and the pupil should explore the problem, discuss procedure for developing it, determine intensity or extent of treatment, and agree upon the probable length of the finished product.   The long term paper does not contribute much to writing competence; the short writing task, concentrating on one or two good writing concepts, is being advocated.   Rewriting is a valuable process, and the short paper lends itself better to revision activities. These involve critical analysis by the pupil himself, his teacher, and his classmates. Best results are obtained if the pupil realizes that only his best efforts will be finally accepted.

As mentioned previously, one of the most hopeful tools for improved teaching of writing may come from the development of generative grammar that has a direct application to the writing of English sentences.

Other communication skills.   To maintain proper balance and emphasis, other activities in the English language arts curriculum also need attention.   These include such subject-matter items as spelling and vocabulary, and such subject-matter courses as dramatics, journalism, and speech.   In most schools these classes are now part of the regular curriculum.   In a few schools they are still used in extraclass arrangements.

Vocabulary and spelling raise special problems.   Every pupil should develop a good vocabulary, and the techniques for encouraging such development are well understood.   However, it must be emphasized that the ability to handle the communication symbols of thought is basic in all educational activities, and the English teacher, like teachers of other subjects, can be but a cooperative agent in the development of vocabulary.   As for spelling, it is overemphasized, particularly in junior high school.   Surveys reveal that from 25 to 50 percent of language arts time in junior high is devoted to spelling, an amount of time far out of proportion to its importance.   Such inordinate emphasis may be due to pressure of people who can easily spot a spelling error in the work of their secretaries, but who cannot tell a good English sentence from a bad one. A suitable English language arts program should deal with vocabulary development and spelling in a proper balance, not at the expense of written composition, the study of rhetoric, or the learning of the structure of our language.

How can motivation for the study of the English language arts be revitalized?

It may be a gross oversimplification to contend that the major problem in the teaching of the language arts today is one of motivation. A collapse of morale is evident, however. It is extremely difficult to motivate lower- and average-ability pupils who can see no need for communication skills beyond the ones they possess and who have experienced nothing but failure in any effort to improve. Even many of the better pupils find the study of the language arts unstimulating or unchallenging. Finding a purpose for study is difficult. Teachers may imply a purpose in such questions as "What will happen to you next year in English?" or "What will happen to you when you go to college?" or "How are you going to pass your year-end examinations?" But threats do not supply true motivation.

Educators have subscribed for years to theories of individual growth and differences of ability among pupils. Yet in the field of the language arts, much of the teaching has been given to pupils in groups which are illogically based on intelligence scores, verbal ability, and past performance. As the pupils progress through the school, they are doomed to the same placement regardless of growth or failure to grow. Since this is likely to be a monotonous, repetitive situation, the ingredients for exciting and challenging learning situations will be lacking. The great boredom that characterizes so many secondary English classes is due to the breakdown of morale among pupils who lack high verbal ability. These pupils should be grouped according to accomplishment, and programs should be adjusted to provide individual challenges leading to purposeful activity.

The differences in pupils widen as they grow older. No two pupils are alike; no two progress at the same rate. Some are word conscious; others, thing conscious. Some grasp abstractions quickly; others lack the intelligence even to understand moderately high level abstractions. Some come from homes of high cultural values; others come from homes where conversations consist of a few gutteral sounds. With such a variety of learning experiences, it is not realistic to think that the same increments of subject matter, each year based on the preceding year, can be presented to all pupils. Communication skills are personal, and instruction must be presented in such a way that each pupil can see a reason to improve. First steps in improvement will come from the pupil's own efforts. A benevolent insistence from the teacher that no work will be accepted for evaluation until the pupil has done himself justice may encourage improvement, and the pupil will be further motivated if he finds that his efforts contribute to the solution of his own problems.

The study of the language arts can be fascinating. If it is approached as a meaningful whole rather than as a collection of unrelated skills, types of language, levels of language, and the interesting history of language can be explored.

How can conditions conducive to good teaching be maintained?

This issue appears more acute in the field of English than in any other subject-matter area. A prevalent idea is that anyone can teach English. Many regularly assigned teachers of English are sub-par in their training and experience. Since the subject is usually required in all grades, there are often overflow classes which may be assigned to the shop teacher or the athletic coach. Occasionally these teachers do a creditable job, but such instances are the exception. English teachers condemn this situation and point to the fact that unqualified teachers are rarely assigned to science or mathematics.

Since English is a required subject, classes are frequently overcrowded. Many teachers are assigned as many as 200 pupils per day, and frequently there is little effort to group these pupils according to ability or accomplishment. The language arts involve a limitless number of relationships that require skillful work on the part of trained teachers, but with overcrowded classes they have no time for good planning, individual attention to accomplishment, or evaluation of learning. It is poor administration and false economy to jeopardize the effectiveness of good teachers with impossible teaching conditions. Some school systems are reducing pupil-load to below 100 pupils per teacher; others are experimenting with lay-readers. English teachers welcome the reduction of class size but are sharply divided in their opinion of the effectiveness of lay-readers.

A third condition that needs attention in many schools is the tendency to use the English classes for anything remotely related to language activities. Because English is a required subject, the English class forms a convenient avenue for reaching all pupils for a general school activity. Contests of all kinds and fund raising and collection campaigns are frequently assigned to these classes. This is an administrative convenience, but an educational atrocity. Only a step less objectionable, but even more time-consuming, is the practice of using the English period for orientation classes, instruction in developing study habits, distribution of career information, training for taking college entrance exams, teaching research techniques, or even teaching the Dewey Decimal System. One school uses the English classroom as the site of the Christmas party. The uselessness of these activities to the mastery of oral and written communication is self-evident. Language arts classrooms must be freed of this conglomeration of unrelated activities, and teachers must be given the time to get on with the tasks that are rightfully theirs.

Improvement of teaching conditions for English teachers probably will result from a study made by The Commission on English. The Commission was established in 1959 by the College Entrance Examination Board to encourage and facilitate improvement in curriculum and methods of classroom instruction. Its members, all teachers of English, made a thorough study of secondary school English and published their findings and recommendations in 1965. The report, *Freedom and Discipline in English*, lists fourteen recommendations. Eight deal with teaching conditions, course load, pupil load, and class size; the others concern teacher training and the English curriculum.

PROJECT ENGLISH

Impetus for improvements in the language arts field has come from research projects, national documents, and English teachers' professional organizations. Probably the most notable project is "Project English," a cooperative venture between the United States Office of Education and major universities around the country. Sixteen different university centers are working on programs covering the total school structure from kindergarten through the first two years of college. Some are focusing attention on college-bound tenth, eleventh, and twelfth graders. Others are working with written composition research at every level from kindergarten through high school. Reading and language materials are being developed for grades seven through nine in depressed urban areas.

Project English has five major objectives:

1. To develop a composition program for grades ten through twelve which will lead to the maturation of writing skills in clearly defined sequential steps
2. To develop a reading program for grades ten through twelve which will lead to the maturation of reading skills in clearly defined sequential steps
3. To develop lists of readings, syllabi for composition, and teachers' manuals for both reading and composition
4. To demonstrate the utility of the reading and writing program by installing them in several high schools on an experimental basis
5. To evaluate the reading and writing programs through tests given in the cooperating schools

Many new programs are being introduced to English teachers in summer institutes. With National Defense Education Act funds, about 105 institutions have up-dated the knowledge of about 4000 English teachers. Project English and English language art institutes have resulted in a large measure from the cooperative work of the National Council of Teachers of English, the Cooperative English Program, and the College Entrance Examination Board English Institute Programs. The National Council of Teachers of English expressed its concern over the changing state of language arts and made its recommendations in one of the most widely read documents in its history.[10]

[10] *The National Interest and the Teaching of English* (Champaign, Illinois: National Council of Teachers of English, 1961).

Another major influence on what should constitute the secondary school English curriculum was the Anglo-American Seminar on Teaching of English held at Dartmouth College in the summer of 1965. The focus at Dartmouth was not on a definition of English as a subject but more on the clarification of the nature of the pupil and his needs and potential for growth. The concern was more for teaching style rather than substance, more on how English properly taught can help pupils reach their full linguistic potential rather than on what areas of content are most important to learn. Curriculum planners in the field of English should make a comprehensive study of Herbert Joseph Miller's Dartmouth Seminar report.[11]

One of the leading strategies of the proponents of status quo is to point to the slow progress of change. The field of English has certain fertility for the growth of opposition to impending improvements. A recent study in the New England states shows that only 30 percent of a thousand responding teachers gave an affirmative reply as to whether they taught linguistics. Less than 12 percent mentioned the use of structural forms of analysis, less than 10 percent used generative transformational systems, and 5 percent reported the use of miscellaneous innovative methods.[12]

A study of 2,247 students who took the College Board English Composition Test shows that the writing activities most commonly used in their English classes were: proofreading a paper before handing it in, writing outside of class on a teacher-assigned topic, and doing grammar exercises in a workbook. Despite research evidence that negates grammar exercises as a mode for improving student writing, these students report they did grammar exercises three times more frequently than they rewrote papers that had been gone over by the teachers.[13]

The basic point surrounding all innovations in the field of language is that the scholars have little doubt, based on their knowledge, research, and experience, that the changes coming into their discipline are improvements. They realize their limitations and deficiencies in plotting the steps of the route, yet they are confident it is the right road. They all have faith in the importance of language as man's highest achievement, and the courage, the persistence, and the dynamism to find new ways of improving their teaching of it.

[11] Herbert Joseph Miller, *The Uses of English: Guidelines for the Teaching of English from the Anglo-American Conference at Dartmouth College* (New York: Holt, Rinehart and Winston, 1967).

[12] Ted Debries, "This World of English," *English Journal* (January 1970), p. 140.

[13] Anthony Tavatt, "This World of English," *English Journal* (February 1970), p. 283.

CONTINUED EMPHASIS ON
ENGLISH LANGUAGE ARTS

English is well on the way to becoming an international language. More than half of the world's newspapers are printed in English, most of the scientific journals are printed in English or have an English edition, and many of the schools of the undeveloped countries use English. Since language is one of the main avenues for understanding of culture, the use of English for world communication is a prime means for promoting the tenets of democracy.

The spreading use and understanding of English in much of the world intensifies the need for its improvement at home. Adequate solutions of the issues involved in the English language arts field, acceptance of the newer theories of learning, and better articulation of learning experiences both within and without the school will contribute to this improvement.

Several future developments have been predicted for the English language arts curriculum and instructional areas. The language arts will be interrelated by the use of thematic units within a humanistic context that will show a better balance between utility and value. In composition, the trend will be away from structure as an entity, but teachers will continue to recognize its importance in relation to writing that is clear and well-organized. Linguistics studies will intensify the teaching of standard usage rather than prescriptive grammatical rules. The teaching of sentence structure will change as research reveals more about language. There will be greater stress on semantics and the history of language. Teachers will use inductive, problem-solving techniques that will involve the individual pupil in a realistic situation.

TOPICS FOR STUDY AND DISCUSSION

1. Evaluate the effects of modern linguistics programs on the purposes and objectives of teaching grammar in the secondary schools.
2. What are the advantages of teaching the language arts through the use of thematic units?
3. If you were a consultant to a language arts curriculum committee, what advice would you offer for improving the teaching of literature?
4. If special emphasis is given to the mastery of grammar, will it enhance or impede a pupil's ability to do creative writing?

5. Are the linguists actually going to provide a "new" approach to the teaching of structural English?

6. Evaluate the problems likely to be encountered in giving literature a humanistic dimension.

7. Why is the teaching of writing skills considered the most difficult of the language arts activities?

8. Are the problems of pupil motivation more difficult in the teaching of English than in other comparable subjects?

9. Make a critical analysis of the possibility of the English language becoming a force in the promotion of democracy throughout the world.

10. Analyze the problems facing school leaders in implementing the numerous approaches to the teaching of grammar.

11. Prepare a comprehensive report on the Dartmouth Seminar and give identity to its likely influence on the teaching of English.

SELECTED REFERENCES

BLACK, MAX. *The Labyrinth of Language.* New York: Frederick A. Praeger, Inc., 1968.

This book contains a reaction to replacing discredited, irrelevant, traditional grammar with the more academically respectable, but still irrelevant, modern grammars. It also raises serious questions concerning the focus on grammar at the expense of other facets of language study.

BURTON, DWIGHT L., and SIMMONS, JOHN S. *Teaching English in Today's High Schools.* New York: Holt, Rinehart and Winston, 1970.

This volume lists major statements of theory and practice by prominent teachers of English. It points to the position of being at the watershed of a new reform in English and suggests changes in the secondary school English curriculum to bring it in line with the recommendations of the Dartmouth Seminar and to reflect current linguistic principles in language learning.

CHISHOLM, WILLIAM. *The New English.* New York: Funk and Wagnalls, 1969.

This is an ambitious attempt to describe the radical changes being made in the teaching of English. The book explains new theories and methods in language teaching. It provides good descriptions of structural linguistics and generative-transformational grammar.

FAGAN, EDWARD R., and VANDELL, JEAN. *Classroom Practices in Teaching English: Humanizing English.* Urbana, Illinois: National Council of Teachers of English, 1970.

This book reviews twenty-seven selected practices in teaching English. Represented in the group are those related to independent study and those that individualize instruction in a humanizing way. Good practices are revealed on motivating and evaluating writing. Techniques and content are identified throughout the material. It should be helpful in curriculum planning.

KOUTSOUDAS, ANDREAS. *Writing Transformational Grammars.* New York: McGraw-Hill Book Company, 1966.

This volume gives ways of writing grammars based on a theory of language description originated by Chomsky. It could serve as an introduction for a course in syntax. It has both theoretical background and practical procedures.

LEFEVRE, CARL A. *Linguistics, English, and the Language Arts.* Boston: Allyn and Bacon, Inc., 1970.

The author emphasizes his own personal brand of linguistics. He presents a structural bias of transformational grammar and includes listings of teaching suggestions for aiding beginning teachers. He advocates the theory that secondary teachers stress intellectual inquiry and not try to make their students "junior linguists."

LOBAN, WALTER, et al. *Teaching Language and Literature.* New York: Harcourt Brace and World, Inc., 1969.

This book has explicit suggestions about teaching in every chapter. The details about method are plausibly based in a theory of teaching that emphasizes process over predetermined ends. The second edition reinforces the book's position as a leader in textbooks on the teaching of English in the secondary schools.

MALONEY, HENRY B. *New English, New Imperatives.* Urbana, Illinois: National Council of Teachers of English, 1971.

Material is suggested for the English department that is ready and willing to engage in a comprehensive self-study. It stresses the theory that English should be involvement and experience with language and literature rather than learning *about* them, and laments the many misdirected approaches in secondary school curriculums.

MORSEY, RAYOL J. *Improving English Instruction.* Boston: Allyn and Bacon, Inc., 1969.

This volume presents a wide range of ideas on teaching literature, grammar, usage, written composition, and oral composition. The ideas are offered as hypotheses designed to help solve problems confronting all English teachers. It stresses ways for teachers to test both formal and informal ideas about the teaching of English.

MURPHY, GERALDINE. *The Study of Literature in High School.* Waltham, Mass.: Blaisdell Publishing Company, 1968.

This book was designed to integrate theory and practice in the teaching of literature. It discusses the nature of literature and suggests objectives for teaching. It is a good treatise for curriculum planners since it presents lists of appropriate works, study guides, illustrative lesson plans, and creative writing assignments suitable for students of varying degrees of motivation and intellectual abilities.

STEEVES, FRANK L. *The Subjects in the Curriculum.* Indianapolis: Odyssey Press, 1968.

This is a collection of readings dealing directly with the subjects in the curriculum. They stress the use of the disciplines as curriculum content and how to select what to teach. Part Two contains material for the consideration of English and language arts curriculum field.

CHAPTER 6

Fine Arts

The emphasis the curriculum maker puts on the fine arts is one of the real tests of his faith in a comprehensive school program. Here, many critics of the school confuse values. The so-called fundamental subjects are always assured of a secure place in the learning experience of the pupil, but the arts are usually considered of secondary importance and their fate fluctuates according to societal whims or economic pressures. Considering the fine arts mere entertainment and ignoring the meaningful values in them that ennoble and elevate will only foster mediocrity in an age searching for excellence.

The youth of the nation are criticized for their vulgar taste in music, their sloppiness in dress, and their weird affinity for fads and off-beat choices of entertainment. They confuse their elders by eccentric behavior and participation in activities that accentuate their youthful independence from accepted social values. Yet, critical adults who argue for the strengthening of mathematics and science in the school curriculum are not in favor of equal emphasis on aesthetic and cultural subjects as represented by the fine arts. They do not appreciate the purpose of educational experiences that go beyond vocational competencies to develop aesthetic values and discriminating tastes that enable an individual to live a fuller and richer life.

Instead of producing merely specialists who can fit into technological slots, the schools must produce generalists who can improve the art of living. The truly comprehensive curriculum lays emphasis on all types of learning activities. All pupils need experiences in understanding music and the various art forms. These experiences should be extensive enough to include something for those who create, those who perform, and those who consume. Pupils need to learn how to exercise social responsibility in making personal and group decisions about the arts. School programs should reflect a balanced image of social and artistic values.

One of the basic tenets of a good education is the development of discriminating taste. The school should help pupils to be as critical of a singer without a voice, or an art form without imagination, as they would be of a public official without integrity. In many respects the fine arts help prepare youths to take part in making civic decisions that will not be stereotyped or prejudiced. Each individual is responsible for the quality of art in his home and the aesthetic choices he advocates in his community. The arts are involved in his decisions on civic planning, housing, and urban renewal. If the aesthetic and cultural levels of society are to be raised, it will result from the educational insights youths gain from the fine arts program of the schools.

The increased leisure of an affluent society gives cause for greater stress in the schools on those learning experiences that contribute to purposeful, intelligent, and satisfying use of leisure time. Growing patronage at art exhibits, the ballet, symphony concerts, and other aesthetic and cultural activities indicates that interest does exist. Youths need educational experiences with music and art forms as preparation for even greater understanding and enjoyment of such profitable leisure time ventures.

ART

Art, one of the most sophisticated forms of visual experience, is the visual language of all people. It is an integrating process of sensing, thinking, feeling, and expressing. To understand art, one must understand his fellowman and the many forms of visual expression man employs. The development of such understanding is not an easy process; it is frequently deep and complicated. The infinite subtleties employed in visual expressions require artistic sensitivity for interpretation. This is an educational learning activity that should have a place in the secondary schools.

National interest

It is hardly necessary to stress the importance of art in the life of a nation. It is paradoxical, however, to compare the lofty position art occupies in the cultural affairs of this nation and the indifference it receives in the nation's schools. An increased emphasis on art in public life may be noted. Galleries are crowded and new ones are being built. Great works of art are topics of conversation. A sympathetic government offers financial encouragement to art projects, and large mail order houses are adding original painting to their lists of merchandise. In the commercial world, advertising, product design, packaging, and television programing are constantly seeking new artistic and colorful ways of increasing product appeal. Communities, large and small, are engaged in serious planning for improved artistic appearance and creative architectural design.

There may not be exactly a renaissance of art, but a favorable climate for a flowering of the arts certainly exists. However, a survey of the programs of the nation's public schools does not reflect a fervent activity in the field. Research data indicate that the pupils either do not have the opportunity or are not availing themselves of the opportunity to pursue art courses. This is especially true of the secondary schools: slightly higher than 50 percent of them offer art courses and around 15 percent of the pupils are enrolled. Only a limited number of the small schools attempt to teach art. Practically all of the programs are in the large urban schools.

Art and pupil needs

It is a simple matter to say that art affects everybody, that a civilization without art is impoverished, and that the person who is dependent on others for providing him with vicarious artistic experiences is barren indeed; but to demonstrate the value of art in the school, such courses must have a prominent position in the curriculum, and getting administrators to include them is not easy.

To do so one must stress the fact that art provides pupils with experiences that are satisfying and directly useful to them in their daily lives. Through art, pupils develop their critical faculties and discover constructive avenues for emotional expression that enable them to contribute artistically to the creation of a more satisfying environment.

Future citizens must learn to create wholesome, satisfying experiences beyond those necessary for making a living. Since they live in a world of colors, forms, lines, textures, space, and motion, they need to develop the ability to explore things creatively through their senses. Every pupil has a relative amount of talent in creative expression. Each one should have an opportunity to work on some of his own ideas, concerns, and imaginative projections.

Administrative problems

Very few administrators would deny the value of art as a school subject. They would generally agree to its inclusion in the curriculum of the elementary school but, as has been suggested before, there is a marked lack of support in the secondary schools. The secondary school people contend their curriculum is overcrowded with more basic requirements. They also point to their inability to secure qualified teachers.

However, the inclusion of subjects in the secondary school curriculum is determined partly by the significance attached to the subject.[1] There is no research to prove that one subject is more important than another for all pupils. Once it is decided that art is a valuable area of instruction, its status in the secondary school curriculum will be improved. The next problem will then be one of scheduling. Numerous scheduling patterns are feasible. No doubt some type of flexible scheduling will make it possible to enlarge the scope of curriculum offerings that are necessary to take care of the ever-increasing experiences needed by secondary school youth. Questions such as, How much art should be required? How many times per week should art classes meet? How long should the class period be? and What should be the size and composition of art classes? are all problems to be settled by local curriculum planners. Some phases of art instruction can be handled well in large groups, while other types will need individual attention. Certainly, every secondary school will want to encourage the very talented pupils to do creative work in depth. This can be done in individual studio cubicles.

Solving the problem of an adequate teaching corps is a formidable task. Consideration of the quality, experience, expertness, special abilities, and limitations of art personnel is necessary if good results are to be secured. This is a situation where training and qualifications do not always insure adequate teaching. And conversely, art classes cannot be assigned to any inept member of the staff who happens to have a vacant period. One answer to the teacher problem will come through encouraging more young people with artistic ability to enter teacher education. Until such a time as an adequate supply of teachers is available, several things can be done to alleviate the shortage. Larger classes can be used for basic instruction. Certain aspects of art instruction, mainly those involving individual direction, lend possibility to the use of staff members with limited training but a reasonable amount of ar-

[1] John A. Varmecky, "Relating Art to the Secondary School Student's Environment," *School Arts* (September 1971), pp. 38–39.

tistic ability.   It is not unreasonable here to suggest the incorporation of talented lay people.   They could be used effectively in extraclass art activities.

Necessary skills

Frustration comes in the classroom when pupils become dissatisfied with their shortcomings.   Teachers may accept this as a signal to change projects rather than as an opportunity to help pupils develop sufficient skills to enjoy the thrill of accomplishment.   A learning program in art is certain to present a number of problems of technique and design.   If pupils are not sufficiently skillful in mastering these problems, they are likely to lose interest in a project.

The art teacher should strive at every experience level to develop sufficient skills in each pupil to solve his immediate problems.   This might be illustrated in the field of drawing.   Drawing ability can be a major hurdle between conception and completion of a creative idea.[2]   Drawing is a skill that can be learned.   This does not mean that copybook methods need to be employed or that pupils must draw photographically, but it does allow for imitative experiences under the skilled guidance of the teacher.   These imitative activities can be drawn from the works of the masters and the skills of the teacher.   Each pupil needs to draw well enough to express what he wants to say.   The ability to see and the ability to express reactions to the visual world are closely aligned.   Each reinforces the other; each motivates the other.   As ideas become more complex, the need for expression motivates the development of greater skills.   As skills develop, the urge to originate new situations leads to still greater creativity.

The experience of creating pleasing utilitarian objects and arranging them in satisfying visual situations is a practical aspect of art.   Pupils must understand art as a visual means of communication through drawing, painting, sculpture, and the creation of personal symbols.   This means that skills need to be developed through experiences with a variety of graphic and structural media.

Some art authorities are suggesting that pupils be encouraged to delve more deeply into a single experience and carry it through with a single process for greater development of skill and understanding.   Some schools are experimenting with individual project ideas whereby a pupil has the opportunity to be creative

[2] Shirley Liby, "A Case for Curriculum in the Arts," *School Arts* (September 1969), pp. 8–9.

with material that is important to him and is of his own choosing. The pupil uses such an approach, not for the sake of being different, but as a tool for learning and as a basis for creativity.

It is questionable if a good teacher would constantly change materials and activities in order to hold the interest of the pupil. To do so is to push the entertainment or novelty value of art. Pupils like to improve in what they are doing rather than constantly dashing through new experiences. Creativity achieved through depth study and with adequate skill brings personal satisfaction. Art has a built-in motivation. It is fun to do when it is done well.

Creativity

In all programs of education, emphasis is on the creative approach and the experimental attitude. In fact, the concept of creativity has permeated the educational world so deeply that it is now in danger of becoming a cliché. Basically, every art teacher more or less looks upon her job as one of fostering creativity. The problem is to agree on what is meant by creativity.

The judgment of what is or is not creative essentially depends upon the degree of difference that may be noted between any two given objects. This means that every art object occupies its own unique position in space and is thus separated from all other objects. It exhibits visible, physical differences from any form made before. The creative pupil produces art objects unlike those produced by other persons.

In its purest sense, the creative act is based on standards of visual differences. It cannot be classified as either good or bad, beautiful or ugly, and it is inconsequential whether it is functional or nonfunctional. The question of whether creativity can be taught is worth pondering. Generally, all pupils possess some ability to perform creatively, but the teacher's role in helping pupils express themselves creatively is unsettled. In the broadest sense, the teacher would merely act as a critic who corrects the pupil's work according to standards of visual difference.

Advocates of the purest forms of creativity contend that the methods of teaching must be personal, expressive, and as creative as the expected aesthetic product itself.[3] They hold that the pupil must be freed from prototype learning where the obvious thing to do is to copy the works and styles of the masters. They believe the creative teacher does not produce in the pupil the image of the

[3] Florion Merz, *Pop Art in the Schools* (New York: Van Nostrand Reinhold Company, 1970), pp. 78–96.

teacher.   When aesthetic ends are predetermined and developed creatively, the growth of essential skills are concomitant in the process.   This does not allow for the usual method of developing skills by checking errors against the ideal model.

Modifications in approaches to creativity.   One of the pivotal points of discussion in the matter of creativity in art concerns the cause of pupil discouragement, usually occurring when a pupil feels that he can no longer successfully pursue the task at hand.   Those who disapprove of imitation or copy work claim the pupil finds himself in this position when he is unable to produce the objects he has been urged to copy, and this leads to discouragement, causing him to cease painting and drawing altogether.   Counterclaims of those who believe in the necessity of imitation for the development of basic skills point to the possibility of the same result if a pupil grasps creative ideas that are beyond his skill to produce.   Hence, it appears that the counterclaims of one group nullify the claims of the other, giving cause for indecision on the part of the curriculum planner.

The psychologist might ask why the assumption is made that imitation and creativity are mutually exclusive.   Such an attitude does not hold with an intelligent diagnosis of imitative behavior. It suggests that imitation does not tolerate variations, elaborations, refinements, or simplifications.   It denies that the pupil who imitates has the ability to develop more personal images with the help of a good teacher.   Actually, there must be some imitation in all creative activity.   According to the gestalt hypothesis the pupil brings to the learning situation his own learning environment, a collection of at least partially imitative experiences.

The extent to which creative people have imitated others is difficult to determine.   It is questionable to say that pure originality allows for no outside influence.   This would mean that pupils do not influence each other and that a teacher's influence must be negated.   Such instructional theories bewilder the practical educator.   He has accepted the idea that pupils should have creative experiences and that art is a suitable vehicle for these experiences, but his practical sense causes him to question the omissions of the development of basic skills and techniques for such experiences.

Arts and crafts

It is not the purpose here to consider the various curriculum divisions of art education, but "crafts" are sufficiently important to deserve separate mention.   Some art authorities contend that a number of very fuzzy ideas have developed concerning crafts as a form of art education.   They say these have resulted in wrong ideas toward the whole field of art.

In schools where art classes are labeled as "Arts and Crafts," art is associated with the gifted learners and crafts with the slow learners.   This is an unfortunate dichotomy because the same patterns of learning are inherent in the programs for both.   The matter of design is an illustration.   Design is a fundamental ingredient in all art.   The role of the designer is basic in the crafts, and craftsmanship is indispensable in achieving worth in an art product.

Design is the ordering of thought and feelings as they are expressed through visual and tactile qualities of materials.   It may be concerned with abstractions such as the relationship between colors, values, and symbols.   Design brings subject matter, technical skills, and perceptions together into a coherent and meaningful experience in art.   Whether this is in drawing, painting, sculpturing, or jewelry making is unimportant.   Good art education includes experiences with as many art forms as possible.

The teaching of crafts also develops sensitivity to visual environment and the ability to think creatively—values usually associated with art.   Ingenuity and improvisation in special uses of tools and materials can be real problem-solving experiences. Teaching objectives for crafts should include acquaintance with a wide variety of materials and their uses, methods in designing and planning products, the broad use of color, practical application of products, and study of creative solutions applied by artists to problems throughout the ages.

Program of study

Art authorities are in general agreement that the first experience pupils have in art ought to be general in nature.   General courses should include work in several mediums such as drawing, design, oils, and crafts.   These courses should be exploratory, so that pupils may probe their interests, abilities and skills.   It is logical that general courses should be supplemented with specialization courses according to pupil interests and aptitudes.   Art appreciation and art history ought to be included in a well-rounded art program. These courses have both vocational and aesthetic value, for many areas of art lead to job opportunities in the business world, and the possibility of a great artist emerging can challenge curriculum builders everywhere.

"Art Education in the Secondary School," an article in a recent issue of *The Bulletin* of The National Association of Secondary School Principals, lists the following manipulative activities that ought to be included in an art education program:

A. Drawing

The process of portraying an object, an idea, or a feeling with lines, shading, and texture in one or more colors. Drawings may be executed with pencil, charcoal, pen and ink, crayon, or brush.

B. Painting

The application of pigment to a surface in order to secure an effect involving forms and colors. Paints may be water colors, tempera, or oils, while painting surfaces include such materials as paper, canvas, wood, or plaster.

C. Printing

The stamping or impressing of a design upon a surface by any one of various methods. The design to be printed may be cut into vegetables, erasers, linoleum or wood blocks, or into metal. In lithography the design is drawn on a special stone or metal, and in silk-screen printing an impression is created by forcing pigment through silk in the unblocked areas of the design.

D. Constructing

Constructing or building implies the combination of one or more three-dimensional materials in the evolution of a space design. Such things as models, mosaics, mobiles, soldered jewelry and sculpture, puppets, and stage sets are illustrative of creative constructions.

E. Forming

The fashioning of three-dimensional designs in relief or in the round. This includes modeling, building up from a mass of material; and sculpture, which usually involves removing a part of the material in developing the finished composition. Such media as clay, plaster, paper, papier-maché, wood, wire, and metal are utilized in this activity.

F. Weaving and Stitching

The evolution of designs from pleasing combinations of such materials as yarn, thread, roving, raffia, reed, and cloth.

"The Arts in the Comprehensive Secondary School," a report of the Curriculum Committee of the NASSP, sets up goals for visual arts, suggesting that each pupil, according to his abilities and interest, should have the opportunity to do the following:

1. Recognize that creativity exists when art is produced.
2. Understand how visual arts help to make real and explain the attitudes and values of our society and help to carry them from one generation to another.
3. Develop an awareness of the great variety of visual art in today's world; for example, advertising and industrial design, architecture and city planning, textile and dress design, theatre and television design, the handcrafts, painting and sculpture, photography.
4. Understand the role of design in form, line, color, texture, and their dynamic interaction with each other.

5. Think critically about the contributions of others and develop judgment and independent taste in all of the visual arts.
6. Develop a sense of responsibility for and become involved in the aesthetic improvement of the environment by such activities as working toward better planned communities, more handsome architecture, well-designed appliances and tools, uncluttered transportation, and more emphasis on the use of original painting and sculpture in everyday life.
7. Understand the characteristics and potentialities of many materials, tools, and processes.
8. Realize how art experiences potentially may help to develop and maintain emotional stability.

Art and special education

Art has much to contribute to the special education field, both at the academically talented level and at the mentally handicapped level. There is no doubt that the really gifted artistic people come from the higher intelligence levels of the social order. The artistic future of the country is crucially dependent upon the identification and encouragement of potential artistic leadership. The future painters, designers, craftsmen, and architects will provide the resources for the aesthetically enlightened consumer. Many pupils among the academically talented have artistic talent, but they frequently lack enough exposure and educational encouragement to discover their potential.

In some instances, the inability of the talented pupil to enroll in art is a scheduling problem. In other instances, it results from a pseudo-erudite attitude among school people that art is not exactly scholarly, or that it is not a likely college preparation subject. More flexibility in scheduling will help solve the first problem; the problem of attitude is something else. School administrators who really believe in the comprehensive school are going to consider art a basic subject and afford it an important place in the educational program.

A strong case can be made for the need of art in the educational program of the academically talented. These pupils should have experiences with visual and sensual images; otherwise, they fail to develop the ability to make adequate aesthetic and perceptual judgments and discriminations, since so much of their work deals with the factual, analytical, and verbal abstractions. These pupils have few opportunities for innovative creative behavior. They need the freedom provided by art.

Attention in special education must also be given to those who represent the opposite of the superior ability group. While about 15 to 18 percent of the school population are considered academically talented, about 6 percent are mentally handicapped. This group is not inartistic, but it does need a more sympathetic approach. These pupils require a careful selection of art activities that convey a sense of permanence and solidity. Tentative conclusions from limited research indicate that a program of studies for the mentally handicapped must be qualitatively different in methods, activities, and tools.

Drawing and painting are meaningful to retarded pupils in the early grades, but as they mature they adjust better to work with crafts such as copper, leather, and clay.

Present trends

It is difficult to identify curriculum issues in art education. They are somewhat philosophic in nature and do not lend themselves to categorical treatment. Art educators tend to group themselves into what might be labeled progressives and conservatives. The approaches of these two groups parallel division of thought in many other sections of education.

The progressive art educators are in the residual stream of progressive education. Theirs is the psychological and sociological approach associated with freedom of expression. The most fervent abhor any form of copying and would de-emphasize drawing. They would have the teacher act as a keeper of material and a guide for pupils who venture into experiences of self-expression. The teacher would enter the classroom without plans of any kind, taking her cue from the interests and desires of the pupils. Of course, just as practices were modified following the heyday of progressive education, so have modifications been effected in art education today. The progressive group has continued to lay emphasis on creativity.

The conservatives also aim at creativity, but they identify and develop it differently. The conservative group would emphasize the development of skills and techniques. They hold that drawing ability is basic to a pupil's growth in art. They would stress visual accuracy and perspective. They contend that basic art education is learning to draw cubes, cylinders, and human figures. Extreme conservatives would have each art lesson be a drawing lesson. They contend that to copy well is a virtue, not a sin. They hold that nonverbal perceptual and expressional skills are essential to understanding. The conservative approach to creativity points to the necessity of having skills and techniques commensurate with desired creative expression.

It is fortunate that the extreme view of neither the progressive nor the conservative group dominates curriculum planning in art education at the present time. The best programs reflect a conciliatory attitude toward the desirability of pupil proficiency in both skills and creative expression. It is true, however, that the approach to creativity continues to be a point of debate.

Future trends

Every indication is that art programs will continue to be exploratory. They will involve a wide variety of broad units of experience based on the role and function of art in all of man's ideas. This concept is based on the thesis that man is revealed in part through his visual artistic expression and these revelations are unique in particular art forms. It suggests that a major function of art education is to teach pupils to incorporate themselves in art expressions and identifies a difference between *doing art work* and really *being deeply involved in it*.

More stress will be put on the development of *understanding* of art and the art method. In the past, too much emphasis has been put on *appreciation* of art. Pupils have been encouraged to appreciate art for art's sake, or because it is the cultural thing to do. Little thought has been given to the idea that real appreciation can only come through understanding; that is, art can be liked or disliked by the pupil according to his reactions to what the art form really means and not simply because a teacher has said it is good art and ought to be appreciated.

Less emphasis will be placed on the learning of technical processes as an end in themselves or in the building of specialized, sequential skills for college studio training. A pupil's art experiences will be evaluated more in terms of the effect these experiences have on his total behavior. The art product will be only one continuum in the art process. There will be an orientation of art experiences toward personal enjoyment of all social living, including home and family relationships.

There is no doubt that art curriculums are going to reflect more diversity in purpose from both the artistic and practical standpoint. Differentiation of programs both for the gifted and the mentally retarded is indicated. Exploration will be continued in the use of art as a therapy for the mentally retarded and the physically handicapped. There will be more concentration upon the "service" aspects of art programs in school and community life. The practical function of artistic knowledge for use in community beautification appeals to the average layman who is asked to support art programs in the school.

A discernible trend in curriculum experimentation may be seen in the movement to use art history as a point of departure for pupil experiences. This involves a reduction of time spent in the manipulation of art mediums and an increase in time devoted to surveying outstanding works of art with attention to understanding how they were created. This may indicate a pendulum swing from overemphasis on direct experiences.

In the final analysis, art is a highly individualized enterprise. It is the rightful inheritance of every school youth, and it is entitled to a secure position in the school curriculum. With the present emphasis on individual learning, art is especially worthwhile, since it offers extensive opportunities for the realization of this important educational objective. The highly personal quality of response to visual design, inherent in individual experience in art expression, helps youths to develop their own aesthetic standards and values. In time these become the standards and values of the nation and its people.

THEATER ARTS

The place of theater arts in a fine arts curriculum is not usually one of prominence. If there is a good dramatics program in a school, it is generally associated with extraclass activities rather than being a part of regular classroom work. Theater arts deserves a more prominent position in the educational spectrum than it now occupies.

One of the problems in getting school administrators to accept theater arts as an educational learning activity is its designated lack of academic value. They cite the fact that teachers are more interested in presenting a copy of the Broadway theater than they are in advancing educational ideals and objectives. Many of these teachers have had very little training in the field of dramatic art. They are "drafted" to do the school play and for the most part, being untrained in theater arts, are presenting rich material so inadequately that the pupil has little opportunity to become acquainted with the important humanistic values involved.

There is no doubt that talented teachers can do a good job with theater arts activities in extraclass sessions, but more adequate results can be secured if teaching of the drama is recognized in the regular school program and pupils look upon such work as vital to their total educational program. Pupils should have theater experiences in all avenues of acting, writing, and producing. This means familiarity with both craft and techniques. It means real insight into what a playwright is trying to convey to his audience.[4]

[4] Mary P. Pierini, *Creative Dramatics* (New York: Herder and Herder Co., 1971), pp. 48–89.

A good theater arts program will help each pupil learn that a good dramatic production can convey a message. A good program will acquaint him with the many facets of the theater, and it will help him to learn the value of effective communication in his personal life. Good theater arts will bring to the pupil the realization of the power of dynamic dramatic methods in making education a more meaningful experience.

Theater arts objectives are identified in the publication of the Curriculum Committee of the National Association of Secondary School Principals, entitled, *The Arts in the Comprehensive Secondary School.* The listing follows:

Each pupil, according to his abilities and interests, should have the opportunity to:
1. Understand and evaluate the literary form of the play, the dance, or opera, the quality of acting, differences in the uses of speech, lighting and stage design, the staging and choreography, and the costume design.
2. Acquire a knowledge and appreciation of dramatic literature, including the skill of reading to visualize staging and acting.
3. Become aware of the influence of the theater arts in his daily life and the influence of theater as a social force, especially its help in understanding other national and cultural groups.
4. Experience a wide variety of theater, including the best in classic and contemporary production in order to have a basis for making his own independent judgments.
5. Discover values derived from participation such as knowledge of avenues of expression, control and use of voice and body, stimulation of the imagination, the discipline of working creatively with others, and how to contribute to the aesthetic experience of others.
6. Discover how theater experiences can help individuals develop and maintain emotional stability.

This same publication suggests the following elective courses for a theater arts program: the study of playwriting, monologues, poetry, and creative writing; theater production, casting, directing, and acting; stage design, costuming, and make-up; creative dance; and oral interpretation.

The development of dramatic skill can involve many desirable educational experiences. Playing a part in a play or designing a set calls for an intensive study of the meanings and motivations that lead to human characterizations. It calls for an understanding of language and its use.

In curriculum planning for the fine arts area, the educational theater should be an integral part of the total program. Participation in theater activities can give the pupil a sense of individual dignity and accomplishment. It can bring enrichment to his emotional life and afford him a glimpse of the vast panorama of his heritage.

MUSIC

Position of music

Among the fine arts, music probably enjoys the most stable position in the curriculum. Music educators are winning the struggle for general acceptance of music as part of the regular curriculum offerings. The transistor tube has brought the possibility of music into every waking hour of an individual.

Not too much space is needed here to identify the value of music in the educational experience of youth. Music has the facility for widening the cultural horizons of a nation. It is part of the culture of all peoples, whether primitive or highly sophisticated. The history of America can be traced through the folk music of its people, and Brahms, Beethoven, and Bach are symbols of old world culture.

Music provides an insight into what is beautiful, artistic, and intellectual. It has companionship with art, poetry, and drama. As a pupil is exposed to better music, he learns to understand it and his musical tastes are raised. As a consumer of music through all the popular mediums, he will desire better quality and gradually the cultural taste of his age group will improve.

The music program of a school, by exposing pupils to meaningful tonal and rhythm patterns, gives them an increased sensitivity to music that can make all future musical experiences more enjoyable. The music curriculum should not be designed to make musicians out of all pupils, but rather to help them to be musical to the extent that their experiences will be more enjoyable and worthwhile. Music offers unlimited opportunities for the gifted and interested pupil whether he specializes or not.

Even though they are not stressed in a music program, there are definite vocational possibilities inherent in it. It is estimated that about 11 percent of the adult population earn all or part of their living through some association with music. The school program can either be basic or supplementary to the training of future wage earners in the field. A well-rounded curriculum in music will take care of the many and varied abilities and interests of the total school population.

Music educators have two major curriculum objectives. One is to give music status in the curriculum as a recognized discipline and the other is to make music available to all pupils.

Music as a discipline

There is convincing evidence that music is worthy of recognition as a valuable subject in the curriculum. The basic contribution it makes to daily living pleasures and the promise it holds for purposeful use of leisure time in a technological society could be sufficient reasons for making it part of the general education of youth, but music educators claim that music is inherently comparable to the accepted disciplines even without these supporting relationships.

It would be regrettable if schools in a space age society neglected music, which is so much a vital part of the humanities. Music has form and design, cause and effect. It is a means of communication as important and eloquent as the written word, perhaps even more so, and it is intelligible to all people if they have experience in its interpretation. It serves both the mind and the spirit. Music illustrates literature and history—it brings civilization to life.

Music draws its sources from great novels, sonnets, and biblical texts. The librettos of opera illustrate the ties between music and literature. Although it has been said many times, the fact remains that music is truly a universal language. It is structured around symbols that are linguistic in nature. These convey impressions, express ideas, communicate thought, and create moods.

Music compares very favorably as a discipline with the highly respectable fields of mathematics and science. To understand music thoroughly requires a rigorous mathematical intelligence. It involves thinking in terms of precision, exactness, and quantitative as well as qualitative analyses. Music has a theory and value system. This involves ratios, numerals, fractions, measurements, and arithmetic symbolization. In its most sophisticated areas, such as composition, harmony, and counterpoint, music requires the same high level of abstract thinking as does mathematics.

Any dichotomy between music and science is related to purpose and use rather than basic values. Both encompass systems of knowledge and both are capable of dissemination of this knowledge. The tenets of science are order, balance, symmetry, and proportion. These are analogous to the tenets of music, and both scientists and musicians are probing for the truth through experimentation, exploration, and logic.

General music program

The second major objective of the advocates of music in the curriculum is to make musical experiences available to all pupils. Music educators claim there is no such thing as a genuinely unmusical person and that even a monotone is not incurable. Jerome Bruner contends that any subject can be taught effectively in some intellectual form to any pupil at any stage of development. The kaleidoscopic nature of music offers experiences for every pupil through singing, playing, creating, or listening.

Heretofore, the music program in the secondary school has consisted of choral groups and instrumental groups. The pupils involved were selected for their interest or ability in performance. This necessarily limited the opportunity for musical experiences. In order to overcome this limitation, general music education programs have been introduced into the secondary schools.

General music education programs are designed for all pupils who want to enjoy the benefits to be derived from all forms of musical study.[5] Those with no previous background or those with a lack of interest in music are encouraged to enter the program. They are provided with exploratory experiences in singing, listening, and playing. Desirable musical skills are matured and new ones discovered.

More success with general music courses has been enjoyed in vocal music than in instrumental. Too often the instrumental teachers support the idea in theory, but in practice they are happy to have every other pupil join the vocal classes if those with high intelligence, excellent motor coordination, healthy lungs, and money to buy an instrument are assigned to them. Singing should be a basic activity in the general music program, but this does not mean that instruments should be neglected. Instrumental work should also be included, even banjo, guitar, piano, and organ.

Regardless of the organizational pattern of the general music education program, certain fundamental objectives need to be met.[6] Basically, pupils should be provided with opportunities for exploring and understanding music as a cultural force in society, individual talents should be discovered and developed, and discrimination that leads to understanding and appreciation of worthwhile music should be stressed. General musical experiences should include a study of the theory of mechanics of music. And probably more important, every pupil should have the opportunity to participate in some form of music for pure personal pleasure.

[5] S. G. Rankin, "Forging a Junior High General Music Program," *Music Educators Journal* (December 1966), pp. 31–32.
[6] Theodore A. Tellstrom, *Music in American Education: Past and Present* (New York: Henry Holt and Co., 1971), pp. 57–104.

Administrative problems

There are several problems in music programs that need attention by curriculum designers. Mostly administrative or philosophic in nature, such problems affect the ultimate outcome of the program. One of the problems is associated with a common attitude of music teachers. Too frequently they are "performance" centered. Their programs are centered around marching bands and public appearances of choral groups. While school officials may stress the public relations value of these things and parents may get satisfaction out of the public performance of their sons and daughters, the real values of music lie in the opportunities given pupils to experience a variety of musical activities in depth.

The full fruition of a musical program is frequently hampered by scheduling problems, allotment of academic credit, and correlation with other activities of the school. Imaginative programs of flexible scheduling can do much to alleviate the scheduling problem. No pupil should be denied an opportunity to have music as part of his schedule because he has other important subjects he must pursue. If music is accepted as an academic discipline, allotment of academic credit becomes an academic matter. A ridiculous procedure is to substitute marching in the band for physical education credit or to allow less credit for music because it is not one of the "solids." The correlation of music with other activities of the school can be exceptionally fruitful to the total school program. Music has much to offer, both supplementary and complementary. This should be a desirable administrative accomplishment.

Another problem is the common complaint of music teachers that their classes are overloaded with undesirable pupils. It is claimed that vocal music classes are frequently dumping grounds for such pupils. If music commands the proper respect in the school and the general objective is to have every pupil share in the music program, there should be no undesirable pupils in any music class. The solution to all these problems hinges on better curriculum planning and mutual respect and cooperation between music teachers and their administrative superiors.

Music education issues

The major issue in music education today is the selection of content or subject matter to be presented to pupils and how this content or subject matter is to be used. Much of the controversy centers around the questions of whether the music selected for the learning experiences of the pupil will be confined to the so-called classics and whether it will be presented in its original form. Some music educators are vehement in their defense of classical music unadulterated. They hold that the only way pupils will be able to judge the barrage of musical stimuli they hear daily is to develop aesthetic judgment and discriminating taste through introduction to a wide repertory of the world's foremost music and then to pursue depth study of as much of it as time permits. These music educators warn against the questionable procedure of pre-digesting music for pupils or adulterating it by removing all difficulties and complexities. They use such terms as "mutilation" and "homogenization" of musical art.

One of the strongest advocates of the use of the pure classics is Charles B. Fowler. He has this to say about the issue:

Detouring the pupil away from what is necessarily difficult in music, sparing the pupil effort, predigesting music to the point where the composition hears for the listener, instead of forcing him to make his own response—all contribute to the formulation of a tepid, flaccid, and debased musical art. Continual reinforcement of such a concept of music indoctrinates youth toward a predisposed and singularly deficient musical taste, and results in stifling the establishment of self-evolving, individual value substantiation. To withhold, conceal, or suppress the musical art in any way tends to envelop pupils in a partial picture which smothers sensitivity, curiosity, receptivity, and insight.[7]

Fowler's point of view is reinforced by the Report of the Yale Seminar on Music Education. This report, the result of a twelve-day deliberation of thirty-one musicians, scholars, and teachers, lists nine things wrong with the music repertory of elementary and secondary schools. The report criticizes the quality and scope of school music, charging that music is corrupted by poor arrangements, touched-up editing, erroneous transcriptions, and tasteless parodies.[8] And more significantly, the report emphasizes the fact that the pupil's ability is constantly underestimated by such activities.

Music educators who desire a wide variety of musical experiences for youth hold that the avowed purpose of music education should be not only to transmit the great musical heritage of the past, but also to lend direction in shaping the future. They have no quarrel with challenging the pupil's ability to reach the various levels inherent in music, but they hold that some music must be

[7] Charles B. Fowler, "The Misrepresentation of Music," *Music Educators Journal* (April–May 1965), pp. 38–42.
[8] K. A. Wendrich, "Music Literature in High School: The Yale Curriculum Project," *Music Educators Journal* (March 1967), pp. 35–37.

altered and others deleted in order to fit the pupil's level of ability. They contend that an important task of music education is to bring the pupil and music into congenial and beneficial association.

The liberal group believes that pupils deserve opportunities to grasp the impact and value of the widest variety of musical art.[9] This includes contemporary serious music as well as so-called "popular" music. Contemporary music may be distasteful to those who will not admit changes are occurring in music. New aesthetic values are involved. Acceptance of these values means the acceptance of unmusical sounds that may be labeled "noise," and there is always conservative resistance to innovation. But future musical history will recognize the landmark contributions of many of the contemporary composers. Criticism heaped on Leonard Bernstein for his efforts to bridge the gap between classical and contemporary music may give his name musical immortality.

The liberal viewpoint does not denigrate the value of acquainting pupils with Bach and Wagner; it merely holds that pupils' knowledge of the classics should be supplemented by association with perishable popular music and the tuneful music of Broadway shows so that they will have a wider field of experience. Classical rigidity excludes too much desirable music from youth. Boredom, sometimes associated with stereotyped music, may account for some of the extremes in musical fads that youth pursue outside the school music program.

There is some contention over what attitudes pupils should develop toward music. This is identified with the difference between "liking" and "interest" and between "entertainment" and "pleasure." The sensible position would appear to be held by those who say that the immediate *liking* of a piece of music is not a valid criterion for including it in a music program. Many fine pieces of music require repeated hearings and close attention before pupils like them. It is unlikely that all pupils will ever like all music. What is important is that pupils find it *interesting* enough to explore and discover musical meaning. This leads to the development of musical insight.

Stage bands

The recognition of so-called "stage bands" in the music program of the school arouses a difference of opinion among music curriculum planners. Those who oppose the stage band hold that it cheapens a good music program. They point to the mediocre type of music used, contending it appeals to the senses rather than the intellect.

Other music educators take a much more liberal view of

[9] Joseph A. Leeder and William S. Haynie, *Music Education in the High School* (Englewood Cliffs, N.J.: Prentice-Hall, Inc., 1960), p. 165.

the stage band.   They believe it helps to develop the musicianship of a pupil by giving him a more flexible style.   They see the stage band as an instrumentality for expanding the desire for a better grade of popular music.   They contend that popular music is a recognized style of legitimate music.

The stage band furnishes an attractive, enjoyable outlet for school musicians.   There are some 8,000 of these bands, mostly in the junior and senior high schools.   They are engaged in festivals where tone, intonation, blend, balance, precision, dynamics, rhythm, and interpretation, as well as arrangements and presentation, are being adjudicated.   These festivals are educational and at the same time can be enjoyable.

If pupils are restricted to only one kind of music they may become lopsided musicians.   They should be permitted to play in stage bands only if they are also members of groups playing serious music.   The stage band activity should be a bonus.   Its acceptance in the school musical program may be dependent on whether the instrumental teacher believes that good playing of music in one medium is good playing of music in all media.

Somewhat akin to the permissive inclusion of stage bands in the school music program is the question of the use of musical organizations in public performances.   It is doubtful that there is any question over the value of scheduled public performances of bands, orchestras, or choral groups to demonstrate the musical accomplishments of the school musicians.   Controversy arises over the so-called misuse of school musicians to pep up athletics, cover lunchroom din, fill embarrassing holes in other programs, or be constantly available for public parades.   School administrators consider these activities as part of public relations programs. Many music educators accept them as necessary nuisances.

Every school should establish criteria for evaluating public performances.   To a certain extent all kinds of public performances are enjoyed by youth, and parents also derive vicarious satisfaction from seeing their children in such performances.   The educational image of the school can be enhanced by public performances, especially if there is good playing of good music.   However, safeguards should be provided to avoid exploitation of youth in non-educational activities and to prevent excessive absences of school musicians from other important areas of their regular school program.

Teaching innovations

Probably the two predominant methods of teaching music are group and individualized instruction.   Music educators, however, have been experimenting with other forms of instruction, such as programed learning and team teaching. Most of the features of programed learning can be incorporated in the teaching of music. The procedures—providing numerous steps in learning, active involvement, reinforcement, instant grading, feedback, and succinct instruction—all adapt very well to musical instruction. This is especially true in the teaching of instrumental music and certain phases of general music.

Team teaching is one of many current attempts to find new solutions to old problems. Music teaching lends itself well to individual and small-group instruction and there are opportunities for large-group instruction in the many phases of musical education. Certain innovative and imaginative procedures are being tried in large-group instruction. Such procedures usually involve opportunities for pupils to share the talents of the competent specialists. If team teaching can do no more than penetrate the conservative aura of music instruction, it will have served a purpose.

Many of the major trends in education continue to center around individualized instruction. Music educators are not unmindful of the need for conversion in their field.[10] Both from the standpoint of theory and practice, music curriculum planners are trying to provide individualized instruction through systems approach, computer-assisted instruction, programed instruction, and learning packages.

General goals

An *ad hoc* committee of the National Association of Secondary School Principals developed a set of general goals for music education. The committee was composed of music educators, school instructional leaders, and classroom teachers. The committee suggested that each pupil, according to his abilities and interests, should have the opportunity to do the following:

1. Develop skills in music so he may:
   a. participate in some kind of musical performance either as an individual or as a member of a group;
   b. listen to music with understanding and enjoyment;
   c. associate the musical score with what is heard or performed;
   d. improvise and create music of his own.
2. Become an intelligent critic of jazz, folk music, popular music, parade music, and the major types of serious music.

[10] Miriam B. Kopfer, "The Evolution of Musical Objectives," *Music Educators Journal* (February 1970), pp. 61–63.

3. Develop a sense of responsibility for exercising his critical judg-ment for the improvement of the musical environment of his community, including offerings on radio and television as well as live performances.
4. Recognize music as an international language and a vehicle of international goodwill.
5. Acquire such knowledge about music as history of music, form and design of music, symbolism of the music score, the quality of tone and other characteristics of the various musical instru-ments and the ranges of the human voice, the combinations of instruments and voices, the role of composers in various his-torical periods, and the relation of music to such other disci-plines as science, mathematics, and literature.
6. Understand how emotional expression as a part of normal, healthy, happy living can be enhanced by music.
7. Desire to continue some form of musical experience both in school and following graduation; for example, select and use recordings and tapes, engage in small vocal and instrumental ensemble work, and participate as performer and listener in community musical activities.

A survey of these general goals will reveal a wide coverage of music instruction and activities. They are a good summary of the objectives of music educators and are in harmony with the trends in music education.

The Tanglewood Declaration

The Tanglewood Declaration is already a landmark in music edu-cation. This declaration was formed at a symposium held at Tanglewood, Massachusetts, summer home of the Boston Symphony Orchestra, during the summer of 1967. The Tanglewood Sym-posium was composed of philosophers, scientists, labor leaders, philantropists, social scientists, theologians, industrialists, and government officials. The field of music was represented by music educators and professional musicians. The symposium addressed itself to the theme, "Music in American Society." The major ac-complishment of the Tanglewood Symposium was the *Tanglewood Declaration*.[11] It is well on its way to becoming a benchmark in American music education. It is a starting point for curriculum

[11] Robert A. Choate, "The Tanglewood Symposium," *Music Educators Journal* (November 1967), pp. 48–50.

planning in the secondary music field.   The text of the Tanglewood Declaration follows:

> We believe that education must have as major goals the art of living, the building of personal identity, and nurturing creativity.   Since the study of music can contribute much to these ends, *we now call for music to be placed in the core of the school curriculum.*
> The arts afford a continuity with the aesthetic tradition in man's history.   Music and other fine arts, largely nonverbal in nature, reach close to the social, psychological, and physiological roots of man in his search for identity and self-realization.
> Educators must accept the responsibility for developing opportunities which meet man's individual needs and the needs of a society plagued by the consequences of changing values, alienation, hostility between generations, racial and international tensions, and the challenges of a new leisure.

Music educators at the Tanglewood Symposium agreed on the following points for curriculum implementation of the Tanglewood Declaration:

1. Music serves best when its integrity as an art is maintained.
2. Music of all periods, styles, forms, and cultures belong in the curriculum.   The musical repertory should be expanded to involve music of our time in its rich variety, including currently popular teen-age music and avant-garde music, American folk music, and the music of other cultures.
3. Schools and colleges should provide adequate time for music in programs ranging from pre-school through adult or continuing education.
4. Instruction in the arts should be a general and important part of education in the senior high school.
5. Developments in educational technology, educational television, programmed instruction, and computer-assisted instruction should be applied to music study and research.
6. Greater emphasis should be placed on helping the individual student to fulfill his needs, goals, and potentials.
7. The music education profession must contribute its skills, proficiencies, and insights toward assisting in the solution of urgent social problems as in the "inner city" or other areas with culturally deprived individuals.
8. Programs of teacher education must be expanded and improved to provide music teachers who are specially equipped to teach high school courses in the history and literature of music, courses in the humanities and related arts, as well as teachers equipped to work with the very young, with adults, with the disadvantaged, and with the emotionally disturbed.

Trends in music education

The ultimate purpose of a music program will be served when pupils come into meaningful contact with the vistas of musical heritage and have experiences that carry them beyond their present expectations. A pupil is musically educated when he can make aesthetic quality a matter of choice rather than chance.

To this end music programs will emphasize objectives that develop significant musical competence, musical understanding, and a knowledge of the whole range of music literature. Essential aims of a music program will continue to be emphasized. These give pupils a measure of musical independence—the ability to sing, to play an instrument, and to read music.

New courses are being introduced in listening and in the understanding of musical literature. Listening courses are geared to challenge the emotions, stimulate the imagination, and engage the mind. Stress is laid on the ability of the pupil to discriminate quality in performance and composition and the ability to perceive elements of form within the abstract.

Specialized courses in both history and theory of music are being made available for gifted and interested pupils. Music theory courses provide pupils with opportunities to improvise music and to write rounds and canons. They may not learn to write masterpieces, but they will be making discoveries that underlie mature musical achievement. Part of this is learning to isolate rhythm from melody and harmony.

Curriculum guidelines in music are being directed toward having pupils arrive at a level of musical and intellectual comprehension that is challenging. Programs feature a variety of styles and periods, media and performance, and musical forms. Significant proficiency in performances is being stressed. The curriculum organizational pattern will vary from school to school, but the best programs will be the ones that include musical experiences for all pupils according to their interests and abilities.

It may be noted that extensive space here has been devoted to this field. It is out of the conviction that the fine arts are going to loom large in the future lives of the citizenry. It has been suggested that a balanced program of instruction is a desirable curriculum goal. Proper emphasis on the fine arts will make this a realistic goal.

The pleas of music educators for recognition of music as a discipline should not go unheeded by curriculum planners. Their job is to balance the amount of study and performance in the arts with the peripheral and materialistic experiences of other areas of the curriculum. It is time that any unwarranted faddish aura be dispelled from the whole field of the fine arts.

TOPICS FOR STUDY AND DISCUSSION

1. Some school administrators still hold that certain subjects have more Carnegie unit credit worth than others. If you were a member of an art or music curriculum committee, how would you convince your school head that your subject is worthy of equal credit with any other secondary school subject?
2. What would be the impact on the fine arts curriculum if the hypothesis were accepted that both art and music should provide experience for those who create, those who perform, and those who consume?
3. Evaluate the curriculum objective in art that says the teacher should foster creativity within the discipline imposed by technique and skill, avoiding the tendency to teach these techniques and skills as ends in themselves.
4. General music classes are advocated for all secondary youth. What would be the merits of such emphasis on general art classes?
5. What is the validity of the claim that the state of art in the secondary schools reflects the state that the arts occupy generally in American life and culture?
6. What position should the secondary school curriculum planner take in regard to the type of music that ought to be included in the secondary school program?
7. What implications are there in the hypothesis that objectives in the fine arts should stress understanding rather than appreciation?
8. The major issue between authorities in the field of fine arts concerns the relation between the development of creativeness and the development of skills. Develop a dialogue on the pros and cons of this issue.
9. Identify the position of music and art in a comprehensive education. Should all pupils be exposed to both fine arts areas in the secondary school curriculum?
10. Should theater arts be incorporated in the regular school curriculum or should this be an extraclass activity? How may a position on this issue be justified?
11. What are the relationships between the music objectives of the school curriculum and the type of music youth supports as public entertainment?

12. Make a critical analysis of the salient points in the Tanglewood Declaration.
13. Why are music educators assuming leadership roles in the individualization of instruction? Why not art educators?

SELECTED REFERENCES

CAPERS, ROBERTA M., and MADDOX, JERROLD. *Images and Imagination: An Introduction to Art.* New York: The Ronald Press Company, 1965.

This book is a unique discussion and analysis of art. It is a conservative presentation of concepts and techniques for modern art education. Theory and philosophy of art are applied to the development of principles and objectives.

CHEYETTE, IRVING. *Teaching Music Creatively.* New York: McGraw-Hill Book Company, 1969.

New methods are described for making music intelligible and enjoyable. It is a source book as well as a book on fundamentals. It includes a good discussion dealing with music as an art and a discipline.

CYR, DAN. "The Visual Language." *School Arts* (November 1966), pp. 32–36.

This article develops the thesis that because objects of art are expressive, they implicitly constitute a language. Each art form has its medium and mode for a specific kind of communication.

HOFFER, CHARLES R. *Teaching Music in the Secondary Schools.* Belmont, California: Wadsworth Publishing Co., Inc., 1964.

The author provides practical suggestions for interesting youth in the study of music. He emphasizes the aesthetic basis for the study of music in the schools. Special attention is given to the problems of integrating music into the total school program.

HUBBARD, GUY. "A Review of the Purpose for Art Education." *Art Education* (February 1966), pp. 7–11.

This article summarizes the purpose of art education and shows what revision is needed. It contends that art education lies *at the center* of the education that all people need.

LOWENFIELD, VIKTOR, and BRITTAIN, W. LAMBERT. *Creative and Mental Growth.* 4th ed. New York: The Macmillan Company, 1964.

This book is an extensive treatment of creativity in art and growth and development of the creative process in the pupil.

Recent research findings providing greater insight and understanding of creativity are incorporated throughout the discussion.

MADSEN, CLIFFORD K. *Experimental Research in Music.* Englewood Cliffs, N.J.: Prentice-Hall, Inc., 1970.

This volume deals with broad classifications of music topics for research and describes concisely experimental research methods and their application to music. It would serve as a good addition to the curriculum planners reference material.

MILLER, WILLIAM HUGH. *Introduction to Music Appreciation.* Philadelphia: Chilton Book Co., 1970.

This book is based on the theme that everyone is capable of some degree of music appreciation. It proposes the integration of psychology, philosophy, and general aesthetics with music and the fine arts. It provides a new approach to music appreciation.

NATIONAL ASSOCIATION OF SECONDARY SCHOOL PRINCIPALS. "The Arts in the Comprehensive Secondary School." Washington, D.C.: Bulletin of the National Association of Secondary School Principals (September 1962).

This consists of a position paper developed by an ad hoc committee of NASSP. It represents the opinion of authoritative art educators.

OSTRANSKY, LEROY, ed. *Perspectives on Music.* Englewood Cliffs, N.J.: Prentice-Hall, Inc., 1963.

This book offers a collection of readings covering all aspects of music. It presents interesting viewpoints on the various approaches to music education. The material is related to the many music activities outside the regular school program.

REIMER, BENNETT. *A Philosophy of Music Education.* Englewood Cliffs, N.J.: Prentice-Hall, Inc., 1970.

This volume identifies fundamental values of music and music education. It gives a functional and systematic rationale for the relationship of all types of musical behavior and furnishes a good basis for curriculum planning in the secondary school music field.

WASSERMANN, BURTAN. *Modern Painting.* Worcester, Mass.: Davis Publications, 1971.

This book presents useful material for planning course content on modern art. It is helpful for understanding what is modern and what is art. It goes on to describe what to look for in a painting or sculpture, how art trends develop, and what materials are used. It is suitable for secondary school art and humanistic classes.

CHAPTER 7

Foreign Languages—
Modern and Classical

MODERN LANGUAGES

The scene is a convention of national educators. The program is a presentation by exchange students from countries throughout the world. The students in their native dress bring greetings and interesting interpretations of their homeland to the appreciative American audience. At the end of the two-hour program a standing ovation is given to the performers.

Later, small groups of school principals and superintendents meet in their hotel rooms to evaluate the program. The chief topic of conversation is not what the visiting foreign students said, but how they said it. In almost envying tones the evaluators comment on the ability of the foreign students to speak with such capability in a foreign land and in a foreign language. They admit that their own American students would probably fall far short of such standards of achievement.

The low capability of American students to speak a modern foreign language is not the result of lack of interest or ability on the part of the student, but rather the result of the narrow objectives established for teaching foreign language. Emphasis traditionally has been on grammar and structure for translation and reading purposes and not on functional speaking use. The approach has aimed at aesthetic and cultural objectives rather than at active communication. However, the rapid development of the space

age, evaporating time and distance, has made the world c(
a startling reality.   Today, the United States has respons'
over the world, and language barriers are not only distr⌐_.
extremely dangerous as well.   The understanding of a language ıs
often the key to understanding a culture.   The learning of a language must change from a purely intellectual task to a functional,
desirable skill.

Changing emphasis

The realignment of objectives in the modern language field is
slowly but surely taking place.   It has resulted in a flurry of study,
discussion, planning, and cooperation involving language teachers,
administrators, governmental leaders, and colleges and universities.
Their goal is one never seriously considered before in this country—
mastery of at least one modern foreign language by a substantial
segment of pupils.[1]   Some enthusiasts speak of the day when
every high school graduate will be bilingual.

Two main objectives are emerging.   The first recognizes
that listening comprehension and speaking should come before
reading and writing, and the second sets as its task the mastery
and retention of a complex of skills.   The realization of both objectives requires consistent, steady work over a considerable period of
time.   It involves teaching a language, not *about* a language.

Recognition of the merits of this "audio-lingual" system of
teaching languages resulted from experiences during World War II,
when an urgent need existed for trained personnel who could speak
native languages.   The armed forces established language training schools at which students were given intensive training in a
language for nine months through speaking and listening to the
language, analyzing its structure, and some reading and writing.

Linguistic scientists contributed to the World War II language schools and have continued to analyze the soundness of
audio-lingual methods.   They see language as a living, vital, ever-
changing force that is intimately involved with people and their
culture.   They claim that a static concept of language, made up
of isolated sounds, words, and grammatical rules, fails to teach a
language as it really is.   They point to the need for a phonemic
analysis of characteristic foreign sounds as pronounced by a native
followed by training in recognizing phonetic variations of sounds
as influenced by their position in words or sentences.   The words
must be incorporated in and taught as part of a thought sequence.

[1] Gail Inlow, *The Emergent in Curriculum* (New York: John Wiley and
Sons, Inc., 1966), pp. 131–132.

Grammar is mastered through cultural patterns of speech. Thus, reading and writing become secondary in importance and should be attempted after structural patterns have been established.

Program modification

Many language programs are undergoing basic modifications because of the experiences of the armed forces and the recommendations of the linguists. Curriculum development leadership in the modern language field has been furnished by the Modern Language Association, and financial support has come from foundations and from the National Defense Education Act. The United States Office of Education, state and local school systems, and colleges and universities have participated in a coordinated effort to improve modern language teaching. Further impetus has been furnished by the Staff Utilization Studies of the National Association of Secondary School Principals. Teachers, students, parents, and employers now realize that too little time has been allotted to language teaching and that traditional language teaching fails to produce competence in speaking the language.

It might be fair to chide the Modern Language Association a little since it was their recommendation in the 1920's that placed emphasis on the ability to read a language in a two-year sequence. Many teachers who favored the aural-oral approach at that time protested the recommendation, but emphasis on reading dominated the secondary school teaching of modern languages until recently. Thus, through better than three decades pupils have studied modern languages with little functional use in communication and limited reading ability.

The renaissance in modern language teaching, accompanied by the general acceptance of the audio-lingual approach, has raised several troublesome questions. When should modern foreign language study begin? and How long should the sequence be? Who should study which language? What are the competencies of the audio-visual approach? How effective is the language laboratory? How can pupil progress in foreign language study be evaluated? How can the study of foreign languages be articulated if started earlier than the secondary school years? Where will capable teachers be found?

When should modern foreign language study begin? No general agreement exists concerning the time a pupil should begin the study of a modern language or how long the sequence should be. Research is not conclusive in the matter. Some authorities contend the third grade is about right, because by that time a pupil has become accustomed to study and has the desire to learn almost anything. At that age, the emulation of foreign sounds is still easy because the child has not acquired a linguistic "set."

Other authorities set the seventh or eighth grade as the best time to begin a language sequence. The Curriculum Committee of the National Association of Secondary School Principals recommends the introduction of a modern language no later than the ninth grade, preferably in the seventh or eighth grade. It recommends a minimum of four years of sequential study—as long as such study is profitable—through the tenth or eleventh grade, even though third and fourth year classes may be small and individual study and practice may be necessary. It is contended that patterns of speech and communication skills established in the first language greatly reduce the difficulty of progress in a second. The four-year sequence would give the pupil time to study a second foreign language if he desires.

Another school of thought believes that the first grade or even the preschool years is the time to introduce foreign language study. Very few modern language authorities would disagree with the early introduction of language teaching, but they are very apprehensive about certain practical aspects of such early introduction. For one thing, it may lack seriousness of purpose. The school may use it to impress patrons, with no plans for continuity or evaluation. Such procedures could dull the pupil's curiosity and interest in languages and cause him to avoid language study in later years. Too, any lapse in study of a language is a serious detriment to progress. A final factor that causes language authorities to question the early introduction of modern language study is the lack of capable language teachers in elementary grades.

The United States Office of Education sponsored an experimental program for the introduction of foreign language in the elementary school. It was called, logically enough, Foreign Language in the Elementary School (FLES). As a stimulator the program enjoyed reasonable success. Elementary school enrollments in foreign language jumped from 200,000 in 1955 to 2,000,-000 in 1965.[2] There is little evidence that any substantial number of programs have been instituted below the first grade. Most of the programs start at the third or fourth grade. The recent trend, however, has been to move to the seventh or eighth grade. This has been due to practical problems of financing, staffing, and articulation.

There are many testimonials of successful programs in the elementary schools, but evidence is less than conclusive of the

[2] Robert Pillet, "Foreign Language," *Nation's Schools* 84 (August 1969): 41–42.

unequivocal acceptance of foreign language as an integral part of the elementary curriculum as advocated by exponents of FLES. Many students in the FLES program change to another language when they enter secondary school. This defeats the basic purpose of a six- to eight-year sequence. The teaching of foreign language probably will continue to be more of a major task of the secondary schools than of the elementary schools.

Who should study which language?   The question of who should study a foreign language has not been resolved.   In theory, the objective of modern language administrators is to make every high school graduate bilingual.   Curriculum requirements established by a limited number of school systems will eventually lead to the fulfillment of this objective. Whether it is a sound or attainable objective for all systems, is uncertain, however. A far more realistic approach would probably be to give all pupils the opportunity to study a foreign language for as long as they can do so profitably according to their interest and ability.   Exceptionally proficient pupils in languages should be encouraged to study a second foreign language while continuing a first. Counseling and guidance are preferable to stated requirements in the modern language field.

Principals and counselors have devoted a great deal of time to helping pupils decide which foreign language to study. Many foreign language authorities question the importance of this procedure. They contend that the selection of a foreign language is inconsequential; any modern language *well* learned will be useful. When language study is functional, and the pupil is able to achieve proficiency, the manner of learning one language usually carries over into learning another. Therefore, the important part of language study is the process of understanding the structure of a language and the culture using the language, regardless of the language being studied.

Spanish, French, German, and Italian, in that order, are the modern languages most widely offered in the nation's schools. The study of Russian and Chinese is desirable, but the supply of teachers is extremely limited. Unless competent teachers, continuity in program, and appropriate instructional materials can be secured, it is nonsense for schools to initiate the study of Russian or, indeed, any other modern foreign language. The study of Asiatic and African languages is frequently suggested, but a realistic evaluation of the study of these languages would suggest that for the time being they be confined to the colleges and universities.

There are two practical aspects to the curriculum selection of modern languages. The first is based on the supply of good teachers. The second deals with the sociological makeup of the

communities served by the schools. Efficient teaching in any .
ern language makes that language desirable, but if the study c
specific language can help members of a community understai.
their own cultural heritage it has added value.

What are the competencies of the audio-lingual approach?   The
audio-lingual approach is probably the best way to teach languages
if the objective is that of practical communication.   Many authorities contend that in the final analysis this approach will also
do a better job in the writing and the reading of the language.

　　　The audio-lingual approach to modern language teaching is
not startlingly new, nor is it a radical departure from the traditional fundamentals of good language teaching.   It is more a rearrangement and a shifting of emphasis.   After the initial orientation in English, the modern foreign language becomes the language
of the classroom.   Pupils are encouraged to think in the foreign
language, not translate it word for word into their native tongue.
On seeing or hearing the Spanish "manzana" a pupil does not
decode it into the English "apple"; he thinks in Spanish of a fruit
to eat or to shine and give to the teacher.   The language being
studied is considered adequate for communication in its own
right, without recourse to English or any other language.   Formal
translation from English to the language being studied is avoided
during the first two years of class work.   No pupil is asked to
read what he does not aurally understand.   Grammar is acquired
initially by imitation and repetition in natural situations and not by
formal analysis.   A study of formal grammar and the reading of
the language are delayed until the advanced stages of study.   The
contention is that the ability to comprehend the written word is
more thoroughly developed if adequate time is spent on learning
to hear and speak the language. When these primary skills have
become automatic in informal discussion, reading and writing
can begin to play an important role in language behavior.   Furthermore, efficiency in the use of the language must be supplemented
with the knowledge of how it works in a society.   A concomitant
value in the mastery of techniques may be in the ease with which
a pupil may learn another language in the future.

How effective is the language laboratory?   Important progress has
been made in providing instructional materials and equipment for
developing listening comprehension and mastery of speech patterns.   Well over 5,000 electronic language laboratories are now
in use, and good tapes and films are available.   The rapid growth
of language laboratories has been a mixed blessing.   As might
be expected, inexperience and inefficiency have produced some
questionable results.   However, it must be kept in mind that the

language laboratory is not an end in itself, but merely a supplement to classroom procedures with well-controlled authentic experiences.   Another complicating factor is rapid technological development of equipment.   Many of the early laboratories are obsolete.

Since language learning is so largely a process of habit formation, all pupils need regular, systematic oral practice.   Skill in speaking will quickly deteriorate if it is not practiced.   Listening practice of ever-increasing difficulty and practice in self-expression can be greatly implemented by intelligent use of available electronic equipment.   The satisfaction of using the language for communication and the sense of achievement as one well-defined goal after another is reached will keep pupils motivated and prevent boredom commonly associated with traditional drill.

How can the study of foreign languages be articulated if started earlier than the secondary school years?   Another problem associated with the development of extended language programs is that of articulation.   If language study is inaugurated in the elementary school with emphasis on auditory comprehension, a smooth transition must be provided to the reading and grammar taught in the later years.   Even if the introduction of modern languages is delayed until the junior high school, articulation problems remain unless the entire secondary school span is carefully administered.   Longer sequences of language teaching are of value because they give pupils a greater advantage in gathering information in another subject and in enjoying another literary heritage.

Where will capable teachers be found?   A final problem inherent in changing from the more traditional methods of teaching modern foreign languages to the audio-lingual method is the securing of competent teachers.   There apparently are not enough trained teachers to go around.   Such teachers must be fluent in the language they teach and their pronunciation, intonation, and language structure must be near perfect.   Incorrect habits and skills learned by pupils are extremely difficult to eradicate.   The teachers must also have had adequate professional preparation to teach aural understanding, reading, writing, language analysis, and culture.

Two recent developments promise some help in overcoming certification barriers for otherwise competent people.   The first is the release of proficiency tests by a reputable testing service for teachers and advanced students.   The second is a movement by state certification agencies to permit citizens of foreign countries to have teaching privileges limited to foreign language areas.

Measuring success of the audio-lingual approach

Some authorities contend that modern foreign language teaching is approaching a new crisis. The audio-lingual method has not lived up to expectations. The NDEA institutes failed to stimulate major improvements in language learning and language laboratories have not been efficient replacements for live teachers. As a result, many students and teachers are questioning the relevance of foreign languages in modern education.[3]

Detractors from the success of audio-lingual methodologies probably find data for their criticisms in early large-scale evaluations. One of the most significant of these was that done by Educational Testing Service through questionnaires presented to students who took College Board modern language achievement tests in French, Spanish, or German in the 1965–66 academic year.[4] As might be anticipated, the picture emerging from the resulting data was not clear-cut. Critics of the audio-lingual method might find support in a number of survey findings:

1. The preparation of written translations both from and into a foreign language continues as a frequent practice in all secondary school grades.
2. Use of English to explain vocabulary or grammatical points is still used extensively.
3. Students expressed little faith in their ability to speak a foreign language.
4. Students indicated reading of the language as their best accomplishment with listening as second. Writing and speaking follow at some distance.

On the other hand, a number of findings from the College Board survey tend to support the opinion that audio-lingual techniques have had a reasonably widespread effect at the high school level:

1. There was evidence of a reasonable emphasis on the development of listening and speaking skills at all grade levels.
2. More than half the students used a language laboratory during the final three years of secondary school.
3. Almost two-thirds of the students were introduced to their study of French, Spanish, or German through a preliminary phase of instruction devoted entirely to the spoken language.

[3] William E. Bull and Enrique E. Lamadrid, "Our Grammar Rules Are Hurting Us," *Modern Language Journal* 55 (November 1971): 449–454.
[4] Neale W. Austin and John L. D. Clark, "A Survey of the Teaching of French, Spanish, and German in Secondary Schools," Copyright © 1969 by Educational Testing Service. All rights reserved.

4. More than half the students were taught the basic structure of the language without the presentation of formal grammatical rules.
5. Students' confidence in their listening comprehension ability far exceeded their assessment of their writing ability.

The future of modern foreign languages

Due to lack of evidence of overwhelming success of audio-lingual methods of teaching modern languages, the trend is toward a more eclectic approach.   There is a broadening of interpretation of the guidelines setting parameters for audio-lingual teaching. Increasing latitude is given to the introduction of reading and writing skills.   Researchers warn of the dangers of excessive reliance on pattern drills that can lead to boredom and fatigue.[5]   They also warn of excessive reliance on pupils' ability to discover for themselves principles that underlie patterns of language.   It is suggested that grammatical instruction be interspersed to prevent the mere parroting of set phrases.

The curriculum of the comprehensive school must continue to contain an adequate amount of modern foreign language teaching.   Curriculum leaders should be cognizant of the importance of another language for the well-educated pupil.

Emphasis must be given to the general education values of foreign languages.   Stress needs to be put on intercultural linguistic values rather than the so-called training of the mind.   Although utilitarian values are important, they are not, in themselves, a major reason for having a complete language program. The understanding of other cultures that leads to the understanding of their people is the real objective.

An important advantage on the part of a student in the study of a modern foreign language is to equate the language with actual living conditions of the people using the language.   Much is to be gained by a student studying French in a French school and living in a French home.   Many schools work out exchange programs with other countries whereby students live abroad for a year.   Exchange students coming to this country serve the dual purpose of improving their study of English and contributing to the language classes in the school where they are based.   These procedures have far more merit than the limited junkets sponsored by modern foreign language tour groups.   Frequently, the tour communication procedures are mundane and do not contribute to the development of language skills.

[5] Walter V. Kaulfers, "High School Foreign Language: Developments and Prospects," *Educational Forum* 34 (March 1970): 383–393.

CLASSICAL LANGUAGES

The future of classical language teaching in the secondary schools is problematical. As far as enrollment is concerned, Latin is more than holding its own, but Greek is practically nonexistent. Little or nothing is being written about Greek and only a few schools offer a course. Surprisingly, the teaching of Latin is not losing ground. The flow of pupils into Latin classes has been steady all during the increased emphasis on the modern foreign languages.

Increasing use of either of the classical languages is going to depend on the number of teachers available to handle the teaching assignments adequately. Most of the present teachers are nearing retirement age and the supply of beginning teachers is small. Prospective Latin students should begin the study of Latin in the secondary school with a minimum of three years' work. If this study is started in the seventh or eighth grade and then dropped until the college years, a problem of continuity arises. Very few students will continue the study of a language after a period of disuse.

The history of the teaching of Latin presents an interesting paradox. Although Latin ceased to be used as a vernacular language by 800 A.D., it was still taught as a spoken language in the sixteenth and seventeenth centuries because it formed a universal means of communication. The practice of teaching it as a spoken language was followed in the early American schools. Thus it may be seen that the teaching of the language was started in this country by the oral-aural method. As the country developed, and French became the language of diplomacy, it became more difficult to perpetuate the teaching of Latin as a spoken language. Hence, the transformation from the oral-aural method to the grammar-translation method. This change did not bother the puritan philosophy of devotion to the training of the intellect. Rather, it enhanced it. It also decided the method of teaching other languages from that point until modern times.

Teaching methods

Today, teaching methods in Latin are in stages of experimentation and revision, especially at the college level, and the experimentation probably will be reflected in the future training of teachers. Changes in teaching methods are being approached in different ways. Most of the revised programs stress the reading of the language; a few emphasize the development of oral ability.

Extensive experimentation on the oral-aural method of teaching Latin has been done by Waldo E. Sweet of the University of Michigan and Father Most of Loras College. They have combined the direct method with a scientific linguistic method. Their premise is that learning a language is the same as learning a set of habits in any other activity. This involves extensive drill and repetition of language patterns. It is doubtful, however, that the oral-aural procedure will ever be used as extensively in Latin as in the modern foreign languages, since Latin is not a means of modern communication. It is likely that the reading of the language will continue to be stressed more and more, with a marked curtailment of grammar-translation.

Who should study Latin?

Because of the tradition that has developed around the study of classical languages, and because of the character and operation of the elective system, pupils studying classical language do not represent the broad spectrum of pupil ability. Pupils who enroll for Latin are likely to come from the upper third of the ability range. Those who are enthusiastic about the teaching of the subject accept this as a desirable situation. They would encourage pupils with proven linguistic ability to enroll in a three-year minimum program somewhere between grades 7 and 12. This could either precede or follow the study of a modern foreign language or perhaps run concurrently with it. None of the advocates of Latin consider it a general education subject suitable for all pupils. What, then, will be the future of Latin? Interest and enthusiasm for the subject remain constant among the pupils and parents, but curriculum emphasis varies according to educational objectives. Where scholarly and cultural objectives are foremost, Latin is firmly entrenched. Where the practical and functional uses of a foreign language are the main objectives, Latin may become an early mortality.

The future of Latin and Greek

There is no doubt that Latin and Greek will continue to be studied by classical scholars on the college level. The future of the teaching of the classical languages at the secondary school level is far more uncertain. As has been stated before, Greek has almost disappeared from the secondary school scene. But it is hazardous to predict the future of Latin with any certainty.

Those who predict an early demise of Latin claim that it is

a dead language, and it is a waste of time to teach it except to satisfy the needs of a few classical scholars. These people mean, of course, that Latin is no longer a means of communication and therefore lacks any practical use in the marketplace.

The proponents of Latin deny the fact that it is a dead language. These classical scholars and curriculum planners place much of their faith in the future of Latin on the continuing popularity of the subject as reflected in secondary school enrollment figures. It is the second most popular foreign language being taught in the public high schools of the nation. There are 1,167,-000 boys and girls studying Latin in grades 7 to 12 and, in seventeen states, it has a higher enrollment than any other foreign language. The advocates of Latin contend that the reason pupils continue to enroll in the subject is because both they and their parents have a high regard for its value. They also claim it makes a direct contact with the classical past from which western civilization sprang. It gives direct access to the thoughts of people who lived during one of the most important periods in the history of humanity. They brush aside the argument that the study of history and literature can do the same thing in a much easier fashion. They hold that it is a fallacy to substitute the abstract for the concrete in cultural and humanistic areas when the concrete is essential.

Probably the strongest argument for the continued teaching of Latin comes from those who point to the contribution it has made to the modern foreign language field. It is the mother of five important languages of Europe and the Western Hemisphere. Over 30 percent of English words are derivatives of Latin. There is also the contention that Latin is the only foreign language in which stress is still placed on grammar. Many of the critics of present-day education believe that the American pupil needs a sense of grammar and style, and they can get it more easily and concretely from the inflected language than from its modern counterparts. Hence, the study of Latin makes a valuable contribution to the understanding of English as well as the modern foreign languages.

TOPICS FOR STUDY AND DISCUSSION

1. Is there justification for calling the traditional two-year foreign language programs a waste of time?
2. Why would the head of the romance language department of a large eastern university level a fine of fifty cents on every department member who used the word "translate" within the course of an academic year?

3. To some people, the use of the word "hardware" is rather harsh when applied to a good modern foreign language laboratory. Why do the critics use such a word?
4. What factors are important in determining the starting grade level of foreign language teaching?
5. Weigh the educational values of foreign languages being (a) disciplinary, (b) practical, and (c) cultural.
6. Why do linguistics scholars claim that English and Latin grammar are more different than they are alike?
7. Evaluate the thesis that a language becomes the means of penetrating the culture of a given society in the broadest anthropological sense.
8. Probe the conclusion that many languages are interchangeable as far as disciplinary values are concerned.
9. What factors will determine whether Latin will continue in the secondary school curriculum?
10. Play the Devil's Advocate and develop the thesis that the audio-lingual approach to the teaching of foreign languages has been oversold.
11. Prepare a positive or negative argument on the similarity of a linguistic approach to the teaching of English and the teaching of a foreign language.

SELECTED REFERENCES

BROOKS, NELSON. *Language and Language Learning.* New York: Harcourt Brace & World, Inc., 1960.

This book presents a very good coverage of the problems related to foreign language teaching in the schools. It touches on objectives, methods, procedures, and philosophy. It places in proper relationship the teaching of literature and the languages.

BULL, WILLIAM E. *Spanish for Teachers: Applied Linguistics.* New York: The Ronald Press Company, 1965.

This volume represents a new departure in the teaching of Spanish. It evaluates the application of contemporary linguistic principles and bridges the gap between theoretical knowledge and classroom practice. We think it is one of the better treatments of applied linguistics.

JOHNSON, MARJORIE C., ed. *Modern Foreign Languages in the High School.* Bulletin No. 16. Washington, D.C.: United States Department of Health, Education and Welfare, 1958.

This is a good treatment of the transition stages in the teaching of modern foreign languages. Modern approaches are thoroughly analyzed and suggestions are made for curricular changes. The effective use of language laboratories is advocated.

MODERN LANGUAGE ASSOCIATION OF AMERICA. *Reports of Surveys and Studies in the Teaching of Modern Foreign Languages.* New York: The Association, 1961.

The Association presents a good survey of best practices in the teaching of foreign languages.

PARKER, WILLIAM R. "The Case for Latin." *Classical Journal* (October 1964), pp. 1–10.

This article develops the thesis that the most defensible reason for studying any foreign language, including Latin, is that such study brings acquisition of a skill and gives a completely new medium of expression and introduction to a new cultural pattern.

PARKS, JOHN H. "The Classics in the Curriculum." *Peabody Journal of Education* 46 (May 1970): 331–339.

This article includes an evaluation of the traditional reasons given for maintaining the classics in the curriculum. It offers as a substitute a justification of the classics along the same lines as those usually given for modern foreign languages.

POLITZER, ROBERT L. "The Foreign Language Curriculum: Background and Problems." *Journal of Secondary Education* (April 1965), pp. 156–163.

This article contends that more time is needed for foreign language study and identifies the study procedures as audio-lingually oriented and deeply influenced by linguistic science. It ranges from early strict control of pupil's responses to final self-expression.

―――――. *Teaching French: An Introduction to Applied Linguistics.* Waltham, Mass.: Blaisdell Publishing Co., 1960.

This book describes and demonstrates the application of linguistics to the teaching of French. It presents the advantages of linguistic methods.

―――――, and STAUBACH, CHARLES N. *Teaching Spanish: A Linguistic Orientation.* Waltham, Mass.: Blaisdell Publishing Co., 1961.

This volume presents the teaching of Spanish on the basis of linguistic knowledge. It gives practical linguistic concepts as well as a general consideration of methodology.

RIVERS, WILGA M. *The Psychologist and the Foreign-Language Teacher.* Chicago: The University of Chicago Press, 1964.

This book identifies major assumptions of the audio-lingual method, critically examines each assumption in the light of modern learning theories, and suggests ways of improving foreign language teaching practices.

STACK, EDWARD M.   *The Language Laboratory and Modern Language Teaching*.   New York: Oxford University Press, Inc., 1966.
This volume carefully follows the optimum sequence in language teaching: hearing—speaking—reading—writing on the university and high school levels; hear—say—see in elementary schools.   It discusses systems, types, construction, and administration of language laboratories.   A new chapter on magnetic recordings provides up-to-date information on tapes, channels, and speeds.

CHAPTER 8

Home Economics

Many stories have developed around the theme of a lifelong search for an ideal or a precious object that is ultimately found on the searcher's own doorstep. In curriculum studies, this is the story of home economics. Curriculum makers look constantly for subject matter related directly to the lives of pupils—subject matter that has practical application and will lead ultimately to a vocational pursuit. Home economics involves learning activities that meet these requirements, yet it is a field that has been received with something less than enthusiasm by administrators, parents, and pupils. In many instances, it has been a subject forced on all junior high school girls and relegated to the slow learners in the senior high school.

Parents often take a negative attitude toward home economics, although it is a subject that will be involved in the lives of all pupils who someday will be establishing their own homes. It is a subject that some parents would deny the right to be in the curriculum, contending that mothers should teach their daughters the art of homemaking in their own homes. There has been a sparse enrollment in home economics for many years. It is only recently that enrollment figures show some tendency to increase.

Home economics is an area of education that has as its major concern the total well-being of the family. Chaotic social conditions in many sections of the country have caused educational planners to reevaluate the responsibilities of the family. Home economics programs need to be restructured to accommodate mobile families with multiple parental obligations.

TITLE CHANGES AND DEVELOPMENT

A brief look at the history of the field of home economics reveals changing attitudes and objectives. At one time, the field was known as "domestic science," probably because the title sounded scientific and imposing. In those days, the two main subjects were cooking and sewing, with pupils enrolled for cooking one semester and sewing, the next. The present title, "home economics," became associated with the subject as increased emphasis was placed on economics as applied to the home and family.

Home economics gained stature in 1917 with the passage of the Smith-Hughes Act, which allocated federal money for the support and development of home economics as a vocational subject. The use of the additional term "vocational home economics" began at this time. This legislation and others that came later were designed to emphasize the contribution of home economics education to the vocation of homemaking. This required the broadening of the field to include child care and guidance, family relationships, and home management. It also meant the inclusion of principles of other disciplines such as science, psychology, sociology, and economics.

A dualism exists in home economics curriculums of the secondary schools of today. A school will have either vocational home economics or nonvocational home economics. This is determined by whether or not the school receives federal funds for the support of the program. It is also marked by the certification of teachers to perform in either one type of program or the other. Federal legislation dealing with vocational home economics sets up definite time schedules for teachers that enable them to plan work with pupils in school that carries over into the activities of the home. Vocational teachers are hired on a twelve-month basis with fringe benefits including a paid vacation and travel allowance. This means that pupils are also enrolled in a twelve-month program. Although they do not report for daily classes during the summer months, they are expected to pursue home projects under the guidance and supervision of the teacher.

Critical views

The field of home economics has its usual share of critics who would change the trend of things and limit developments. Some of these people contend that as it is now conceived, home economics is not a field at all, or at best it is entirely synthetic. They point to the fact that principles of science are involved in health and housekeeping practices, principles of psychology and sociology determine child care and family relationship, and principles of economics are basic to the whole structure of family finance. These critics propose to retain these learning principles in the setting of their own discipline and thus save valuable pupil time in already overcrowded curriculums.

Other critical groups are alarmed at the invasion of home economics into the sacred tenets of the home. They hold that marriage, child rearing, and family intimacies are too complicated for secondary youth to comprehend. They would have the school confine itself to the teaching of the fundamentals. These alarmists are never too specific as to what the fundamentals are.

Some critics of vocational home economics claim there is too much federal dictation in the programs. However, most administrators of schools that have the vocational programs work on the assumption that federal directives can be instrumental in the development of good learning situations. Recent surveys show many nonvocational programs with offerings broadened to include the same comprehensive activities as the vocational classes. (Heretofore these nonvocational programs have involved mostly cooking and sewing, and even after revision many of them have inherent limitations.)

Regardless of the critics, home economics is enjoying its best enrollment of pupils to date. Over 95 percent of all public secondary schools of the nation have classes in home economics. Close to 50 percent of all girls take one or more courses in the field. About 1 percent of the boys pursue the subject. There is little doubt that homemaking of some form or other will continue to be taught in the secondary schools.

Should boys enroll?

As has been noted above, boys constitute about 1 percent of the present enrollment in home economics. Some authorities contend that 25 percent of the boys in the school should be enrolled in any given year.[1] Occasionally schools will set up special programs for them. In other instances they will be enrolled in regular classes. A thought might be given to whether more boys should enroll.

A good case for the affirmative can be made when consideration is given to the changing conditions in family life.

[1] Elizabeth J. Simpson, "Challenges in Curriculum Development in Home Economics," *Journal of Home Economics* (December 1968), pp. 767–773.

Where working wives are concerned, it is logical to expect the husband to assume part of the burden for homemaking. The expanding programs in home economics offer experiences needed by both boys and girls in such things as child care and guidance, family relationships, and home management. Some proponents of home economics for boys point to the vocational possibility in training to become chefs. This is a limited prospect, however, since most programs do not deal with preparation of large amounts of food. Such a program would interfere with more general objectives, and this type of training probably should be assigned to a regular vocational school. Either at the vocational school level or at the college level, programs are being developed for training men in food management for restaurants, hotels, college residence halls, etc. There are also vocational opportunities to specialize in textiles and clothing design. The pertinent question here is whether secondary school home economics courses should furnish the preparatory background for this specialized work.

The negative side of the question of whether home economics is a subject for boys is represented by the boys who enroll in classes as a "lark" or as an escape from more "difficult" subjects. They can become a nuisance and impede the progress of pupils with more serious purposes. Some authorities contend that boys would be better off in the behavioral sciences where they can secure adequate concepts of masculinity and better understanding of the need for emotional stability in their future wives. Whether more boys enroll in home economics or not, it is doubtful whether the subject will be functional and purposeful for any great number.

HOMEMAKING IN A CHANGING SOCIAL ORDER

In recent years the term "homemaking" has been used more and more in connection with home economics. Altough there are numerous vocations in the field of home economics, such as home demonstration agents, home economists for utility companies, and several types of government positions, the chief vocational pursuit is homemaking. It furnishes a practical application of classroom teaching, and requires no on-the-job training. Everybody agrees it is important, and few can escape the ultimate need for its basic content. Homemaking in the modern social order is an inclusive process involving foods and nutrition, clothing selection and construction, child care and training, family relations and social graces, home furnishings and equipment, consumer education and money management, and the many problems related to family health.

The field of home economics, like most of the other subjects in the school curriculum, is bound to be affected by the changing social order in an automated, technological society. Those making curriculum decisions concerning home economics must be very conscious of the social forces that are shaping modern family living.[2] If the subject is to be worth a prominent position in the curriculum of the comprehensive secondary school, it must earn this position through the vital contribution it makes in helping pupils face the complexity of modern living.

It is of little value to compare the modern home with the nostalgic image of a patriarchal father reading the Bible and conducting family prayers before an open fireplace. Those are days of another era. Home life today must be evaluated in terms of a changing social order. The home must be assessed as a changing social institution. What is viewed by some as the collapse of the home and family life is nothing more than necessary adaptations of the institution for survival in a culture now predominantly urban and technological rather than rural and agrarian. The employment of both father and mother outside the home calls for mutual responsibility in homemaking, although women will necessarily continue to carry major responsibility for operation of the household and for the spiritual, intellectual, and aesthetic tone of the home. Any going back to the simple life is impossible. The job of the school is to teach people to live well in an urban culture in an imaginative and creative way.[3]

As had been stated before, challenges in curriculum development in home economics are greatly increased by the complexity of American life. An inflationary economy practically necessitates multiple wage earners in the lower- and middle-income families. A modern home in the $30,000 to $40,000 price range, soaring prices of all commodities, and increased economic tax burdens negate the possibility of economic survival with only one wage earner.

The homemaker-wage earner is a new image emerging in the home economics field. Curriculum adjustment within home economics programs and development of interdisciplinary courses related to modern family problems are resulting necessities. Statistics identify the working mother as 38 percent of all women who work out of the home, and women make up 35 percent of the labor force. Half of American mothers bear their last child at the age of 30, hence more than half of their lives remain for

[2] Marguerite C. Burk, "In Search of Answers about Family Economic Behavior," *Journal of Home Economics* (June 1966), pp. 440–444.
[3] Mary Lee Hurt, *Current Developments in Vocational Home Economics Education* (Washington, D.C.: United States Department of Health, Education and Welfare, 1970), pp. 1–21.

gainful employment.   Care of children of working mothers is an acute problem.   Surveys show 8 percent of children of working mothers are expected to take care of themselves while the mother is at work.   Divorced, separated, and abandoned mothers create the problem of one-parent families.   Six million children, nearly one in ten, are living in one-parent homes.

There is no doubt the secondary school home economics curriculum should include programs adjusted to the needs of prospective homemaker-wage earners.   Content for such programs should emphasize human relationships applied to both family and job responsibilities.   Principles of management, including decision making, goals, values, standards, and nature and use of resources should be included in content.   Integrated subject matter should include budgeting and consumer education.   Materials and activities from physical education that emphasize physical well-being through nutrition, recreation, and exercise should be included.   Child care and child guidance has a special kind of identity in the program for the part-time mother.   The dual role that women play today in homemaking and wage earning complicates and broadens the scope of home economics education.

Thus it may be seen that modern home and family life needs to be analyzed critically by curriculum planners in the field of home economics.   The schools serve all social, economic, and cultural levels.   If the teaching of homemaking is to be the responsibility of the secondary schools, and if this responsibility is to be met realistically, the homemaking curriculum needs all of the characteristics common to other secondary school fields, such as ability grouping, problem solving, content adjustment, and sensitivity to a changing technological order.   Of particular concern to the homemaking field are such social factors as the mobility of people, crowded living conditions in urban life, stress of rapid change in employment conditions, necessity for living in diversity, and the need for a common value structure.

HOMEMAKING AT DIFFERENT ECONOMIC LEVELS

It is difficult to identify the modern home.   It has different characteristics on different cultural and economic levels.   There are really three homes to be considered.   While certain common denominators may be found in each, there are many problems of family living peculiar to each.

In the upper income brackets, both parents are likely to be college graduates leading active and busy lives.   The father will be out of the home much of the time in business pursuits. The mother may not be a wage earner, but she will be busy with countless social and civic activities. Much of the education of the children, both in and out of the home, will be done by tutors or in private schools. There is little likelihood that these children will be enrolling in courses in home economics. Those with sufficient mental capacity will be college bound. However, the need for homemaking skills is as great in this group as in any other.[4]

Homemaking is complex. Exceptional skills and capacities are needed to carry out family living. There is need for an understanding of the dynamics of human behavior, a perception of personal and family relationships, and an appreciation of the obligations and responsibilities of parenthood. It may be assumed that children of well-to-do families receive such instruction in a liberal arts education. It is difficult to determine whether this is true or not. Excessive divorce rates in these families raise a question.

Home conditions are quite different in middle-income families, the so-called white-collar group. There is a devotion to family activities in this group. It is true that both parents are very active, with the mother holding down a full-time position in many instances, but parents tend to do more things with their children, such as little league baseball, scout work, and other forms of recreation and sports. These families are together more. But here again, the children are likely to be college bound and the parents do not look to the secondary schools for teaching the art of homemaking. Classes in home economics will be pursued on an occasional elective basis.

The lower income families, frequently referred to as the blue-collar group, probably contribute more children to the school system than either of the other groups, and more pupils will be enrolled in home economics classes from this group. This is true because fewer of these pupils are college oriented and many of them are facing early marriage and parenthood either by choice or necessity. Among the lower income families, the roles of the father and mother are quite contrasting. The father and mother tend to lead separate lives. Most of the responsibility for homemaking falls entirely on the mother. The father is out of the home much of the time. He does his eight-hour stint in a factory or mine and then spends most of his other working hours in pursuits of personal satisfaction such as bowling or fraternal lodge attendance. In these homes, children are tolerated, often lacking in security and affection. The role of the wife is a lonely one. There is a great need for a common meeting ground for satisfactory family life.

---

[4] Doris E. Hanson, "Which Family," *Journal of Home Economics* (December 1966), pp. 777–779.

FACTORS INFLUENCING THE HOME
ECONOMICS CURRICULUM

Planning a home economics curriculum today is complicated by problems different from any previous societal order. Research in family activities reveals new sets of values, all cogent to subject-matter content in home economics classes. Education of family members has a higher priority than ever before. The value of an education has been accepted even among lower income families. Planning for the education of the children is a major family problem. And beyond the education of the children is the continuing education of the parents. Adult education has a greater enrollment than any other educational enterprise, and this will increase as life expectancy increases. Fortunately, the field of home economics has been a pioneer in adult education. This is true particularly of vocational home economics.

Securing an education may tie in well with family ambitions. The desire of the average citizen to get ahead and have the best for his children calls for careful financial planning involving savings accounts, insurance policies, and sagacious investments. Also involved here is the need for security in the home. Most families are ambitious to own their own home. This requires good money management.

The automation of the home along with efficient management provide time for many leisure-time activities. These pursuits can add much to the togetherness and enjoyment of family life. Careful planning can provide possibilities for creative expression in the areas of art and music. Hobbies and sports can be valuable and rewarding leisure-time activities. This phase of family living is increasingly important for its contribution to both physical and mental health. Relief needs to be found from the pressures and frustrations of modern living. The incidences of cardiac cases and mental breakdowns point to this need.

The personal well-being of each family member is part of good family planning. This revolves around the necessities of food, clothing, and good health. Well-balanced diets, good eating habits, proper personal grooming, and sensible care of the body are all ingredients of such planning. Two very personal facets of the home concern family ties and religion. Gregariousness of human beings is a natural instinct which is inherent in good family relationships. Love and respect among family members give meaning to such relationships. Wholesome religious experiences can be additional factors. Planning for church attendance and family worship are part of the American heritage.

SUBJECT-MATTER ARRANGEMENT

The content and sequence of course work in home economics is of primary concern to curriculum planning. A survey of existing curriculum reveals two common patterns. One pattern shows a series of separate courses in sequence of relationships and difficulty. Such courses cover such topics as foods, clothing, home management, health and home nursing, family relationship, child development, and consumer buying. The second pattern has yearly courses designated as Homemaking I, II, III, and IV. Each year a series of topics is covered. Parts of these topics are repeated in succeeding years, but in increasing difficulty and application. The proponents of this plan contend that it provides for the establishment of interrelationships among the topics.

Two major problems are found in the home economics programs of many schools. The tendency is to require the subject in the junior high school for at least two of the three years. This tends to dull the eagerness of pupils to enroll in senior high school classes, which are usually elective. Senior high school teachers are critical of the fact that too much work of an advanced nature has been attempted in the junior high school, with the result that pupils either lose their zest for the subject or complain of forced repetition. This problem is likely to be present when programs are set up on a yearly basis labeled home economics, I, II, III, and IV. It takes careful planning to avoid boring repetion in such programs. One of the hardest things to do is to control the degree of difficulty.

If the plan of a yearly series of topics or units is followed, placement and sequence might be made on this basis:

junior high school:
1. nutrition and health
2. personal care
3. making friends
4. room arrangements
5. safety in the home
6. care of young children
7. care and construction of clothing

senior high school:
1. clothing selection and construction
2. food for the family
3. child development
4. home planning and furnishing
5. home entertaining

6. family relationships
7. family finance
8. home nursing

Research shows that these are the topics pupils, parents, and teachers consider important. Parents and pupils suggest certain emphasis in these topics, such as more help in child training rather than child care, and more attention to moral and spiritual values in the home rather than skills of housekeeping.

PRESENT TRENDS IN THE FIELD

The best thinking among curriculum leaders in the field of home economics is consistent with curriculum development in other subject-matter areas. In meeting the needs of the wide variety of pupils found in a comprehensive school program, it is necessary to build curriculum content on basic concepts and generalizations. Results of extensive research and conference planning suggest five major divisions of content for home economics courses. These include:

1. human development and the family
2. home management and family economics
3. food and nutrition
4. housing
5. textiles and clothing

The above five major areas of content are not suggested in any sequence or order. They are only purposes of identifying what constitutes the field. Arrangement, adjustment, and application of this content will differ from school to school. Learning should be established in problem-solving situations where the development of skills and the evaluation of experiences are major objectives. Independent study and clinical activities may be provided by study in depth of such subjects as personality development or family financial security. Special survey courses may be arranged for the college bound, for business education pupils, or for seniors who for some reason or other have never had the opportunity to take work in the field. Special school projects may be part of the program. They would include child care centers, clothing repair centers, and centers for social graces.

A closer look at the textile and clothing unit will illustrate a suggested approach. The skills necessary for the design and construction of clothing continue to be basic and necessary, as is an understanding of the values and uses of textiles. The major emphasis, however, is put on an understanding of the uses of textiles and clothing as a means through which roles in life may be identified and expressed.

Through problem-solving situations, pupils become acquainted with the basic values and purposes of clothing in communicating personality and desired impressions. An individual can reflect and express personal values through clothing. Certain consequences can result from clothing choices. Impressions can be striking or subtle. Values can be established or destroyed. The history of societies and civilization can be traced through clothing choices. Thus it may be seen that a knowledge of the uses of clothing can be of far greater impact than skill in design and construction. Fame and fortune may come to the limited few who design clothing; a certain satisfaction may be gained by those who construct their own clothing; but the responsibility for intelligent wearing of clothing is the problem of all.

According to Ruth P. Hughes, there are three trends in the home economics field of uppermost importance:[5]

1. Awareness of sociological and psychological characteristics of students which have necessitated curricular changes. One change important enough to be noted as a separate trend is a greater emphasis on vocational education.
2. Careful analysis and appropriate use of empirical findings relevant to home economics education. Of particular importance is current work both in psychology of learning and sociology for the classroom. These require a research orientation among staff in home economics education.
3. A broader concept of teacher education to include not only the traditional preparation of secondary teachers but others whose mission is some form of innovative teaching.

The sociological and psychological changes in the characteristics of students affecting curricular changes relate to the so-called sexual revolution of today. The open warfare between the proponents and opponents of sex education courses in the schools has perplexing aspects for the experienced secondary school principal. In a previous era sex education was neither emphasized nor identified. Content areas in biology, health education, social studies, and home economics included units of material related to reproduction, child care, health hazards, and social implications of promiscuity. If queried, most principals could identify their sex education program, but they would be surprised at the question being put in such form.

The sex education controversy has implications for home economics education. Whether the sex education program aspects

---

[5] Ruth P. Hughes, "Trends in Home Economics Education," paper delivered at the West Virginia Home Economics Association Annual Meeting (February 1971).

related to home economics are part of an integrated program of the school or continue as part of the home economics curriculum will vary according to the mores of different communities. The fact remains, however, that sex is a basic integral part of family life and as such is in the providence of responsibility or home economics education. The major task is in the restoration of the role of the family as the behavior-constraining and behavior-defining agency for youth. Readily available contraceptives, high physical mobility, and a consumer-oriented economy with its explicit approval of self-indulgence do not uncomplicate the problem. Possible solutions for the sex education problem as well as the many other problems in the home economics curriculum field will be found by teachers benefiting from broader concepts of teacher education emphasizing the use of empirical research and problem-solving techniques.

THE HOME ECONOMICS
CURRICULUM OF THE FUTURE

The vocational aspects of home economics undoubtedly will continue to be stressed. It is a field that fuses theory and practice. Surveys of future job opportunities for young people reveal two general types of employment. One will be in positions associated with technology and will require well-developed technological skills. The other will be in positions of service to people. Here, too, skill and training will be necessary for those who want to be in the best competitive positions. Home economics can contribute to the vocational preparation of pupils for both technological and service jobs either directly or indirectly. In the case of very capable pupils preparing for jobs of a technological nature, the role of home economics may be limited to the homemaking responsibilities of these pupils. This touches on the question of whether intellectually gifted pupils should enroll in home economics classes.

In the past, only a limited number of the very intelligent girls enrolled in home economics work. Yet 95 percent of American women marry and have an average of three children each. This means that regardless of training and job position, a girl is almost sure to be a mother and a homemaker. Therefore, it is reasonable to assume that part of her preparatory education should contribute to this ultimate responsibility. Some authorities lament the waste of womanpower in the present technological order. These authorities would load the secondary school preparation of capable girls with science, mathematics, and foreign languages. Psychologists maintain, however, that no school subject is markedly superior to another for "strengthening mental power," and the undeniable need for educating homemakers is merely avoided. The question that faces the planners of home economics curriculums is one of designing home economics classes that will challenge capable pupils. Instruction needs to reach the rich potential these pupils have both intellectually and artistically. This instruction should include concept development and critical thinking on a high level. It is the responsibility of the comprehensive secondary school to prepare pupils for the dual role of making valuable contributions both within and without the home.

The need for people in service occupations has developed rapidly with the urbanization of the population. People living within limited space and lacking opportunities to be self-sufficient need the services of many others. These service jobs have become more and more specialized, so that those who render the services must be trained. Whether the home economics curriculum should include vocational preparation for all service jobs is an open question that should be answered. Much of the content of home economics classes in the past has been applicable to the training for service jobs, but it has been homemaking oriented. A brief listing of some of the service jobs needs will illustrate this: child care services; clothing services—dry cleaning, etc.; institutional work—hospitals, motels, hotels, etc.; housing and home furnishing—florists, gift shops, department stores, etc.; and specialized services such as companions to the elderly, and shopping guides.

If the home economics curriculum of the future is to fulfill its role in a comprehensive school, there is no doubt that adjustments must be made. Practically all girls, including the intellectually gifted, will be future homemakers. If all girls and a substantial number of boys enroll, instruction must be adjusted to ability, as in any other subject. Many of the pupils who will pursue service jobs are already in home economics classes. New content and training in new skills will be necessary to adequately prepare these pupils. Home economics programs face a new urgency in helping youth adjust and make discriminating use of available resources, both human and physical. The pupils must learn to make sensible decisions in order to gain maximum satisfaction and contribute significantly to the building of good homes and good communities.

TOPICS FOR STUDY AND DISCUSSION

1. What should be placed in an outline of learning experiences for both boys and girls in a family living course that would contribute to their readiness in establishing their own homes?

2. Weigh the values of home economics courses for general education, vocational education, personal development, and family life.
3. What common threads should permeate curriculum areas of home economics, health education, sociology, economics, and business education? Are there other areas that should be included?
4. Explore in depth the vocational home economics program sponsored by the national government as to its rigidity, its emphasis on motivation by contents, and its relations to modern family living needs.
5. Explore the theory that home economics should not be offered as a course in the secondary school curriculum—that it lacks subject-matter content and the concepts involved ought to be developed in other more appropriate subjects.
6. How can the imbalance in home economics enrollment between the junior and senior high schools be justified?
7. Analyze the changing roles of men and women in a technological social order. What are the conclusions for curriculum planners in secondary school home economics?
8. If home economics curriculum planners are to come to grips with such vital problems as sex education, what should be the approach?

SELECTED REFERENCES

BROWN, MARJORIE, and PLIHAL, JANE. *Physical Home Environment and Psychological and Social Factors.* Minneapolis: Burgess Publishing Company, 1969.

This is a good source for evaluation of the physical make up of the home. It furnishes guides for establishment of experiences with manipulating sensory stimuli such as colors, sounds, physical arrangements, etc. It would be helpful for curriculum decisions in this phase of course content.

FLECK, HENRIETTA. *Toward Better Teaching of Home Economic.* New York: The Macmillan Company, 1968.

This book furnishes material for home economics education seeking answers for family living in relation to scientific and technological developments, affluence and poverty, the population explosion, the growing role of government in family life, and the changing functions of the family that characterize contemporary American society. Special attention is given to new approaches in curriculum development.

HALL, OLIVE A., and PAOLUCCI, BEATRICE. *Teaching Home Economics.* New York: John Wiley and Sons, 1970.

This is the second edition of this popular textbook in the

field of home economics. One of the new chapters gives special attention to deviates in the learning process, both retarded and accelerated. Both the affective and psychomotor domains are given analytical treatment.

KILANDER, FREDERICK H. *Sex Education in the Schools*. New York: Macmillan Company, 1970.

This volume is aimed at helping educators organize and conduct meaningful learning experiences in family life and sex education. Emphasis is on the acquisition of knowledge and the development of wholesome attitudes. Part One contains chapters 1–13, dealing directly with family living aspects of sex education in the schools.

New Directions for Vocational Home Economics. Washington, D.C.: Report of a National Conference, American Home Economics Association, 1971.

Over four hundred home economists assembled for the purpose of finding what directions educators in vocational home economics should pursue. This report contains the major addresses given at the meeting. At least three of the addresses may furnish guideposts for the next decade.

SIMPSON, ELIZABETH JANE. *The Classification of Educational Objectives, Psychomotor Domain*. Washington, D.C.: United States Department of Health, Education and Welfare, 1966.

This report is most influential on the development of a classification system for educational objectives, psychomotor domain in taxonomic form. The field of home economics is finding new directions from this report.

CHAPTER 9

Industrial Arts

Industrial arts programs run the gamut from almost complete obsolescence to sparkling modernity. The recent experience of a state university curriculum coordinator illustrates the point. He received an enthusiastic invitation from a young industrial arts teacher to visit his new shop. The coordinator was pleased to find the shop housed in a modern addition to the school sufficiently isolated from the main building to prevent noise problems. His enthusiasm cooled, however, as he approached the new shop area and sniffed the familiar odor of fresh sawdust. His suspicions were confirmed as he entered the shop proper. The commodious area was filled with woodworking tools and woodworking power machinery, and the neatly piled lumber rack was well stocked with new lumber.

The university visitor was discouraged to find such a limited concept of a modern industrial arts program. His main consolation came with the remembrance of shop programs in other parts of the state which provide high school pupils with experiences in metals, woods, plastics, graphic arts, application of electricity and electronics, application of design and drafting, and research in the production of industrial products. These shops represented the best in industrial arts programs.

Studies of curriculum guides for industrial arts in the various states reveal a diversity of programs. In some states it is difficult to find published materials. In other states there is an abundance of material dealing with drawing, woodworking, metal working, electricity, and radio. Far less attention is given to plastics, graphic arts, and power mechanics. Most of the curriculum guides concern themselves with the use of hand tools, the operation of machines, and related information concerning materials. It is difficult to find agreement on what should be taught. From a perusal of the available curriculum materials, it is reasonable to conclude that industrial arts in the hinterlands has not progressed very far from the concept of teaching basic hand tools and machine processes. Too often, the making of the "take home project" is the ultimate objective. Most individual arts curriculums need reorganization, both in their concepts and in their objectives.

CHANGING CONCEPTS

While the term industrial arts is now in good usage by those connected with the field, and the laboratory for learning activities is properly labeled the industrial arts shop, this has not always been the case.[1] The earliest term used in the field was manual training. Objectives were related to the development of skills in the use of hand tools, and woodworking was the major activity. Frequently, mechanical drawing was taught as a related subject. In some instances, courses in woodworking and mechanical drawing were given in alternate semesters; in other cases the courses were given during the same semester, on different days of the week. Enrollment in manual training was confined mostly to boys.

As increased technological knowledge brought new products and new industrial processes into everyday living, curriculum planners sought to incorporate this new information into the shop classes. There was a feeling that pupils needed a wider knowledge of materials and processes of industry. They also needed information on the use and maintenance of the many modern conveniences and labor-saving devices coming into the home. To cover this wider scope of activity, the term manual arts came into use. Learning activities in the manual arts shop included the use of plastics, graphic arts, textiles, bookbinding, etc.

The use of manual arts as a term to identify the field never gained wide usage, and it soon gave way to the current term, industrial arts. Programs of industrial arts have both technical and aesthetic aspects; many processes in the arts, such as ceramics, and different forms of crafts, such as weaving and leather working, are taught. The increased emphasis on a wide variety of activities in the industrial arts field soon identified it with the purposes of

[1] Marshall L. Schmitt and Dale W. Chismore, "Definitions for Industrial Arts," *Industrial Arts and Vocational Education* (March 1967), pp. 100–119.

143

general education.   Out of this grew the concept of the general shop.

Emphasis in industrial arts has never been on vocational education.   Confusion sometimes arises over this matter.   The vocational overtones in industrial arts are secondary.   Vocational education demands specialization and depth preparation that are not stressed in the industrial arts shop.   Primary objective is to give pupils a wide range of preparatory experiences that will lead to later vocational choice or avocational pursuits.   The theory behind the general shop is that pupils with wide experiences in industrial processes will adjust to the rapidly changing demands of a technological order.   It presupposes that the job training of today may not be usable tomorrow.   Vocational specialization too early may be wasted, but purposeful, planned experiences in a wide variety of industrial processes can result in intelligent vocational choices as opportunities occur.   Even if no vocational choice results, avocational skills learned in general shop may result in personal satisfaction and worthwhile leisure activities.

Industrial arts experiences are for both boys and girls.   Both are involved in the technological culture.   It is doubtful whether any great number of girls will enroll in shop classes, but there is no reason to assume that they lack aptitude for it or that their needs are not as great as boys.   Women are engaged in all phases of industrial life.   They also share equal responsibilities in homemaking and recreational pursuits.   Perhaps more experimentation is necessary for discovering the feasibility of a commonalty of experiences between industrial arts courses and home economics courses.

CURRICULUM OBJECTIVES

One of the earliest lists of industrial arts objectives is *The Standards of Attainment of Industrial Arts Teaching*,[2] published by the American Vocational Association in 1934.   Objectives emphasized the manipulative skills in the use of hand tools and the execution of simple basic operations.   The list remained essentially the same through revisions in 1948 and 1953, with the exception of added objectives for health and safety.   It was a good listing at the time it was made, and it still contains many of the fundamentals of a good industrial arts program, but it does not reflect adequately the needs of the modern industrial order.

A study of industrial arts objectives recently compiled by

[2] American Vocational Association, Inc., Industrial Arts Division, *Standards of Attainment of Industrial Arts Teaching* (1934).

leaders in the field shows a definite effort to meet the needs of youth in a complex society. These objectives include emphasis on problem solving, design, and experimentation as facets of a more wholesome approach to learning through intelligently organized experiences that help orient the student in the realm of industrial and technological subject matter. The proper emphasis given to the manipulative activities continues to be an issue, but more stress is being placed on the correlation of science and mathematics and the relation of various industrial processes to lifelike situations.

The report of a U.S. Office of Education conference in 1960 includes four rather broad objectives.[3] These objectives were the result of extensive surveying and summarizing of previously established objectives by recognized authorities in the field. They were meant to provide experience for the slow learner as well as the gifted and are worthy of careful analysis.

1. To develop in each student an insight and understanding of industry and its place in our culture.

There is no doubt that this objective is ordinarily the responsibility of courses in economics, sociology, and physical sciences, but industrial arts can show both the theoretical and the functional aspects of the occupational and productive activities of society. Industry is a dominant element of the modern social order. The school shares a heavy responsibility for helping each student understand this industrialization. Industrial arts can furnish basic training in skills, techniques, and information that will be of value for those who enter industry and the phases of business associated with industry. A desirable background also can be furnished for those who expect to go into advanced work in the various professional areas related to industry.

2. To discover and develop talent of students in the technical fields and applied sciences.

The fulfillment of this objective would bring a new type of pupil to the industrial arts shop. The stigma of being a dumping ground for disinterested pupils of questionable ability would rapidly disappear. Pupils would be guided into industrial arts courses as a result of their identification with scientific and technological pursuits. Future technicians, engineers, and production workers would gain basic experiences suitable to their aptitudes and needs.

The discovery aspect of this objective is worth careful analysis. The academically capable pupil is often cloistered in abstract subject-matter areas where the premium is on storing

[3] Office of Education, *Improving Industrial Arts Teaching* (Washington, D.C.: United States Government Printing Office, 1960), pp. 3–18.

knowledge rather than applying it to practical situations. Part of these pupils graduate from secondary schools completely inept in the simplest of applications. Experience in industrial arts would not only aid in discovery of technical abilities, but would give confidence and satisfaction in use of such abilities.

3. To develop technical problem solving skills relative to materials and processes.

Problem solving continues to be a cardinal process for learning. There is a concentration of emphasis on problem solving in most of the subject-matter fields that are undergoing significant change in content and teaching techniques. When properly directed in industrial arts, this approach leads to creative thinking, the application of principles of science and mathematics, and technological know-how. The use of tools and materials divorced from problem solving may be glorified busy work, and this does not satisfy basic needs of pupils, regardless of whether they are of high ability or low ability.

4. To develop in each student a measure of skill in the use of the common tools and machines.

This is one of the oldest objectives in the industrial arts field and it still is fundamentally sound. The skilled use of tools is essential in the many phases of industrial arts. This skill needs to be developed beyond the mere manipulative phases of the use of tools and machines. It leads to a necessary understanding of industrial processes and gives the pupil an opportunity to develop his talents in technical fields. This ability is a means to an end in problem-solving ability.

A recent visitor to the Argonne Laboratories in Chicago observed what appeared to be an ordinary workman soldering wires on an electrical panel board. It was on a Sunday afternoon and the laboratories were deserted except for the solitary workman. His appearance and the work he was doing gave credence to the belief that he was a technician called in to do a special job. The visitor was quite surprised to learn that he was observing one of the best physicists in the nation. Here was an example of a top-ranking scientist making use of manipulative skills in the world of experimentation.

The basic objectives of industrial arts programs should be concerned with the contributions that can be made to general education. They must satisfy the ramifications of complex industrial experiences, as well as patterns of general civic and human relationships. Industrial arts experiences, if indeed they have progressed beyond the hand tool stage, need to be broadened beyond the materials and processes of modern industry to include unique patterns of human relations such as those involved in the delicate balance between labor and management.

INDUSTRIAL ARTS IN THE COMPREHENSIVE SCHOOL

The role of industrial arts in the comprehensive school needs better delineation.   For example, a basic concept of the comprehensive school is the proper balance of curriculum offerings to meet the needs of all pupils.[4]   The connotation of balance appears to mean that pupils should have experience in subjects contributing to the educational, vocational, and citizenship aspects of their lives.   It is sometimes referred to as a balance between the academic and practical, or between the academic and the manipulative skills. Industrial arts represents a balancing subject in the curriculum as well as a subject that can exhibit balance within its own subject-matter area.

The industrial arts shop is unique as a facility for bringing together and synthesizing the various phases of a good educational program.   Functional industrial arts should exploit this uniqueness and extend its benefits to all pupils.   Those things that make specific contributions to all youth should be emphasized.   Industrial arts has the subject matter and activities to challenge the more able pupils.   Attention should be given to the establishment of special, high-level classes that will attract pupils interested in science and engineering.   Extensive experience in dealing with the less capable certainly ought to aid in charting sound programs for their needs. A minimum program for all abilities is a good objective.

The increasing complexity of our industrialized society and the increasing amount of mechanization encountered everywhere makes it essential that industrial arts experiences be regarded as basic and fundamental for all youth.   There is definite evidence of need for reorganizing industrial arts objectives and content around modern industrial development and basic problems of industry, incorporating the accepted objectives of the comprehensive school.

There is no doubt that industrial arts as a part of general education can provide profitable and valuable experiences to all pupils in the public schools.[5]   There are opportunities within its bounds to make positive contributions to the teaching of moral

[4] William G. Floyd, "Industrial Arts: A New Approach," *Bulletin of the National Association of Secondary School Principals* (March 1967), pp. 24–31.
[5] Roy W. Roberts, *Vocational and Practical Arts* (New York: Harper and Row, Publishers, 1971), pp. 16–47.

and civic responsibilities. It can also be an important adjunct to scientific research and experimentation.

There is a tendency to adjust industrial arts programs to provide more meaningful experiences for the college bound pupil. This idea is commendable and has merit for those who plan to specialize in any form of engineering or highly developed industrial pursuit. However, the terminal pupil continues to deserve major emphasis in the industrial arts program.

The shop teacher would doubtless prefer to have pupils of average and above average intelligence, and if vocational objectives are to be fulfilled in areas of industrial management and technological skills, this is a worthy preference. The ability to conceive from abstract ideas, to bring to life on the drawing board, and to execute a finished product from raw materials is the ultimate objective of every industrial arts teacher. This does not mean that industrial arts cannot fulfill worthy objectives for pupils of lesser academic ability. Research studies continue to show that academic proficiency as expressed by IQ and other mental measurements has no correlation with the success of students in subjects that are primarily of the manipulative type.

In addition to providing pupils with knowledge for hobby pursuits and home mechanics efficiencies, industrial arts is in the pleasant position of being able to offer knowledge, skills, and techniques that can be used directly and immediately in gainful employment. It might be argued that this is vocational education and perhaps would include all vocational aspects, but no experience that becomes basic for life's work can be divorced from vocational experiences. The need for draftsmen, mechanics, and technicians is ever present. Many skilled hands are needed between the drawing board and the launching pad.

It must be repeated, however, that industrial arts objectives are different from those of vocational education. The responsibility for preparing youth for job situations is the function of vocational education and should be identified as such. It is more important for pupils in industrial arts courses to learn of the complexities of American industrial culture and the resulting effects on the lives of people. The more technology and science expand, the more important it becomes for a person to understand industrial processes.

The unit shop and the general shop

The unit shop represents one of the prize creations of curriculum planners in the industrial arts field. It has come to symbolize the best aspects of depth instruction in several industrial processes, since pupils gain enough information to understand these processes and to make decisions as to possible vocational pursuits. The wide variety of experiences usually offered by a unit shop program include work with woods, plastics, metals, graphic arts, electricity, drafting, etc., and serve to introduce pupils to design, formation, and utility of materials. These experiences afford the pupils enough of a basic understanding of the uses of industrial materials for personal consumer practices or vocational choices in an area of specialization.

There are those who contend that the unit shop will gradually fade out of the industrial arts program. They believe future programs will not be divided into specific areas such as wood, plastics, and metals; content will deal more with principles and concepts of industrial procedures. Emphasis will be on application of mechanisms, methods of production, influence of automation on labor and economics, and creating new ideas and new products. These same authorities see innovations in teaching methods that will involve experimentation, research, and problem solving. Changes in content and method will necessitate revamping of industrial arts laboratories and classrooms. This probably means the unit shop will lose much of its identity.

The general shop represents another industrial arts innovation in curriculum planning. It differs from the unit shop in emphasis rather than organization. While the unit shop tends to stress depth instruction in sound industrial processes, the general shop covers in breadth more of the expanding field of industrial processes. Advocates of general shops give less emphasis to the preparation of pupils for particular industrial positions. They consider the general shop in keeping with the general education objectives of the comprehensive secondary school. Perhaps general shop concepts are better oriented with present curriculum trends.

CURRICULUM TRENDS

There is a problem in bridging the gap between philosophy and theory in the new industrial arts programs. There are detractors as well as advocates of plans that feature technology as the basic content ingredient and the increased use of classroom activity procedures at the expense of laboratory experiences. There are those who contend the tendency is to make programs with too many classroom activities and too few laboratory activities. The problem is to use industrial and technological processes as content and keep relevant learning activities in the laboratory. If industrial arts is to be a vital subject in the curriculum, ways must be found to coordinate laboratory experiences with all phases of the program.

Those who advocate increased use of classroom experiences in industrial arts programs point to the major responsibility the subject has for carrying out the aims of occupational education.[6] These are classified as: (1) development of technological and industrial awareness, (2) encouragement for exploration of individual aptitudes, capabilities, interests, and characteristics, and (3) development of skills and habits of hand and mind.

Technology approach

Although industrial arts has been a part of the secondary school curriculum for a long time, industrial arts educators continue to defend its legitimacy and struggle with semantics of identity. They continue to make statements such as "Industrial arts *is* a school subject and is important in the general education pattern of all students."[7]   This same authority holds that industrial arts curriculum building concerns only content, that curriculum starts and ends with content.   Outcomes are not part of curriculum, but merely describe what values are to be achieved from the study of subject matter.   Neither are methods a part of curriculum design, only an explanation of how subject matter is taught.

In contrast to the above, another industrial arts educator explains curriculum as the medium through which the aims, purposes, and objectives of education are implemented and realized.[8] He introduces the word "structure" (used interchangeably with the word "model") as the vehicle for establishing various content levels to meet changing knowledge requirements.

Despite differences in approach, there is a growing agreement among industrial arts educators that the dominant objective of industrial arts should be that of providing an understanding of American industry and an awareness of its changing technology. Programs using this as the basic objective are identified with a technology approach.   In its simplest form this approach redefines the old objective of "a degree of skill" as an understanding of the necessity for skillful use of tools rather than skill in the use of tools.   In more complex form technology as related to industrial arts is conceptualized as a study of man as the creator of technology

---

[6] Leslie H. Cochran, *Innovative Programs in Industrial Arts* (Bloomington, Ill.: McKnight and McKnight Publishing Co., 1969).
[7] Robert S. Seckendorf, "Where Should We Be Going in Industrial Arts?" *The Bulletin of the National Association of Secondary School Principals* (November 1969), pp. 98–107.
[8] Paul W. DeVore, "Structure and Content Foundation for Curriculum Development" (Washington, D.C.: The American Industrial Arts Association, November 1970), p. 1.

incorporating the fundamental technical and cultural elements of the several areas of technology.

Paul DeVore proposes that an industrial arts curriculum based on the study of man and technology has the following characteristics:[9]

1. Provides a better base from which to implement the purposes and objectives of general education;
2. Is not limited or isolated by geographical boundaries, thereby evidencing the true nature of disciplined inquiry;
3. Is concerned with man as the creator of technology regardless of national origin;
4. Provides a meaningful relation between technology and man's culture. Historical, anthropological, social and economic elements of the culture are important to the understanding of man's technology, and a knowledge of man's technology is vital to the understanding of any culture; and
5. Identifies a knowledge area meeting the criterion of a discipline in the truest sense of the term.

DeVore structures the organization for content in a technology-oriented industrial arts curriculum around three technical areas:[10]

1. *Production*—providing goods and services of economic value for man's needs and wants. Instruction would center around tools, materials, processes, machines, and organization and management of procedures related to fabrication, processing, and constructive technology.
2. *Communication*—providing information dissemination, storage, retrieval, and use. Subject matter would be related to information about sensing, encoding, transmission, signaling, receiving, and decoding systems through the use of radiant energy and mechanical-chemical and electro-mechanical means.
3. *Transportation*—providing movement of man, materials, products, and services. Content would include information on propulsion, guidance, control, structural and suspension systems for the solution of problems related to terrestrial, marine, atmospheric, and space environments.

If the proposals for an industrial arts curriculum based on technology are incorporated into the comprehensive secondary school program, industrial arts will undoubtedly take on a new image. Its position in general education will be solidified and its integration with other subject-matter areas will be axiomatic. It will necessitate retraining of teachers and the opening of the industrial arts curriculum to the entire school.

9 Ibid., p. 2.
10 Ibid., p. 12.

Enterprise—Man and Technology

A new industrial arts program for secondary schools has been devised at Southern Illinois University. The program is entitled "Enterprise—Man and Technology." The students, either individually or in groups, decide on a certain enterprise to develop. The initiation, conduct, termination, and consequences of the enterprise are the responsibility of the student or groups of students. The program calls for laboratory experiences, homework, classroom activity, field trips, and a work cooperative.

Laboratory activities involve work experiences whereby students learn to integrate specialized work tasks with efficient production. They design a salable product or service, arrange to finance production of the same, design and prepare tools and fixtures, rent equipment, procure supplies, hire and train a work force, and produce a predetermined number of units or services. They arrange for distribution of products and evaluation of the results.

Homework in the enterprise consists mostly of readings agreed upon by student and teacher. The material relates to the enterprise involved and the broader aspects of technology. Homework assignments can also entail production planning and preparation for laboratory and classroom activities to follow.

The major portion of classroom activities is devoted to the study of a productive society. Classroom consideration of man's role in technology involves discussions related to the student's experiences in the laboratory. Topically, the major headings include planning, organization, control, and evaluation. The selected categories of technology are: electronics and instrumentation, visual communications, materials and processes, and energy conversion and power transmission. Resource people are involved and use is made of multimedia.

The Enterprise program makes extensive use of community resources. Planned visits are made to commercial, industrial, civic, and recreational facilities. Whenever possible, students are encouraged to make arrangements for on-the-job training relating to their enterprise. The proponents of the Enterprise idea believe that students encounter the fundamental problems of a technological society. They discover the kinds of competition that develop when technological and human innovations are put to work. They are brought face-to-face with the basic need for expertise in the world of work. Leadership in secondary education is turning to the community as a base resource for the curriculum. An important phase of the open school idea is its outward thrust.

Other programs

Industrial arts curriculum planners may want to take a closer look at one of the following programs as described by Eugene R. Flug. Each program has some of the characteristics of the two programs previously described, although each program has specific features of its own.[11]

Industrial Arts Curriculum Project.   This project lists three main objectives: (1) to create an understanding of the concepts, principles, generalizations, problems, and strategies of industrial technology as a body of knowledge; (2) to develop an interest in and an appreciation for industry as an integral part of the economic system that provides industrial goods for human wants; (3) significant value for occupational, recreational, consumer, and sociocultural purposes.

The Partnership Vocational Education Project.   Students study the unity or wholeness of industry and explore underlying functions that relate to possible vocational choices.   Stress is placed on information that shows the correlation of industrial-technical subjects with other academic areas.

Galaxy Plan for Career Preparation.   The purpose is to bring activities of business, agriculture, home economics, vocational-technical education, and industrial arts closer together in order that students can explore career possibilities in the world of work.

Orchestrated Systems Approach.   This approach aims at development of knowledges and competencies for understanding and participating in the production of goods and services that contribute to betterment of life in an industrialized society.   Product-producing and servicing experience are features of this program.

More use of research

One of the most encouraging aspects of curriculum development in the industrial arts field is the amount of research going on and the availability of results for industrial arts teachers.   There has been a substantial increase in the number of studies using good research

11 Eugene R. Flug et al., "Roundtable: Comparing Programs in Industrial Arts," *Industrial Arts and Vocational Education* (January 1970), pp. 24–26.

techniques. These studies are based on sound analytical endeavors to identify, classify, and organize content and experiences of industrial arts students.

As is true in so many fields in education, a discouraging thing about research in industrial arts is the lack of consistent findings, particularly those dealing with techniques and modes of teaching. There is little experimental evidence to indicate comparative superiority of any teaching method for any specific subject matter or any group of learners. The number of variables influencing teaching effectiveness is apparently so great that researchers have not been able to isolate and identify these variables precisely enough to permit accurate description of "best" teaching methodology.

Regardless of outcomes, it is encouraging to find so much research and experimentation going on in the field. It is a harbinger of improved techniques for the future. At present the questionable quality of many of the instructional strategies no doubt contributes to the lack of consistency in the findings of methodology studies. The experience of curriculum workers indicates that several revisions based on large-scale field tests are required to produce quality instructional materials and methods.[12]

THE FUTURE OF INDUSTRIAL ARTS

Industrial arts curriculum planners face a dilemma in deciding what direction programs should take. Involved are several pertinent questions. Will shop class teachers acquiesce to administrative pressures to make their special charge the less capable pupil who cannot make it in other areas of the curriculum? Will the shop idea be replaced by area program developments? Will industrial arts programs become theory-centered classes and primarily feeders to technical education?

Probably the best answers to the foregoing questions will be found in analyzing the stature industrial arts ought to maintain in a comprehensive school. Without doubt, the field has much to offer the slow learner and, especially, the handicapped. This is a responsibility that industrial arts teachers ought to capitalize on rather than reject as a thankless task. Second, industrial arts is made to order for the contributions that can be made to a technological social order where increasing demands are for purposeful leisure time pursuits. The great "do it yourself" mania that has

[12] Daniel L. Householder and Alan R. Suess, "Current Research in Industrial Arts Is Increasing," *Industrial Arts and Vocational Education* (September 1970), pp. 4–5.

swept over the nation has not come about by accident. These needs are genuine and they should be planned for in the education program of a comprehensive school. The industrial arts shop should be a laboratory for the development of purposeful industrial and leisure time skills. Finally, industrial arts teachers must be cognizant of the impact technology is making on American industry. The body of science, techniques, and skills related to industrial development must be constantly reviewed for the purpose of making proper adjustment in industrial arts programs so as to attract and retain pupils of ability commensurate with the increasing difficulty of such programs.

There is a strong possibility that industrial arts theorists will outdistance practical thinkers in the rush to bring sophistication to the field. It may appear to the practical-minded industrial arts teacher that his shop is to become a citadel for physical science and mathematics rather than a place where pupils use skilled hands to shape industrial products, as formerly conceived. And indeed, this may be true. There are those who see the industrial arts program of the future rich in applied science. Principles of physical science will be evident in a large percentage of problem-solving, project-making activities of the future shop.

Those who would bring greater sophistication to industrial arts see pupils involved in making telescopes and studying astronomy, learning the lapidary art from geological investigations, and engaging in a wide study of electronics involving the building and understanding of radio equipment, high-fidelity sound, and even satellite tracking. Such programs would forego the regular auto mechanics course and teach the broad field of power, its resources, its conversion and use. The industrial arts shop would be an extension of the science laboratory. Pupils would see meaning in scientific principles by associating phenomena with familiar products and daily operations.

Industrial arts can make a real contribution to the secondary comprehensive school program. The opportunity is present for the development of an industrial arts program that will be vital in the lives of secondary school youth. Courage and vision on the part of industrial arts leaders can open many new vistas in the field.

TOPICS FOR STUDY AND DISCUSSION

1. What authenticity is there to the statement that industrial arts may have the unhappy distinction of being the most misunderstood subject in the secondary school curriculum?

2. What are the points of delineation between industrial arts and vocational education?

3. Surveys show there is a tendency to stress industrial arts more in the junior high school than in the senior high school. What objectives would determine this?

4. Industrial arts teachers are usually conscious of the "dumping ground" stigma attached to their field. What assessment of responsibility may be made in this matter?

5. Contrast the development of industrial arts in different size school districts according to community needs.

6. What logic is there in the proposal that industrial arts has aesthetic as well as technical value?

7. Identify the commonalty of experiences for pupils enrolled in courses of industrial arts and home economics.

8. Prepare a report for a local school board that would justify or reject industrial arts as a required subject in the secondary school curriculum.

9. Where should emphasis be placed in curriculum planning for a good industrial arts program for modern needs—on the unit shop or the general shop?

10. What answers should be given to those who ask why a good industrial arts program should have precedence over a specialized vocational education program in a comprehensive secondary school?

11. The requirements of engineering schools sometimes suggest mechanical drawing as a desirable subject for college preparation. Should provisions be made to separate this subject from the regular industrial arts program?

12. Refute the charge that increasing industrial and technological content in the industrial arts curriculum tends to limit laboratory experiences.

13. Critics of DeVore say his proposals are too theoretical and not likely to be implemented in the industrial arts field. Do you agree or disagree and why?

SELECTED REFERENCES

BROWNELL, JOHN A., and KING, ARTHUR R., JR. *The Curriculum and the Disciplines of Knowledge.* New York: John Wiley and Sons, 1966.

This book sets forth the current condition of knowledge as a pluralism of the disciplines. It proposes a model to devise a theory of curriculum practice that affirms the centrality of the disciplines of knowledge. Chapter One discusses the various aspects of man in relation to the technologies.   This is the new direction for many industrial arts educators.

Components of Teacher Education.   Twentieth Yearbook, American Council of Industrial Arts Education.   Bloomington, Illinois: McKnight and McKnight Publishing Company, 1971.

This is a good compilation of material on industrial arts content.   Each chapter is written by a different authority.   Materials covered include: technological dimensions of content, theoretical bases of content, scope and sequence of content, and elements of instructional methods.

DeVore, Paul W.   *Structure and Content Foundations for Curriculum Development.*   Washington, D.C.: American Industrial Arts Association, 1967.

This is a valuable pamphlet on the relationship of the industrial arts field to technology.   The function of industrial arts as a part of formal education is reviewed.   This pamphlet proposes the body of knowledge called technology contains the content reservoir from which industrial arts curriculum content can be derived.

Industrial Arts in the Technologies.   Morgantown, West Virginia: West Virginia University Publication, 1970.

This is a brief report of five pre-doctoral and five post-doctoral students who spent an academic year in building a model for industrial arts education.   The result is a detailed rationale and structure of a model program for the education of teacher-scholars in technology.   It forms the basis for a new type of industrial arts curriculum for secondary schools.

New Concepts in Industrial Arts.   Thirtieth Annual Convention Proceedings.   Washington, D.C.: American Industrial Arts Association, 1968.

The contents include selected addresses from the thirtieth annual convention of the American Industrial Arts Association meeting. A wide range of topics is included.   All the material is pertinent to problems related to industrial arts curriculum planning.

Roberts, Roy W.   *Vocational and Practical Arts Education.*   New York: Harper and Row, 1971.

This book contains a historical development of the field.   It sets forth guiding principles for curriculum decisions.   An attempt is made to put in proper perspective the relationship between vocational and industrial arts education.   The use of the words "practical arts" in the book title will bother many industrial arts educators.

CHAPTER 10

Mathematics

The relevance of almost any subject in the curriculum may be debated. Mathematics is an exception, because it has been considered one of the fundamentals for a long time. A revolutionary advance in both the development and use of mathematics has been associated with the launching of space missiles which have come to be recognized as symbols of the great development of scientific knowledge that started early in the twentieth century. The important advances in the use of mathematics, among other things, made the space age possible.

The new uses of mathematics constantly being discovered in the fields of physics, chemistry, and engineering are to be expected. But even more astonishing uses are being found in other fields. The biologist is applying mathematical theory to the study of inheritance, industry is using mathematics in scheduling production and distribution, the social scientist is using ideas from modern statistics, and the psychologist is using mathematics of game theory. The mathematics curriculum of the secondary school must move rapidly to keep pace with the needs and development of these new applications.

The new uses of mathematics require greater understanding of the structure of mathematical systems and less manipulation of formula and equation. There is more emphasis on the construction of mathematical models and symbolic representation of ideas and relationships. Most computation previously done by human beings is now done by machines. Both the changed emphasis and the increased use of mathematics cause the subject to be more and more a part of the total cultural pattern.

New programs, developed for both the elementary and secondary schools, are designed to attract more youths into the study of mathematics and to give a more realistic preparation to those who pursue the subject.   A number of experiments have demonstrated the feasibility and advantages of teaching new topics in secondary school courses.   New ideas, language, and symbolism help to give a better understanding of mathematics.   Obsolete material is being replaced with more significant subject matter.

THE BEGINNING OF THE NEW MATHEMATICS PERIOD

During the period when important changes were first being made in the mathematics curriculum, quite a controversy raged over the use of the word "new."   While the difference of opinion was largely one of semantics, certain authorities took issue with the idea of calling the various reorganizations of subject matter new mathematics.   To avoid this relatively unimportant argument, other authorities decided to use the term "modern mathematics" rather than "new mathematics."

For purposes of clarification, it should be noted that the mathematics in the programs being introduced were not new as far as being recently discovered was concerned.   What was new was the emphasis given to topics that were not previously treated. This did not mean a rejection of large amounts of traditional subject matter, but an extensive reorganization of curricular material.

Probably the most important characteristic of the new mathematics was not in the content but in the spirit in which mathematics was approached.   To emphasize the underlying unity and coherence of the subject and the interrelationships among the basic concepts, the new programs included such unifying elements as the concept of sets, the structure of the number system, coordinate geometry, inequalities along with equalities, and appropriate mathematical language.

The new programs eliminated subject matter that had little relevance to modern needs.   Elaborate and special cases of factoring, obscure geometry theorems, and logarithmic solutions of all the special cases of triangles by trigonometry were gone.   Algebra was no longer presented as a collection of isolated techniques and formal mechanical procedures for solving verbal problems.   Instead, the unified basic structure of algebra was used in developing algebraic skills.   Such a point of view gave the pupil more opportunities to explore and discover mathematical concepts on his own and to learn what constitutes mathematics and how a mathematician thinks.

In a broad sense, all mathematics since the time of Descartes and Newton, around 1650, might be labeled "new" because a new era in mathematics dawned with the renaissance of the subject in western Europe. A more limited time might be assigned to the development of modern mathematics starting with the turn of the century when ideas that had been developing in the latter half of the previous century came to fruition.

Specifically, the term *new mathematics* was best associated with such contemporary activity as that used in matrix algebra, topology, linear programing, stochastic processes, and electronic computers. Again, the question might be asked, what was new? Was it the mathematics or was it the terminology? Was it the curriculum organization, or was it the method and emphasis? The answer probably lies in the assumption that it was the combination of all these things.

A survey of authorities writing on school mathematics reveals certain innovations as characteristic of the new mathematics.[1] These were innovations of content such as the notion and language of sets, systems of numeration, the real number systems of algebra, elements of logic, and the nature of measurement. There was more emphasis on abstract ideas such as the concept of closure, the inverse of an operation, and the extensions of the number systems. Increased attention was given to logical rigor. This was illustrated by explicit emphasis on such ideas as undefined terms, related propositions, and the meaning and significance of implication.

The critics who claimed the only thing new about the new mathematics was the terminology pointed to the use of such language as "open sentences," "truth values," "simple curves," "natural numbers" and "real numbers," "sets," "sub-sets," and "proper sub-sets." There was an insistence upon precise language invoking subtle distinctions and formal definition. Examples included "number" and "a numeral," "the roots of an equation" and "the solution set," and "functions" and "relations."

It was really unimportant to make an issue of the degree of newness in the field of mathematics. What was important was the fact that more pupils were studying mathematics and enjoying it, and many mathematics teachers were excited about the attention their subject was getting. Organization, methodology, and terminology are closely associated with matters of content

[1] Charles H. Butler et al., *The Teaching of Secondary Mathematics* (New York: McGraw-Hill Book Company, 1970), pp. 42–46.

and ideas. These are the elements for study in the mathematics curriculum.

CURRICULAR IMPACT OF MODERN MATHEMATICS

Educators responsible for curriculum development in mathematics may be uncertain as to whether modern mathematics is catching on or whether those who adopted one of the several new programs have made the right move. It would be helpful for those in doubt to review a progress report made by the Commission on Mathematics.[2]

Since the major reforms in mathematics may be traced in part to the influence of the Commission on Mathematics of the College Board, it is of major significance to find what impact the recommendations of the Commission have had on the mathematical content of the curriculum of the secondary schools.

A little over a decade ago the Commission on Mathematics was formed by the College Board. The Commission recommended the following nine-point program:

1. Strong preparation, both in concepts and in skills, for college mathematics at the level of calculus and analytic geometry.
2. Understanding of the nature and role of deductive reasoning —in algebra as well as in geometry.
3. Appreciation of mathematical structure ("patterns")—for example, properties of natural, rational, real, and complex numbers.
4. Judicious use of unifying ideas—sets, variables, functions, and relations.
5. Treatment of inequalities along with equations.
6. Incorporation with plane geometry of some coordinate geometry, and essentials of solid geometry and space perception.
7. Introduction in grade 11 of fundamental trigonometry—centered on coordinates, vectors, and complex numbers.
8. Emphasis in grade 12 on elementary functions (polynomial, exponential, circular).
9. Recommendation of additional alternative units for grade 12: either introductory probability with statistical applications, or an introduction to modern algebra.

The progress report made by the Commission based on a survey conducted by the College Entrance Examiners Board reveals how well the nine-point proposal of the Commission is being

[2] S. Irene Williams, "A Progress Report on the Implementation of the Commission on Mathematics," *The Mathematics Teacher* (October 1970), pp. 461–468.

implemented. Data were obtained by means of questionnaires sent to 2,718 seniors who participated in College Board examinations. The general format of the questionnaire was relative to what the students had studied in secondary school mathematics.

The study indicates positive evidence of the Commission's recommendations being incorporated in the secondary school mathematics. The following examples are pertinent:

1. Structure and properties of the number system had been studied by 85 percent of the students—more than three-fourths prior to their junior year.
2. Approximately 90 percent of the students had studied inequalities along with equations.
3. Almost half of the students reported their geometry course as including some coordinate geometry, one-third some solid geometry, and one-fifth both solid and coordinate geometry.
4. Indirect proof had been studied by 80 percent of the students —propositional logic by about 65 percent.
5. Approximately 95 percent reported encounter with trigonometric functions prior to the twelfth year.
6. While only 35 percent of the students had studied complex numbers and 55 percent had studied the solution of triangles by logarithms, approximately three-fourths had studied complex number systems.
7. The data show an acceptance of sets as a unifying idea in mathematics. There is a general increase in acceptance after grade 7.
8. The terms domain and range of a function, period of a function, and amplitude and frequency of a function had been encountered by more than half of the students.
9. Measures of central tendency and interpretation of data had been studied by about 40 percent of the students and measures of dispersion by about 20 percent.
10. Seventeen percent of the students had enrolled in advanced placement courses in mathematics.

The data from the survey indicate that innovations by the Commission on Mathematics and other curriculum reform groups have begun to appear in the programs of secondary school students and that recommended topics are being integrated into mathematics programs rather than attached in a superficial way.

HOW MAY MODERN MATHEMATICS BE INTRODUCED INTO THE CURRICULUM?

The selection of a program and materials to supplement it should be done by the present mathematics teachers and the curriculum leader, considering the objectives, not only of the mathematics department, but of the entire curriculum. Many schools through-out the nation have made a complete changeover to the modern mathematics program, and many others are in a state of transition. It would be helpful if the experiences of those who have made the change, or who are now in the process of making the change, could be compiled into a manual for those who still have the task before them. There is no reason to believe that any school will be immune to the necessity for change.

When introducing modern mathematics into the school curriculum administrators must decide which of the several new programs to consider and if the teachers will be able to handle the new material. The availability of in-service training programs, the number of staff members who may have had limited experiences with a certain program, and the type of new teachers who may be secured are all items to be considered in the selection of a program.

It is doubtful that many schools would agree to a totally new staff of teachers for any new program; therefore the solution to the teacher problem lies in the retraining of the present staff. Experience with many traditional mathematics teachers indicates that teachers have more trouble shifting to the new programs than pupils do. Over the years these teachers have built up certain reactions and language patterns that they use when confronted with a mathematical problem. In most cases the new programs have changed the approach, the language, and the symbolism. The pupil sees this material for the first time and sees nothing strange about it, but the teacher must unlearn and forget many thought processes inherent in the older approach.

Nevertheless, mathematics teachers generally are more than willing to update themselves in the new concepts, and new textbook material and many types of in-service training programs are available. The National Science Foundation Summer and Academic Year Institutes are popular, and the financial assistance offered makes them feasible and practical. Leaves of absence are granted for attendance on a college campus. Demonstration classes may be conducted by experts at the local level. Many schools have engaged mathematicians to conduct in-service extension courses for their teachers. A number of voluntary study groups have been formed, often without the assistance or insistence of administrative leaders. Many of the teachers in these groups comment that they have never before worked so hard or enjoyed it more. They soon discover that the mathematics in the new programs is not easy and it is not watered down; it is interesting and challenging.

It is assumed that the recently trained teachers coming into the schools will be prepared to handle modern mathematics programs. This responsibility, of course, rests with the teacher education institutions. Any teacher working with the new programs must understand the new mathematical content and must know the proper techniques for teaching it.

THE DEVELOPMENT OF MODERN MATHEMATICS PROGRAMS

The origin of modern mathematics programs is not difficult to determine. No program had a significant superiority over another, and the ultimate objectives of each of the programs were relatively similar. A cogent factor in the choice of a program was the contention by some teachers that a certain program would work better with certain types of pupils, or the fact that the teachers were partial to a particular program because they had some experience with it. Some principals contended that after a thorough examination of all available programs and after extensive consultation with their colleagues, they could choose a program by the toss of a coin.

Probably the best known and most widely used of the modern mathematics programs is that of the School Mathematics Study Group (SMSG), which was formed at a conference of mathematicians sponsored by the American Mathematical Society and financed by the National Science Foundation. In this program, pupils continued to manipulate numbers, but the prime objective was to develop an awareness of the basic properties of numbers. SMSG developed units of material for grades 4 through 12, testing the material in each unit extensively before publishing it as a textbook. Each unit presented topics and problems for mathematical analysis, repeating the topics in sequence for deeper treatment and continuous review. These concepts and their relationships form the structure of mathematics; therefore the program makers assumed that they were central to all mathematics.

SMSG courses dealt with relatively conventional topics rather than introducing new topics, but the organization and method of presentation had undergone definite change. The familiarity of experienced teachers with many of the topics was the basis for adoption of the SMSG materials, since the teachers could use the SMSG units with relative ease, following the directions provided in the teaching manuals.

In grades 7 and 8 the SMSG material covers elements of the total secondary sequence: abstract concepts, the role of definition, development of precise vocabulary and thought, experimentation, and mathematical truth. Although the course for grade 10 is predominately plane geometry, there is some material on solid geometry, an introduction to analytic geometry, and a review of algebra.   Grade 11 includes trigonometry, vectors, logarithms, mathematical induction, and complex numbers. There are two divisions of the material for grade 12.   One division is a study of elementary functions such as polynomial, exponential, logarithmic and trigonometric operations.   It includes an introduction of geometrically meaningful methods of handling areas, tangents, and maximum-minimum problems that give pupils an intuitive background for calculus.   The second division is an introduction to matrix algebra, including problems involving systems of linear equations and geometry.   Careful attention is given to algebraic structure.

From this review of the secondary school area of SMSG mathematics, it may be seen that the old compartmentalization of subject matter has been dissolved[3] by problem-solving techniques that require the use of the interrelated facets of the whole field of mathematics.   These techniques place a utilitarian value on mathematics.

The movement in mathematics which was most concerned with curriculum reform started with the formation of the University of Illinois Committee on School Mathematics (UICSM) in 1951.   The committee grew out of a desire of the colleges of education, engineering, and liberal arts to improve their freshman mathematics courses, but soon the interest and emphasis of the committee shifted to high school mathematics.

The UICSM program (often referred to as the Beberman Program, in honor of its director, Dr. Max Beberman) presents mathematics as a consistent, unified subject.   Pupils are led to discover principles for themselves and to develop manipulative skills necessary for problem solving.   It is an active process, with the pupil doing mathematics rather than being told about mathematics.   The secondary school program, for grades 9 through 12, consists of eleven units organized around the following topics: (1) the arithmetic of real numbers; (2) pro-numerals, generalizations, and algebraic manipulations; (3) equations and inequations, applications; (4) ordered pairs and graphs; (5) relations and functions; (6) geometry; (7) mathematical induction; (8) sequences; (9) exponential and logarithmic functions; (10) circular functions and trigonometry; and (11) polynomial functions and complex numbers.   Units 1 through 4 are intended for grade 9, units 5 and 6 for grade 10, units 7 and 8 for grade 11, and units 9 through 11 for grade 12.

[3] Evelyn B. Rosenthal, *Understanding the New Math* (New York: Hawthorn Books, Inc., 1965), pp. 28–32.

In theory, the UICSM program was designed for all students. In practice, it is likely that the first two years are basic and the final two years are for advanced pupils. Some teachers feel the whole program is for only the more capable pupils. This opinion could result from the inexperience of the teachers in the use of the material or from the faulty background of the pupils. Reliable evaluation of the effectiveness of the material is still in progress.

The University of Maryland mathematics project deals exclusively with grades 7 and 8 of the junior high school. It has for its objectives development of precision in using the language of mathematics, appreciation of the structure of number systems, facility in the use of inductive and deductive methods of reasoning, and acquisition of an understanding of metric and nonmetric geometry. A strong thread of algebraic concepts runs through the program.

In order to assure understanding of basic concepts, verbal and operational components are developed together, and both the vertical and horizontal aspects of each mathematical component are given careful attention. This procedure is based on the theories of Gestalt psychology, which suggests that learning should be by related wholes rather than fragmentary parts. The Maryland program is aimed at the development of carry-over values that are necessary for classroom activities in any subject. Among these are the ability to recognize and use space, time, and number relationships. The pupils learn to observe, describe, and classify numbers as well as to draw inferences and develop understanding.

In grade 7, the Maryland program includes such topics as properties of natural numbers, systems of numeration, symbols, factors and primes, mathematical systems, points, lines, curves, and planes. Attention is also given to proofs and equations in the system of real numbers. The grade 8 topics include the system of rational numbers, the system of real numbers, and the system of integers under addition. Logic and number sentences, equations, fractional number phrases, plane figures, and scientific notations for arithmetic numbers are covered. The Maryland program covers part of the material formerly presented in grades 9 and 10, and some question has been raised as to whether it is within the learning ability of all pupils in grades 7 and 8.

Several other modern programs for the teaching of mathematics have been developed within the last decade. Each is meritorious in its own right within identifiable objectives. These programs include the Greater Cleveland Mathematics Program, the Syracuse University-Webster College Madison Program, the Suppes Experimental Project, and the Ball State Experimental Program. Important contributions were also included in the *Re-*

port of the Commission on Mathematics by the College Entrance Examination Board.

CONTROVERSY CONCERNING GEOMETRY

Curriculum reform will continue to center around the nine expectations of the Commission on Mathematics. A puzzling issue remains unsettled. That is what to do with geometry. There is strong disagreement among authorities as to content, length of time to be studied, and integrating relationships with other mathematical subject matter. It appears that the early introduction of geometric concepts on an intuitive level will be continued, the usual synthetic geometry will be changed to incorporate increasingly certain characteristics of coordinate geometry, and strong leanings toward treatment of geometric transformations will emerge.

Great strides have been made in the development of the mathematical curriculum for elementary and secondary school pupils. Since the new mathematics was introduced more than a decade ago, programs for arithmetic and algebra have been developed with a certain amount of universal acceptance. This has not been the case with geometry. A real dilemma has developed.[4]

It is comparatively easy to reach agreement on the fact that the objective in the teaching of algebra is the development of properties for the fields of rational, real, and complex numbers. It is easy to grasp the notion of a field. In geometry, however, there is not even agreement on what the subject is about. Frequently it is necessary to fall back on the often-quoted truism of any field, "Geometry is what geometers do."

To some geometry is the study of geometric figures, while in the minds of others it is identified with a method of proof. Many authorities contend geometry is the study of the invariants of transformation groups. Much of the controversy in the secondary mathematics curriculum area centers around the question of whether transformation geometry is the answer. There appears to be emerging a modified "yes."

The many different classifications of geometries further complicate mathematics curriculum decisions. For example, there is Euclidean, affine, non-Euclidean, projective, algebraic, and differential geometry. Each of these may be studied in two, three,

---

[4] Richard H. Gast, "The High School Geometry Controversy: Is Transformation Geometry the Answer?" *The Mathematics Teacher* (January 1971), pp. 37–40.

four, or any number of dimensions. In fact, the problem is so complicated that agreement is almost nonexistent.

Presumably, curriculum designers must decide on objectives for the formation and content of geometry. There are several ways this may be done. Two examples are cited. The first deals with the way a composite of authorities may be used. For a long time mathematics teachers have been aware of the inadequacies of geometry courses based on abbreviated versions of Euclid's *Elements*. A listing of changes in course composition that have been tried in this and other countries might include:[5]

1. The use of modified versions of the axioms.
2. The simultaneous development of plane and solid geometry.
3. The early introduction of metric ideas such as length of segments, angle measure, and area of plane figures.
4. Reliance on the properties of the real-number system.
5. The introduction of coordinate geometry.
6. The use of vector methods.
7. The use of those transformations of the plane, called isometrics, that leave the distances between points unchanged.
8. The inclusion of some non-Euclidean geometry.
9. The development of Euclidean space as a vector space with an inner product.
10. The development of the Euclidean plane as a coordinatized affine plane, with the real-number system used as the set of coordinates on a line and with a perpendicularity relation introduced in the plane.

Two of the new mathematics programs developed in the United States are based on part of the listing above. The School Mathematics Study Group used the first five in varying proportions in their two courses "Geometry" and "Geometry with Coordinates." The University of Illinois Committee for School Mathematics emphasized number 9 in the above listing.

A second example of how to reach a decision on the formation and content of geometry courses in the secondary school mathematics program would be to follow objectives as formulated by a recognized authority. Allendoerfer offers both objectives and approaches for the teaching of geometry.[6] His objectives include:

1. An understanding of the basic facts about geometric figures in the plane and geometric solids in space.
2. An understanding of the basic facts about geometric transformations, such as reflections, rotations, and translations.
3. An appreciation of the deductive method.

[5] Irving Adler, "What Shall We Teach in High School Geometry?" *The Mathematics Teacher* (March 1968), pp. 226–228.
[6] Carl B. Allendoerfer, "The Dilemma in Geometry," *The Mathematics Teacher* (March 1969), pp. 165–170.

4.   An introduction to imaginative thinking.
5.   Integration of geometric ideas with other parts of mathematics.

Allendoerfer offers a selection of one of three approaches. First, the synthetic approach. This is the method used by Euclid and is familiar to all mathematics teachers. Second, the analytic approach. This method solves geometric problems by means of algebra through the use of coordinate systems. And third, the vector approach. Vectors are used to develop theory through the use of standard vector algebra.

The controversy over geometry is academic in nature, but the decision as how to incorporate the subject into a mathematics program of a secondary school is real. Authorities in mathematics, both as individuals and in groups, have much to offer as to objectives and approaches, but the final decision must be made on the understanding of the nature of geometry and the conception of goals individual teachers are trying to reach.

COMPUTER-ASSISTED INSTRUCTION

Many technological devices have promised hope for the improvement of instruction in the schools. Among these are motion pictures, television, language laboratories, programed instruction, and teaching machines. For one reason or another, none of the above devices has lived up to its early promise.

With the development of the electronic computer, a new technology raises new hopes for improved procedures in education. Computer-assisted instruction (CAI) promises to provide some of the quantum jumps that have been hoped for in the past. Computer-assisted instruction has the flexibility and capacity for individualizing learning processes necessary for adaptive education.

The three fundamental characteristics of computer applications to mathematics instruction as well as other subject-matter areas are: (1) the ability of a pre-stored program in a computer system to evaluate a student's responses and provide information regarding the correctness of these responses; (2) the active responding by the student; and (3) the opportunity to individualize instruction not only at the level of achievement, but in reference to specific interests and abilities of the student. The above three characteristics involve individual pacing, logical presentation, small step development, and immediate reinforcement.

Computer-assisted instruction has an impact on instructional methods. There is increasing concern for developing techniques that extend theories of learning to the actual learning situation.

In view of the fact that a computer facility makes possible an environment for careful control of complex variables purported to contribute to effective and efficient learning, it behooves curriculum planners in mathematics to investigate the effects of feedback variables, types of review, and levels of achievement on growth of understanding for immediate and delayed retention.

Sophisticated computer-assisted instruction has been developed in the field of mathematics. The same thing is true for science, music, social studies, and English. Materials in other fields are under construction.

The impact of the electronic computer on the curriculum of the student cannot be over-estimated. Elementary concepts of numerical analysis are mathematically based. There is need to acquaint students with the capabilities, limitations, and idiosyncrasies of computers. Equations and algorithms are part of computer formulation, certainly with the use of flow charts.

MATHEMATICS IN THE COMPREHENSIVE SCHOOL

It is evident that mathematics plays an important role in the development of a comprehensive school curriculum. The subject matter is constantly growing, not only in advanced mathematics, but also in the elementary phases of the subject. Mathematics is being called on today to meet a wide variety of needs that could not possibly have been anticipated a few years ago.[7]

One of the main factors pointing to the significance of mathematics in a comprehensive school program is the changing of emphasis in the field. It is moving away from human computation to an understanding and construction of symbolic representation of factors that relate to scientific or social situations. As has been previously suggested, new mathematical ideas, language, and symbolism are being introduced to give a better understanding of the subject, thus widening the range of pupil abilities to comprehend and enjoy the subject.

The cooperative effort of college mathematics professors and elementary and secondary classroom teachers in developing new programs of mathematics will lead to better articulation between secondary school and college mathematics programs. Practical applications of mathematical material, and better integration of mathematical subject matter with the total curriculum, will

[7] Bruce E. Meserve and Max A. Sobel, *Mathematics for Secondary School Teachers* (Englewood Cliffs, N.J.: Prentice-Hall, Inc., 1962), pp. 266–270.

give greater continuity to the total school program and involve more pupils in math than ever before.

One of the problems surrounding the introduction of modern mathematics programs into the curriculum is the determination of what level of pupil ability is best suited for such programs. There is contention that most of the programs favor the superior and college-bound pupil. Only experience and valid research will furnish the answer to this question. A good program in any subject-matter area in a comprehensive school will provide for the talented as well as the slow learners.

Accelerated programs leading to advanced placement should be part of the mathematical offerings of a comprehensive school. In many cases this acceleration allows the pupil to be exposed to a full year of calculus while still in high school. A competent secondary mathematics teacher will enrich her classes for superior students with simplified or intuitive level topics that are sure to be studied in college-level mathematics.

Unfortunately, among average and slow learners there has developed a distaste and fear of mathematics that may be carried throughout their lives. Teachers have the task of convincing students that mathematics is worth learning, that there is a purpose in the mathematics program. In mathematics, learning is cumulative and the slow learner will fall hopelessly behind if the program is not adjusted to him. The slow learner goes through substantially the same mental processes as his more favored friends, but he has a different rate of perception. A well-adjusted program of mathematics in a comprehensive school makes provision for all rates of learning.

PROBLEMS OF ARTICULATION

The emergence of a sound mathematics program in the comprehensive secondary school will depend on the establishment of modern mathematics programs from the kindergarten through grade 12. Major problems are being encountered in the middle school years. The adjustment of materials and teaching procedures for slow learners is troublesome. However, there is no doubt that pupils in slow learning groups can master mathematics appropriate to their needs if program adjustments are made. Efforts in this direction are exemplified by the approach to teaching fractions in the new Illinois programs.[8]

[8] Peter Braunfeld, Clyde Dilley, and Walter Rucker, "A New UICSM Approach to Fractions for the Junior High School," *The Mathematics Teacher* (March 1967), pp. 215–221.

Authorities disagree on what changes in elementary school mathematics are most urgently needed.   Some caution against blind acceptance of modern programs.   Even Beberman counseled that too rapid a change in the elementary grades may prevent pupils from learning to make computations.[9]   He suggested that teachers must always be ready for change but that the changes ought to be made gradually and experimentally.

Some authors, such as Morris Kline, reject the principles of modern mathematics.[10]   In proposals he makes for the high school mathematics curriculum, Kline contends that mathematics must be developed constructively, not deductively, and that intuitiveness should replace vigor in presentation.   It is safe to say, however, that the number who caution against or reject modern mathematics programs are in the minority.   The programs are generally accepted and are well on their way to establishment.

Probably the most assuring voices concerning the values of modern mathematics programs came out of *The Cambridge Conference Report of 1963*.[11]   The Cambridge Conference, organized by Zacharias and Martin, was composed of twenty-five leading scientists and mathematicians.   The report says in part: "A student who has worked through the full thirteen years of mathematics grades K-12 should have a level of training comparable to three years of top-level college work."

It is a mistake to evaluate modern mathematics programs on the basis of materials rather than methods.[12]   Poor teaching will not enliven the best of materials.   The modern programs emphasize method, content, and the learning process, placing the implementation of the curriculum back into the hands of the best teachers.

TOPICS FOR STUDY AND DISCUSSION

1. Evaluate the conundrum there is nothing "new" in the "new" mathematics.
2. How will the new mathematics change the lament of the school youth who says he likes mathematics but he does not like to do "thought" problems?

[9] Francis J. Mueller, "The Public Image of New Mathematics," *The Mathematics Teacher* (November 1966), pp. 618–623.
[10] Morris Kline, "A Proposal for the High School Mathematics Curriculum," *The Mathematics Teacher* (April 1966), pp. 322–330.
[11] Irving Adler, "The Cambridge Conference Report: Blueprint or Fantasy?" *The Mathematics Teacher* (March 1966), pp. 210–217.
[12] Brother L. Raphael, "The Return of the Old Mathematics," *The Mathematics Teacher* (January 1967), pp. 14–17.

3. What deductions may be drawn from these two statements: (a) Factors important in a pupil's success in mathematics are native intelligence, cultural background, and motivation. (b) To many people, mathematics is an emotional blindspot.
4. What would be the position of a course in general mathematics in a modern mathematics program?
5. Substantiate the conclusion that modern mathematics is a change in presentation rather than content.
6. Occasionally, a critic declares that modern mathematics programs are doomed to failure. Develop a refutation.
7. Prognosticate the outcome of the controversy over geometry.

SELECTED REFERENCES

BEBERMAN, MAX. *An Emerging Program of Secondary School Mathematics.* Cambridge, Mass.: Harvard University Press, 1958.

This is a detailed description of the Beberman—one of the orginators of the "new" mathematics—approach to the teaching of mathematics and the Illinois program. The approach involves new nomenclature and emphasis on discovery techniques.

BUTLER, CHARLES H., et al. *The Teaching of Secondary Mathematics.* New York: McGraw-Hill Book Co., 1970.

This is the fifth edition of a very popular and authoritative textbook on the teaching of secondary school mathematics. It gives a good background for curriculum decisions in building a mathematics program and offers extensive material for teaching selected topics.

FAWCETT, HAROLD P., and CUMMINS, KENNETH B. *The Teaching of Mathematics from Counting to Calculus.* Columbus, Ohio: Charles E. Merrill Publishing Co., 1970.

The authors say their sole purpose in this book is to give their interpretation of "the discovery approach." They contend that a sure way to stifle the spirit of mathematics is to emphasize the "finished product" at the expense of the *process* which produced it.

KIDD, KENNETH P., et al. *The Laboratory Approach to Mathematics.* Chicago: Science Research Associates, Inc., 1970.

This book identifies educational concepts of the laboratory method of instruction, including active learning, student involvement, student participation, and relevance. It lists pertinent questions for decision making in adopting the laboratory approach.

KLINE, MORRIS. "A Proposal for the High School Mathematics

Curriculum." *The Mathematics Teacher* (April 1966), pp. 322–330.

A significant article because it does not subscribe to the modern mathematics curriculum but proposes a new set of principles and a curriculum adhering to them. It contends that mathematics must be developed, not deductively, but constructively.

NATIONAL COUNCIL OF TEACHERS OF MATHEMATICS. *Historical Topics for the Mathematics Classroom.* Thirty-first Yearbook. Washington, D.C., 1969.

A format of overviews and capsules depicting the use of the history of mathematics in the teaching of mathematics. It points to a meaningful and consistent system of notation in the various branches of mathematics as part of the history of mathematics.

————. *The Teaching of Secondary School Mathematics.* Thirty-third Yearbook. Washington, D.C., 1970.

This book deals with the forces shaping today's mathematics programs. It identifies special outcomes for mathematics programs and gives examples of various classroom applications.

WILLOUGHBY, STEPHEN S. *Contemporary Teaching of Secondary School Mathematics.* New York: John Wiley and Sons, 1967.

This volume is for experienced mathematics teachers who have not been able to keep abreast of all recent developments in mathematics education.

YOUSE, BEVAN K. *An Introduction to Mathematics.* Boston, Mass.: Allyn and Bacon, Inc., 1970.

The author includes an introduction to the nature and spirit of mathematics.

CHAPTER 11

Physical Education and Health

The new addition to the high school building had been formally opened. It was a gymnasium to all intent and purpose, but the voters passing the bond issue had been advised that it was to be a physical education building to be used in the development of strong bodies for all boys and girls in the school. A textbook salesman, making his rounds, had casually dropped in on a boys' class in the new building. He was quite impressed with what he saw. The boys were lined up in military fashion responding alertly to the crisp direction of the handsome, barrel-chested instructor. Close order drill was followed by a snappy display of skill in handling dumbbells and Indian clubs. The session was closed with "free exercise" in rope climbing, sit-ups, ladder walking, half squats, and extensions.

The above scene took place at the close of World War I. If the same textbook salesman had visited the new gymnasium five years later, he would have been surprised at the change. The few remaining dumbbells and Indian clubs would have been gathering dust in a decrepit storage box over in a corner. The ropes and other equipment would have shown the same signs of neglect. One of the pupils would have been refereeing a rough and tumble basketball game on the floor, and the new broad-shouldered physical education teacher would have been in his office designing football plays for the afternoon practice. This was one of the early cycles in physical education programs.

Twenty-five years later another cycle followed the second World War. An alarming number of youths had been rejected for military service because of physical deficiencies. Typically, the blame was placed on the inefficiency of the secondary school curriculum, and logically, the physical education program bore the brunt of the repercussions. Once again, exercise and drill aspects of the program became focal points of emphasis, and physical education classes spent hours deftly weaving their way through old rubber tires strewn round the floor and climbing hastily constructed walls, replicas of military obstacle courses.

The next cycle in physical education was identified with the term "physical fitness." National political figures, including the President of the nation, engaged in activities designed to improve the general physical fitness of the individual. Touch football, jogging, cross-country running, etc., were in vogue. A President's Council on Youth Fitness was formed and the following recommendations were suggested for physical education programs:

1. The identification of the physically underdeveloped pupil and the building of suitable programs of correction.
2. Provisions for a minimum of fifteen minutes of vigorous activity every day for all pupils.
3. Use of valid fitness tests to determine pupils' physical abilities and evaluate their progress.[1]

The main objective of a physical fitness program was the development of strength and endurance. It would change a nation of softies into a nation of muscles. The worthiness of such an objective is acceptable if it does not lead to singleness of purpose and outcome.

The latest area of emphasis in the physical education field centers around the term *motor learning.* A survey of programs for preparing teachers of physical education reveals such courses as "Motor Learning," "Psychological Basis of Activity," "Psychology of Human Behavior," and "Human Motor Performance." Despite the apparent simplicity of the term, there appears to be quite a diversity of opinion as to how it applies to physical education. An all-encompassing view is that all physical education is motor learning. One singular viewpoint stresses experimental aspects— to analyze and apply research findings to the learning of motor skills. Then there are those who discuss human movement from a conceptual viewpoint and talk about such things as time, force, and space. Others are concerned with the physical activity from

[1] President's Council on Youth Fitness, "Suggested Elements of a School Centered Program" (Washington, D.C.: Government Printing Office, 1961), pp. 17–18.

an integrated point of view and stress neurological and perceptual mechanisms.

Motor learning is the unique concern of physical education because it involves movement, and movement is the essence of physical education. Motor learning is the purposive integration of movements into effective patterns of action and by definition is the learning that may be observed and evaluated in terms of relatively permanent changes in motor behavior.

If curriculum objectives in physical education are to be based on motor learning, it brings a new dimension to program planning for physical education in the secondary schools. Curriculum expertise will need to include background in the various branches of psychology, physiology, neuro-physiology, and human development. So much of physical education instruction has involved "how" to do things. Advocates of motor learning are more interested in the "what" to do rather than the "how" to do. It may be noted, however, in the long list of objectives for physical education presented later in this chapter, motor learning is identified, but it does not dominate the listing. It is problematical what the final influence of motor learning will be in the shaping of the secondary school physical education program, but there is no doubt that curriculum planners must recognize its importance and shape programs accordingly.

PURPOSES AND OBJECTIVES

Periods of alternate stress and laxity are not representative of all physical education programs, but, unfortunately, such lack of continuity is the basis for many problems associated with the development of good physical education programs. Both professional educators and lay citizens must determine, once and for all, how to fulfill the objectives of a good program. Although many states have requirements for all pupils to be enrolled in physical education classes, the dodges used by school administrative officials are disturbing. Frequently, marching in the band or blowing a horn is substituted, and the academically inclined student needing an extra subject to go to college is excused from physical education. The development of high powered athletic programs for public entertainment gives the lay citizen a mistaken image of the physical prowess of the entire student body.

It is difficult to understand the inconsistencies among school people regarding physical education. Every set of educational objectives published in the last half century has listed health and physical well-being in categories of major importance. The comprehensive high school stresses the general welfare of all pupils and emphasizes a well-balanced curriculum, including those subjects that contribute to physical and mental happiness throughout life.

Nevertheless, the curriculum planning aspects of physical education have suffered from a lack of agreement on purposes and objectives. There has also been a tendency among advocates of the subject to claim a multiple of outcomes that have not been attainable due to insufficient teaching time, inadequate facilities and equipment, and large enrollments. Objectives range from narrow concepts of body building to wide concepts of general physical fitness and recreational activities.

There are physical education authorities who would go beyond present exigencies and attempt to anticipate societal and cultural changes, necessitating a program with a wide variety of physical and recreational skills. But there is no doubt that the physical fitness aspects of the program continue to be stressed. The sedentary occupations in a technological culture and the excessive use of automobiles make it necessary for all ages of the population to be inculcated with the need for intensity and frequency of exercise. Even athletic coaches are learning that their teams cannot attain peak physical condition by mere practice of the sport. The practice session lacks something that is needed to build strength and endurance.

It is doubtful that sufficient time or continuity of program is available in present-day school physical education activities to ensure the physical fitness of every pupil. However, the value of a physical education program is only partially related to the physical fitness a pupil attains during his school days; the ultimate value must be measured in relation to the desire he develops for, and the satisfaction he derives from, being physically fit the remainder of his life.

The previous statement might lead to confusion as to whether physical fitness assures physical well-being, especially if mental well-being is also implied. It would be unfortunate to make this assumption. There is no doubt physical fitness is a contributing factor, but in the absence of conclusive evidence to the contrary, it might be assumed that the stimulation of physical activity, rather than the strength and endurance developed by muscle-building activity, promotes physical and mental well-being.

This distinction is important in the development of carry-over values. Youths need well-rounded programs of both rigorous exercises and games and milder forms of the same activities, but it is the carry-over potentialities of the milder activities that are more evident in the pursuits from which adults derive physical and mental well-being. The average golfer cannot equate the physical benefits of his game with the rigorous exercise he receives, but he can build a strong case for the stimulation he gets from the physical activity and the exhilarating mental lift he gets from the repartee he enjoys with his playing companions.

Pupils who engage in competitive sports need a greater degree of physical fitness than those who do not, but the direction of a physical education program should not be geared to the necessity of competitive athletics. The major emphasis should be on helping the total school population to obtain the degree of physical fitness and the basic skills necessary for the enjoyment of a variety of physical activities. When the dean of a school of physical education of a major university was called to task by one of his associates for granting two semesters of credit for a course in golf, he explained that it often took two semesters for a student to attain enough skill in the game to really "be hooked."

It is axiomatic that physical fitness is a prerequisite for the enjoyment of any physical activity. It is equally axiomatic that a satisfactory degree of skill is necessary for enjoyment of those physical activities associated with games and other recreational pursuits. Some physical education authorities claim that instruction in skills and intensive physical fitness development tend to be mutually exclusive. This need not be true if curriculum planners provide for a rational balance between the two activities and gear the program to the individual needs of pupils.

THE PHYSICAL EDUCATOR POSITION

Physical education has much to offer in finding solutions to problems of student unrest. Secondary students appear to be bewildered and confused in some respects but conscientious and thoughtful in others. Investigation of the teen-age culture is needed to discover what students need, feel, and care about. This intensifies the relationship between physical and mental needs. It suggests that physical education functionally should stress knowledge and attitudes and the program of students should be designed to meet societal needs. Guidelines established for these purposes by a committee assigned to write a position paper for the American Association of Health, Physical Education, and Recreation include the following:[2]

1. A setting in which experiences will help each student enjoy physical activity, to feel good about himself, and to accept himself and others.

[2] Francis M. Kidd et al., "Guidelines for Secondary School Physical Education," *Journal of Health, Physical Education, and Recreation* (April 1971), pp. 44–48.

2. Opportunities for vigorous activities through which there may be alleviation of frustrations and tensions.
3. Many avenues for self-identification and for identification with sex and peer groups.
4. A variety of opportunities to develop self-confidence, individual initiative, and responsibility to self and society.
5. Experiences which recognize a diverse range of human talents and interests, facilitating the discovery of specialized abilities together with the acceptance of limitations.
6. An atmosphere which relates and integrates the individual with his total environment.
7. Special attention to differences in physical development and maturity of individual students.
8. An environment that supports the rules necessary for the concept of fair play and for the safety of the participants.
9. Opportunities for students with severe structural or functional handicaps to participate in special activities adapted to their individual needs.
10. Coeducational physical education experiences.
11. Attention to the use of books, periodicals, and audio-visual media as resource materials.
12. Knowledge and experience in activities which will encourage and assist the individual to maintain fitness throughout life.
13. Leadership opportunities for each student.

The position paper committee recommends to secondary school physical education curriculum makers a common core of learning experiences for program building that includes the following suggestions:[3]

1. The instructional program has as its foundation a common core of learning experiences for all students. This core of experiences must be supplemented in ways that serve the divergent needs of all students—the gifted, the average, the slow learner, and the physically handicapped. It must be geared to the developmental needs of each pupil.
2. The program should provide for a reasonable balance in those activities commonly grouped as team and individual sports, aquatics, gymnastics, self-testing activities, dance, and rhythms.
3. Sequential progression in the specific skills and movement patterns involved in the activities included in the above grouping is essential
4. There should be opportunity for elective learning experiences within the required program.
5. The acquisition of knowledge and understandings related to the development and function of the human body, and to the mechanical principles of human movement is necessary.
6. Learning experiences (physical actiivties) should be designed to foster creativity and self-direction and to encourage vigorous activity which includes emphasis on safety procedures.

[3] Ibid., pp. 44–48.

7. Physical fitness—agility, balance, endurance, flexibility, and strength—should be developed.
8. Experiences which reinforce the development of behaviors, attitudes, appreciations, and understandings required for effective human relationships are important.
9. Special opportunities should be offered for those students who find it difficult and uncomfortable to adjust to the regular program because of physical, social, or emotional problems.
10. The program should present basic skills which can be employed in a comprehensive intramural, interscholastic, and recreational program for all girls and boys.

Influence of the advocates of motor learning is reflected in the position paper of the American Association of Health, Physical Education, and Recreation. Physical education is defined as being an integral part of the total education program that contributes to the development of the individual through the natural medium of physical activity, hence, human movement. Secondary physical education is described as a carefully planned sequence of learning experiences designed to fulfill the growth, development, and behavioral needs of each student by encouraging and assisting him to:[4]

1. Develop the skills of movement, the knowledge of how and why one moves, and the ways in which movement may be organized.
2. Learn to move skillfully and effectively through exercise, games, sports, dance, and aquatics.
3. Enrich his understanding of the concepts of space, time, and force related to movement.
4. Express culturally approved patterns of personal behavior and interpersonal relationships in and through games, sports, and dance.
5. Condition the heart, lungs, muscles, and other organic systems of the body to meet daily and emergency demands.
6. Acquire an appreciation of and a respect for good physical condition (fitness), a functional posture, and a sense of personal well-being.
7. Develop an interest and a desire to participate in lifetime recreational sports.

PRINCIPLES OF A GOOD PROGRAM

A survey of the best thinking in the field of physical education reveals a consensus as to what constitutes a good program. The major emphasis in physical education should be on instruction.

4 Ibid., pp. 44–48.

This means the teacher should constantly be engaged in teaching knowledge, skills, and attitudes in regard to physical activities. As has been suggested, it is desirable for pupils to improve their physical bodies, and in order to do this it is necessary to engage in strenuous body building exercises. This should not be, however, the end objective. It is most important that pupils acquire attitudes and desires that will cause them to use their knowledge and skills to build strong bodies throughout their lifetimes. One of the main health problems of busy people is the tendency to neglect keeping in good physical condition and then expect the body to respond to a sudden burst of physical exercise in the same manner that it did formerly. This kind of exercise does more harm than good. One of the best outcomes of a good physical education program would be the built-in desire to use physical exercise in a scheduled, consistent pattern.

Instruction in physical education should be arranged in units of four to six weeks' duration. Successful experience in physical activities are just as important as successful experiences in mental activity. Pupils need good exposure to an activity in order to understand purposes and to acquire enough skill to ensure successful experiences.[5] Short, fragmented units often end before a student has a chance to determine any measure of success or evaluation. Units of reasonable length are even more important if the pupils are heterogeneously grouped. The variance in time required for the learning of physical skills by different pupils necessitates extended periods of activity. This does not preclude the introduction of a variety of approaches for the accomplishment of these skills.

Variety is a desirable factor in physical education activities. It is intolerable to repeat the same activities in an identical manner every year. Learning should be purposeful and challenging. The worst offenders among dull repetitious activities are those teaching sport skills such as touch football, basketball, and softball. These games are not too complex and often occupy far more time than learning or even enjoyment justify. Pupils frequently choose to play familiar games, for they derive security and pleasure from participating skillfully. However, the same pleasurable satisfaction can be obtained if the pupils are introduced to a wider variety of the less frequently played games. This procedure will offer many more pupils the opportunity of developing skills peculiar to their abilities. There is no more reason for having the same cycle of physical education activities every year

[5] Charles C. Cowell and Hilda M. Schwehn, *Modern Principles and Methods in Secondary School Physical Education,* 2nd ed. (Boston: Allyn and Bacon, Inc., 1964).

throughout a pupil's school career than there is for repeating American history every year.

Evaluation in physical education is necessary as a measuring device and as a motivating factor. Pupils are intensely interested in the development of their physical prowess, and teachers should be concerned with this development as a fulfillment of their objectives. Adequate tests are available for physical fitness and skills of all types. Cumulative records on all pupils should be part of the repertoire of every physical education teacher.

Evaluation need not be limited to the measurement of physical prowess. Regular classroom evaluation should be made of subject-matter concepts and moral and social values. Pupils will maintain higher respect for physical education as a discipline if sophisticated classroom procedures are pursued. Successful experience is as important to pupil progress in physical education as it is to pupil progress in other subjects. It cannot be assumed that inherited capacity is the sole ingredient in superior performance. Excellence is a product of motivation, ability, and desire. It is relative to the individual pupil. Moral values can be equated, and excellence in performance can be judged, on an individual basis.

Since sports are closely interwoven with physical education programs, attention should be focused on those sports with the greatest carry-over values. Individual and dual sports offer the greatest promise here, namely, swimming, bowling, golf, weight training, tennis, and badminton. Sufficient time and effort should be provided to develop reasonable skills in these sports. If a pupil uses one or more of these activities throughout his active life, then physical education has contributed to his well-balanced development.

Greater attention needs to be given to curriculum materials and class schedules in physical education. Too often, little or no direction is given to planning classes. A well-developed course of study should be an integral part of every program. Administrators should group pupils for a reason, rather than using physical education class as a miscellaneous dumping ground. Class size should not exceed the maximum of classes in any other department of the school. Classes of 60 to 100 pupils are intolerable if proper physical education objectives are to be achieved. No pupils—including varsity athletes—should be excused from enrolling in physical education, nor should they be permitted to substitute other classes.

Although most states require adequate training for certification of physical education teachers, there is still the need for upgrading the professional characteristics of many teachers. Only those who are properly trained should be assigned classes in physical education, and physical education teachers should look upon their teaching assignment with the same respect that any good academic teacher displays. Some school administrators prefer that their athletic coaches teach something other than physical education. The theory here is that too much physical activity is involved in teaching physical education and coaching athletics for a teacher to do a good job doing both. Neither experience nor research furnish a conclusive answer to guide staff assignments in the field.

Physical education and its related activities of health education, recreation, and safety present a real challenge to curriculum planners who believe in a comprehensive school program. This field separates the honest believer from the lip-service advocate. There is probably no area of education so important to the complete well-being of children and youth as health, physical education, and recreation, yet there is no area that has suffered more from indifference, uncertainty, and spasmodic emphasis. Pupils need certain basic experiences that can be provided only through physical education. It is the responsibility of the school to furnish these experiences. They are an inherent part of a real comprehensive school program.

HEALTH EDUCATION

Health education in the secondary schools is of increasing importance. Health educators are struggling for identity of program and independence of operation. In a curriculum sense health education has been neglected and overshadowed by emphasis on physical education. In too many situations health education classes are scheduled in association with physical education and taught by physical education teachers who may or may not be competent in the health education field. In the worst situations health education classes are dependent on whether rainy days preclude physical education classes using the outdoors or whether the gymnasium is available for boys and girls on separate days. A case can be made for the development of an independent health education program taught by health education teachers.

Today many people enjoy a high level of health and a greater life span than ever before, but it is difficult to identify reasons for this in the health education programs of the public schools. It is more logical to assume that the development of new drugs, better public health programs, and improved medical care are primarily responsible. Despite the possibility of a higher level of health and a greater life span, society is plagued by health problems such as heart disease, obesity, lung cancer, mental illness, alcoholism, drug addiction, and venereal disease. A solution to these problems must come in part from better health programs in the public schools, and much of this responsibility is centered in the secondary schools.

The basic concept in health education is to help the pupils see the desirability of achieving and maintaining a reasonable level of health. This is an individual responsibility and must be considered worthwhile by the pupil. The problem is to cause the pupil to see good health as a functional matter in his present life rather than as a delayed benefit. Too frequently, health classes stress physiological aspects of the pupil's life rather than healthy living.

Health is a personal matter. Whatever is taught, therefore, must become a part of the experience of each learner, and subject matter must be established in the context of his life. Knowledge about the structure and physiology of the body is of little value unless it contributes to the solution of actual health problems.

Effective health education needs cooperation between the home, the school, and the community. Attitude and desire for healthy living must be inherent in the total environment of the pupil. In order to be effective, a good school health program must be complemented by reasonably good health activities in the home of the pupil and in the living activities of his associates.

Good health education objectives include the securing of information and the building of good attitudes. This means the pupil needs to understand how his body functions and how to avoid those things that are injurious to it. Equally important is the development of proper attitudes toward living that will ensure good mental health. The carry-over values of the health program are exceedingly valuable. It is here that attitudes are of paramount importance.

Among the important understandings the health program should develop are those dealing with the causes and consequences of disease and illness. This should be related to the necessity of securing competent medical aid. The whole area of quack remedies and patent medicine should be covered. The average citizen faces a continual barrage of chicanery from the pseudomedical experts. While some of the products offered as remedies have limited value, others are worthless, and some are exceedingly dangerous.

A good health education program inculcates temperance and balance in health activity. Youth has a particular need to establish a proper sense of balance between healthy zest for adventure and foolish exposure to unnecessary hazards. In later years this means using good sense in the proper distribution of physical exercise in games and other activities. The social, economic, and psychological consequences of alcoholic beverages, drugs, and tobacco are basic teaching concepts in the health program. And (probably of equal importance in a well-fed nation) temperance in eating and the resulting control of obesity must also be taught.

The responsibility of the health education program is not only to furnish information, but also to guide the pupil's thoughts and actions toward the development of a behavior pattern that will enhance his total well-being. All pupils are required to make health decisions. The adolescent years are of significant importance in the final shaping of personality, a basic adjunct to good mental health. Ability to get along with people and the adjustment to sex as a natural and essential part of human existence are factors in developing a wholesome personality. Sex education should be taught naturally as a normal part of youthful development. Pupils need factual information rather than half-truths and fantasies. A good health program should help pupils understand the role of sex as a basic factor in a normal, healthy life.

SAFETY EDUCATION

There are many areas of the curriculum where it is apparent that safety is integral. Besides physical education, these include athletics, vocational education, homemaking, and all shop and laboratory courses. But since safety is closely allied with physical activities, and since coaches and physical education teachers are often enlisted as driver education teachers, safety education has been associated with the physical education curriculum.

In the more sedentary aspects of the school curriculum, safety is stressed in two ways: (1) by creating a safe environment throughout the physical part of the school, and (2) by using safety subject-matter content in appropriate subject-matter areas. The one part of the curriculum where safety is of major importance is in driver education.

The inclusion of driver education instruction in the secondary school program is a debatable issue. It runs the gamut from being a state requirement for all pupils to being considered an unwarranted "fad." Two factors weigh heavily in favor of driver education as a part of the formal training of youth. The first is the recognition that almost every person who reaches the legal driving age will be driving a car. The second is that the consequences of poor driving are so disastrous to the individual, the community, and the nation that this aspect of safety education simply cannot be neglected.

A good safety education program stresses prevention and control of hazards that lead to accidents. The pupil is provided with opportunities to practice safe and skillful behavior and he is encouraged to prevent complacency and carelessness. There should be continuity of purpose and objectives in the association of physical education, health education, and safety education. Each involves the general well-being of the individual, each demands a degree of self-discipline, and each necessitates the cooperative effort of the home, the school, and the community. The challenge is to create programs that help pupils live a healthy and safe life.

CURRICULUM DIRECTIONS

Curriculum decisions in the field of physical education must be made on a wider basis than the one formerly associated with the subject. Heretofore, physical education has been thought of as an activity related to the physical growth of the body, but today's leaders have a much wider concept than this. The general education values of the field are stressed. Basic objectives of physical education include not only those of physical fitness but also those of social, emotional, and even moral fitness.[6]

In the broader concept of physical education, health education, safety education, and recreation probably will continue to be associated with the field of physical education. With the developing complexity of the field there is reason for curriculum planners to provide for the development of separate identity for health education, safety education, and recreation while keeping each program integrated and allied with the other. Each of these programs necessitates an involvement of the home and community. Specialized aspects such as sex education require certain moral decisions and, to a limited extent, even religious decisions.

If physical education leaders are really going to come to grips with their problems, bolder and broader programs must be planned involving all youth and providing for all of their complicated needs. Youth must be taught to see beyond the necessity of acquiring strength and endurance for physical fitness to the need for building a healthy mind and social maturity for complete physical well-being.

Two examples of the need for bold programs in the field of

[6] Charles A. Bucher, "A Ten Point Program for the Future of Physical Education," *Journal of Health, Physical Education, Recreation* (January 1967), p. 27.

health education and physical education may be found in sex education and in varsity athletics. In the matter of sex education, youths need factual knowledge and truth. Neglect here contributes to health problems, social maladjustment, and moral decay. In the matter of athletics there is an urgent need for sanity and balance in pupil participation and in community emphasis on sports contests. In many schools, varsity athletics are a public entertainment medium and not a physical education activity. Certainly youths need to know *how* to play and *what* to play, but this does not involve vocational training for professional sports careers.

Finally, physical education leaders need to interpret the academic aspects of their field. Scientific understanding of the body and its physical relation to efficient living require coordinated knowledge from anatomy, physics, physiology, cultural anthropology, sociology, and psychology. The respectability of physical education should cease to be the concern of its proponents; their responsibility for meeting today's enlarged concepts should be of constant concern.

TOPICS FOR STUDY AND DISCUSSION

1. Analyze the basic difference in curriculum emphasis between physical fitness and physical well-being.
2. Should courses in health education be based on scope and sequence of subject matter? Develop a position pro or con.
3. Are classes in physical education as important for youth as classes in mathematics? Support a position.
4. How does one account for the ebb and flow of emphasis on physical education?
5. Are there more significant relationships between health and physical education than between physical education and English?
6. What are the compatible characteristics of the fields of physical education and music?
7. Some authorities hold that in the light of some of the more important objectives in the field of physical education, the subject is not properly named. What would be the reasoning in back of such a claim?
8. If curriculum objectives in physical education are based on motor learning, how will physical education fare in the modern educational swirl of cognitive learning and performance based objectives.
9. Evaluate the common core of learning experiences proposed for physical education by the American Association of Health, Physical Education and Recreation.

SELECTED REFERENCES

BUCHER, CHARLES A., et al. *The Foundations of Health.* New York: Appleton-Century-Crofts, 1967.

The health and well-being of the young adult is the central concern. Emphasis is on total health, stressing the interrelationship of physical, mental, and emotional factors that contribute to optimum fitness.

CARRON, ALBERT V. *Laboratory Experiments in Motor Learning.* Englewood Cliffs, N.J.: Prentice-Hall, Inc., 1971.

The experiments will acquaint the curriculum worker with some of the research problems, performance phenomena, and research tools utilized in the study of motor learning and performance.

COWELL, CHARLES C., and SCHWEHN, HILDA M. *Modern Principles and Methods in Secondary School Physical Education.* 2nd ed. Boston: Allyn and Bacon, Inc., 1964.

This book deals with modern techniques and methods of physical education instruction. It incorporates experimental procedures for physical education. Team teaching and individual instruction are advocated. It contains helpful suggestions for physical fitness and physical well-being.

FAIT, HOLLIS F. *Health and Fitness for Modern Living.* Boston: Allyn and Bacon, Inc., 1961.

The author makes a good analysis of the concept of physical well-being. He points up the importance of pupils gaining lasting concepts of the relation of health to successful living. Illustrations of good health programs are included.

GODFREY, BARBARA B., and KEPHART, NEWELL G. *Movement Patterns and Motor Education.* New York: Appleton-Century-Crofts, 1969.

This volume is based on the theory that all learning has its foundation in motor learning. It presents a research-based rationale for a program of movement pattern education. Detailed descriptions include motor patterns required for adequate adjustment, as well as deviations from these patterns and their implications for later learning.

KILANDER, H. FREDERICK. *School Health Education.* New York: The Macmillan Company, 1962.

Material is organized into curricular patterns that encourage orderly and comprehensive planning of health education instructional programs. The approach throughout is practical rather than theoretical. It includes a comprehensive overview of the many topics associated with health education.

MILLER, ARTHUR G., and MASSEY, M. DOROTHY. *A Dynamic Concept of Physical Education for Secondary Schools.* Englewood Cliffs, N.J.: Prentice-Hall, Inc., 1963.

This book presents an overview of physical education in the secondary schools and a good discussion of the many opportunities for creative thinking in the field. Material is rich in supplementary media for physical education curriculum construction.

Physical Education for High School Students. 2nd ed. Washington, D.C.: NEA Publication—Sales, 1970.

A good description of a variety of recreational and sports activities for high school physical education programs is included.

PRESIDENT'S COUNCIL ON YOUTH FITNESS. *Youth Physical Fitness: Suggested Elements of a School-centered Program.* Washington, D.C.: Government Printing Office, 1961.

Parts I and II provide much useful material for inaugurating a school youth fitness program.

VOLTMER, EDWARD F., and ESSLINGER, ARTHUR A. *The Organization and Administration of Physical Education.* New York: Appleton-Century-Crofts, 1967.

The leader in its field, this well-known text has now been brought up-to-date.

CHAPTER **12**

Science

The position of science in the school curriculum is secure. Space research has given great impetus to the training of scientists and technicians, and it is inconceivable that a school board member would ever question the teaching of science in the schools. Indeed, in the dark days following the launching of the space age by an unfriendly power, questions were raised as to whether enough science was being taught in our schools. Hastily contrived surveys revealed that the number of pupils studying science had not declined and the program was stable, but they also revealed an undesirable lag in the curriculum. The content and methods of teaching science had not changed much in fifty years.

Because science is important in a technological society, it would be reasonable to assume that all pupils are pursuing science courses. This is not true. The science education of many pupils is confined to basic required courses, usually physical science and possibly biology. Improvement in the situation may be noted with increased enrollments in chemistry, but the number of pupils taking courses in physics is not in proportion. Earth science is being accepted as a regular offering.

Those curriculum authorities who urge more science for all pupils point to present-day societal needs. Progress in applied science and technology has changed how people live, how they make a living, what they believe, and how long they will live. There are few types of employment in the United States that have not been changed and that do not require a higher level of literacy in science than ever before. The government is spending large sums of money for science and technology. The number and complexity of decisions involving understanding of products, processes, ethnics of science, and the relationship of science to society are ever-increasing. It is reasonable to conclude that if the masses are going to be involved in making scientific decisions, the schools must help all pupils to understand scientific processes.

Possibly more progress has been made in reshaping and modernizing the school curriculum in science than in any other field. Both content and methods of teaching have undergone extensive modifications. Greater emphasis has been placed on the dynamic qualities of the scientific enterprise. What science is and how it operates are considered more important than the results of science.

CURRICULUM OBJECTIVES

The understanding of recent theories and the acquistion of new knowledge must be the main objectives in the science curriculum. Pupils must understand the character of scientific knowledge—that it is dynamic and is likely to shift meaning and status with the ever increasing amount of new knowledge. Illustrations are numerous in each of the disciplines of science. For example, it was long believed in biology that acquired characteristics of a person were not inherited. Recent research may prove this false. In chemistry, the fact was accepted that Group O elements formed no binary compounds, yet it is now known that krypton, xenon, and radon do form binary compounds. And in physics, the dynamic possibilities of the laser are comparatively untouched. Thus, science education should be geared to the continuous changes taking place, and the curriculum must provide for the identification and incorporation of exciting new developments.

Since the continual changes taking place in science are directly related to the physical universe, a second objective in science education should be to help the pupil acquire the necessary tools for interpreting his immediate environment. The teaching of chemical bonding in chemistry is pointless unless the concepts are applied to newly synthesized rare-gas compounds. In physics, electricity and magnetism must be applied to the comprehension of Van Allen radiation belts and conductivity at near absolute zero temperatures. In biology, the effects of radioactive fallout must be brought to bear on everyday problems such as radioisotopes in milk and other food, the contamination of the earth's atmosphere, and the disposal of radioactive wastes.

A third objective in the science curriculum should be to

help the pupil understand the scientific enterprise. The unifying principles of science should be stressed. The pupil should understand science as a process of discovery and should become familiar with the way a scientist thinks and acts. To attain this objective the curriculum must develop the pupil's ability to use thought processes and functional skills in the solution of problems. It must put less emphasis on the technological applications of science and more emphasis on the inherent processes of science.

A fourth objective in science education should be to help the pupil become aware of the nature of man, his knowledge base, his beliefs, and his attitudes concerning the environment in which he lives. As seemingly inexhaustible supplies of natural resources dwindle, man must find replacements and methods of conservation. Brown-outs, black-outs, over-crowded space, chemically contaminated food, dirty air, and polluted water all present major problems requiring scientific and social solutions. Environmental and ecological studies must be part of the science curriculum.

A final objective in science education should be to make the subject more interesting and stimulating to the pupil. It must be presented in terms of modern learning concepts and theories, stressing science as an activity. This approach encourages pupils to develop an understanding of main ideas and concepts rather than memorizing facts and formulas. Emphasis is placed on experimentation and discovery, using the methods of scientists. This procedure is one of the main differences between traditional science teaching and the newer approaches.

THE MODERN PROGRAMS IN SCIENCE

Curriculum work in science involves types of problems which are different from those of other fields.[1] Changes in science are well advanced. Each of the science subjects has undergone extensive study and renovation, and modern, practical programs have been developed. The main decision now is whether to adopt the modern programs or stubbornly hang on to traditional programs. Even the most conservative are finding little reason for resisting the newer programs.

Most of the curriculum decisions in science involve the initiation and implementation of the modern programs in chemistry, physics, biology, earth science, and physical science.[2] These pro-

[1] J. J. Gallagher, "Broader Base for Science Teaching," *Science Education* (July 1971), pp. 329–338.
[2] John I. Goodlad, *The Changing School Curriculum* (New York: The Fund for the Advancement of Education, 1966), pp. 39–55.

grams are the results of several years of careful study and experimentation involving college personnel who were experts in their disciplines, classroom teachers trained in subject matter and method, and hundreds of boys and girls. Extensive tryout and revision were necessary. Usual curriculum decisions, such as the precise boundaries of the educational unit to be studied, and the areas of the subject matter to be considered, were determined. A good science program must involve kindergarten through grade 12, and one of the basic purposes of the new programs is to provide better articulation between the college and the secondary schools. Textbooks, laboratory manuals, and supplementary learning aids are all provided for in the modern programs. Teachers are upgraded and retrained at summer and year-round science institutes sponsored by the National Science Foundation. The main task, therefore, as far as current science curriculum decisions are concerned, is to be sure the school personnel understands the purposes and methods of the modern science programs.

There are two salient differences between the new science courses and the traditional ones: philosophy and content. The pupil is engaged in inquiry and the teacher is a director or guide in the scientific process. Since pupils come to understand science only through active participation, they are not expected to stand by and watch teachers run through demonstrations. Rather than being led by the hand through lectures and field trips, pupils are called on to spend more time in challenging laboratory situations, where real problems of science are explored in a scientific manner. Heavy emphasis is placed on reasoning. Mere memorization of the laws of nature is less important than understanding how these laws affect the lives of people.

The content of the new science material has undergone radical changes. Almost everything taught in science classes in the last thirty years has either been thrown out or greatly modified. This is understandable when it is remembered that scientific knowledge has doubled every ten years since the beginning of this century. Seven new science programs are in use, including two in physics, two in chemistry, and three in biology. Also, new approaches to general science and earth science are in various stages of development.

Physics

A modernized physics curriculum is the oldest and most mature of the science programs. It was developed by the Physical Science Study Committee with support from the Massachusetts Institute of Technology and the Ford Foundation. Because of its sponsoring organization, the "new" physics became known as PSSC physics.

The subject is taught in four major sections, all closely interrelated. The first is a general introduction to the fundamental physical notions of time, space, and matter. From experiments in measuring time and matter, the pupil moves to an understanding of velocity and acceleration, vectors, and relative motion. He then goes on to study matter, developing the concepts of mass and of its conservation. The pupil gradually understands that in physics, time, space, and matter are united.

The second part begins with light, leading to the particle theory and then to waves. Discussion emphasizes the manner in which virtually all scientific knowledge develops.

Part three takes a closer look at motion, this time from a dynamic point of view. The laws of motion, gravity, conservation of momentum, and conservation of energy are "discovered" through a combination of theory and laboratory exploration.

The last part of the course introduces the pupil to electricity and, through it, to the physics of the atom. Here he uses the knowledge of dynamics gained in part three. Next comes a discussion of magnetic fields and the forces they exert on moving charges. The final section discusses the induction laws, leading to the structure of the atom, and the pupil returns to the basic concepts of science with a new understanding.

The PSSC course emphasizes the basic structure of physics, the acquistion of new physical knowledge, and the necessity for understanding rather than memorizing basic physics concepts. In the laboratory the pupil is directed to first-hand experience in discovering and verifying physical phenomena. The program contains fewer facts than the usual course in physics, but concepts are stressed to be understood and used. About five dozen films are carefully integrated with the textbook, class discussion, and laboratory work.

All through the course, compartmentalization is resisted. The subject of light, for instance, is not disposed of in one great gulp, but reappears in progressively greater depth as the pupil's general understanding of physics deepens. The course also seeks to stress the interconnections between physics and the other sciences, particularly chemistry and biology. PSSC physics is designed for academically oriented pupils whose school programs would normally include a course in physics in the junior or senior year.

Harvard Project: physics

As has been stated before, the PSSC physics course was prepared for college-oriented pupils. It does not cater to the wide variety of abilities found in a comprehensive secondary school. This may be one of the reasons why enrollments in physics continued to decline despite the introduction of PSSC materials.[3]

The Harvard Project in Physics is the outgrowth of the work of several hundred physicists and teachers who formulated, developed, and field-tested materials suitable for a wide range of pupil abilities. It is designed for the average pupil and should be suitable for more than half of the secondary school population.

The Harvard Project content is not unlike the PSSC physics. The difference is in the historical and philosophical approach. The presentation is activity-oriented and makes extensive use of multimedia. The material is so arranged as to encourage physics teachers to assume responsibility for structuring the courses they teach. This provides opportunities for meeting the needs of diversity among pupils.

The Harvard Project in Physics contains units of material on: (1) Concepts of Motion, (2) Motion in the Heavens, (3) Energy, (4) Fields and Waves, (5) Models of the Atom, and (6) Constitution of Matter. Evaluation of HPP shows evidence that pupils respond well to the material and show significant gains on measures of physics achievement. As is the case of most innovative programs, much of the success in use of HPP is dependent on the flexibility of the teacher. The responsibility for structuring the course and the purposeful use of multimedia are very important.

Chemistry

Both of the modern chemistry programs were developed by groups sponsored by the National Science Foundation. The courses are not competitive; they are considered two roads to the same destination. Both advocate a research chemist's approach with meaningful experimentation rather than the use of recipe procedures in the laboratory. There are, however, some basic differences in content, pupil experiences, and pedagogy.

CBA chemistry (the Chemical Bond Approach) deals with the question, "What is a chemical change?" To find the answer, a series of chemical systems is studied in detail, considering changes in bonding, structure, and energy.

Models for atomic and molecular structure are closely related to chemistry's periodic table in the CBA approach. Trends in the properties of elements and compounds are, in turn, related to structural models. The development of these relationships requires discussion of a variety of topics, such as atomic size, nuclear

[3] Fletcher G. Watson, "Why Do We Need More Physics Courses?" *The Physics Teacher* (May 1967), pp. 212–214.

change, ionization potential, modern acid-base theories, and ionic bonding. The importance of making a clear distinction between experimentally determined information and theory is recognized. The course attempts to combine observations with ideas in the text and the laboratory. Model building, both physical and mental, is introduced. The need to modify or discard models becomes apparent to the pupil as more knowledge is gained and he begins to understand the progressive improvement which theories undergo. Thus, chemistry is presented as an ongoing process.

The course emphasizes laboratory work with the idea that a pupil will develop an appreciation of chemistry if he performs the functions of a chemist. The laboratory program helps the pupil identify a problem, design an experiment, carry out the technical operations, and arrive at a conclusion based on his own data.

An attempt is made throughout the course to confront the pupil with the implications of logical argument based on theory. This is done mostly through the discussion of mental models which are introduced as logical devices, based on a set of convenient assumptions. A central concept is that materials consist of atoms held together by forces or bonds. (Chemistry has been described as the making and breaking of these bonds.) Chemicals, therefore, have structures and can be conceived in geometrical terms.

CHEMS chemistry (the Chemical Education Material Study), like the CBA, emphasizes models and model systems. The course begins with an introductory section designed to help the student gain some familiarity with scientific methods and models, and with such concepts as uncertainty in measurement, phase changes, chemical reactions, energy, molecules, the mole, conservation of atoms, kinetic theory, the electrical nature of atoms and ions, and chemical periodicity.

A second major section is devoted to the development of other important principles of chemistry, starting with a closer look at energy effects, rates of reactions, and chemical equilibrium. These ideas are then applied to solubility, acid-base chemistry, and oxidation-reduction. Atomic structure and bonding are treated in some detail and related to molecular architecture, properties as a means of substances, and the periodic table. The final section uses organized descriptive chemistry as a means of applying and reinforcing the concepts developed earlier.

Like the Chem Bond material, the CHEMS course relies heavily on experimentation in the laboratory. In contrast to CBA, however, CHEMS makes the laboratory an integral part of the learning process. Principles are developed through the pupil's laboratory discoveries. An excellent set of films reinforces the learning procedures.

Both the CBA and the CHEMS programs have been released to the public domain and are now part of several modern chemistry textbooks. Most of the material in the new textbooks is from the CHEMS program. Laboratory texts and multimedia materials are available.

Biology

There are three new biology programs, all of which were developed by the Biological Sciences Curriculum Study (BSCS). These courses differ from traditional courses in that they place greater emphasis on molecular and cellular biology, on community and world biome, and on the study of populations. They stress investigation and principles and higher levels of organization.

Nine unifying concepts run through the three versions of BSCS biology:

1. Changes of living things through time-evolution
2. Diversity of type and unity of pattern of living things
3. Genetic continuity of life
4. Biological roots of behavior
5. Complementarity of organisms and environment
6. Complementary of structure and function
7. Regulation and homeostasis—the maintenance of life in the face of change
8. Science as inquiry
9. Intellectual history of biological concepts

About 65 percent of the content of the three biology courses is identical. For purposes of clarity, the three versions were labeled yellow, green, and blue. These versions do not represent a simple revision of old thinking in high school biology. On the contrary, all three are completely new starts based on the most up-to-date thinking. None of the three courses were written for advanced or slow students; all can be taught with equal facility to the average tenth grader. The difference between versions is essentially in the approach to biology.

One version approaches biology from the ecological point of view, starting with cycles of energy in the biosphere, turning to the basic biological unit—the individual—then examining populations, communities, and ecosystems. The next unit covers taxonomic diversity of animals, plants, and microorganisms. Other units deal with ecological diversity on land, in fresh water, and in the seas; the history of life; and the major biogeographical regions of the world. Subjects discussed in the various units include cells and the cellular structure of organisms; the physiology, reproduction and development of plants and animals; heredity, evolution, and behavior; the structure and functioning of the human animal; and finally, the human animal in the midst of his biological setting.

Another version approaches biology as a molecular study. Essentially the same material is studied, but the student begins with the emergence of the smallest and first living organisms. Using these as "building blocks," more and more complex matters are studied—cells, organs, individuals, societies. Half the course is given over to the molecular study of systems within organisms— the reproductive, transport, respiratory, digestive, regulatory, photosynthetic, and skeletal systems, among others, are taught. Other subjects covered include heredity, the human species, integrated organisms and behavior, populations, societies, and communities.

A third version is a cellular treatment, differing from the others in that students primarily inquire into the biology of cells (structure, functions, chemistry, reproduction, etc.), microorganisms (viruses, bacteria), and plants and animals. A treatment of evolution is followed by units on man and his world.

All three BSCS versions include laboratory manuals, teachers' handbooks, laboratory teaching units, specially prepared films, and other materials. As in the other modern science programs, the pupil is taught science as a way of thinking, stressing underlying concepts and understandings. The pupil is given practice in drawing generalizations, seeking relationships, and finding his own answers.

All three BSCS versions were revised in 1968 and are scheduled for revision in 1973.

Earth science

Procedures similar to those used in BSCS biology programs are being used by the Earth Science Curriculum Project (ESCP), sponsored by the American Geological Institute, in developing earth science materials for use in the ninth grade.

The ESCP approach to teaching earth science departs from the usual pattern. The concept of "science as inquiry" is stressed throughout. The textbooks being developed are not merely a collection of facts, but are designed to lead the pupil into his own investigation of the earth. For example, instead of stating that the diameter of the sun is so many miles, the textbook encourages the pupil to measure it with simple equipment.

Pupils introduced to the use of significant figures, the various types of error, and the use of graphs. Mathematics used in the ESCP materials is not complicated, but it is used as the language of science. Fact is carefully kept separate from theory. A new departure in the material is the introduction of the interface concept.   The theme of cyclical phenomena is used extensively and includes such cycles as the hydrologic cycle, the rock cycle, sunspot cycle, and various climatic cycles.

Space here does not permit a review of the many science programs developed for elementary schools, middle schools, or junior high schools.   Sufficient to say, many of the programs relate to the secondary school science curriculum since they include the seventh, eighth, and ninth grades.

Physical science

Physical science has gradually replaced general science as the basic course in the junior high school.   In some schools earth science performs the same function.   The junior high school science course should unify subject matter for conceptual understanding since it serves as a foundation for senior high school science that includes the disciplines of biology, chemistry, and physics.

Instead of organizing each course in junior high school around a major discipline of science, the courses at each grade level should be organized around central themes.   Thus, each major unit, or block, taught each year should be concerned with the development of the basic themes that run like threads through the entire year's work.

Many science educators felt the muliplicity of topics in general science programs was unmanageable.   As scientific knowledge broadened, more and more areas of study were added to general science, and nothing was deleted.   The result was an unworkable course to which neither the teacher nor the pupil could do justice.   The sensible solution was to give the pupils fewer areas of study and to treat these in greater depth.   This has been an objective in the junior high school physical science course.

Another criticism leveled at general science programs was too much emphasis placed on the introduction of varied household technology: too much study of water faucets, heating furnaces, and automobile engines.   While it is true that some technological applications must be included for pupils to understand basic science principles, it must be remembered that technology is a *result* of the application of these principles, not a *cause*.   Physical science programs emphasize scientific behavior as exemplified by spirit of inquiry and a quest for new understanding.   Pupil participation in laboratory experiences are stressed.

A final factor that is very important in reshaping science courses is attention to vocabulary.   Since this will probably be the first formalized course the pupil may have in science, he must be able to read intelligently in the field.   More and more pupils are coming into junior high classes with reading problems. Teaching of reading is a problem for all teachers, and science teachers are no exception. Educational studies reveal that a science course presents pupils with a new vocabulary equal to that of a beginning class in a foreign language. Yet, too frequently, it is assumed the pupil will master these new words by a process of mental osmosis.

The science curriculum that guides the classroom teacher should give attention to reading skills and vocabulary building, as well as to the mastery of scientific concepts. The primary objective of a physical science course in the junior high school should be to give the pupils a firm foundation and a sustaining interest in science for the years beyond.

SCIENCE AND THE ENVIRONMENT

Implementation of the Harvard physics material and the Earth Science Curriculum Project (ESCP) into the secondary school science curriculum marks more than two decades of major curriculum overhaul. The conclusion might be drawn that there is no further need for changes in the science curriculum. This is not the case since the nature of science is a continuous process of discovery and change.

Science educators are conscious of the growing concern over the destruction of the environment resulting either directly or indirectly from scientific discoveries. As the scientist uncovers the basic principles of nature, technology applies these principles to developing new products and new techniques. Frequently the process of manufacturing the new products and the resulting consumer use by great masses of people are destructive to man's environment.

Technology and progress are often equated. Business equates growth with progress, and the depletion of natural resources is referred to as the development of natural resources. Industrial processes can cause pollution in all of its insidious forms. Degradation of the environment and extinction of species are justified as necessary in supplying man's needs. Industrial leaders contend that technology will ultimately solve environmental problems in the same fashion they were created. Evidence is offered in the form of smog devices, desalination plants, floating cities, and high-yield food production.

Preparation for solving environmental problems of mankind resulting from technological development of scientific discoveries must begin in the schools. This means accommodations within the curriculum centered around problems of how to utilize technological possibilities in such a way as not to instigate social-cultural upheaval.[4]

The science teacher is likely to need help in dealing with the broad scope of environmental problems. The social science teacher can have responsibility for developing concepts of man's place in nature, and the English teacher can guide students into contemplations of man's role in controlling his environment. This can be reflected in the study of utopian and dystopian novels. Many of the best teaching techniques of the present-day school can be employed by science educators in developing curriculum procedures for helping secondary youth understand the crucial environmental problems created by scientific discoveries and technological development.[5] Team teaching and the planning of interdisciplinary materials can be suitable activities.

The following is an outline for a suggested interdisciplinary course with emphasis on problems related to the preservation of a beneficial environment:

I. Chemistry Involved
  A. Historical Background: Early Theories and Experimental Work
  B. Development of the Atom and Atomic Structure
  C. Bonding in Molecules
  D. Bonding of Carbon: Introduction to Organic Chemistry, Biopolymers
  E. Introduction to Solution Chemistry
  F. The Study of the Nucleus: Radioactivity
  G. Effects of Radioisotopes
II. Environmental Control
  A. Air Pollution: Chemical, Biological, and Physical Problems
  B. Water Pollution: Chemical, Biological, and Physical Problems
  C. Solid Waste Removal
  D. Radiochemical Pollution
  E. Biological, Chemical, and Physical Methods of Pollution Control
  F. Long-range Effects of Environmental Alteration
III. Natural Resources
  A. Current World Supply of Natural Resources: Renewable and Nonrenewable

[4] R. Thomas Tanner, "The Science Curriculum: Unfinished Business for an Unfinished Country," *Phi Delta Kappan* (March 1970), pp. 353–356.
[5] Alfred T. Collette and Walter A. Thurber, *Teaching Science in Today's Secondary Schools* (Boston: Allyn and Bacon, Inc., 1968), pp. 83–117.

B.   Sources of Resources
C.   Present and Projected Rate of Consumption
D.   Waste of Natural Resources: Methods of Reusing Resources
E.   New and Potential Techniques of Extracting Resources
F.   The Replacement of Natural Materials by Man-made Materials
G.   Relationship of Natural Resources to National and World Problems

IV.   Ecology
A.   Necessary Biological Background Material
B.   Selected Examples of Ecological Systems
C.   Current Problems and Possible Solutions
D.   Potential Future Problems

V.   Quality of Life
A.   Population: Its Relationship to Available and Future Food Supplies and Natural Resources
B.   Advances in Medicine
C.   Genetics: Its Present Status and Potential Future Impact

VI.   The Outlook for the Future
A.   Concepts Expressed through Literature
B.   Legal Aspects of Control
C.   Physical Well-being
D.   Contemplative Relationship between Science and Technology

THE ROLE OF SCIENCE IN GENERAL EDUCATION

Leaders of education thought in this country generally subscribe to the proposition that the primary goal of secondary education is the provision of a broad general education for all.   This is a rationale that underlies much of the present curriculum in the comprehensive school.   However, though the importance of science is never questioned and quite a bit of lip service is given to the concept of science for all, it never seems realistic for all pupils to pursue science when the courses continue to follow the compartmentalization of the science disciplines and are academically oriented.[6]

Biological taxonomy and ionization equilibria are un-

[6] "School Science Education for the 70's," Committee on Curriculum Studies: National Science Teacher Association, *Science Teacher* (November 1971), pp. 46–57.

doubtedly important, but whether such subjects can be mastered by all pupils is an open question. Heretofore, the approach to science for all pupils has been through watered-down versions that usually are of little value as far as the development of scientific concepts are concerned. The main significance of science for many pupils should be as a way of thinking or an approach to problem solving. This approach can be developed through an understanding of the nature of science and the role of science in human endeavor.

Perhaps new programs of science should be developed to take care of general education objectives if the modern science programs are not adaptable. These new programs should attempt to describe the nature of science by showing how science has developed. The continuing theme should be the impact of science and culture on each other. Emphasis should be placed on the fact that man must continually change his concepts of natural phenomena.

Important developments in the history of science might be the central theme of a science course for general education purposes. Such events as the proposal of the heliocentric theory, the downfall of the phlogiston theory, the discovery of the laws of heredity, and the development of analytic geometry could form the subject matter. A study of the culture and the mores of the times surrounding these events could be the basis for the pupil's ability to comprehend modern scientific developments. Such a course could contribute more to a pupil's understanding of science from a general education viewpoint than so-called "practical" adoptions of traditional science courses or even attempts to redirect the modern programs.

All curricular changes should include experiments that encourage investigation. The history of science is filled with the thrilling experiences of pioneers who dared to probe the unknown. Youth's hero worship need not be confined to the temporal fields of entertainment.

SCIENCE AND THE SLOW LEARNER

If the general education objective of science for all pupils is to be reached, more attention must be given the slower learners. Heretofore, too many of these pupils have been bypassed because it was assumed that science was too difficult. And this will continue to be true if science continues to be taught as a series of abstract verbalizations.

Like all learners, slow learners must structure their think-

ing, see relationship, and build mental models if they are to understand and appreciate a concept.[7]   The main problem for teachers
is to slow down the process to keep from applying too much pressure. The slow learner will accept a challenge if he anticipates any
chance of success, but if the challenge is beyond what he can accomplish with reasonable effort, he faces frustration.

In Bruner's *The Process of Education,* he encourages the
teaching of slow learners when he says there is no reason to believe
that any subject cannot be taught to any pupil at virtually any age
in some form, provided that basic notions are divorced from their
mathematical expressions and abstract paraphernalia.[8]

Perhaps another clue to teaching the slow learner in science
may be found in the approaches to the BSCS biology. It is assumed
in these approaches that there is nothing better for the slow learner
to study than the modern biological concepts found in the BSCS
material.   There is evidence that a wide variety of pupils can follow the same general course when they are permitted to choose how
deep and how fast they will go.   The structure of science is the
same, regardless of the intensity or the speed with which it is
studied.   Rather than teach a different set of ideas to different
levels of pupils, it is better to teach less, but teach it thoroughly.

There is consensus among those who have worked with
slow learners that these pupils have aspirations and goals.   They
appreciate evidence of accomplishment and will work toward that
end if they are motivated rather than frustrated.   Programs in
science geared to the maximum interest span of the slow learner
must include a variety of activity, immediate praise, and frequent
evaluation.   Like all learners, slow learners must do worthwhile
things within their capabilities.

SCIENCE FAIRS

The school science fair is an example of a potentially valuable experience for pupils that has been badly misused.   The basic objective of a science fair is to give pupils an outlet for individual depth
study of a scientific problem.   It can involve field or laboratory
work, library research, discussions with scientists, industrial visits,
and many other worthwhile activities. The end product, either a
written report or a technological construction, can be displayed at
the science fair.

[7] Fletcher G. Watson, "Teaching Science to the Average Pupil," *Science
Teacher* (March 1967), pp. 24–26.
[8] Jerome S. Bruner, *The Process of Education* (Cambridge: Harvard
University Press, 1960), pp. 33–54.

The potential of the science fair for the encouragement of the pupil's study of science is considerable. Beyond the satisfaction gained from the teacher's evaluation and encouragement is the gratification gained from a public display of scientific attainment. The science fair can be an elaborate undertaking, viewed by hundreds of interested and influential citizens. It can illustrate dramatically the many activities associated with science courses and can promote a community's interest and support for the total school program.

Unfortunately, the potential factors for making a science fair valuable can also destroy the integrity of science and the integrity of the pupil. If the activity is turned into a contest in which projects are judged and prizes are awarded, it can be the basis for many questionable procedures. Frequently, the teacher, unwittingly or not, gives too much assistance to the pupil in order to promote a superior science fair. When the teacher contributes too much, in order to help a pupil win a contest, the pupil cannot develop independent research power.

In many instances, parents are more guilty of misguided assistance than the teacher is. If a talented parent assumes even partial responsibility for a pupil's project, he makes a mockery of the pupil's effort. Parents' entrance into the activity can result from several causes. If the school decrees that all pupils must prepare an entry for the fair, the disinterested or nontalented pupil, in order to avoid embarrassment or humiliation, may turn to a concerned parent for help. Too frequently, parents assume total responsibility, so the fair becomes a display of parental, not pupil, efforts. Even the capable pupil may turn to parental help if winning the competition becomes the major reason for the activity.

Another cause for concern by many science educators is the time allotted to preparing for science fairs. The amount of time ordinarily available to the pupil precludes adequate laboratory study or carefully controlled experimentation. Therefore the emphasis is on building something that can be seen rather than representing a basic scientific activity. The amount of time and care spent in preparing the display of the pupil's project may exceed the time spent on the basic research, since a pupil rarely wins, regardless of the quality of his research, if he has a deficient or uninviting exhibit.

A final detrimental factor related to the positive value of a science fair can be in the judging of the projects. Obviously, if the fair is a contest, it must be judged. The securing of competent judges is difficult, and the time allotted for judging is often inadequate. The damage done to educational objectives by incompetent judging can be irreparable. Even with exceptionally competent judging, it is difficult to convince all participants of the validity and fairness of the results.

Science educators who reject the concept of science fairs are convinced that they are not beneficial to the pupils, and that the prime function is the aggrandizement of the image of the school or of the science faculty. In spite of such criticism, the activity should not be discarded until an accurate assessment of the positive values are made. Little research is available on such activities. Answers are needed to such questions as whether pupils actually engage in scientific research and experimental activities, whether the fair stimulates a free flow of ideas among the pupil scientists, and whether the participants actually continue their investigations after their accomplishments have been exhibited.

UNANSWERED QUESTIONS

Despite the fact that science programs have undergone extensive changes and many science educators believe the main task now is to implement these programs, there remain some unanswered questions for curriculum builders to ponder. One is the question of integration. There are some authorities who believe all secondary school science should be integrated.

There is nothing new about integrated science. Boundaries between the disciplines began to disappear some forty years ago. Advocates of further integration of science courses contend that natural phenomena have no inherent properties that make them exclusively chemistry, physics, or biology. (A careful examination of PSSC physics and CHEMS chemistry will reveal a unity of purpose and materials, and an integrated course might be worth experimentation.) Scientific inquiry has evolved processes and theoretical concepts that are basic to all science disciplines. These same science educators are convinced that science teaching must be kept general if there is to be a scientifically literate citizenry.

A second unanswered question concerns the need for greater specialization of courses. Should such things as microbiology or radioisotopes be taught in the secondary schools? Science educators who advocate microbiology as a specialized course point to the fact that these related organisms are so different from higher cells they form a separate kingdom of plant, animal, and protista. It is contended that a course in microbiology is well adapted to the secondary school, since it is interesting and exciting and the nomenclature and taxonomy are much less complicated than even those of biology. It fits well into a secondary school laboratory situation because the manipulations require a minimum of skill and the organisms grow quickly. Excessive cost of equipment and lack of trained teachers might deter some schools from adding such a course, and a small section of BSCS biology includes microbiology.

Only a few schools have introduced separate courses in radioisotopes. Those who advocate such a course contend it can be challenging for advanced pupils and can prepare these pupils for specialization in college science courses. The normal procedure has been to include material concerning radioisotopes in chemistry, physics, and biology courses.

There is a constant effort to answer these questions through study and experimentation. Projects are in progress all over the country and the results will soon be available to curriculum planners.

EVALUATING SCIENCE EDUCATION

The point has been well established that there has been a change-over in science from traditional materials to the so-called new, modern materials. The basis for change has been the reorganization and updating of science information and the adoption of modern psychological concepts of learning. The pupil has been re-directed from factual memorization of formulas to active participation in the science enterprise through individual study and problem solving. The results of these changes ought to be reflected in curriculum organization and the behavioral patterns of pupils.

Regardless of what they are called, science courses in the secondary schools ought to reflect the development of basic scientific concepts. The junior high school years ought to include concepts of matter (chemistry and geology), life (biology), energy (physics), and space (astronomy). The senior high years ought to provide for the college bound and the non-college bound. The modern programs in chemistry, physics, advanced biology, and earth science should be used. Earth science and applied science should be basic for the non-college science pupil.

Course organization may form the vehicle for the mastery of scientific concepts. Functional evaluation of the science program can be made only in the behavioral development of pupils. The emphasis in the modern programs is on the participation of pupils in science activities. If a pupil's progress in science is going to be measured by what he can do rather than what he can tell about, then evaluation should be made accordingly. Ambiguous objectives such as "provide understanding" or "enable a pupil to do critical thinking," should be avoided. The growth of pupils in science should be measured by their ability to apply learned concepts. The following is a brief listing of examples:

Classify a set of objects and state the basis of classification.
Distinguish between observation and influence.
Construct a graph from a table of data.
From a given set of data, state a prediction or formulate a hypothesis.
Design an experiment.
Construct a three-dimensional picture of an object from two-dimensional views of the object.
Apply a rule and calculate the conversion of a quantity into other units of measurement.
Demonstrate how to test a prediction.
Formulate an operational definition from certain data.
Construct a model to fit said data.
Apply a rule to a new situation.

The kind of behavioral activities suggested above will cause pupils to be doing science rather than learning what science has already done. If science learning is arranged to teach the pupil basic scientific concepts, and if his learning is measured by his ability to apply these concepts, then modern science education objectives will be fulfilled.

TOPICS FOR STUDY AND DISCUSSION

1. Evaluate the curriculum track system for determining the assignment of pupils to science courses.
2. If you were a secondary school biology teacher, how would you determine which of the BSCS biology versions you would use in your various classes?
3. Curriculum experts in the area of physics hold that the physics textbook of a decade ago is more out of date today than a ten-year-old textbook was in any previous period. Analyze the scope, sequence, and control of the PSSC physics with that of an older physics book.
4. What are the significant differences between chemistry classes using the Chem Study and the Chem Bond materials?
5. A constant question confronting curriculum workers in science concerns the relationship between generalizations and facts. How should this question be resolved?
6. If a school system reorganizes its administrative units into a 4-4-4 plan, what science courses should be placed in the middle school?

7. Make a comparison of the science programs in the secondary schools of today with those of the pre-space age.
8. Compare Harvard Project physics content with PSSC physics.
9. Prepare a statement to convince the science curriculum committee that a modern physical science course is more in tune with the needs of boys and girls than the older general science courses.
10. Evaluate the need for ecology and environmental problems in a secondary school science curriculum.

SELECTED REFERENCES

DISCH, ROBERT. *The Ecological Conscience.* Englewood Cliffs, N.J.: Prentice-Hall, Inc., 1970.
Sixteen different contributors identify environmental problems that may determine survival. Much of the material can be used for determining course content in up-dating the science curriculum.
FISCHER, ROBERT B. *Science, Man and Society.* Philadelphia: W. B. Saunders Co., 1971.
This is a good source book for philosophic discussions of scientific content in the curriculum. The author claims most science courses are *in* science. He claims his material is *about* science. The author further claims that an approach to science that does not emphasize both substance and relevance is incomplete and unbalanced.
HURD, PAUL D. *New Directions in Teaching Secondary School Science.* Chicago: Rand McNally and Co., 1969.
The author examines recent trends in secondary school science curriculum development and the perspective they provide for new directions. He discusses the nature of science, identifies past and present problems, and points to future goals. A good treatment on the evaluation of new science curricula, both social and philosophical aspects, is included.
OKEY, JAMES R. "Goals for the High School Science Curriculum." *Bulletin, National Association of Secondary School Principals* (January 1972), pp. 57–68.
This article recommends goals for the high school science curriculum. The entire issue of the *Bulletin* is devoted to the theme: Scientific Literacy Imperative for Survival. The role of the high school principal is clearly defined in developing a science curriculum. Outstanding science curriculum authorities are contributors.
TAYLOR, ALTON L. "Curriculum and Instruction Evaluation in Science." *Science Education* (September 1970), pp. 237–239.

Evaluation procedures for science teaching are rather scarce. This article offers good suggestions for both curriculum and instruction evaluation. A systematic testing program is suggested for quantitative feedback.

THURBER, WALTER A., and COLLETTE, ALFRED T. *Teaching Science in Today's Secondary Schools*. Boston: Allyn and Bacon, Inc., 1968.

This is an updated edition of a standard in the field of science teaching. It incorporates most of the new ideas on science curriculum and furnishes a wide range of examples for application to modern educational needs. A critical analysis of the latest programs in each of the secondary curriculum areas is offered.

WELCH, CLAUDE A. "Evolution Theory and the Nature of Science." *The Science Teacher* (January 1972), pp. 26–28.

While this article is written on the theme of evolution, it contains many interesting deductions concerning the nature of science. It offers good suggestions for determining the way science course content should be organized and the purposes of instruction.

WOLFE, DEBORAH P. "Trends in Science Education." *Science Education* (March 1970), pp. 71–76.

This article provides good material for updating science curriculums. It discusses progress of the various science programs in the elementary and secondary schools. It contains a listing of fourteen trends in science education. Certain predictions for the future are made.

CHAPTER 13

Social Studies

Several years ago a large metropolitan newspaper administered a factual information test on material from the social studies to a sampling of pupils in selected secondary schools. The results were so poor that the paper decided to use them to castigate the teaching of social studies throughout the nation. It is beside the point that the test was poorly constructed and placed little emphasis on relationships or understandings. The incident illustrates the misconception that arises over the purposes of the social studies, not only in the public mind, but also in the professional approach.

Much ferment has developed in the social studies field. Part of it is due to the anxieties and frustrations related to world problems and part is due to increased emphasis placed on the need for curriculum balance in the comprehensive secondary school. A long-time objective associated with the social studies has been the teaching of good citizenship. Consequently, in a nation where crime rates, particularly juvenile crimes, are ever-increasing, social studies teaching in the schools is carefully scrutinized. The citizenship goal, the eclectic nature of content, and the changing social values make the social studies particularly sensitive to all kinds of pressures seeking to remold educational purposes. The vulnerability of the social studies curriculum is apparent in selection of textbooks, teaching of controversial subjects, and decisions concerning the teaching of ideologies. A major problem in the social studies is to delineate scope and refine objectives. Social studies cannot be a panacea for all social ills.

THE ROLE OF HISTORY
IN THE SOCIAL STUDIES

The role of history in the social studies field poses the basic problem of proper perspective and balance in curriculum making.   The zealous advocates of the importance of history would dissociate it entirely from the social studies field.   These advocates admit that the two are interdependent, since history provides data for most of the social studies and uses principles and concepts derived from each of the disciplines involved in the social sciences; however, they contend that history is the foundation of the social studies rather than the social studies being the foundation of history.

The heaviest attack on the social studies by the proponents of this point of view is made in the area of contemporary problems. The contention is that pupils who are preoccupied with contemporary affairs in programs of social studies are deprived of the ability to profit from the whole past experience of mankind.   It is the study of history, not the history of contemporary problems, that provides real problem-solving situations.

In trying to resolve the proper relation of history to the other social studies and the emphasis it should receive in the secondary school curriculum, it might be well to take a look at the values proclaimed for the study of history.   The authorities advocating a separate identity of history say it reveals how institutions, ideas, and customs arise and are developed.   It makes available to pupils factual information to enrich their thinking.   It is a source of criteria for critical evaluation of the present and offers alternatives in thought and action for the future.   With a knowledge of history, the pupil draws on the experiences of all mankind.   Vicarious experiences in the study of the subject bring him knowledge beyond his grasp in any other way.   History reveals the infinite variety of human experiences and the infinite potentialities of mankind.   While it does not predict the future, it provides the pupil with information for wise choices.   While it does not guarantee the choices will be wise, it enhances the possibilities.   In addition to this imposing list, many other valid reasons for the study of history are advanced.

The value of history is not a point of debate.   Some of the most relevant content for understanding contemporary society is found in the study of ancient civilizations.   But the question at issue is whether history must be pursued in curriculum isolation in order to gain this understanding.   Those who contend it must would separate history from the social studies field, train teachers in a well-delineated manner, and adjust the curriculum accordingly.

Other advocates of the proper emphasis of history in the social studies curriculum have a more conciliatory attitude.[1] They take a rather paternal position and view history as a basic subject in the social studies field. This position is predicated on the feeling that other approaches to the study of human society besides the historical one are useful, proper, and necessary in the secondary school. Its advocates see history as a coordinating thread that weaves through the social studies fabric and forms a structure through which the other areas are supplemented, explained, and enriched. According to this point of view, there is a need for a more effectual way to combine the social studies and history. History should be treated as a genuine investigation of the past rather than a collection of information or pious indoctrination. It should serve as a basis for dealing objectively and vigorously with real situations. This school of thought does not hold with the idea that historical investigation is merely a recording of events. There is too much information available to record all details fully. The writer of history must establish a purpose as a basis for choice of material. He arranges subject matter, hunts causes, and explains events. He is dependent on judgment evaluations of the total social order and records events that appear relevant to his purpose.

A third approach to the issue of the relevance of history in the social studies field is taken by those who contend that curriculum makers cannot decide by fiat what subject is basic to another. They would resolve the issue by deciding what concepts are important to teach and then guiding the pupil through a problem-solving approach that will help him find in one field the answers to contradictions, evasions, and inequities in another field. As they see it, the job of the teacher is not to transmit a quantity of subject matter or teach values and attitudes, but rather to emphasize concepts the pupil ought to know in order to acquire the capacity for inquiry and critical thinking. A more rigorous selection of content would be made in the teaching of history. The monotonous re-covering of well-traveled patterns of previous courses would be eliminated. The effort would be to relate every subject in the social studies area continuously and usefully to basic ideas that are essential in order to think clearly about human affairs and the attendant social problems.

The choice is not between history and the exciting new

[1] Daniel M. Feins and Gerald Leinwand, *Teaching History and the Social Studies in the Secondary Schools* (New York: Pitman Publishing Corporation, 1968), pp. 416–472.

vistas that are opening for the social studies. Those who contend that history is incompatible with the newer approach because it lacks structure are not realistic. Other social studies, such as economics, political science, anthropology, and social psychology, have historical significance and furnish the necessary structure for supplementing the content of history. History should continue to synthesize the social studies. It should never be divorced from them.

PROBLEM-SOLVING APPROACH TO THE
TEACHING OF THE SOCIAL STUDIES

There may be some question of whether a "new" approach is needed for the teaching of social studies or whether a variation of the standard approach will do. In the sense that "new" is used in other subject-matter content, social studies can benefit from a "new" approach. In fact, one of the basic new procedures used in the other areas is the extensive use of problem solving.[2] A realistic use of this procedure is long overdue in the social studies. Heretofore, problem solving has not been dominant in social studies instruction. If used at all, it seldom has been interpreted psychologically or logically in such a fashion as to foster intellectual growth in pupils.

In order to use problem solving effectively, it is necessary to structure the subject-matter material. A lack of structure has been responsible for the tendency to amass facts that have little relevance in the understanding of social problems. Those who argue pro and con about the value of facts are generally agreed that to have value a fact must be used in relation to understanding and concepts. While this is a worthy objective, it is far from being an accepted practice in the classroom.

Advocates of structure in the social studies contend that every social order possesses certain basic characteristics in common with other societies.[3] Social problems in one society are merely variations of problems in another society. Structure can be achieved in the social studies curriculum by a developmental approach to the social studies that cuts through the mass of subject-matter presentations and identifies a limited number of basic

[2] *Handbook for Social Studies Teaching,* The Association of Teachers of Social Studies of the City of New York (New York: Holt, Rinehart & Winston, Inc., 1967), pp. 302–333.
[3] Dorothy M. Fraser, *Social Studies Curriculum Development, 39th Yearbook* (Washington, D.C.: The National Council for the Social Studies, 1969), pp. 50–74.

social concepts that are consistent in the experiences of mankind. These conceptual themes must be adaptable to the growing mass of new information.

Those who point to the need for structure in the social studies are not necessarily suggesting fusion of subject matter. Some of the past efforts at fusion resulted in a mishmash. Nor does the determination of structural concepts mean that the various social studies disciplines are searched for themes that are consistent in each subject-matter area. (This too was part of the fusion idea in the past.)

The present structural concept approach involves pre-determining those concepts or themes that are consistent in all social cultures and then searching the various disciplines for material that leads to understanding. According to good psychological principles of learning, this understanding will be more meaningful if it comes through problem-solving procedures. Skillful teaching will help pupils identify problems in present-day social, economic and cultural interaction.

A problem is any unanswered question that requires information and a choice of hypothesis for a decision. It is a perplexity that must be felt, not merely comprehended, by a pupil. Problems cannot be programed and handed to pupils on ditto paper. In helping pupils search for understanding and beliefs, the problem-solving approach leads them to encounter realistic problems.

Those who would place history in a dominant position in the social studies curriculum complain that problem solving is not applicable to the teaching of history. This is true only as long as history is viewed as a chronological narrative couched in factual terms free from concepts or generalizations. From that view, the historian is considered infallible, and any attempt to challenge his generalizations reflectively reduces the pupils' faith in historical knowledge. Another reason for rejecting problem solving as an aid to teaching history is the misconception that once a problem is solved it ceases to be a problem. But problems can be historic as well as contemporary. The historic problem of imperialism can be as challenging as the contemporary problem of how to end war. Both of these problems could arise out of a concept of man's struggle for freedom. Use of the problem-solving approach in the social studies would emphasize the importance of all the subject-matter contributions to the understanding of social culture. An example here would relate to the complex problems surrounding the emphasis on ecology. While the conservation of dwindling natural resources involves both political and scientific solutions, the social behavior of man will determine ultimate implementation.

SCOPE AND SEQUENCE
IN THE SOCIAL STUDIES

Some curriculum workers disdain any consideration of scope and sequence in the arrangement of subject-matter material within a secondary school subject.   They contend that this emphasizes the subject matter rather than the learning needs of pupils.   Nevertheless, scope and sequence is one of the real issues in the social studies field.   It involves the larger problems of structure and subject-matter coordination and arrangement.

In consideration of the many proposals for arrangement of curriculum material in the social studies, it must be kept in mind that no evidence has been produced—historic, philosophical, statistical, or experimental—to demonstrate the superiority of any pattern of social studies disciplines or concepts over any other pattern as far as instructional purposes are concerned.   Most of the proposals come from deep-seated convictions resulting from extensive teaching experience on the part of those making the proposals.

The issue of a proper curriculum pattern involves much of the present-day ferment in the social studies and gives rise to several questions.   The most pertinent of these questions include the following:

1.   What is a proper succession of courses?
2.   How much social studies should be required?
3.   Can history and the social studies be more effectively combined?
4.   Should there be more electives in social studies programs?
5.   Should more attention be given to nonwestern culture?
6.   How can rational inquiry and critical thinking be developed?
7.   How can content be made consistent with selected objectives?
8.   How can statutory requirements be met?
9.   How can overlapping and duplication of subject matter be avoided?
10.   How can the vast amount of subject-matter information be brought within workable limits?
11.   Would a national social studies curriculum be desirable?
12.   How can structure be obtained?
13.   How can facts be made relevant?

All these questions are concerned with the establishment of scope and sequence in classroom instruction.

An *ad hoc* curriculum committee for the social studies from the National Association of Secondary School Principals had honest differences of opinion concerning proper scope and sequence of subject matter. After lengthy consideration the committee, composed of experts in the field, decided on three possible approaches. The only admonition they gave curriculum planners was that they should be responsible for a logical development of these patterns, avoiding unnecessary repetition, and keeping in harmony with established local objectives.

Approach One

Grades 7 and 8	American history to 1870; local, state, and federal government, and United States geography.
Grades 9 and 10	World geography and world history, both courses organized according to culture areas.
Grades 11 and 12	United States history (since 1870, with a brief overview of the history prior to 1870) and modern problems.

Approach Two

Grades 7 and 8 (first semester)	Broad field, geographic-centered, socioeconomic units on key and representative regions and nations of the world.
Grade 8 (second semester)	The citizen and his local, state, and national government (functions, relationships, structures, and agencies featured).
Grade 9 (first semester)	Introduction to the understanding of peoples and their institutions (major anthropological and sociological concepts).
Grades 9 (second (semester) and 10	History of selected eras, peoples, areas, and nations of the world with full attention to contemporary aspects and problems.
Grade 11	United States history and government (with important economic units).
Grade 12	Contemporary problems that challenge the citizen (limited to 6 to 10 live issues—political, economic, and social —local to international in scope).

Approach Three

Grade 7	World vistas—history of the peoples of Eurasia and Africa.
Grade 8	History of the United States to 1876.
Grade 9	A. History of a state.
	B. American government and citizenship—national, state, and local.

Grade 10	History of the United States since 1876.
Grade 11	World cultures—Western and non-Western.
Grade 12	Contemporary problems at home and abroad.

A single subject-matter approach to scope and sequence is advocated by some authorities who would make the study of history the foundation for the study of the social sciences. To guarantee the integrity of teaching in the social studies, these authorities would have the secondary school offer a systematic, wide-ranging, cumulative program in history. Labeled as history, organized as history, taught as history, such a program would be faithful to the standards of accuracy and objectivity that history is supposed to impose. The sequence would look something like this:

Grade 7	—American history, with considerable emphasis on exact geographic knowledge.
Grade 8	—Ancient and medieval history with attention to literature and the arts.
Grade 9	—History of Europe (including England) from the sixteenth to the twentieth century
Grade 10	—World history, stressing international relations and giving attention to geographic elements.
Grade 11	—American history, enlarged basis for comparison and evaluation with specific attention to foreign relations.
Grade 12	—A systematic study of one of the social sciences. Likely choice would be political science with emphasis on the constitutional system and comparative systems. Elective courses in economics and geography. Defer sociology, anthropology, and social psychology to the University.

With this approach, the teacher is charged with responsibility for an expression of firm convictions. Any opinion-type of discussion would be relegated to the extraclass area.

Many of the curriculum planners in the social studies field are not too concerned with scope and sequence. They would seek out subject matter that lends itself to structural organization. From the structure of the social sciences they would develop social concepts that pervade the social cultures of mankind.

One such plan organizes social structure into four basic elements:

1. The societal goals of America
    (a) Concepts and values of a free society
    (b) Effective participation in group processes
    (c) Necessity of interdependence
    (d) Orderliness in change
    (e) Competence in critical thinking
2. The heritage and values of Western Civilization
    (a) The solutions of Ancient Egypt and Persia to "the prob-
         lem of empire"
    (b) Pure democracy in the Hellenic city-states of Greece
    (c) The concept of law in Rome
    (d) The piety of the Middle Ages
    (e) The swelling burst of nationalism which characterized
         the nineteenth century in the Western World
3. The dimensions and interrelationship of today's world
    (a) The ongoing and accelerating scientific revolution
    (b) The contracting world of complex international relations
    (c) The current population explosion
    (d) The penetrating influence of public policy in all phases
         of life
    (e) Changing economic structures and patterns
    (f) Changes and conflicts in values and ethics
4. A specific process of rational inquiry and the tenets of good
    scholarship
    (a) The problem approach
    (b) Techniques of research
    (c) Skills of good scholarship
         Locating material, interpreting verbal and graphic ma-
         terial, a sense of time and chronology, evaluating ma-
         terial, synthesizing material, comprehending material,
         and presenting material

Another idea for the structural concept of social studies
content suggests that a general renaissance will occur in the field
when modern conceptionalizations come into use in the secondary
classroom.   An enriched perception will be inherent in the use
of new concepts.   It is suggested that the following be a basic set
of tool concepts: culture, custom, mores, values, enculturation,
acculturation, cultural lag, manifest function, latent function, and
institutions.

A state committee engaged in the revision of the social
studies curriculum was advised to make sure that pupils were
provided with regularly recurring emphasis on the basic ideas or

concepts in terms of which all human experiences are explained. Suggested basic concepts for this purpose included culture, man in a culture interacting with the forces of nature, social groups, economic organization, political organization, freedom, interdependence, and science.

It is appropriate to determine scope and sequence in the social studies, but it is only a matter of orderly convenience. Greater reassurance for lasting values will come from classrooms that stress intelligent attitudes and purposeful problem solving. It is good to arrange what is to be taught, but it is far more significant to assess what is learned.

PATTERNS OF INSTRUCTION
IN THE SOCIAL STUDIES

Social studies is an evolving, changing field. It is incumbent on curriculum planners to be flexible, tolerant, and warmly receptive of changing emphasis. Social studies need definition. Otherwise, just about anything may be included under the title.

In defining social studies it is necessary to delineate the relationship between social studies and the social disciplines. The latter is a term associated with college instruction. Edgar Wesley, dean of the social studies educators, gives this definition: "The social studies are the social disciplines simplified for younger learners." To many people this does not present an accurate picture since the social studies are not tied to any one social discipline but rather represent an interdisciplinary combination of all of the social disciplines.

Careful scrutiny of the field of social studies will reveal at least three different approaches to the formation of social studies subject matter and social studies instruction. These approaches might be identified as: (1) social studies as citizenship transmission; (2) social studies as social science; (3) social studies as reflective inquiry.[4]

Citizenship transmission

Citizenship transmission connotes content known in advance that should be taught or transmitted to youth. This idea permeates much of the traditional curriculum. It is based on the assumption

[4] James L. Barth and S. Samuel Shermis, "Defining the Social Studies: An Exploration of Three Traditions," *Social Education* (November 1970), pp. 743–751.

that there is a set of important concepts that should be organized and taught as subject matter. The teacher's function is to acquaint students with events, people, phenomena, and ideas that are worthy of being learned. The implied assumption is that these things possess intrinsic importance and although they may be irrelevant now, they will be valuable in the future.

Advocates of the citizenship transmission theory rely on the teacher to alternate description with persuasion. Although teachers are expected to present "both" sides of an issue, they ultimately must help the pupil to see the rightness and wrongness in value judgments. Through such a process it may be seen that parliamentary democracy would become the best possible form of government, and the story of America would be one of uninterrupted progress—the type of progress that is always good.

The social studies educators who challenge the citizenship transmission theory contend it is based on two questionable assumptions. First, the assumption that the way to teach citizenship is to transmit a body of content to be stored for future use in decision making. Second, the body of content is usually formed by a consensus of expert opinion and is unconcerned with the needs of students living in a socially disturbed world.

Social studies as social science

The social scientist advocates the acquisition of knowledge. The process is self-justifying and self-validating. No motive is needed for gaining new knowledge. It is good for its own sake. Since the purpose of the social scientist is to generate knowledge and not citizenship, there seems to be an explicit assumption that possession of knowledge and tools of a particular social science will somehow create a good useful citizen. There is no explicit connection between social science and citizenship, only an expectation that acquisition of the attitudes and knowledge of the social scientist will of itself prove sufficient.

The influence of the social scientist on the social studies curriculum presents a paradox. The social scientist as a teacher is academic and traditional. He considers his teaching assignment as one of imparting knowledge, and the task of the pupil is to consume as much of it as possible. The behavior of the social scientist, however, as an inquirer or a researcher contrasts sharply with his behavior as a teacher. As an inquirer he defines significant problems and defines mode of inquiry related to these problems. He speaks of the structure of knowledge within a particular discipline, i.e., history, sociology, political science, etc. He identifies important concepts within a discipline and sets about to gain important knowledge about these concepts.   If the social scientist would conduct his teaching as he does his research, he would qualify for membership among the most forward-looking social studies teachers of the day.

Social studies as reflective inquiry

The most striking characteristic of the "new social studies" is the emphasis on reflective inquiry. In itself, reflective inquiry is not new, nor is its suggested application to the social studies new. In identifying reflective inquiry as applied to the social studies, it might be well to point out what it is not. Inquiry is not leading students to conclusions one wishes them to reach. It is not wandering carelessly among a variety of topics to motivate and attract pupil attention. It is not a purposeless rap session devoid of evidence or supportive data, nor is it a reward session for time consumption after the material has been "covered."

Reflective inquiry operative in the social studies is a method whereby the teacher and pupil identify problems of considerable concern to them and the social order and then search for solutions based on relevant facts and values. Inquiry in the social studies is interdisciplinary. To be interdisciplinary it involves the use of data from all of the social sciences as well as other disciplines. From the standpoint of reflective inquiry a problem is not a problem unless it is sensed, defined, or perceived by particular individuals as a problem. Solutions to problems result from rational, calm, reflective thinking. Enthusiasm is to be desired, but strong, emotional debate without researched information is inconsistent and irrational. To assume the position that a problem is a good problem because it "turns students on" is not tangential, nor is it consistent with the best objectives of reflective inquiry.

PROJECT SOCIAL STUDIES

During the past decade there has been a mild revolution in the formation of the social studies curriculum. Emerging from this ferment is a format called the "new social studies." The effect will probably be as far-reaching as the "new math" and "new science."

The backbone of the changes in the social studies curriculum is based on the 110 research projects related to various facets of the social studies curriculum sponsored by the United States Office of Education and other cooperating agencies. Many of these projects are completed and ready for publication.

A brief summary of the findings and recommendations of the finished projects might include the following:

1. Emphasis on ideas and methodology from anthropology, sociology, political science, economics, and social psychology. History and geography are not de-emphasized, but these subjects no longer dominate the subject-matter field.
2. There is a distinct flavor of an interdisciplinary, integrated approach to curriculum development. This is particularly true of much of the new history material. Most of the discipline-oriented projects incorporate ideas from other fields.
3. Most of the projects show concern for the structure of knowledge. Patterns of concepts and generalizations are identified. The building of knowledge structures is considered an essential part of instructional strategy.
4. Practically all the projects claim to use discovery or inquiry teaching strategies. Some formalize inquiry into patterns such as problem solving, the scientific method, inductive thinking, or deductive thinking. Others claim discovery strategies alone are more interesting and more effective.
5. A concern for values is evident. Most of the projects attempt to teach students to identify and analyze values in context.
6. More social realism and areas of conflict are suggested for the social studies classroom. Problems related to violence, profanity, social class, sex, and personal-social conflict are advocated.
7. Cross-cultural studies are a common means for contrasting values, establishing models for complex cultures, and perceiving uniformity and variety in human behavior.
8. Added emphasis is on the non-Western world. Studies of Africa, Asia, and Latin America are highlighted. The new social studies materials reflect extensive field testing. There is an abundance of materials for both teachers and students. Sources of raw data are identified and the use of multimedia instruction is emphasized.

Probably the most significant thing about the new social studies is the stress put on discovery or reflective inquiry. While this concept is not new, the new social studies presents raw data in such a form that it practically forces teachers to use methods of inquiry.

PROBLEMS OF PUPIL MOTIVATION

Enthusiastic advocates of the social studies would contend that young people need deep insights into their democratic heritage and firm loyalty to its values. They would further contend that youths who acquire information about man's continuing struggle for freedom will develop a sense of personal dedication and loyalty to free institutions. Such youths will obtain an abiding faith in their American heritage, and they will accept responsibiltiy for preserving and improving the ideals represented. Truly, these noble sentiments should be inherent in the exciting challenges of the social studies classroom. Unfortunately, this is not always true.

Secondary pupils are making some of their lowest scores on scholarship tests in the social studies. One of the main reasons for this is the lack of motivation resulting from boredom with the organization and presentation of social studies material. Emphasis on unrelated facts and dull repetition of subject matter are contributing factors. American history is a case in point. In the traditional cycle formation, American history is often taught three times. Each teacher assumes the pupils are having the material for the first time, and she proceeds to teach the whole chronological story with little or no effort to bring depth or understanding to the important concepts. When this happens, the course is reduced to a superficial perusal of the subject and pupils are not permitted to develop a feeling for history.

One way to stimulate interest in the social studies, which has been practiced in some quarters, has been to make the content interesting and attractive by making it easy. This is certainly a step in the wrong direction because the same students who dislike social studies are hard at work on difficult problems in science and mathematics. So-called easy things are seldom challenging. It is the lack of purpose and the uselessness of content against which pupils rebel. Making it easy or difficult does not solve this problem.

Curriculum planners too often do not recommend method or content that is consistent with their stated objectives. It is customary to write social studies objectives that cover all human endeavor. These objectives need to be geared to actual learning activities of pupils. Content acquires meaning and interest for pupils when its relevance to current problems is perceived. The teacher's job is not to transmit knowledge or quantities of subject matter or even to teach values and attitudes. It is to establish concepts that pupils ought to know, helping them to develop capacity for inquiry and, through critical evaluation, to arrive at their own conclusions.

Attempting to teach values to pupils may be another contributing factor to their hostility to the social studies. Many teachers justify the teaching of facts on the basis that through the facts they teach values. The questions are, Whose values? What kind of values? Are they values that have meaning to pupils or are they preconceived adult values that are not consistent with the social order of the day? Does the well-meaning teacher want to teach pupils to be good?   Can this be done without in-doctrination, and when is "good" relevant?   Pupils are presented with a paradox.   They are urged in school to achieve excellence and they live in a world outside that is often socially, morally, and politically inconsistent with such behavior.   There is no question but that pupils must establish values—a culture is dependent on the way values are maintained and modified.   But instead of ex-pecting pupils to gain values through stray facts, teachers must help them to develop capacities for determining values.   This can be done best in classrooms where pupils are encouraged to ex-perience value decisions.

It is not necessary to sacrifice basic values in making the social studies classroom exciting and challenging.   Those responsi-ble for planning the social studies curriculum need to include more realistic content.   With the ever-increasing amount of knowl-edge, it is impossible to include everything.   Subject matter must be planned that is relevant to the understanding of selected social concepts.   This will eliminate needless repetition and meaningless survey efforts.   Teachers can revitalize social studies classrooms by providing more active participation in challenging, problem-solving situations.   This does not mean problem solving involving how many trash cans should be located on the school campus, but rather whether a democracy being charged with imperialism is really imperialistic.   In such classrooms, teachers will not associate trivial problems with complicated solutions, and they will not exercise their inclination to abstract and generalize.   There will not be a ritualistic quality in instructional purposes, nor will the methods be those of prescription and indoctrination.

Environmental crisis

Environmental problems are of deep concern to young people.   A realistic approach to the study of environmental problems may be one of the answers to pupil motivation.

The world faces an environmental crisis.   Resources are being depleted at an alarming rate, the air is being polluted beyond human tolerance, chemical waste is destroying both land and sea life, in fact the whole ecological imbalance of the earth is reaching a danger point in the survival of man.[5]

While the problems involved in the environmental crisis af-fect most of the subject-matter disciplines, there can be no doubt that the social behavior of man is the center of the problem.

[5] George L. Fersh, "Environmental Crisis: Lodestone for the Social Studies," *Social Education* (January 1971), pp. 53–55.

Herein lies an unsurpassed opportunity and responsibility for social studies teachers to develop an overriding concern for dealing with environmental problems in order that individuals, private enterprise, and governments at all levels will unite in seeking solutions to such problems.   There needs to be developed a national and world citizenry dedicated to this objective.

Through involvement processes pupils must learn how to relate and deal with nature.   The development of value judgments, attitudes, skills, and concepts for solutions to environmental problems are transferrable to the host of other social problems.   Effective learning about environmental needs, problems, and issues can develop essential knowledge for the type of citizen that appreciates the interrelatedness of all resources and recognizes alternatives and consequences in the decision-making process resulting in a respect for the dignity, worth, and values of others.   This is the type of citizen that has an awareness of the realities and probabilities of the tempo with which change and solutions can be achieved. Young people equipped with the fundamentals necessary to meet environmental problems can apply such skills in seeking solutions to problems and issues associated with human rights, social behavior interaction, and international relations.

There can be plus values in moving subject matter concerning the environmental crisis into the center of social studies curriculum.   Focus on environmental problems will necessitate moving out of the classroom atmosphere in dealing with physical and cultural realities as well as social and economic behavior.   It will be necessary for learners to investigate the interests and concerns of the neighborhood, the state, the nation, and much of the world.   Air polluters from factories in the local town, the peril of the disappearance of the Atlantic salmon by Danish fishermen, the building of honky-tonk communities in the Maryland wetlands, and the flooding of the dolly sods in West Virginia all are part of the problem in the environmental crisis.

For those who complain of the dullness and irrelevancy of secondary school social studies classes, a frontal attack on the problems of man in saving his environment may be a sinecure. Most environmental issues involve a blending of theory and pragmatism for solution, an assignment of personal and civic responsibility, a shading of idealism and materialism, a tempering of necessity and justice, and a viable relationship between freedom and survival.   These are what life is all about.   The social studies are what life is all about.   Youth may not be correct in its assessment of the irrelevance of much of the secondary school curriculum, but there are sufficient grounds for concern in the social studies.   Teachers who stress chronological order and sequential detail compound the problems.

ROLE OF THE SOCIAL STUDIES TEACHER
IN TEACHING CONTROVERSIAL ISSUES

Fulfillment of social studies teachers' responsibility for helping young citizens to assume their rightful roles in the democratic order lies more in the way they teach social studies than it does in the type of offerings. Democracy is dependent upon the right of people to study and discuss issues freely. Equally important, it is dependent upon a citizenry which exercises its rights, keeps well informed, and makes decisions after divergent points of views have been thoroughly explored. Responsibility for democratic citizenship cannot be developed within a vacuum. It must come from a study of societal problems and active participation in the solution of such problems. Every school should have a vital, active, student governing organization.

The question of teaching controversial issues is a persistent one. It is closely allied with the question of whether social studies teachers should teach by prescription and indoctrination.[6] In one sense of the word, there is no vital social problem that should be left undiscussed. But in order to keep from destroying the long-term objectives delineated for good citizenship, certain ground rules must be observed. Equally true is the fact that any teacher who can successfully avoid indoctrinating students with his viewpoints is certain to be an insipid and uninspiring teacher. Here again, ground rules apply—chiefly those of respect for opposing viewpoints.

The *ad hoc* committee on social studies set up by the National Association of Secondary School Principals established certain principles for teaching controversial issues that bear quoting:

1. The topic is significant or related to a persistent problem so that the information acquired about it will be of continuing usefulness.
2. The issue is suitable for the maturity level of the students.
3. Sufficient material, of appropriate difficulty, is available so that students can gather essential data and study the major points of view concerning the issue.
4. Time is available to study the topic adequately for present needs.
5. The teacher has enough background on the subject to provide adequate guidance to pupils.

[6] Allan A. Glatthorn, "What Place for Controversy," *Bulletin of the National Association of Secondary School Principals* (September 1966), pp. 1–8.

6. The topic can be studied and discussed reasonably in the local community. But school officials must seek board of education approval for responsible discussion of issues that presently lie buried by general agreement. The responsibility of the social studies goes beyond mere support of the *status quo*. The horizons of free discussion must be vigorously extended through a comprehensive public relations program designed to elicit official and general approval for discussing more issues. Students need to feel that what they say and do is important. The public should recognize that a social studies program avoids sterility by studying controversial issues and equipping students for active and productive living in a democracy.

The same committee also suggested certain rules of conduct for social studies teachers. The urgent need to teach controversial issues carries with it heavy responsibilities for the teacher:

1. He uses the issues to teach respect for the opinions of others and to develop critical thinking and a desire to participate actively in the democratic process.
2. He is sure that all points of view are presented fairly.
3. He develops a classroom atmosphere in which pupils feel free to express their opinions and challenge ideas.
4. He is sure that students learn to seek and value information, that they do not become satisfied with a mere exchange of opinions.
5. The teacher exhibits in discussions and action the characteristics which he desires to teach.
6. He is a perpetual student of the social sciences in order to have the background needed to guide pupil study.

Many issues which face this democratic nation sharply divide its people. The problem of equal rights for all citizens and the problem of federally supported education are two examples.

A third issue, closer to being resolved but still quite pertinent, is the question of informing young people of the tenets of communism. A number of states have taken official recognition of this problem. Some states have statutory requirements for all public schools to include units about communism in the social studies curriculum. While most curriculum workers abhor statutory curriculum requirements, this illustrates the intensity of purpose on the part of lay-citizenry concerning the issue. Other states, probably more wisely, have established state educational governing boards to develop broad policy statements with recommended courses and guidelines. Very few states have taken no recognition of this problem. The gap has been bridged by using the phrase, "teaching about communism rather than teaching communism." In a sense, most teaching is teaching about something.

It is apparent that ideological experiments on the left or right are a menace to the traditions and tranquility of this great nation.   It behooves the citizenry to be fully informed of the strength and weaknesses of such adversaries and to understand their intent and purposes in world affairs.   The schools of this nation bear the responsibility for a systematic and objective study of the comparative merits of democracy and communism.   It is no longer a controversial issue.

PROBLEMS TO BE SOLVED

Curriculum problems in the social studies field will continue to be perplexing.   The conflict between balance and dominance, and the stresses of a disturbed social order, are ever present in curriculum-making decisions.   However, the emergence of the comprehensive secondary school concept helps to implement curriculum balance. The importance of the social studies in the secondary school curriculum has been revitalized by the establishment of several national studies by professional and governmental organizations.

Improvement in a subject-matter field should be continual. Social studies teachers must become alive to crucial issues.   While historical scholarship might be the specialized goal of some pupils, it certainly is not appropriate for all.   The classroom ought to be a laboratory for developing intelligent thinking and thoughtful citizenship.   If world citizenship is to be realized, pupils must learn to accept both diversity and pluralism.

From a survey of curriculum activity in the field of social studies, it can be assumed that future programs will be identified by their conceptual framework; for example, new approaches to citizenship deal with moral imperatives related to the idea that human dignity requires protection by democratic government. Principles of government are presented in the light of how they support a pluralistic society.   Discriminating judgment and accuracy of facts are imperative.

Increased attention to the non-Western world will involve reshifting subject matter in world history courses.   There has been a tendency to stress the fact that the world is a dangerous place in which to live and therefore it is important to get along with peoples of other cultures.   This idea blurs the differences of people and ignores factors of national interest and power.   It suggests an approach to international relations that has a kind of virginal innocence and idealism, but does little to make the world more understandable.   The primary object should be to understand those things that make people alike and those things that make them different, both demanding mutual respect.

Economic education, disregarded for many years as unessential to social studies programs, is returning as a center of interest,[7] with emphasis on economic opportunity, incentives, and rewards as means of securing full productive use of the nation's human and material resources. The keynote of the resurging economic education is a belief in man's capacity to identify and analyze problems of living and working together. It involves positive thinking in policy making and social planning, both public and private.

New dimensions are also developing in the field of geography,[8] which was, until recently, a grade school factual subject of places and products. The new geography, especially that being advocated for secondary school use, emphasizes the study of the earth as the home of man and proposes to help pupils understand the social, political, economic, and ideological relationships existing between people and places.

In the new social studies curriculum, classroom instructors will train pupils to think through issues for their worth rather than accepting preconceived textual solutions. Outmoded content and interpretations will be discarded. This will mean breaking with traditions that have no pertinence to modern problems. Solutions to the problems resulting from the complexities of modern society call for critical dialogue between teachers and pupils. The whole curriculum venture rests heavily on the willingness of instructional staffs to adopt new social studies conceptualizations and to experiment with new curricular structures.

TOPICS FOR STUDY AND DISCUSSION

1. Would a nationwide curriculum in social studies satisfy objectives for the perpetuation of democracy in this country? Defend your position.
2. Is there a dichotomy between curriculum emphasis on concept development and the stressing of factual and chronological order in social studies?
3. Evaluate the thesis that pupils are justly bored with much of the content of the social studies curriculum.
4. Analyze the position of patriotic zealots who contend that the teaching of American history insures the perpetuation of democracy in America.

[7] John E. Maher, *The Subjects in the Curriculum: Economics* (New York: The Odyssey Press, 1968), pp. 125–132.
[8] Randall C. Anderson, "Trends in Geography Instruction," *Bulletin of the National Association of Secondary School Principals* (February 1967), pp. 10–19.

5. Analyze the contention of some historians who say history is a unifying subject drawing together many strands of human experience in relation to the organizing principles of chronology.
6. It is generally assumed that the teaching of citizenship is the unique responsibility of the social studies field. What are the implications of such an assumption?
7. Scope and sequence are frequently of major concern in the deliberations of social studies curriculum committees. What is the logic of such concern?
8. Modern social studies educators tend to place more emphasis on reflective inquiry and less emphasis on facts and chronological development. Assess the paradoxical aspects of this position.
9. Prepare an assessment of the value of the Project Social Studies.

SELECTED REFERENCES

CRABTREE, CHARLOTTE A. "Inquiry Approaches: How New and How Valuable." *Social Education* (November 1966), pp. 523–528.

An examination of some of the assumptions, practices, and empirical support for inquiry approaches in the social studies is presented. Concept learnings and reflective thinking skills are evaluated in relation to inquiry approaches.

FENTON, EDWIN. *Teaching the New Social Studies in the Secondary Schools.* New York: Holt, Rinehart and Winston, 1966.

This book attempts to stimulate constructive thought about subject matter and teaching strategies of the social studies. It sets up a model for inductive teaching. Much of the material is drawn from the 100 or more social studies projects in progress all over the country. It draws on the contributions of many of the leaders in the new teaching movement.

GARDNER, WILLIAM E., and JOHNSON, FRED A. *Social Studies in the Secondary Schools.* Boston: Allyn and Bacon, 1970.

This is a valuable book of readings in the social studies curriculum field. Included are the following topics: "Social Studies—Rule in General Education," "The Changing Social Studies," "Methods and Techniques of Instruction," "Improvements and Innovations in Social Studies," and "Research and Evaluation in Social Studies."

KRUG, MARK M. *History and the Social Studies.* Waltham, Mass.: Blaisdell Publishing Co., 1967, pp. 46–98.

The approach to history is essentially humanistic. It offers suggestions for how the social sciences should be organized for instructional purposes and questions the current emphasis on structure.   It is a good source for answers as to the *what* and *how* for curriculum construction in the social sciences.

————, et al.   *The New Social Studies.*   Itasca, Illinois: F. E. Peacock Publishing Co., 1970.

The authors set out to discover to what extent the materials for the new social studies meet the objectives claimed for them by their creators.   They point out that not all of the approaches and materials are equally valid or suitable for use in the secondary curriculum.

McLENDON, JONATHON C.   *Social Studies in Secondary Education.*   New York: The Macmillan Company, 1965.

This volume introduces the basic elements of social studies instruction.   It includes established practices and noteworthy experiments.   The junior high school social studies program is given special attention.   Curriculum and instructional problems are given special attention throughout.

PLOGHOFT, MILTON E., and SHUSTER, ALBERT H.   *Social Science Education.*   Columbus: Charles E. Merrill Publishing Company, 1971.

This book for prospective teachers brings together the emerging characteristics of the "new" social science and projects a practical scheme for classroom use.   It stresses the social inquiry approach by means of problem cases and situations.

ROGERS, VINCENT R.   *A Source Book for Social Studies.*   New York: The Macmillan Company, 1969.

This is an excellent source of material for course content in secondary school social science curriculum.   It is an attempt to cull out the seemingly bottomless pit of ideas, information, and facts that are of relevance to social science content.   It tries to answer the question of what is worth knowing.

CHAPTER 14

Vocational
and Technical Education

Vocational education might be termed "crisis education," since the federal government has turned to vocational education for solving manpower problems in times of both military and economic crises. At such times, educators and lay citizens are likely to reach an early conclusion that social and economic problems can be solved by preparing youth for some type of useful and gainful employment. However, too little effort is made to discover whether the problems are inherent in changing economic and social conditions, or whether vocational education has any relation to the solution of the problems.

Vocational education is unique in that it was the first, and for a long time the only, federally supported education. During the period following the Civil War, when competent persons were needed in agriculture and the mechanical arts, the Morrill Act gave land to the states to establish agricultural and engineering colleges. When a similar shortage of trained workmen in agriculture and industry followed World War I, financial assistance was sent into the secondary schools through the Smith-Hughes Vocational Education Act. Approximately seven million dollars was to be distributed to the states for support of vocational education in agriculture, trade and industrial education, homemaking and, later, distributive education. World War II brought the George-Barden Act, to help furnish a fully trained work force, and the War Production Training Act, to provide crash training for war production workers.   The Korean conflict necessitated the Nurse Training Act to relieve a critical shortage of nurses.

VOCATIONAL EDUCATION ACT OF 1963

The Vocational Education Act of 1963, the most significant and far-reaching congressional action in the vocational education field, was not the result of a war crisis but of the accumulation of social and economic conditions caused by an unprecedented peacetime economic boom that began between 1956 and 1958 as a result of space exploration.   This economic prosperity was the result of scientific and technological industrialization.   However, the automation of industry, which had been going on at a startling pace, eliminated scores of jobs and created a need for totally different kinds of employment.   The nation was faced with the perplexing situation of widespread unemployment in a booming economy on the one hand and a critical shortage of skilled technicians on the other.

The main factor that brought about the Vocational Education Act of 1963 was the discovery that the unemployment had created an unbelievable amount of poverty in what had been termed an "affluent society."   A distressing number of poverty pockets were found in the Appalachian coal fields.   Government advisers decided that the only real solution to poverty problems was the retraining of workers.   This required the extension, expansion, and improvement of vocational education.   The recommendations of a panel appointed by President Kennedy to study the situation resulted in the Vocational Education Act, which not only poured vast amount of money into vocational education, but left the doors wide open for sweeping readjustments and the building of imaginative new programs that involved more than five-sixths of the nation's population.

The act authorized matched grants to the states for assistance in maintaining, extending, and improving existing programs and developing new programs.   It also provided funds for part-time employment of needy youth so that they could afford to continue training.   It stated specifically that persons of all ages should have access to vocational training or retraining.   This meant those still in school, those who completed or dropped out of school, those already in the labor market, and those with any kind of educational handicaps.   The training should be part of programs designed to train persons for gainful employment as semiskilled or skilled workers or technicians in recognized occupations.   Obviously, this excluded professional training or the preparation for jobs requiring a college degree, but it included pre-service and in-service training of vocational and technical teachers. This teacher-training provision and the 10 percent of the funds set aside for research, experimentation, and the development of pilot programs indicated the intentions of the act to upgrade vocational education.

Significant amendments to the Vocational Education Act of 1963 were added in 1968. These amendments go a long way toward reordering the original act. Perhaps the most important implication of this legislation was its comprehensiveness. It directed federal funds to a wide variety of services and programs at every level of education. Vocational education had to be considered by the educational community as one of the major missions of the public schools. The 1968 amendments called for the participation of private training sources, and for the use of resources of industry and other employers in making opportunities accessible to all. The legislation called for the relating of academic work to real-life situations. This fundamental concept was to be taught in the context of occupational preparation orientation.

WHO SHALL BE INVOLVED?

A broad interpretation of the Vocational Education Act with the 1968 amendments would say that vocational education is a must for all people, but discussion here will be concerned mainly with the secondary school phases of the programs. Vocational preparation, a basic objective of terminal or continuing secondary education, has been associated with the middle and lower ability pupils who have pursued courses in vocational agriculture, vocational home economics, distributive education, trades and industry shop classes, and business education.

Unfortunately, vocational education classes have had pupils who lack either mental or manual skills to successfully participate in such courses. This has been a twofold detriment to vocational education. These pupils have caused the experiences of the more capable pupils to be ineffective and the chances of these low ability pupils of getting and holding demanding jobs have been almost nil.

Sights must be raised and service broadened if vocational education is going to fulfill the promises of a golden era. Vocational education must include opportunities for students of all levels of intelligence, capability, and aptitude, and must retain flexibility for rapid change.

The middle and lower ability pupils will continue to form a sizable part of the vocational education field, and they must be fitted with appropriate technical skills for the jobs they are to hold. Determining what skills are necessary is a major educational task which is made difficult by the rapid obsolescence of present industrial processes and the veiled mystery of future ones. A whole new range of programs must be established to prepare the lowest ability pupils for unsophisticated service jobs. The number of service jobs available promises to be the economic salvation of these future wage earners. Even for these jobs, however, lack of suitable training or social maladjustment will render such persons useless.

A totally new approach to vocational education will concern the top-level pupils. An effort must be made to capture the number of capable pupils who heretofore have left school without completing any useful program. This group includes many who have the ability to enter the highly technical fields but have deferred professional objectives. The secondary schools can provide sophisticated, challenging programs that will prepare these students for technical institutes or junior colleges.

Inclusion of the entire range of secondary youth in the scope of vocational education may help solve problems of dropouts, unemployment, and other social and economic ills. The greatest detriment to success will be failure of the programs to keep pace with new scientific and technological developments.

VOCATIONAL VERSUS GENERAL EDUCATION

Curriculum planners must bridge the dichotomy between vocational education and general education to determine the extent of the vocational education program. General education extremists would practically eliminate any formalized vocational training for secondary school youth (some would also omit it from the baccalaureate program), contending that the best vocational education is a good general education.

Those who oppose the establishment of strong vocational education programs in the school raise the question of what kind of vocational education really makes sense. They hold that automation will render today's skills useless in the industrial complex of tomorrow. A common prediction is that job skills will change three times in the life of every worker. Industrial leaders are quoted as urging the schools to leave the learning of technical skills to on-the-job training and to produce pupils well-grounded in the humanities and commercial skills—persons with general intellectual alertness, ability to read and solve problems, and ability to communicate and get along with other people. Studies show that the greatest number of workers lose their jobs in industry through their inability to get along with people rather than their inability to do the work.

The advocates of general education urge curriculum planners to guard general education carefully and keep vocational education as small as possible. They suggest that the purpose of the secondary school is to prepare youth for the fullness of living and that the preparation for vocational proficiency should be left to other institutions and agencies. Naturally, advocates of vocational education do not share this viewpoint, but they must tolerate it so that they can gradually change it and encourage educators to provide for general and liberal concepts in their vocational programs.

SCHOOL ORGANIZATION FOR
VOCATIONAL EDUCATION

In view of the Vocational Education Act, the foregoing discussion of vocational education versus general education may be somewhat academic. With the amount of financial assistance being offered by the federal government and the current social and economic problems, there will be few school districts that will withstand the clamor for some type of vocational education. The important question becomes how to organize and house the programs. Educators are sharply divided on this issue.

The Vocational Education Act encourages the establishment of area vocational schools, and the strongest advocates of vocational education believe the special vocational school is the only answer. On the other hand, there is a strong continguent of educational leaders who are dedicated to what Conant called the "really distinctive American school"—the comprehensive secondary school. In this school, vocational education is an integrated part of a comprehensive school program. The choice of school organization is a perplexing problem for curriculum planners, and it demands a careful weighing of evidence before decisions can be made.[1]

A separate vocational school is expensive to build and expensive to operate, but the advocates of such schools are sure the costs can be justified and the programs can be made really effective. They hold that a certain amount of comprehensiveness can be maintained in a special vocational school. They point to the large number of these schools in Pennsylvania, Ohio, New Jersey, and New York where the quality programs of the past decades have originated. The status of the large city schools may influence the thinking of those who do not want to break with the past.

One of the most telling arguments for the separate vocational school comes out of an evaluation of the social status of its

[1] Clayton E. Farnsworth, "Trends in Vocational Education," *Industrial Arts and Vocational Education* (January 1967), pp. 23–25.

pupils. It is the contention of vocational school leaders that where vocational education is part of a comprehensive school it receives little respect. Operating funds are not adequate and there is a glaring lack of administrative and supervisory attention. In too many instances, vocational education facilities are housed in Quonset huts, abandoned storerooms, basements, or isolated wings of the regular school building, and opportunities for participation in the total educational and social program of the school are curtailed. Therefore, an undesirable status attitude is developed toward vocational pupils. If the pupils are already suffering from economic, social, and educational impoverishment, the situation becomes intolerable. Vocational people do not deny the comprehensive values of the school, but they strongly condemn a situation that makes second class citizens out of pupils. A comprehensive program should not come at the expense of a pupil's self-respect and his status among his peers.

Whether the new vocational schools, such as the area schools, can acquire a desirable status remains to be seen, but there are many factors in their favor. Many of the pupils will be receiving a technical education that will be far more sophisticated than former programs, and the school population will have a better balance of pupil ability and achievement. Vocational leaders believe that comprehensiveness can be achieved in a vocational program without merging it with the academic school program. They think such programs should augment and complement each other. The vocational secondary school program should be so organized as to provide a complete range of opportunities for all pupils to explore and experiment with the different clusters of occupations.

The National Association of Secondary School Principals is on record as favoring the comprehensive high school. According to the NASSP, this type of secondary school provides opportunity for pupils from various socioeconomic groups, and with different aptitudes and levels of ability, to live and work together. The publications of the Association's Curriculum Committee describe the comprehensive school as one that offers the best structure and content for fulfilling the American ideal of adequate educational opportunities for all youth.

From the foregoing definitions, it may be concluded that the comprehensive school is everything to everybody. This makes it difficult to deny its virtues. Theoretically, it should contain, among other things, a completely functional program of vocational education. In order, then, to identify the advantages of the comprehensive school in relation to vocational education, it is necessary to point out the weakness of separate vocational schools.

Adverse criticism of separate vocational schools can be summarized under the headings of articulation problems, rigidity of curriculum, and unfavorable social relations. It is claimed that where vocational schools exist, a youth is forced to commit himself too early. Opportunities for vocational choice should go much beyond fourteen or fifteen years of age, yet once a pupil has been in a vocational program for a period of time, spending at least half of his time in the shop, he finds it difficult to change his course. If he returns to his home school, he is retarded academically. It is equally difficult for an older pupil to make a late commitment to a vocational school. He has to begin almost from scratch in his shop work and his academic work is not always applicable. These conditions could exist in a comprehensive school, but the proponents claim it is far less likely.

One of the heaviest criticisms of the vocational school concerns its curriculum. Too frequently, it follows the pattern of the Smith-Hughes Act. This means that at least four periods a day must be devoted to shop work, a plan which does not take into account variability in job requirements or in pupil capacity or ability. Curricular patterns change slowly, mainly because machinery and equipment is expensive. Yet the rapid development of technology brings quick obsolescence to job requirements and hence to the equipment used in training for these jobs. It is also contended that the vocational school curriculum is too heavily weighted with trade training considering that trade unions are reluctant to admit graduates to their rank without apprenticeship.

Minority groups are adverse to vocational schools because of the schools' tendency to de facto segregation. They claim that guidance counselors influence their children to select vocational schools because the counselors continually misunderstand the children's aspiration levels. Another type of segregation is caused by the unwarranted idea that the vocational school is the only salvation of low ability pupils and prospective dropouts. Thus, the social stigma attached to attending vocational schools becomes one of the most serious handicaps to overcome.

Antagonists, and even many advocates, of separate vocational schools doubt that such schools will survive. Some of the large cities that have had special vocational schools are now turning to comprehensive schools. The administrators still contend the vocational school is educationally efficient, but they recognize signs of grave social maladjustments that prevent many students from enrolling. Authorities in one large city, for example, after an extensive study of their schools, found that many qualified pupils, in spite of good guidance help, preferred to remain in their neighborhood high school. Convenience, sentiment, prestige, and family influence affected their choice. Therefore, the authorities concluded that the needs of most youths were not being met in vocational schools and they turned to the building of extensive vocational programs in comprehensive high schools.

Attempts have been made to reshape the structure of the separate vocational school. Tracks for special technical training have been developed to attract the more able pupils, attempts have been made to facilitate the flow of pupils between the academic and vocational schools, and curriculum structures have been altered for technological needs. However, the demonstrated social advantages of community pupils living together in a community school probably sound the death knell of the separate vocational school as it has been conceived in the past.

VOCATIONAL TECHNICAL SCHOOLS

The demand for unskilled hands is rapidly diminishing. The complexity of modern jobs calls for greater sophistication of preparation. Service occupations such as health, law enforcement, fire protection, sanitation, pollution control, and education are adding technical classifications constantly. Business occupations in data processing, distribution, transportation, finance, and management are also developing technical categories. The production and manufacturing occupations continue to be centers of automation where only those with technical skills have any chance of survival. The program of the secondary school will continue to furnish terminal preparation for limited skills positions, but a technical school's program will be needed for these more complicated occupations.

The term "technical school" has many connotations. As used here, it refers to a school which trains youth to be highly skilled artisans and technicians—a community college, a junior college, or a comprehensive secondary school expanded to include the thirteenth and fourteenth years. It is both unfeasible and impractical to provide such training in the usual span of the secondary school years.

Curriculum planners must pay increased attention to articulation, so that pupils in the comprehensive schools will be prepared to continue their training in a technical school. Preparation should be adequate for both the terminal student in the technical school and the student who plans to continue on toward the baccalaureate degree. This means an added dimension for vocational education at the secondary school level. Spiraling job requirements and the increasing need for breadth of preparation will cause curriculum patterns to be pointed toward post high school matriculation. This ought to raise the status of vocational education, since most of the pupils will be "pre-college," or at least "pre-junior college."

FUTURE TRENDS

It does not take too much clairvoyance to predict that new types of area vocational schools will be developed, due to financial stimulation offered by the Vocational Educational Act.[2] The type of programs developed in these schools, however, is an open-end question. In sparsely populated sections, the schools may accommodate pupils from other schools in the area who will attend technical classes for part of each day, then return to their home school for academic and social experiences. In other situations, students may attend courses requiring from one to six weeks for completion. Most likely, the area schools will specialize in technical training and adult education; they will not serve as the permanent base for the pupil's entire secondary education. The area vocational schools in urban centers will probably offer highly technical, advanced programs.

School leaders in both Cleveland and New York are committed to the comprehensive school, and this may become a trend in the larger cities. Reasons for this trend involve such factors as population developments, dropout records, socioeconomic conditions, employment opportunities, and the changing character of large cities. Pilot programs in large cities show that youth with impoverished backgrounds frequently show both aptitude and talent when a favorable climate is provided. This favorable climate is augmented when pupils are able to attend school in their home community with friends and neighbors. U.S. Office of Education statistics show that the secondary school is the last formal schooling for more than four-fifths of the school population. It follows that the comprehensive school is the best type of school organization to meet the many needs of so large a segment of youth.

For a secondary school to be truly comprehensive in meeting the needs of vocational education, it must offer a variety of vocational, technical, and occupational classes to enable pupils to develop marketable skills. The curriculum must also offer reading improvement courses and such special services as work experience programs for in-school and out-of-school youth and for on-the-job training.

[2] Grant Venn, "Vocational Education for All," *Bulletin of the National Association of Secondary School Principals,* vol. 51, no. 317 (March 1967), pp. 32–40.

Guidance programs will take on added significance in a comprehensive school. Since the pupil does not have to commit himself at any particular time, he needs continuous advice and counsel for his vocational preparation. This should affect the dropout rates, because youth will not be bound to an unsatisfactory program or school. Greater flexibility of programing is possible in the large comprehensive school, permitting greater freedom of choice according to the interest, achievement, and readiness of the individual pupil.

One of the desirable trends in urban areas is the development of regional skill centers. It may be argued that these regional skill centers are sophisticated forms of the regional vocational school. To a certain degree, this is true. Transfer to a regional skill center may be on a full-time basis, but most likely the pupil will remain a member of his home school and attend the skill center on a part-time basis. Planned for pupils who, through their aptitude and achievement, qualify for high cost specialization that is not practical in a comprehensive school, the center may include advanced placement and honors programs of a technical, vocational nature. Courses of study involve such subjects as aeronautics, automatic transmissions, cosmetology, data processing, and electronics.

NEEDS OF VOCATIONAL EDUCATION

The Vocational Education Act of 1963 with the 1968 amendments gives vast sums of money for the building of imaginative new vocational programs. The question is, What will be the most effective program?[3]

The task of preparing youth to earn a living remains the primary goal of all education. The secondary school, being the preparatory school, fails in its objective when it permits youth to drop out or graduate without positive evidence of realistic occupational knowledge. The occupational concerns of the pupil ought to be an inherent part of the school curriculum. In the past, a high school diploma was the passport to satisfactory employment, but many high school graduates are now unemployed. Their preparation is not applicable to the changing world of work.

The task faced by vocational education curriculum planners is both difficult and hazardous because of the inherent problems and the uncertainties of a technological order. The first problem

[3] Gerald Somers and Kenneth Little, *Vocational Education: Today and Tomorrow* (Madison, Wis.: The University of Wisconsin Press, 1971), pp. 68–72.

that should be attacked is misguided official attitude. School administrators and their faculties have developed false and distorted ideas about vocational education. This has come about through a lack of knowledge and understanding of the field. The principal and his staff need to take an objective look at the obligations of the school for preparing youths to be functionally effective in their social order. The gap between the "white-collar" worker and the "blue-collar" worker has narrowed to the point where both are in the same relative area of sophistication. Both need the science and mathematics laboratory; both need the ability to think in problem-solving situations; and both need the ability to get along with other people.

A second problem that detracts from the value of vocational education is the idea that college preparation represents the only real value in education. Pupils are classified as going to college or not going to college. The not-going-to-college group become second-class citizens—vocational pupils. Administrators should realize that going to college involves vocational preparation and that college-bound pupils will enter the labor force. Irreparable damage is done in the secondary school when attention is focused on the college-bound group and equal status is denied all others. If the school is sincere in its desire to meet individual needs, it will expand its view of all vocational obligations, which are equally honorable and equally valuable.

A third problem in vocational education is the ever-changing employment needs. A curriculum that does not keep pace can result in pointless waste of school funds and scores of disillusioned pupils. Certain facts need continual evaluation: local employment statistics are subject to periodic revisions, mobility of the work force on a state and national basis affects job preparation, and the turnover of employment in each occupational area warrants careful attention. Good survey practices call for involvement of many people beyond the school staff. Help should be enlisted from leaders in business and industry, parents, pupils, state and national divisions of vocational education, employment bureaus, and placement services. Survey results will call for carefully planned procedures tailored to fit the individual needs of pupils in each local school area.

Another facet of vocational education that needs increased attention is the work-study program. The Vocational Education Act furnishes finanical assistance for the development of such programs. Work-study programs have grown haphazardly in the curriculum for several years. In many instances, they have lacked vitality and any real integration in the vocational preparation programs. Too often, work-study arrangements have been made for pupils as a means of financial assistance to enable them to stay in school.   While this objective is not without value, it should not be a determining factor in deciding which pupils should be involved in work-study activities.   The selection should be based on vocational education objectives and sound educational principles. Work-study programs should be an integral part of job-training, furnishing job environmental experience which will enable the pupil to set worthwhile educational goals for himself.

A NEW LOOK

It is problematic whether there will be a new look in vocational education or whether it will be the old look transferred to a new setting.   There are, however, two or three interesting experiments going on that give promise of new approaches.

In Quincy, Massachusetts, a group of behavioral scientists from the American Institute for Research worked with vocational educators in designing a curriculum that demonstrates the increased effectiveness of instruction derived explicitly from analysis of behavior on the job.   Eleven job families were analyzed to determine, specifically, what the worker does on the job and what skills and knowledge he needs.   A training sequence for each of the jobs within the family of jobs was established, the idea being that a selective type of vocational training would be valuable for a "cluster of jobs."   If the pupil elects to leave the training program before completion, he has developed a minimal ability for several jobs within the cluster he pursues.

In Richmond, California, experiments were conducted in dovetailing technical and academic subjects.   Shop and laboratory programs were used to dramatize the relationship between theory and practice.   Teachers from various disciplines were formed into teams to coordinate classroom, laboratory, and shop experience. When heat was being taught in physics, the mathematics class covered appropriate equations, laboratory work involved the conducting of heat experiments, and the English class developed oral and written reports on the subject.

A project at the Massachusetts Institute of Technology, involving over 100 vocational educators, was based on the thesis that a major overhaul of instructional methods, techniques of teacher preparation, and school organization was necessary.   In examining the many facets of the problem, the group concluded that present-day schools were not taking full advantage of the built-in motivation that stems from the desire of young people to do things.   They recommended the development of new curricular materials and instructional media, beginning at the junior-high-school level.   In contrast to the traditional approach, with its dependence on the written and spoken word, the new pattern would utilize the potential of experimental and investigative activity as a springboard to the acquisition of skills, understanding, and the ability to think.

There are educational authorities who would change the image of vocational education by redubbing it "career education." These authorities claim students are disenchanted with education that does not lead to a meaningful goal.[4]

Enthusiasts for the relevancy of career education say it is not intended as a substitute for vocational education as such, nor is it intended as a substitute for general education or college preparatory education. They hold it to mean all education experiences geared to preparation for economic independence. Career education should permeate the whole public education program, K through 14, and be a part of the curriculum for *all* students. The proponents of career education envision sufficient flexibility to enable the switching of options within a wide range of occupational choices, including the option to go on to college.

Curriculum planners in career education would offer fifteen clusters of occupations, each student having the opportunity to explore three—perhaps in the middle school or junior high school. Specialization in occupational training would be offered in the senior high school and beyond. All students would receive work experiences before graduation or leaving school.

Vocational education curriculum planners propose three models for career education outside the schools. One would be industry or employee based, one home based, and one a special residential facility based model. The latter would offer special intensive programs and services for teen-agers and adults in residential schools and possibly camps.

The goals offered for career education are consistent with those offered for vocational education in general. These goals are:

1. Meeting manpower needs of society.
2. Increasing the options available to each student.
3. Serving as a motivating force to enhance all types of learning.

It is a matter of semantics whether the title of vocational education is changed to career education or whether it retains its well-established identity. What is important is that a large segment of educational planning will be directed toward improving skill levels and productivity that will provide job satisfaction for a wider number of youths and would remove some of the class and status considerations that too long have been associated with the world of work.

Vocational education is on the threshold of its greatest

4 Walter M. Arnold, "Career Education—New Relevancy in Our Schools," *Industrial Arts and Vocational Education* (November 1971), pp. 6–8.

hour.   The schools of the nation are dedicated to the responsibility of providing the best possible education for youth.   The influence that social and economic forces exert on the school must finally be resolved into courses, experiences, and programs.   A technological-minded society has forced vocational education into a clear perspective, and the implications are explicit for both creative and functional planning.   Vocational education planners are faced with the pleasing prospect of infiltrating the school curriculum with their type of education from the early school years to the final stages of adult life.   It is a worthy challenge, and it can be a valuable accomplishment.

TOPICS FOR STUDY AND DISCUSSION

1. Are cities like Cleveland and New York justified in de-emphasizing separate vocational schools?
2. Is vocational education the strongest answer to the dropout problem?
3. Is the continuous education idea a pipedream or is it a definite reality? Reinforce your answer.
4. It is frequently stated that many pupils who should register for vocational courses in the secondary schools do not. Why is this true?
5. What factors are relevant in a decision of whether there is a dichotomy between vocational education and general education?
6. What are the advantages of area vocational schools? What level of work should be offered in area vocational schools?
7. What is the validity of the view of those who contend that vocational schools force an early vocational choice on youth?
8. Assume a community had to make a choice between a vocational school and a junior college. What factors would be relevant in the decision?
9. The U.S. Office of Education has adopted career education as its major thrust. Show how career education either negates or enhances vocational education.
10. Analyze the amendments added in 1968 to the 1963 Vocational Act for their possible benefits to secondary school vocational programs.

SELECTED REFERENCES

DEPIANTA, HAROLD J. "Work Experience: The Necessary Link." *Bulletin of the National Association of Secondary School Principals* (September 1969), pp. 71–79.

This article points to the fact that for many students education is too theoretical and lacks practicality. It suggests a program combining classroom work with on-the-job training. Objectives and procedures are given.

DUGGER, RAY. "The Vocational Act of 1963." *Bulletin of the National Association of Secondary School Principals* (May 1965), pp. 15–23.

The author of this article advises educators that they are faced with the challenge of achieving full benefits from the Vocational Act in order to utilize the best talents of more people for a full and balanced economy. He includes a good survey of the provisions of the act.

EVANS, RUPERT N. *Foundations of Vocational Education.* New York: Charles E. Merrill Publishing Co., 1971.

This is a refreshing modern treatise on vocational education. It suggests an organizational pattern for vocational education and identifies future trends.

KIMBRELL, GRADY, and VINEYARD, BEN S. *Succeeding in the World of Work.* New York: McKnight and McKnight Publishing Co., 1971.

This is a work-study textbook that brings together the essentials every student needs for analyzing job selections. It deals with the meaning of work and appraises student interests, abilities, and aptitudes.

NELSON, HILDING E. "The Vocational Curriculum: Patterns of Experimentation." *Bulletin of the National Association of Secondary School Principals* (November 1969), pp. 108–119.

The author draws extensively on his experience as the director of two national institutes on innovative curricula in vocational-technical education. He identifies patterns of curriculum activity and gives a limited prognosis of each.

ROBERTS, ROY W. *Vocational and Practical Arts Education: History, Development, and Principles.* 2nd ed. New York: Harper & Row, Publishers, 1965.

This book traces the history and development of vocational education and practical arts education. It makes a worthy effort to show that the new concepts in the field are similar and should involve close cooperation.

SOMERS, GERALD G., and LITTLE, KENNETH. *Vocational Education: Today and Tomorrow.* Madison, Wis.: The University of Wisconsin Press, 1971.

This volume deals with the pressing issues confronting vocational education. It analyzes the impact of 1963 Vocational Education Act and the 1968 amendments.

VENN, GRANT. *Man, Education and Manpower.* Washington: American Association of School Administrators, 1970.

This author delineates the role of education in the development of manpower needs in a highly technological society. He suggests specific action that should be taken to support education in the urgent task of meeting comprehensive manpower needs.

WILHELMS, FRED T. "Vocational Education: What Are the Big Questions?" *Bulletin of the National Association of Secondary School Principals* (May 1965), pp. 3–7.

This article is a proposal for a new phase of vocational education to take care of the vocationally inept who have been making vocational education a "dumping ground." The proposal suggests a three-phase program.

WILLIS, BENJAMIN C. "The Changing Story of Vocational Education and What's Needed Now." *Nation's Schools* (February 1963), pp. 57–58.

The superintendent of a large school discusses the importance of vocational education, describing how concepts are changing.

PART III

Issues and Action Outside
the Subject Areas

CHAPTER 15

Extraclass Activities

In the old world, academic scholarship was the sole purpose for a school's existence, but a dualism has developed in American secondary schools. In addition to scholarship activity in the classroom, a whole series of educational activities has developed outside the classroom. Some over-enthusiastic proponents of extraclass activity even claim that this activity program comes closer to supplying basic educational needs than the regular academic program.

The origin of the extraclass activity movement probably could be traced to the first time a school administrator became interested in the games pupils were playing outside the jurisdiction of the school and invited them to bring their activities into the regulated area of the school. Development was rapid, because parents were invited to see their pupils perform and the pupils liked the exaltation of having spectators. Teachers became willing sponsors, because they enjoyed the break from the formality of the regular classroom.

Status was established for extraclass activities when college directors of admission began to consider them important enough to be listed on secondary school transcripts and employers began to use pupil participation in extraclass activities as criteria for evaluating potential job success. Both these developments reflect the current feeling that pupils learn from these activities many things that are important for successful participation in adult life. In particular, they suggest that human relations can be developed better in extraclass activities than in academic classrooms.

In many schools, a pupil's social status depends on the extent and type of his participation in extraclass activities. The students who are in positions of leadership or who participate in prestige clubs have the highest status. In the rapidly developing suburban areas, parents relate their children's social status in school to the social prestige desired by the adult suburbanite. The "blue-collar" parents encourage their children to grasp the reins of leadership as basic training for quite a different role. Extraclass activities furnish the experiences pupils from laboring families need for labor leadership roles.

The various terms used to describe extraclass activities illustrate a changing emphasis on their educational importance. One of the most frequent terms used is "extra curricular." This connotes curricular status, but extra, or beyond the realm of the regular curriculum. "Cocurricular" is also used in many schools. Apparently used to establish equal status for all learning activities, whether inside or outside the classroom, the term suggests a cooperative basis for extended activity beyond the academic classroom. In many situations, curriculum leaders have given regular classroom status to activities that heretofore have been considered outside the curriculum. School bands, choral groups, and orchestras have been scheduled as regular class periods, usually with full academic credit. The school newspaper is the main activity of the secondary school journalism class, and the school annual may be prepared in a regular classroom situation.

The use of the term "extraclass" suggests that everything a pupil does under the sponsorship of the school is an extension of the classroom. This situation may be the result of a desirable improvement in comprehensiveness—a balance of emphasis on all learning activities of the pupil. Thus, athletic contests and band concerts become classroom learning situations, and the Latin club is pragmatic evidence of a good language learning situation.

ISSUES INVOLVED

The expansion or reduction of extraclass activities is one of the issues that continues to trouble secondary school administrators and their faculties. School evaluators stress the importance of these activities and attempt to measure the effectiveness of the school in terms of pupil participation. The various accrediting associations cite schools for unusual ventures into fields of new activities. It would appear there would be no reason for curtailment of extraclass activities, but this is not an accurate deduction.

Overinvolvement and underinvolvement

Both overinvolvement and underinvolvement of pupils are trouble-some problems in regulating extraclass activities.[1] So many activities are available, faculty sponsors may compete among themselves for the time of the capable and popular pupils. These overactive pupils are often also carrying a heavy schedule of academic work. Parents complain of overworked, exhausted, and frequently emotionally disturbed children. Church and civic leaders blame the school for their inability to capture the time of pupils for community work. Many schemes have been used to curtail and regulate pupil participation. The most common one is a simple regulation of the number of activities in which a pupil is permitted to participate each semester. Some people question such regulations. They hold to the oft repeated statement that it is the busy person who really gets things done. They say participation is a matter of individual needs and should be accompanied by intelligent guidance on the part of the school.

It is possible that underinvolvement is a more serious problem than overinvolvement. Most of the dropout studies show that pupils dropping out of school are not participants in extraclass activities. Their school activities are confined to regular classroom work, and continued failure or boredom haunts their lives. It is thought that maladjusted pupils would find success and interest in the less restrictive boundaries of extraclass experiences. Therefore, school administrators have turned to forced participation through graduation requirements. However, forced participation might remove valuable spontaneity from such activities. Probably the most satisfactory answers to pupil involvement will come through intelligent guidance and the development of appealing activities.

From the standpoint of the curriculum, the issue of pupil involvement in extraclass activities may be solved by giving curricular status to many of the activities that have not been considered worthy of regular school time. Rejection of this idea has been a foolish hobgoblin of those who would not temper the sacredness of the so-called solid subjects. A realistic educational objective would be to bring vitality and purpose to all classroom activities and then let these qualities flow over into the extraclass hours. Another aid to greater pupil participation will come through the development of more flexible scheduling, so that the relative values of these activities can be adjusted to their needs.

[1] Glen F. Ovard, *Administration of the Changing Secondary School* (New York: The Macmillan Company, 1966), pp. 298–329.

Meeting the changing needs of society

One of the most critical issues related to extraclass activities concerns the question of whether they can be adjusted to meet the changing needs of society. These changes obviously affect the curriculum. It has been pointed out before that the United States is a highly urbanized, industrial nation with an affluent society pockmarked by racial discord and poverty. Adults in industry are working fewer hours, and unskilled youths are finding work scarce. Persons who wish to take an active part in society's affairs soon learn they cannot be heard unless they join like-minded individuals in voluntary associations.

Although chronological age is consistent, social maturation of youth is occurring earlier than in the past. Former college activities are now part of the high school milieu, and junior high youngsters are having proms and formal dances. A teen-age subculture has developed, exhibiting a wild fascination for fads and offbeat social ventures and alternately worshiping the ridiculous and the serious. It purposely strives to confuse its elders, but it is a force that demands and secures recognition. The commercial entertainment business has been revolutionized to meet its needs: recording of teen-age music has become a multibillion dollar business; motion pictures are slanted to adventure, horror, and sex; and a major television network openly admits that its programs for the new season will be aimed at the twelve-to-sixteen-year-old group. This teen-age culture, operating on the outer limits of the school program, presents a problem for school planners, but a mistake will be made if the school does not adjust its programs to capitalize on the serious longings this group is covering up with its loud flamboyance.

Youth—idealistic, as always—is in search of a cause. It longs to be heard, struggling against the impersonality of the day and seeking to change its own lot and the lot of others. It suffers from boredom thrust on it by financial security and by the fact that it is not needed in the work stream of the social order. Youth necessarily has been shunted out of the mainstream. It is conscious of the lack of important things to do.

Solutions to the problems of youth are complex, and school officials cannot be blamed for groping, but certain ground rules are evident. The overwhelming success of the Peace Corps suggests that youth wants to work at something worthwhile in order to feel necessary and important. The risk of life involved in joining intense racial demonstrations shows a deep-rooted desire to do something for others. Young people constantly struggle to be accepted as partners by adults. Perhaps the aimless frivolity of some of the extraclass activities of the school has caused administrators to underestimate the capacity of youth for serious social decisions. They must reevaluate objectives of extraclass activities considering teen-age cultural propensities.

Realistic evaluation

A third issue in the extraclass field is how to evaluate activities properly. To date, much of the evaluation has been based on opinion rather than controlled research, so many of the claimed benefits are more theoretical than realistic. There is always the possibility of claiming too much on one hand and failing to develop full potentiality on the other. Character-building and leadership development are usually credited to extraclass activities, although this evaluation has not been substantiated. A Texas high school principal, to justify the identification and grouping of football players in physical education classes, says his boys get their start here for professional football contracts. An over-zealous dramatics teacher attempts to dominate the life of a budding female actress to the exclusion of parental advice and guidance. The jazz trumpeter in the stage band is filled with delusions of fame and success by his admiring classmates and the unwise forbearance of his band director.

Another phase of the evaluation problem concerns decisions on the extent of the school's extraclass program. Where does the responsibility of the school end and that of the community begin? Is the school performing functions that can be done better by community agencies? Should the school or an outside agency sponsor recreation? Should the school sponsor dances or merely teach pupils to dance? Is the school attempting to shoulder too much of the responsibility for youth's out-of-school hours? These decisions are especially important if the school's existing program is ineffectual and no other agency has a youth program.

Probably the greatest need for careful analysis of the school's function lies in the area of overstressed athletics and marching bands. In a pedagogical sense, athletics and other performance activities are considered extraclass activities, but the unreasonable emphasis put on these things by some schools raises the question of whether they are educational activities. In those schools they are more of a form of entertainment than of an educational venture. Stressing the importance of having a winning team, excessive firing and hiring of coaches, and overindulgent solicitude toward varsity athletes are all marks of maladjusted educational objectives. School bands are used at athletic contests to provide additional entertainment.   In a struggle for a share of the gate receipts, an argument sometimes arises over whether the football team or the band has more entertainment value at the game.   Certain communities think so much of the "chamber of commerce value" of the high school band that they raise thousands of dollars to send it across the nation to participate in spectacular parades.

Some educators accept this overemphasis by rationalizing that the activities are good public relations and that the pupils gain educational travel experience.   This is certainly a distorted viewpoint, and it is hard to believe that any serious-minded school leader, who sees extraclass activities as the purposeful extension of regular classroom work, can accept it as a valid educational evaluation. In several states, secondary school principals have banded to form voluntary associations for the purpose of bringing all extraclass activities under centralized control.   Accrediting associations also have given these activities added attention.   Surveys consistently show that thoughtful patrons are more interested in the basic educational purposes of the school than in public performance display of its pupils.   Could it be that where excessive overemphasis exists, school administrators are being misguided by outspoken minorities?

BASIC AREAS OF ACTIVITIES

Whether activities are made a regular part of the curriculum or whether they remain in the extraclass category, they are usually classified as clubs, student councils, publications, dramatics, athletics, and assemblies.   There are two general types of clubs: those closely allied to the classroom, such as the Future Homemakers' Club (a requirement in the vocational home economics program), and the hobby-type club somewhat removed from the mainstream of classroom work, such as the camera club or the ham radio club. Theoretically, the best purposes of education are served when the club is an extension of classroom learning.

The success of all club work is dependent on the enthusiasm of the pupils and the devotion of the faculty sponsors.   The two types of clubs—associated classroom and special interest—call for different types of sponsors and appeal to different types of pupils. In the associated classroom type of club, the sponsor has inherent capability due to his knowledge of the subject-matter field and his interest in enriching his classroom learning.   A number of an accrediting team expressed amazement at the extensive activity of one school's Latin club.   From a school population of around a thousand pupils, the Latin club enrolled over two hundred and fifty.   The club met during the noon hour and membership was entirely voluntary. The secret of the club's success could be found in the outstanding ability of the Latin teacher, whose pupils were excited about Latin activities both within and without the classroom. It was difficult to discover where one began and the other ended.

The special interest, or hobby, clubs appeal to pupils who desire a less formalized activity. These clubs are usually developed from the expressed interest of pupils who persuade some faculty member of like interests to sponsor them. It has been said that a successful camera club takes a real "photography nut" for a sponsor. It must also be added that it takes pupils who are keenly interested in photography. Sometimes financial ability to buy equipment and supplies determines the pupil's participation, but it is usually more a matter of interest.

Needless to say, the securing of capable and interested sponsors is a major administrative responsibility. With the coming of negotiated contracts, teachers are demanding compensation for all duties beyond regular classroom instruction. While there is no doubt as to the justification of teachers seeking extra pay for excessive demands made on their time in sponsoring extraclass activities, such as clubs, it does tend to remove part of the spontaneity of an informal relationship, and in cases of restricted school finances it will probably reduce the number of clubs a school can support.

From a curricular viewpoint, school clubs should fulfill two objectives. First, they should integrate the educational purposes of the school. Second, they should provide wholesome enjoyment for pupils. Criteria for evaluating club activities and sympathetic stimulation of pupil participation should be administrative objectives.

STUDENT COUNCILS

The student council represents one of the best agencies in the school for putting into practice all the objectives for democratic citizenship. In the opinion of many evaluators, a good student council is one of the best identifications of a good school. It is difficult to understand why any school principal would fail to recognize this, yet in some schools, the principal is either lethargic in his backing of the council or downright hostile to its existence, claiming that pupils have no right to interfere in the administration of the school. This must be the mark of administrative insecurity or an autocratically directed school.

In the early days of student participation in administrative affairs of the school, the term "student government" was used. Unfortunately, pupils were directly involved in such things as the discipline of their classmates. Elaborate systems of student courts were established, and penalties and fines were levied. This type of pupil participation was doomed from the start. Pupils should share in the administration of the school, but they should not run the school. Leaders in the student council movement have worked hard to establish the principle of separation of powers between the pupils and the administration. There ought to be mutual understanding and rapport between the council and the principal, and each should know where authority begins and ends.

The function of a student council is to determine the wishes and desires of the student body and make them known to the administration and faculty.[2] This group of elected leaders coordinates extraclass activities, school improvement, and school morale. The council should have extensive authority in determining the operation of pupil affairs that are outside the classroom but within the jurisdiction of the school—the part of school life that closely resembles community responsibility in the adult neighborhood. Through the student council, pupils can gain realistic experiences in procedures of democratic government.

The constitution of the student council should clearly define its powers and responsibilities. Many pupil activities can be given over completely to the council, others can be shared with the faculty, and still others should be out of the council's jurisdiction. The faculty and administration can take pride in the extent to which pupils can carry responsibility for their own growth and development. But they must be prepared to help pupils right themselves if they stumble and fall.

The organization and extent of student council activities will vary from school to school. In one school, council members, selected by their peers in a student council conducted election, are assigned to council activities as part of their regular class schedule. The sponsor of the council attends daily council meetings as one of his teaching assignments. The following listing presents the activities of the council committees in one given year:

1. Assembly Committee
    a. Plans weekly assemblies
    b. Contacts teachers and groups concerning their assembly duties
    c. Schedules assemblies, provides for preliminary part of assembly (announcements and introductions)

[2] Arthur Kent, "And Finally—A Definition of Student Council," *School Activities* (May 1966), p. 11.

    d. Determines student seating arrangements

    e. Evaluates assembly programs and student reaction

2. General Welfare Committee

    a. Handles traffic regulations and car registrations

    b. Handles lost and found department

    c. Determines ways and means to command respect for school and personal property

    d. Requests meeting with faculty guidance committee in cases involving student welfare

3. Social Committee

    a. Maintains a school social calendar

    b. Takes care of school bulletin board

    c. Arranges for special school decorations

    d. Acts as clearing house for all social activities

    e. Arranges for chaperones

    f. Keeps scrapbook of all student activities

Note: Special committees to carry on special functions are appointed as the need arises.

Recent critics of student councils warn of the pitfalls such organizations may encounter.[3] They contend that a homogeneous membership, weak student leadership, and the wrong advisor, all can culminate in a meaningless program. Membership should reflect all segments of the social order of the school, else the council will be composed of a homogeneous group of the "right" students. Rejection of such a group on the part of many students renders the council impotent. Good leadership is essential but difficult to secure. Unfortunately, leadership characteristics that have been in vogue in the past are detrimental in the present-day student milieu. For example, a good way for a student council leader to become ineffective is to appear too supportive of the school administration. Finally, the right sponsor is vital to the success of a council. He certainly should not be an inexperienced teacher, nor the old war horse type. Neither should he be one who tries to direct too much. Obviously, he must be able to communicate and be accepted by today's youth.

The success of a student council is largely dependent on the principal and his faculty. A sympathetic, friendly, and cooperative faculty can give a council so much help and support that success of almost any council venture will be assured. An apathetic, unconcerned faculty, too busy to extend time or effort in support of

[3] Allan A. Glatthorn, *The Principal and the Student Council* (Washington, D.C.: The National Association of Secondary School Principals, 1968), pp. 1–47.

council projects, can render the organization ineffective in short order.   Much of the responsibility for faculty attitude toward the student council rests with the principal.   It is his task to interpret the pupil's objectives to the teachers, and the teachers' wishes to the pupils.   He can help afford the council the prestige it rightly deserves.

SCHOOL ASSEMBLIES

In schools where student councils are responsible for arranging school assemblies, the assemblies are considered part of the extraclass activity program.   This attitude involves a partial abandonment of the formalized atmosphere of chapel exercises involving religious and character-building objectives.   Emphasis is shifted from faculty responsibility to pupil responsibility so that the assembly becomes an outlet for pupils' talent for entertaining rather than a platform for teaching "moral lessons."

This change of emphasis does not mean abandonment of faculty responsibility.   It means the development of cooperation between pupils and faculty with the pupils accepting more responsibility for direction and planning.   The faculty must still make sure that school assemblies are worthwhile and that they fulfill established objectives.   In a publication of the National Association of Secondary School Principals entitled *The Student Assembly*, the following objective for school assemblies are found:

1. Build school spirit.
2. Help pupils develop poise and stage presence.
3. Furnish training opportunities for leadership development.
4. Provide inspirational experiences for pupils.
5. Serve as a forum for educational information.
6. Furnish purposeful and tasteful entertainment.
7. Help improve the cultural experiences of pupils.
8. Develop better listening habits.
9. Serve as an extension of good classroom activities.
10. Promote better school and public relations.

The foregoing publication also lists a number of guiding principles to be followed in planning school assemblies.   Included in the listings are the following:

1. Adequate faculty supervision is essential.
2. Programs must be run as has been suggested, according to the principles which the administration has established as school policy.
3. General student participation should be encouraged.

4. Inspiration, information, and entertainment must be presented in a balanced "diet."
5. If the student council is made responsible for school assemblies, it must realize the importance of delegating the responsibility for programs.
6. It is important to utilize school and community resources— human and material.
7. There must be long-range planning.

INTERSCHOLASTIC ATHLETICS

As has been mentioned earlier, it is debatable whether interscholastic athletics are any longer an extraclass activity for they are over-emphasized and out of harmony with good educational objectives. However, in the minds of thoughtful educators, athletics in proper perspective should and must remain a truly extraclass activity. Because of the potential for controversy and the magnitude of the problems involved, athletic programs must be directed by those who are willing to make judgments based on sound principles. The extensiveness of an athletic program, including interscholastic athletics, may make the delegation of authority a necessity, but the responsibility for its relation to the total educational program must remain under central administrative control.

Efforts at regulation have probably been greater in athletics than in any other school activity. Objectives and standards have been established, debated, and reestablished. School officials, athletic officials, accrediting associations, special committees, and even governmental agencies have been active in establishing regulatory principles for conducting athletic contests. Probably statewide activities commissions, organized and operated by secondary-school principals, have been the most progressive and most effective agencies operating in this area. Over half the states have established such commissions, which regulate the entire range of extraclass activities involving interscholastic competition. (A complete discussion of these organizations is presented later in the chapter.)

Enthusiastic advocates of interscholastic athletics claim it is one of the best sources for realization of educational objectives because of the intense interest involved and the highly emotional situations that develop. This claim is based, of course, on the supposition that the program is well-organized and well-conducted. If it is not, the potential for adverse outcomes is equally great. Athletic programs in which pupils are exploited to entertain the public, advertise and earn money for the school, or enhance the professional reputation of the coach have no place in educational institutions and should not be tolerated.

There are sensible and reasonable ground rules that can be set up for an athletic program. In the first place, all activities should be conducted as an integral part of the total educational program. Athletics, including interscholastic games, should supplement rather than substitute for a good physical education program. Equal time should be given to each game when planning intramural athletic contests or providing experiences in games such as tennis, golf, bowling, and archery. Administrative control of interscholastic athletics must remain with the central administrator of the school. The physical welfare and safety of participants must be a primary objective; permitting injured or poorly equipped players to take part in games is intolerable. Finally, if good sportsmanship and good citizenship are to be outcomes, rules and regulations of officials and regulatory bodies must meet with cheerful and cooperative compliance.

Some of the most troublesome problems in the area of athletics have arisen in the junior high schools, where athletic programs have tended to become junior replicas of the high school. The same excesses have entered junior high interscholastic athletics, and damage due to the immaturity of the participants is inestimable. The issue is whether junior high pupils should be taking part in interscholastic games. Physical education authorities suggest a limited program adapted to the capacities and needs of junior high school boys. Certainly the physical and emotional immaturity of junior high youngsters should be a determining factor in program establishment. Basic objectives of the junior high school are not tolerant of overadulation of varsity athletes and the "hoopla" of championship games.

In most states, the participation of girls in interscholastic athletics is either limited or banned altogether by athletic conferences or state associations. A survey of the field will reveal a gradual diminishing of female membership on teams engaged in interscholastic competition. Intramural games and playdays appear to be adequate substitutes. In view of the continual growth of female competencies in the so-called "man's world," an inverse argument might be made for the curtailment or elimination of male interscholastic competition. This, of course, is highly unlikely.

STUDENT PUBLICATIONS

Student publications—the newspaper, the yearbook, and the literary magazine—are one of the best examples of activities that should not be classified as extraclass. Formal publications of the pupils have been made part of the curriculum in many comprehensive schools, and in no sense of the word should they be considered "extra," or outside the regular classroom schedule. When the publications are organized and prepared according to good educational procedures, they fulfill two objectives: they are the vehicles for making practical application of writing skills, and they afford opportunities for vocational exploration that might lead to careers in professional journalism.

The school newspaper can add or detract from the image of the school, depending on whether it publishes lively news or adolescent social trivia, or on whether it is a true representation of pupil life or a censored product of the faculty sponsor. Surveys of school newspapers show that as high as 80 percent of the news consists of such nonsensical information as what junior girl is dating what senior boy, and who is carrying a secret torch for the football captain of the school. A good school newspaper should have the same credentials as a regular newspaper. It should report the newsworthy activities of the school accurately, and should reflect the serious thinking of the student body. It should be the voice of leadership for its youthful clientele. The just fate of an unworthy publication is to have its readers lose faith in its purpose or become bored with its stale ideas. Teen-age culture is filled with exciting and intriguing experiences as well as stubborn and baffling problems. The school newspaper should mirror this unsettled growth period.

Some schools publish worthwhile yearbooks. In other schools, however, publishing activities are worthless as educational ventures, because they involve too much deleterious assistance from professional publishers and photographers. Frequently, a school selects a publisher for the yearbook on the basis of how much professional help its agent will render the school. Unfortunately, this help often takes the form of unimaginative advice aimed at rendering greater profit to the publishing house. A high degree of tolerance is given to stereotyped material such as the last will and testament and the senior prophecy, and early submission of such material is awarded a discount, since it helps the commercial publisher maintain a balanced work load. The commercial photographer also has a profit motive. If a large number of group shots are included, he guarantees a certain number of dull informals. Of course, the real profit comes from the sale of individual photographs to the seniors. The school's reward is a photographic cut for the yearbook.

The publication of the yearbook needs careful reevaluation on the part of the extraclass planners. The excessive costs of publication, the sterility of educational content, and the lack of opportunities for practical experiences for pupils, raise the issue of whether the yearbook actually has educational value. To restore vitality to this publication, pupils must be made responsible for arrangement of content and imaginative authorship and photography.

A limited number of schools support a literary magazine. Some of them are exceptionally good, while others suffer from lack of emphasis on the real purpose of such a publication: to provide encouragement for creative writing. Submission of material should not be confined to members of English classes or to seniors. Creativity is the possession of every pupil. The freshman science pupil as well as the embryonic sportswriter in the sophomore class may come up with youthful literary gems.

SPEECH AND DRAMATIC ACTIVITIES

Valuable dramatic and forensic experiences are gained in the formalized atmosphere of the classroom. Good teachers use these activities to bring variety and enrichment to their classroom learning situation. A certain amount of dramatic flair is inherent in children. The alert teacher, capitalizing on their natural tendency to imitate, to exaggerate, and to dramatize, provides them with opportunities for self-expression, development of imagination, and acquisition of self-confidence. The extension of these opportunities form the extraclass activities of dramatics and speech.

School plays, dramatic club offerings, and interscholastic speech contests form the central core of dramatic and speech extraclass activities. The school play is a familiar landmark in American education. Its values are relative and depend on the educational objectives involved. Some schools have a reputation for the highly dramatic effectiveness of their plays. This means a finished product is a basic objective, requiring the asssignment of leading roles to experienced pupils with proven dramatic ability. Educational values are associated with a high degree of specialization. In other schools, dramatic excellence is sacrificed by casting eager, inexperienced, and less capable pupils. Objective here is to afford these experiences to as many pupils as possible.

A well-balanced dramatic program should meet both objectives cited above. Pupils of unusual and superior talents should be given every opportunity to further their growth. At the same time, all other pupils who want to act should not be denied the opportunity. The school should support dramatic clubs of differing purposes and should join the National Thespian Society, a dramatic honorary association for worthy pupils, whose membership encompasses anyone engaged in dramatic effort—actors, stage hands, electricians, directors, etc.

Forensic activities have reached a low ebb in some schools. This is regrettable, because lasting values can be gained from organizing thoughts and effectively communicating them. Many people in industry and public life can trace their success to the ability to communicate orally. Concomitant values assigned to public speaking experiences include the development of research attitudes, the ability to organize and retain knowledge, and the ability to develop critical thinking. Authorities in the speech field are hopeful of a resurgence of scholastic speaking activities. Planners of extraclass activities should consider this area carefully.

SUPERVISION AND CONTROL

The direct control of extraclass activities operating within the school is the responsibility of the principal and faculty. Part of the responsibility is delegated and shared with the pupils. In order to solve the problems which occur when extraclass activities move off campus, school administrators have formed regulatory bodies. The earliest of these were state athletic associations for the purpose of regulating interscholastic athletic competition. Thirty-four of the states have already supplanted these single purpose groups with more inclusive groups for the purpose of regulating all extraclass activities. These organizations are generally known as activities commissions or associations.

The need for more extensive regulation of off-campus extraclass activities partially resulted from the stepped-up activities of high school bands. It is not uncommon for schools to engage in local, district, and state contests to determine the superiority of these musical organizations. They are used extensively for giving pupils "educational trips" and providing "publicity" for local communities. Not only have high school bands been sent from coast to coast, but in several instances they have been involved in foreign junkets. School authorities, sensing the development of problems beyond the control of local power, turned to voluntary state regulating procedures.[4] It appeared logical to include the whole gamut of extraclass activities in the scope of these newly organized activities commissions, although there was no urgent need for regulating many of the less troublesome activities.

The advocates of state voluntary regulating bodies point to the need for united action in any field of endeavor. They contend that the individual school administrator is powerless to with-

[4] James F. Clark, "Legal Status and Jurisdiction of State Associations," *School Activities* (November 1965), pp. 5–10.

stand local pressures and local snap judgments unless group support is given.   Group action is a prerequisite to efficiency and such action is possible only when members of the group are loyal to its ideals and recognize the value of organization.   Policies and regulations must be formulated to ensure a degree of equality in competition and to prevent excesses that might be forced on one school to the detriment of all other schools in the group.

Other forms of off-campus regulation of extraclass activities are furnished by professional organizations and accrediting associations.   The National Association of Secondary School Principals publishes an annual list of approved contests and activities.   The North Central Accrediting Association sanctions this list for its member schools as well as approving the regulations of the various state organizations.   It must be emphasized that all organizations operate on a voluntary basis and in no way attempt to absorb or abridge the legal authority of local or state boards of education. They are simply a means of implementing the authority and responsibility delegated to the local school administration.   In a larger sense they are the means for providing more abundant and wholesome extraclass experiences for boys and girls.

IDENTIFICATION OF VALUES

Assuming the student quest for "relevance" is not met in the classroom, there could be experiences in extraclass activities, resulting from student participation in decision making, that could stabilize his total school experience.   The demarkation between class and extraclass activities is fading in many of the modularly scheduled, independent learning, mini coursed secondary schools, but there still are opportunities for students to promote a number of educational activities that are officially sanctioned and relevant to their needs.   In order to assure relevancy in extraclass activities, care should be exercised to see that they do not become static from year to year.   In a relevant situation activities are born, flourish, and die each year—responsive, as they should be, to student needs at the time.   The future development of extraclass activity will depend on how well school authorities identify and implement the values inherent in these activities.   Basically, they are one of the best potentials for establishing good pupil-teacher relationships. In the informal atmosphere that is characteristic of these activities, a mutual friendship and respect can be developed that enables the teacher to understand the pupil and the pupil to recognize the teacher as an ally or friend.   This rapport can lead to better overall school morale.   Opportunities for better guidance are abundant for a mutual feeling of trust can enable the teacher to gain the pupil's confidence and learn his problems.

Extraclass meetings foster the freedom and informality that is characteristic of adult group meetings. The experience of speaking as a member of the group, the development of leadership roles, and the spontaneous contributions made in an extemporaneous matter prepare the student for similar activities in the adult order.

Extraclass activities provide a vehicle for securing a broad look at possible vocations. Many pupils develop interests in these areas that lead to the pursuit of a future occupation.

Extraclass activity is probably most valuable as a supplement to regular classroom work. The wise teacher uses it to enrich classwork and motivate the pupils to creatively explore vistas beyond the scope of prescribed classroom hours. The total school program can be enhanced by this extension of the classroom learning situation.

Finally, a major health need can be met in the extraclass area. Mental health leading to a general physical well-being can be developed by broad and varied opportunities for pupils to participate in stimulating and challenging activities beyond the scope of the classroom. This can lead to a much improved use of leisure time by both youths and adults.

TOPICS FOR STUDY AND DISCUSSION

1. What criteria should be used regulating participation of pupils in extraclass activities?

2. How may an extraclass activity be evaluated in terms of its contribution to desirable educational objectives for secondary schools?

3. If the personal social development of the pupil is a major objective in extraclass activity, what type of organizations will best meet this objective?

4. Should the right to participate in extraclass activities be based on minimum grade point averages or would desirable objectives be achieved through other qualifications?

5. There is considerable evidence in research that school administrators are frequently disenchanted with the so-called activity period in the daily schedule. Analyze the problems involved.

6. There appear to be two desirable conditions for a good extraclass program. The program must be built on the expressed interests of the pupils, and the faculty must be capable of spon-

soring activities. What course of action should be followed if one or both of these conditions is lacking?

7. There is a tendency in some schools to curricularize most of the so-called extra curricular activities. Evaluate the pros and cons of such a movement.

8. Some critics contend that varsity athletics have lost most of the desirable characteristics of a purposeful extraclass activity. Propose reasons for such a viewpoint.

9. What safeguards should be placed on the management of funds collected and dispensed in extraclass activities?

10. A secondary school authority in a recent talk said, "In a completely flexible school, there are no *extraclass* activities. Individualized scheduling allows pupils to meet as a part of the school day for photography, basketball, stamp collecting, chess, or to participate either as a listener or producer of special assembly programs." What do you think?

11. Assess the value of extraclass activities in the quest of youth for viable alternatives.

SELECTED REFERENCES

BOLMEIER, E. C. "Legal Aspects of the Curriculum and the Extracurriculum." *Bulletin of the National Association of Secondary School Principals* (March 1965), pp. 128–142.

A good summary of court decisions involving legal aspects of school activities outside the classroom is included. The article proposes all extra-curricular activities be curricularized, contending that all school activities are educational and should be for all pupils.

FORSYTHE, CHARLES E. *Administration of High School Athletics.* Englewood Cliffs, N.J.: Prentice-Hall, Inc., 1962, pp. 246–255, 387–425.

The pages referred to suggest that the proper administration of athletics should be consistent with the administration of the total school program and discuss the many facets of athletic administration and athletic control.

FREDERICK, ROBERT W. *Student Activities in American Education.* New York: Center for Applied Research in Education, 1965.

This book updates much of the information in the field. It presents some interesting findings concerning the types of activities that are most important to the pupils.

GOLDBERG, ENID A. *How to Run a School Newspaper.* Philadelphia: J. B. Lippincott Company, 1970.

The many phases of operating a good school newspaper

are discussed. Emphasis is put on proper journalistic procedures, selection of student staff, sound financial procedures, and types of relevant news. The delicate problem of administrative censorship is discussed.

HELLEN, MELVIN P. "School Activities Need an Open Door Policy." *Clearing House* (September 1965), pp. 42–43.

This article contends that many schools are making pupils who might benefit the most ineligible to participate in extracurricular activities.

HOLLAND, ALLYNE S., and HOLLAND, ROBERT G. *The Student Journalist and the Literary Magazine.* New York: Rosen Richards Associates, 1970.

This book fills a void in the area of good procedures for the literary magazine. This phase of student journalism has much to offer for the development of good unity. The whole field of student journalism is evaluated and objectives and outcomes are proposed.

KARLIN, MURIEL S., and BERGER, REGINA. *The Effective Student Activities Program.* West Nyack, N.Y.: The Parker Publishing Co., 1971.

This book analyzes the strengths and weaknesses of an effective student activities program. It establishes objectives for administration, faculty, and students. It offers many good suggesions for working with youth in an extraclass setting.

KLEINERT, JOHN E. "Effects of High School Size on Student Activity Participation." *Bulletin of the National Secondary School Principals Association* (March 1969), pp. 34–46.

As indicated in the title of this article, it relates to the effects of school size on student activity participation. As school size increases, the ratio of students taking part in extraclass activity decreases. Many helpful suggestions are made for overcoming this dilemma.

LANE-PALAGYI, ADDPE. *Successful School Assembly Programs.* West Nyack, N.Y.: The Parker Publishing Co., 1971.

Effective assembly programs are a needed factor in a good student activity program. This book offers a great deal of help for the harassed secondary school administrators. The changing values of assembly programs are assessed and suggestions made for effective procedures.

SAXE, RICHARD W. "Manifest and Latent Functions in Educational Activities." *Bulletin of the National Secondary School Principals Association* (January 1970), pp. 41–50.

This article identifies certain sociological concepts that affect educational activities. It presents the principal's rationale as to how the fortunes of the football team relate to the general morale of the school.

CHAPTER 16

Adult Education

In its broadest sense, adult education includes all educational activities beyond the teen-age years, including college. Discussion here, however, will be centered on the continuing education of the large segment of the population that does not secure a college education. It is true that extensive programs of adult education are found on college campuses and college graduates participate in adult education activities in the community, but this participation is somewhat removed from the continuing education program of the public schools.

THE NEED FOR CONTINUOUS EDUCATION

The need for continuous education is closely allied with employment problems. Technological developments have greatly reduced the number of jobs available to people with limited marketable skills and have made it necessary to retrain people for new jobs.

Other problems are perhaps as important as those of employment. Today, citizens must have the ability to make complex decisions; yet eleven million adults are functional illiterates, and too many voters base their decisions on scanty information, prejudiced opinions, and hope for personal favors. Lack of social skills results in tension between peoples of different race, color and religion. Mounting divorce and crime rates emphasize the problems of unsatisfactory social adjustment. Extended life expectancy

272

and the declining number of necessary work hours greatly extend the amount of leisure time available, but too often the new leisure is more frustrating than rewarding.

The potential enrollment for adult education far exceeds the enrollment possibilities of either elementary or secondary education. This makes it one of the most significant educational movements on the American scene.

DEVELOPMENT OF ADULT EDUCATION

Adult education has developed through a variety of patterns and organizations. In the early stages it was entirely vocational education through trade schools. An extensive network of public and private correspondence schools developed later, and colleges and universities began to include a variety of extension courses. World War II marked the entrance of the military into the adult education field in a formal and well-organized fashion. Today, part of the military budget is still devoted to the continuous education of service personnel.

Community colleges and vocational schools are the latest developments on statewide scales. Oregon, among other states, offers financial assistance to communities willing to develop schools for continuing education. In Florida, a series of junior colleges have been well established. In addition to the basic two years of college, they provide extensive vocational and technical programs which are terminal. Plans are well under way for a program of continuous education from kindergarten through graduate school at one location.

A series of events have marked the development of the national structure of adult education. The Smith-Hughes Act of 1917 furnished federal funds for extensive vocational agriculture programs—evening classes or other continuing education activities —for adult farmers. Adjustments and extensions of these programs were made by the George-Dean Act of 1936 and the George-Barden Act of 1946.

Latest impetus to the vocational aspects of adult education was furnished by the Vocational Education Act of 1963, which developed out of the growing awareness that vocational education is a tool for the social and economic improvement of underprivileged people. The scope of this act was greatly enlarged by amendments added in 1968.

The first professional recognition of the status of adult education came in 1924, when the National Education Association established the Department of Adult Education. The formation of the Association for Adult Education and the National Home State Council followed in 1926.

The federal government entered the adult education field in a formal way in 1933, when it developed the Federal Emergency Program to provide training for victims of the Great Depression. This involved such programs as the Civilian Conservation Corps, which trained young adults for forest conservation activities. Another federal government activity was the creation of the Armed Forces Institute in 1942. Since its conception, this program has provided for the continued education of thousands of young men and and women in the armed forces. Today, part of the military budget is still devoted to the continuous education of service personnel.

The Adult Education Association, formed in 1951, has conceived many of the national programs and plans for adult education. The Fund for Adult Education, which plans and supervises programs, was established the same year. Thus it may be seen that adult education has had much more federal backing than any other form of education. However, good programs of adult education must be state and locally oriented.

In spite of the fact that most of the traceable development of adult education is largely within the framework of educational institutions, curriculum planners must be aware of the fact that a number of adult education programs are outside this framework. They may be sponsored by museums, libraries, industrial organizations, labor unions, professional societies, military establishments, hospitals, religious organizations, trade associations, state and local governments, prisons, and a host of political, charitable, social, civic, ethnic, and other community organizations.

PUBLIC SCHOOL INVOLVEMENT

The structure for adult learning is formed in the elementary and secondary schools, and the basic and preparatory training of the regular school program must be articulated to the continuing needs of adult learners. Part of the secondary school curriculum is geared to adult education in the formal school period, and adults may continue to take courses in the post-school years. This is true particularly of the subjects with vocational training aspects, such as vocational agriculture, vocational home economics, and distributive education. Formal classes are conducted within the school, and regular school personnel engage in follow-up activity in the homes, on the farms, and in the communities. Late afternoon and evening classes, allied but not directly associated with the regular school program, are part of the curriculum of many comprehensive secondary schools. Their counterpart may be found in the regular schedule of vocational and technical schools.

Available research indicates that public schools are the major agency for promoting adult education, and the evening school is the main organizational pattern. Evening school enrollments have steadily increased since 1955, and there has been a gradual increase of academic subjects and a decline in vocational subjects. There is little uniformity of curriculum structure, since the needs of students vary greatly.

Little progress has been made in preparing teachers for adult education. The usual procedure is to recruit from the regular day school program. Often, however, these teachers do not adapt themselves well to evening school teaching, even though it offers greater financial remuneration.

ADULT EDUCATION OBJECTIVES

The local curriculum planner must make decisions on vocational stress, terminal emphasis, academic continuation, or preparation for leisure-time pursuits, since immediate objectives for these programs will vary from community to community.

There are, however, at least three broad general objectives that ought to underlie all programs of adult education. The first is enrichment of community living and improvement of the social order. Many adult education activities are in themselves community enrichment. This is particularly true of certain social and cultural ventures such as the creation of art galleries, the development of symphony orchestras, and the organization of various cultural study groups. If adult education is to be community centered and financially supported, this objective is realistic.

A second objective that ought to be inherent in well-planned adult education programs is the fostering of respect for human dignity and personality. This objective involves an all-out effort to reduce race tensions and criminal activities and to improve community living conditions everywhere.

A third objective concerns the improvement of the citizen's ability to make the intelligent decisions required by the complexities of modern society. This objective is vital in a democratic society.

These objectives, natural extensions of secondary school objectives, attain fruition in adult education. Their refinement, improvement, and application are part of the opportunities of adult education.

BASIC ASSUMPTIONS FOR
CURRICULUM PLANNING

Curriculum planners for adult education can make certain basic assumptions with a reasonable degree of assurance.[1] Research and experience will be needed, of course, to substantiate these assumptions. It can be assumed that adults, like children, can learn, depending on individual ability and experience. The cliché "too old to learn" will not withstand psychological evidence. Learning ability does not change, except in case of brain damage or related physical deterioration. In fact, learning among adults can be enriched by their broad experience and great dedication of purpose. Some of the most productive years can come late in life. Adults, then, can profit from continued education, and the complexities of modern society and technological development make it necessary for every citizen to update his knowledge constantly.

It can also be assumed that adult education is here to stay and that the local community is the focal point for planning and implementation. It is unfortunate if curriculum planners do not articulate adult education with all related divisions of learning.

The final assumption is a word of caution: a minimum of organization is desirable. Adults want purposeful action; organizational intricacies cause them to lose their patience and interest. The longer adults have been away from the formal structure of the average public school, the more they want structure to fit their pattern of living.

INSTRUCTIONAL ACTION POINTERS

In the operation of adult education programs certain action pointers should be observed. Whether the program is sponsored and operated by a school system or by another community agency, community participation is greatly enhanced by voluntary leadership and association with governmental agencies. In the case of a school-sponsored program, voluntary involvement would be in the area of advisory councils and student leadership activities.

Teachers for evening programs must have patience, skill, and understanding, and they must plan their instruction carefully.

[1] Amiel T. Sharon, "Adult Academic Achievement in Relation to Formal Education and Age," *Adult Education Journal* (Summer 1971), pp. 231–237.

Since attendance is not compulsory, students drop out of programs quickly if they do not like the teaching procedures. They resent being "talked down to" as much as they dislike vocabularies which are over their heads. Techniques that will work in other classroom programs are often unsuccessful with adult students.[2] Extensive lecturing, for example, may result in a decline of interest. The program must offer them freedom of choice and freedom in learning development. Above all, its values must be apparent and practical. Student involvement in problem solving is one of the soundest teaching procedures. This means the teacher consults with the student to help identify problems, helps gather data for solutions, furnishes the technical advice needed for the formation of hypotheses, and gives the student ample latitude to reach successful solutions. To a certain degree, the whole realm of adult education should be geared to upgrading intelligent decision-making ability. Decisions in the voting booth, the market place, the public forum, and the family circle require greater acumen than ever before. Good citizenship requires ready ability to analyze an issue, study the facts involved, and come to a clear, valid, and unbiased conclusion. Too frequently the average adult is unaware of the necessity or even the desirability of making a decision.

Adult education programs should help mature people do the intelligent thinking so necessary for solving the ever-increasing political, economic, and social problems. Here again, actual experience is important. Descriptions of the processes and techniques of decision making must be supplemented by realistic experiences.

Any plan of action for adult learning activities should include a word of caution concerning the disturbance of deep-lying prejudices. A frontal attack here can be fatal. This is where the best techniques of nondirective teaching must be used. The teacher must skirt the edges of these prejudices to help the student extend his horizon beyond their petty confines. This calls for problem solving of the highest order.

It is very important in adult education to avoid any aura of remedial learning. The concept of a "second chance" education is not desirable. The pride of an adult learner can be hurt if he feels he is compensating for deficiencies of earlier experiences. Learning can be adjusted to the learner's level, however elementary, but the learning activities should be developmental rather than remedial.

It is not feasible to analyze the dropout problem here, but it is important to raise the question of whether the term "dropout"

[2] Robert H. Schacht, "When Programs Fail, Find Out Why," *Adult Leadership* (September 1971), pp. 91–92.

is accurate or deserves the stigma frequently attached to it. Basically, for one reason or another, potential dropouts are maladjusted and disenchanted with their present school.   If adult education programs are properly developed in association with the public schools, the dropout will merely become a transfer.   The main change in his status will be from a youth to an adult.   His educational program may be different, but it will be continuing.

TRENDS IN THE FIELD

For curriculum planners to solve the numerous problems of adult education, the public must recognize its intrinsic values, and educators must establish coordinated curriculum patterns.   The stumbling blocks are diversity of authority and diversity of opinion concerning the field's rationale.   While vocational education is important, it should not continue to dominate program planning. Adult education is well beyond the narrow confines of vocational training.   It also exceeds the limited academic outline formerly adhered to.

The general ability level of adult students will continue to rise, and the facilities provided for their use will expand gradually.[3] Differentiation of curriculum and instruction will occur as the body of knowledge about adult needs and abilities increases. Concurrent with these developments will come a clarification of the unique role of adult education.

The trend of learning emphasis in the regular school program will soon affect adult education.   As teachers shift their purpose from the transmission of knowledge to the development of capacity to learn, the curriculum will shift from a subject-mastery organization to a learning-skills organization.   Teachers will become persons who help pupils to inquire.   With this changed concept of education, adult education truly will be continuing education.   Everyone will continue to seek new information throughout his lifetime.

One of the chief factors in adult education curriculum determination is the point of dissemination.   Both public and private agencies are engaged in the development of formal programs. Most of the private agencies are reputable, but the profit motive tends to influence their objectives.   Public education is in the best

[3] King M. Wientge and Philip DuBois, *Factors Associated with the Achievement of Adult Students* (St. Louis: Washington University, 1966), pp. 34–38.

position to establish an educational continuum.   Financial support for the entire structure of education will be increased by the involvement of the adult population, and a closer liaison will be established between the secondary school curriculum and the adult education curriculum.   It is difficult to envision the "needs" and "wants" of the total post-secondary school population, ranging as it does from out-of-school youth interested in pragmatic affairs, such as job improvement, personality improvement, and home building, to the "golden agers" to whom cultural and purposeful leisure activities are paramount.

There is evidence that emphasis in all social planning is shifting from the technological aspects to the humanistic aspects. This does not mean a slowdown in technological progress, but rather a stepping up of efforts to help people adjust to the problems of a technological order.   This involves continuous adult education for all social groups.

The trend toward the practical and functional will continue. Objectives must include the improvement of public life as well as the improvement of private life through better trained public leaders in business and governmental affairs.

Adult education leaders must put renewed emphasis on the use of voluntary coordinating groups such as central labor councils, educational federations, ministerial alliances, social welfare agencies, federated men's and women's clubs, trade associations, and other civil agencies supporting programs of adult education.   They must also work increasingly with officials of government and leaders of political parties to stimulate the use of educational processes in the performance of legislative, administrative, and judicial responsibilities.

With the fulfillment of the objectives of continuing education will come a better delineation of the responsibilities of childhood education.   The basic purpose of the formal school years should be to provide the skills and knowledge necessary for life pursuits.   If it is achieved, then adult education will enable its students to utilize these educational processes throughout their lives.

CONTINUING EDUCATION

It may be noted throughout this discussion that emphasis has been on continuing education.   This concept has slowly replaced the more limited concept of adult education.   Continued education is necessary for minimum competence as a citizen, and more specialized education is necessary for positions of responsibility.

The greatest problem in the field of continuing education is how to benefit all citizens. In the past, adult education has been too much of a process of educating the educated. Little success has been achieved in reaching those with less than an eighth-grade education, those over 55 years of age, those from lower socioeconomic levels, and those from certain ethnic and cultural groups. These groups must be reached if the concept of continued education for all citizens is to be meaningful.

The acceptance of the concept of continuing education for all people may cause some curriculum planners to start scurrying about for new formulas and new procedures. This is not necessary. While the problems may be somewhat different in scope, the basic learning techniques remain the same. Subject matter probably will continue to be diverse, encompassing such subjects as literacy training, professional and technical education, religion, personal development, speed reading, sewing, woodworking, literature, music, and the arts. Activities will continue to involve correspondence study, apprenticeship, on-the-job training, internship in classes, discussion groups, conferences, lecture series, and community forums. Teaching will still be done by lectures, panels, forums, demonstrations, projects, discussions, teaching machines, and work shops.

TOPICS FOR STUDY AND DISCUSSION

1. It has been said that education does not change very much; it only acquires new labels. Does this statement apply to renaming "adult education" "continuous education"?
2. How can adult education contribute to community enrichment?
3. The solution of major social problems is frequently considered the task of education. What is the role of adult education in this assignment?
4. Is it realistic to leave the implementation of many adult education activities to so-called "volunteer" personnel?
5. Assess the role of the various levels of government in financing, coordinating, and planning programs of adult education.
6. In the past, much of adult education was associated with vocational education. Was this because vocational education met the needs of adults for continuing education or because it furnished saleable skills to the unemployed?
7. Enumerate the likely future trends in adult education in view of the ever increasing life span. Will these trends affect secondary education?

SELECTED REFERENCES

BERGENIN, PAUL. *A Philosophy for Adult Education.* New York: The Seabury Press, 1971.

This book presents a stimulating and concise analysis of what one adult educator believes should be the ideas, principles, and goals that structure adult education in a democratic society.

COMMISSION OF THE PROFESSORS OF ADULT EDUCATION. *Adult Education: A New Impetus for our Times.* The Adult Education Association, 1961.

A report is directed to those who are responsible for planning and conducting adult and continuing education programs. It reports that adult education has begun to develop a curriculum of its own and has accumulated a unique body of theory, knowledge, and practice.

FULLER, JACK W. "An In-Service Program for Adult Education Faculty." *Adult Leadership* (December 1971), pp. 205–206.

Much of the success of adult education depends on the adaptability of the faculty. This article proposes a practical program of in-service training for an adult education faculty. It is based on programed self-instruction.

GILL, MARGARET. "News and Trends in Adult Education: IMPACT." *Educational Leadership* (January 1965), pp. 279–284.

This article describes IMPACT, a three-year adult education demonstration project, showing how public school education is helping to direct social change toward new types of continuing education for all.

KIDD, J. R. *How Adults Learn.* New York: Association Press, 1970.

This volume provides an excellent study of adults and the factors affecting their ability to learn. It has a summation of many theories of learning and an evaluation of current practices in adult education.

KNOWLES, MALCOLM S. *The Modern Practice of Adult Education.* New York: Association Press, 1971.

This is a practical guide to the theory and practice of adult education. It stresses newly emerging technology of adult education based on an original theory of andragogy (the art and science of helping adults learn).

LASSEY, WILLIAM R. *Leadership and Social Change.* Iowa City: University Associates, 1971.

This book provides a collection of papers carefully integrated with introductory chapters emphasizing leadership in terms of communications, organizational change, community change, and small-group structure.

SAINTY, GEOFFREY E.   "Predicting Drop-Outs in Adult Education Courses." *Adult Education* (Summer 1971), pp. 223–230.

This article is one of the few attempts to discover by research the causes of dropouts in adult education.   It points to the need for special assistance techniques for students who are likely to leave programs of adult education due to the lack of any stimulating successes.

SMITH, ROBERT, et al.   *Handbook of Adult Education.*   New York: The Macmillan Co., 1970.

This is an up-to-date revision of a standard in the field of adult education.   It lists objectives, procedures, and instruments for evaluation of adult education.   It should prove very helpful for curriculum planners for adult education for it does a certain amount of crystal-ball gazing about the future of adult education.

PART IV

More Humane
Curriculum

CHAPTER 17

Humanizing the Setting—
Overcoming Barriers

Improving curriculum or anything else requires an analysis of the forces that now maintain the status quo. Some persons blame inept or frightened school administrators. Others place the blame on poor teacher preparation, conservative communities, old buildings, lack of funds, regulations of state departments of education and regional accrediting associations, the universities, and so on. Although most of these factors are indeed straw men, they seem both convenient and dangerous to many persons. Actually, recent court decisions and legislative enactments are giving more local responsibility to those persons in the schools who want to take further steps to individualize learning and professionalize teaching.

Curriculum improvement requires resolving issues and answering questions that confront anyone who plans to make changes. You were directed in Part I of this book to some issues and questions. Parts II and III provided information about developments and issues in the various curriculum content areas. Now we discuss in more detail how content may be organized, some methods of teaching and learning, school schedules, educational facilities, and a number of structural matters. The educational setting may either enhance curriculum improvement or stand in its way. First, we discuss some barriers. Barriers to curriculum improvement include certain concepts of school organization, the use of space and time, school regulations adopted for administrative convenience, and the limitations of partial changes in school programs.

THE SELF-SUFFICIENT CLASSROOM

Today's conventional secondary schools schedule about twenty-five to thirty-five students with one teacher for five periods a week, usually at the same time each day, in what is regarded as a self-sufficient classroom. Most teacher and pupil activities occur in that setting, supplemented only by study halls, libraries, laboratories in some subjects, and homework. This self-sufficient classroom inhibits many of the newer concepts of instruction in the various subject fields. Providing a variety of learning opportunities both inside and outside the school building makes any subject potentially more interesting to the learners.

Chapters 18, 19, and 20 describe how learning activities may be categorized under three headings: independent study, large-group instruction, and small-group discussion. On an average, teachers in self-sufficient classrooms spend almost half of their time lecturing, presenting, demonstrating, showing films, and giving tests—activities for which the size of the group is irrelevant so long as each student can see and hear well. Independent study occurs, but it is difficult to accomplish in this setting because the materials are limited, the students do not have adequate space, and the time is limited by standard periods. Small-group discussion as described in Chapter 20 is also difficult, because the number of students is too large.

Every student and teacher in a school should have access to some thirty different kinds of supplies and equipment, not counting specialized laboratory equipment. Good teaching techniques involve books and other printed materials; overhead, film, and slide projectors of various types; tape and disk recorders and playback equipment, television and video tape equipment, and so on. The absence of any of this equipment limits the opportunities of both the student and the teacher.

Of course, it is unrealistic to suggest that all classrooms have this equipment. The cost of such a program would be prohibitive even in an affluent society, and students would find it difficult to move about with all that material in one room. Moreover, experience shows that even if the equipment were provided, teachers would not use much of it.

Probably the greatest shortcoming of the self-sufficient classroom, from the point of view of the students, is that pupils are limited by whatever competencies their one teacher possesses. Teachers also are restricted. Because the room can accommodate only twenty-five to thirty-five students, educational economics requires that teachers be scheduled into these rooms five to six hours per day, twenty-five to thirty hours per week. Expected to perform most of the teaching services for a given group, the teacher often finds himself providing services for which he is less competent than some other teacher in the same building, doing tasks that interest him much less than some others he might be doing, lacking technical devices to enliven his teaching, and performing many clerical and custodial activities for his group of students.

UNIFORMITY IN TIME ARRANGEMENTS

Today's school typically schedules classes into standard-length periods for all subjects and activities. Once having decided how long periods should be, forty, forty-five, fifty, or whatever minutes, classes meet for that time, usually at the same time each day. Such an arrangement provides a situation in which a student can think about science for only forty-five minutes, then he must stop thinking about science in order to think about history or physical education for an equally short time. The home economics teacher selects recipes that can be completed in forty-five minutes, including getting materials out and putting them back. The length of the class should be determined by the teachers and students, not by an electric clock in the school office. (Chapter 23 describes a number of ways in which schedules are made flexible so that teachers and pupils can make decisions about the use of time.)

THE MULTIPURPOSE CLASSROOM

Excepting rooms for science, fine and practical arts, and physical education, schools tend to build look-alike classrooms that are multipurpose in their conception. An English room looks like a mathematics room except for a few superficial decorations. Everything is supposed to happen in the same room—large-group instruction, small-group discussion, and independent study.

Because they are multipurpose, these rooms are unnecessarily expensive. Proportionately twice as many students could be put in the same space for large-group instruction and 50 percent more for small-group discussion than are allocated according to present requirements in multipurpose classrooms. However, the most important fault in these multipurpose rooms is that the cost of equipping each one adequately is prohibitive, as indicated earlier in this chapter. For example, designing a room to serve as gymnasium, auditorium, and study hall creates compromises that detract from the potential effectiveness of the space.

Some newer schools attempt to push the multiservice idea even further by using movable walls. The theory is that such an arrangement will encourage team teaching. If four classrooms are arranged in a huge square with movable interior walls, one of the four teachers makes a presentation to the total enrollment of the four classrooms when the walls are pushed back. Then the walls are closed and each teacher takes his original class for small-group discussion and independent study. However, the seating arrangement is not good for large-group instruction and the smaller rooms are not appropriate either for small-group discussions or independent study.

THE EDIFICE COMPLEX

Some communities tend to build monuments for schools, rather than facilities primarily designed to improve the quality of teaching and learning. The building itself costs too much in relation to the money spent on supplies and equipment. An immediate goal might be to spend 25 percent less on the building and to use that amount of money to provide better aids to teaching and learning.

Whether caused by the edifice complex or not, another glaring weakness of school buildings is the failure to provide teachers with adequate places to work—an office with some privacy, meeting rooms, and places where instructional materials may be prepared. Clerks and instructional assistants also need adequate space. Including a separate classroom for each teacher is needlessly expensive. (Chapter 28 will suggest other ways to improve educational facilities.)

ADMINISTRATIVE CONVENIENCE

The rules and regulations that school administrators and the public consider necessary for a "smooth-running school" often form another barrier to curriculum improvement. Many of these regulations are designed to free the administration from decision making, since they apply to all persons without exception and can be interpreted by clerks. But individual differences among students and teachers are difficult to recognize by the application of uniform rules and regulations. Illustrative of the regulations are the following: using standardized tests to classify students into ability groups; applying standardized admission policies to graduates of other schools or of elementary schools; resorting to letter-grade requirements for participation in athletics or other extraclass activities or admission to some school subjects; adopting standard rules regarding when a student may leave school or graduate; reducing a pupil's grade arbitrarily in relation to the number of days of unexcused absence he accumulates during a grading period.

Comparable rules may militate against the professionalization of teaching: uniform salary policies, uniform teaching loads, uniform rules for providing clerical assistance, uniform class sizes, and so on. Many standards of state education departments and regional accrediting associations fall in the same category; for example, requiring all classes to meet 200 minutes per week, enrolling no more than 30 students in a class, requiring a given number of books in the library per pupil enrolled, and so on.

The quality of education in a school is not measured by decibels of sound or silence. Clearing the corridors of students except during massive changes at five-minute intermissions between class periods has little virtue per se. Administrative convenience may get in the way of curriculum improvement.

LIMITED TIME FOR TEACHERS
TO WORK ON CURRICULUM

Teachers require much more time during the school year than they now have available to improve the curriculum in the various ways that we propose. No one has established a precise figure of how much time is required. As a start, we propose five hours per week times the number of teachers in the school. Some teachers will spend more time than others.

All departments need to decide what content is required, what is desirable for pupils who develop hobbies or special interests in the field, and what is necessary for pupils who envision a career in the area. In spite of some interest over the years in such designations, very little has been done to accomplish the separations that those purposes require.

Teachers also need time to prepare guidesheets and worksheets or some form of learning packages to direct and stimulate pupils to do more complete and creative independent study. Such materials need to be largely self-directing, self-motivating, self-pacing, and self-evaluating. Even though teachers may consult banks of behavioral objectives, learning packages, textbooks and other learning materials, and a variety of externally prepared examinations, these materials need to be further tailored for the local situation.

Teachers also need time for obtaining feedback from the learning and work centers to help diagnose the needs for further curriculum changes.   They need time for conferences with each other and with consultants who may be brought to the school to help them.   They need time to evaluate the total curriculum.

Our experiences suggest that this time needs to be available to teachers during the school year rather than on an occasional afternoon or day.   A school that individually schedules teachers and pupils can provide more time for some teachers at certain periods during the year as needed.   We find that the quality of teacher productivity is better during the year than in the summer when they are not in close contact with pupils and the program.

A school system has two basic alternatives in providing teachers with time to work on curriculum.   One option is to hire extra teachers, an alternative that is costly and mostly unnecessary. The other alternative, the one we recommend, is to provide differentiated staffing as we suggest in Chapter 24.   Of course, there are good reasons for such staffing changes that go beyond providing teachers with more time to work on curriculum.   A school can achieve the goal largely within existing revenues.

INADEQUATE PLANNING OF CHANGES

Well-meaning teachers and administrators, in the very process of starting innovations and experiments in their schools, may create barriers to further curriculum improvement.   For instance, they may fail to recognize that a systems approach is essential in educational change.   A language laboratory imposed on a conventional system of teaching a foreign language produces only partial gains, or in some cases actually impairs the effectiveness of language teaching. Failure to understand that television is only one form of large-group instruction and that it cannot substitute for small-group discussion or independent study constitutes another failure to recognize the systems approach.

Improved learning outcomes will not occur if team teaching merely means that occasionally two or more teachers put their classes together for large-group instruction and then return to their conventional classes.   Such arrangements fail to accept the notion, expressed in Chapter 1, that changing one part of the instructional system requires changing all the others related to it.

Educational change should involve reeducating teachers. If they continue to teach as they did in conventional classrooms, no particular benefit to themselves or to their students will result.

Methods for evaluating pupil progress must also change, as will be explained in Chapter 26.

TOPICS FOR STUDY AND DISCUSSION

1. Select a school problem, such as how to develop more pupil responsibility for learning or conduct, how to improve attendance or discipline, or how to reduce the number of dropouts. How do present school policies affect the problem? What changes in policies or procedures would lead to improvement?
2. Considering an educational innovation, such as television, language laboratories, computer-assisted instruction, or programed learning, answer the questions listed in Topic no. 1.
3. Interview several teachers to discover the special interests of each, the self-images (what they think they do best or least well), and their ideas for improving schools. Analyze their responses in writing your report.
4. Do the same as in Topic 3, but use students as your interviewees.
5. Some persons today believe the barriers listed in this chapter are so immovable that the only solution is to create new institutions, such as "free schools" or "schools without walls." Prepare to argue for or against such proposals.

SELECTED REFERENCES

BARONI, REV. GENO C. "The Inner City: A New Challenge to Catholic High Schools." In *Catholic Education in Contemporary American Society.* Washington, D.C.: The National Catholic Educational Association, NCEA Bulletin (August 1967), pp. 108–116.

This article presents the problems schools face in larger cities and suggests remedial steps.

BISHOP, LLOYD K. "The Student: Humanizing the School Program." In *Individualizing Educational Systems.* New York: Harper and Row, Publishers, 1971, pp. 175–221.

This chapter emphasizes the student as a co-participant in the educational enterprise and suggests strategies for involving students in school programs.

CAY, DONALD F. "Barriers to Curriculum Building." In *Curriculum: Design for Learning.* Indianapolis: The Bobbs-Merrill Co., Inc., 1966, pp. 136–153.

The chapter in this book discusses problems related to time, money, materials, and teacher personnel.

GOODLAD, JOHN I., and KLEIN, FRANCIS M. *Behind the Classroom Door.* Worthington, Ohio: Charles A. Jones, 1970.

This book shows how teachers resist educational changes and suggests constructive measures.

HICKERSON, NATHANIEL. *Education for Alienation.* Englewood Cliffs, N.J.: Prentice-Hall, Inc., 1966, pp. 73–98.

These three chapters emphasize thirteen curriculum changes needed to provide better education for the economically deprived.

LOUNSBURY, JOHN H., and MARANI, JEAN V. *The Junior High School We Saw: One Day in the Eighth Grade.* Washington, D.C.: Association for Supervision and Curriculum Development, 1964.

This is a provocative report of a "shadow study" in which 102 competent observers recorded what happened to 102 eighth graders in 98 schools in 26 states on May 3, 1962. Read especially, Chapter 2, "The Day's Record," to see the effects of school organization, methods of teaching and learning, and content on pupils.

MANLOVE, DONALD C., and BEGGS, DAVID W., III. *Flexible Scheduling Using the IndiFlexS Model.* Bloomington: Indiana University Press, 1967, pp. 29–39 and 64–78.

These two chapters discuss some myths that should be destroyed and the need for new professional roles for teachers.

TOMPKINS, ELLSWORTH, and GAUMNITZ, WALTER. "Summary: The Case For and Against the Carnegie Unit." *The Bulletin of the National Association of Secondary School Principals,* no. 288 (January 1964), pp. 68–72.

This article lists fourteen reasons why the Carnegie Unit gets in the way of secondary school improvement. The preceding 67 pages describe the origin, history, status, and efforts to change the Carnegie Unit.

WOODS, THOMAS E. *The Administration of Educational Innovation.* Eugene: University of Oregon Bureau of Educational Research, 1967, pp. 33–41.

This chapter describes several inherent "barriers to change" that inhibit educational innovations and suggests constructive actions.

CHAPTER 18

Students Learn
with Alternatives:
Independent Study

How much time is our own? Usually we work with other people. Even our recreation involves many group activities. Yet, everyone needs opportunities to learn and do things his own way, to develop his own special interests and talents, and to be creative. Without these opportunities and responsibilities, he loses his identity in a mass of group functions.

What a person does independently determines his unique personality and helps him maintain good mental health. It can also result in major contributions to the general welfare.

The effective school challenges each pupil to manifest higher levels of intellectual inquiry and creativity. It provides him with opportunities to study and to work apart from the mass. The conventional school, however, schedules most of a student's time into group activities in classes, study halls, laboratories, and other workrooms, and mass examinations and the application of competitive group standards often reward conformity. Such group assignments may deny individual students needed opportunities for independent study and investigation and sometimes bore them with needless repetitiveness or worry them with unnecessary frustrations.

Children in kindergarten and the first grade work independently for a considerable portion of the day even in conventional schools.   Unfortunately, as the children grow older, the school structures more and more of their time in groups under relatively close supervision of their teachers.

THE MEANING OF INDEPENDENT STUDY

Independent study can be defined as "the activities in which pupils engage when their teachers stop talking." Its purpose is to give each student the opportunity to develop his unique talents and interests to the highest possible degree.   That is why personal learning activities constitute the central function of education—the heart of the school.

Independent study has two dimensions for most students. First, the pupils must master the minimum essential knowledge, skills, and other values required in the subject.   Teacher presentations tell them what these essentials are and how to attain them. This aspect of education was called *basic education* in Chapter 2. The second level of independent study provides for enriching knowledge and skills, referred to in Chapter 2 as *depth education*.   Here students manifest their special interests and talents.

Independent study may be an individual activity or it may involve two or more pupils working together.   A group of pupils with similar needs for remedial work may work in a specially equipped laboratory, or an advanced group with special interests may cooperate in a project.   In any case, the emphasis remains on the individual, who has been placed in a learning situation where he may succeed and contribute to others as well as to his own personal development.

Independent study takes different forms.   In one school, pupils who were failing every subject in the conventional program were assembled in a room to work with motors.   The school provided many types of motors—sewing machine, vacuum sweeper, automotive, and others—and some were brought to school by the pupils themselves.   Competent teachers helped pupils to increase their knowledge of motors.   When some of them wanted more information, a reading specialist helped them to improve their reading so they could learn more.   They also learned about motors by listening to taped information and by looking at films.   Ultimately, some of the pupils wrote reports on what they were doing.   In another school, a senior spent twenty-two hours per week doing original research in the school's biology laboratory, involving equipment designed especially by him on the basis of extensive reading and conferences with experts in and outside the school. The student did most of this work outside the conventional thirty-hour school week but some school time was available to him in the school's flexible schedule.

In an effective school, most pupils may spend approximately twelve hours of the usual thirty-hour school week in independent study.[1] Many students will spend additional time in subject fields in which they are competent and have particular interests. Ultimately 60 percent or more of a pupil's time may be spent in independent study. That goal will result from more effective "teacher talk" as described in Chapter 19 and "pupil talk" as proposed in Chapter 20. The combination of a different school schedule, cooperative professional decisions by teachers and counselors, appropriate attendance and reporting procedures, and new evaluation techniques should be established to encourage and to govern personalized independent study. The types of independent study can be illustrated by considering the variety of places in a school where they occur.

LOCATION OF INDEPENDENT STUDY

Five different areas within the school are recommended. Organization of the areas, and the degree to which they are separate from each other, depend on the size of the school and the degree of staff commitment. Since there are many ways to provide these facilities in new buildings or old, the spaces are described in general terms. The five areas are library, resource centers, small-group conference areas, relaxation rooms, and restriction zones. There are also out-of-school study spaces.

Library

The central library serves two basic functions in independent study. First, it provides a quiet place where pupils who prefer that type of environment may work. Second, it provides a storehouse for printed, recorded, and visual materials that students use while doing more sophisticated research. The library is headquarters for the librarian and her assistants, who also help to supervise the resource centers, usually located elsewhere. Because the library is complemented by resource centers, the size of the space and the number of books, recordings, and visual materials stored there are

[1] J. Lloyd Trump, *Images of the Future—A New Approach to the Secondary School* (Washington, D.C.: The National Association of Secondary School Principals, 1959), pp. 8–9.

smaller than the published standards for school libraries usually recommend.

The arrangement described here does not minimize the importance of the library and the librarian.   Quite the contrary, both have strategic roles to play in the independent study program. Many pupils need at times the quiet and the resources that the library provides, as well as the services of the librarian; but they do not need these services all the time.

Resource centers

These special learning areas, essential for every school subject, have two parts.   First, there is the *study area* where pupils read, write, listen, view, think, and at times talk with others briefly. Second, there is the *workroom* where the staff keeps the "tools of the trade" of the particular subject, such as the gymnasium, the art room, the foods laboratory, or the social science workroom.   In larger schools there are advantages in having separate resource centers for each of the subject areas.   Smaller schools may combine the subjects into fewer centers.   The two facilities for each center are located near each other.

The study area includes ten or twelve individual study carrels with walls approximately 5 feet high.   Nearby shelves carry a wide variety of reading materials frequently used by most pupils in the particular subject field.   A simple coding system makes it easy for pupils to find and replace the materials.   Another part of the room has tape, disk, and video players and a stock of frequently used recorded materials.   Recordings of all large-group presentations and of selected small-group discussion sessions are provided.   Some of the recordings are prepared by local teachers or outside consultants for students of different ability and interest levels; others are purchased from commercial sources; some are made by pupils themselves.   As in the case of printed materials, recordings are coded simply.

In another section of the room, screens are mounted on the walls, and magazine-fed 8 mm. motion picture projectors, 16 mm. sound projectors, and film strip and slide projectors are available. Pupils use earphones so that they do not bother those engaged in different activities.   The resource center also houses programed instruction materials and self-teaching exercises prepared by the staff or purchased commercially to help students learn the basic facts and skills in the subject.

Some schools provide computerized carrels or electronically equipped centers where pupils may select and work with materials located elsewhere in the school or outside the school.   Special programs for remedial, average, and advanced instruction are provided.

The study area of the resource center is noisier than the library. Students move about a good deal and occasionally talk to each other, interrupting what they are doing to discuss an important topic. However, the atmosphere is still somewhat subdued, like the quiet area of an office away from the noisy machines.

The other part of the resource center, which we may call the workroom, is a noisier place. Let us consider several examples. Good social science instruction includes student surveys and studies in the school and community with consequent need to tabulate the collected data—so calculating machines are available in the social science workroom. The workroom also provides typewriters for writing reports, duplicating machines, and equipment for making maps, charts, and the like. A teletype machine brings the students the latest information on economics, international affairs, and other local and regional happenings.

Science workrooms include supplies and equipment found in the conventional school's science laboratories, but the emphasis is different. The equipment is more portable and special facilities are provided for more extended and extensive experiments. Of course, the biggest difference between today's science laboratory and the resource center envisioned is that science students also have a room in which they can read, write, listen, view, and think with the science materials at their fingertips.

The physical education workroom differs from today's gymnasium. The emphasis is on activities that students may engage in individually or in very small groups—activities similar to those which they may use for recreation and physical fitness at home or on a fifty-foot lot. The size and shape of the physical education workroom is not dictated by the dimensions of a basketball court. Provision for basketball is in an entirely different room. Adjacent to the physical education workroom is a place where students may read, view, listen, write, and think about health, recreation, and physical fitness with appropriate materials readily available.

The foreign language workroom includes recording and listening equipment to test students' ability to pronounce and speak and to understand the speech of others. The resource center also houses materials in the language for pupils to read, write, listen to, and view.

Special help areas

In addition to the resource centers that meet the needs of most pupils, the school needs to provide regularly for pupils with special interests and needs. The teacher or instructional assistant in the resource centers is responsible for a considerable number of pupils at a given time. The pupil who has difficulty may have to wait too long for assistance or the facilities in the resource center may be inadequate. The school facilities also need to include special help area(s) where pupils who need temporary assistance or a more involved remedial program in any curriculum field can obtain the assistance immediately. The special help we describe requires the assistance of a competent teacher with interest and preparation in the subject field. That teacher will decide when the pupil may profitably return to the other resource centers.

Small-group conferences

Spaces are required where students may gather in small groups of three or four to discuss their projects, exchange ideas, make suggestions for further investigation, engage in preliminary evaluation of their efforts, and work together in other ways. Frequently, a group of students will ask a teacher to sit in on a discussion to make suggestions, help solve a knotty problem, or plan future activities.

Pupils may gather around a table in the school cafeteria for this purpose. Similarly, tables and chairs may be placed in an ordinary classroom or on a patio or in a room near the library. Of course, the noise level of the area may be relatively high because the room is usually full of students talking.

Relaxation area

Pupils spend 40 percent or more of their time in independent study, and this time will increase as teacher presentations and study materials become more sophisticated. They need to relax for a few minutes from time to time, for learning is more effective when periods of concentrated study are interspersed with different activities. In the conventional school, however, the pupils are denied this privilege. Teachers go to the faculty lounge and other staff members take coffee breaks, but the pupils are supposed to work rigorously all day long except for the brief respite between periods. Even then, teachers are often assigned to corridor duty to make certain that the students do not relax too much!

In an innovative school, the relaxation areas is usually a part of the cafeteria. Students may purchase soft drinks or light refreshments at snack bars which are open all day. However, students are not pressured to make purchases; they can bring their own sandwiches if they like. The young people can talk about school work if they wish, but most often they talk about out-of-school activities and events. The pupils do not spend more than fifteen or twenty minutes in the relaxation area; some of them may use it more or less.   Those who abuse the privilege, of course, have it taken away.

Restriction zone

The fifth area for independent study is the study hall of the typical secondary school.   True, the conventional study hall is on its way out and has already disappeared from many schools.   As a place for all pupils to study (in many schools the only place besides the library) it was poor.   Pupils lacked materials and adequate supervision and were not allowed to carry on conversation.   A small study hall is needed as a part of the total independent study program, but its function is now changed.

The school assigns a pupil to a study hall when his actions in the other study areas testify to the fact that he has not developed sufficient responsibility for his own learning.   Temporarily, the staff withdraws his privilege of working in the library, the resource centers, the small-group study area, or the relaxation room.   The study hall is a place of complete silence.   It is supervised by a teacher who helps students to become ready to return to the other independent study areas.

The study hall is a general facility serving all the subjects in the school; therefore, the student has to bring his materials with him just as he does in today's conventional school.   Study halls have dictionaries and a set of encyclopedias, but that is about all. The school goal should be to have no more than 1 to 3 percent of the total school enrollment assigned to a restriction zone.   If more than 3 percent or so are assigned, there is a clear indication that teacher presentations (see Chapter 19) are faulty or the school has inadequate independent study facilities.

Most educators rebel at the thought of a "restriction zone." However, there are always students who interfere with others who want to work constructively, and schools that fail to provide this emergency control have to send a constant stream of offenders to the school offices.   Even enlightened societies still have jails or corrective institutions.

Out-of-school study spaces

Independent study occurs outside of school as well as inside.   The kind of activities and the number of hours per week varies.   Some of the study may be similar to the conventional school's homework, but the assignments should emphasize minimum requirements rather than prescribing in advance a given number of problems to work, the pages to write, or the books to read.

Some out-of-school study may occur in factories, shops, offices, and other places where students are acquiring work experience. The school develops independent study spaces cooperatively with local employers, social agencies, governmental agencies, and others. Study also occurs in museums and institutes. This kind of independent study makes the community school concept a reality.

The rule-of-thumb that the school uses in determining when the pupil is scheduled for independent study away from the building is quite simple. The pupil studies in the community or even at a greater distance away from the school whenever the physical setting, the materials, and the instructional assistant are better out there than the comparable situation which the school can readily provide in the school building itself. An important consideration is that adequate arrangements exist in the locale away from the school for supervising the experience and providing reports of the pupil's progress back to the school.

SUPERVISION OF INDEPENDENT STUDY

Teachers should avoid association with pupils during independent study, so that they will not be tempted to over-supervise. In place of the teachers, carefully selected, qualified instruction assistants may supervise the study spaces. These adult assistants need at least a college minor in the subject field represented by the various workrooms, and should know the subject well enough to answer many questions and to refer a student to his professional teacher when a specialized type of assistance is needed. Three types of persons usually are available: housewives interested in part-time work, advanced college students, and retired teachers.

The instruction assistant is there primarily to maintain order (a simple matter, usually), to recommend any student who needs to be transferred to the restriction zone, to keep the machines and books in usable condition, and to provide other assistance as needed. He is under the cooperative supervision of the chairman of the teaching team in the subject area and the school librarian.

Pupils are scheduled into the workrooms, and appropriate records are maintained so that the school and the parents know where they are and in general what they are doing. Pupils leave the workrooms only with the permission of the instruction assistant in charge. The atmosphere of the workrooms must be relaxed, yet businesslike. Pupils may confer as long as they do not abuse the privilege.   In some schools, pupils who have earned the privilege may, with parental consent, come and go as they wish among the independent study centers.   This "open campus" concept is an ideal toward which all schools may strive.

NEW DIRECTIONS

School personnel must become more sophisticated in assigning pupils to various types of independent study, recognizing the individual pupil's past records, his potential talents, and his special interests (see chapters 19 and 23).   Program success also requires effective evaluation of such diverse student projects as a model, a new discovery, an exposition, the solution of a problem, a proposed reclassification of data or species, a poem, a musical composition, a new tool, a product, or a survey (see chapters 26 and 27).

Both dimensions of independent study—the essential learnings and the opportunity for creative and depth efforts—are for all pupils.   This reiteration emphasizes a concept that is often neglected in schools.   Teachers readily conclude that independent study is meant only for the talented few.   All pupils need to learn the required content with as much freedom as possible from constant supervision and help.   All pupils need to follow their special interests and talents even though some of them achieve mediocre results in relation to other pupils—a contrast which teachers should refrain from highlighting.

Immature young people are highly conscious of the values placed by a school on different types of activities.   Superior presentations may motivate students, and exciting discussions may stimulate them, but they will consider independent study an unwarranted luxury if the school emphasizes the marks on factual examinations.   The school that places high value on the quality and quantity of independent study when it appraises and reports individual pupil progress will reap the benefits of superior work by students.

The school should send parents, colleges, employers, and the general public an analysis of the total productivity of its student body in independent study, as well as examples of excellent individual pupil activity.   This reporting creates a special image of educational priorities.

The teacher's goal is to become increasingly dispensable. He should expect all students to grow in self-analysis, self-correction, and self-direction, for the quality of the student's independent study reflects the quality of the teaching.   Every student failure in independent study should challenge the teacher to help him succeed next time; it should not be an excuse to resort to the easier route of more teacher domination and control. Independent study is the ultimate educational objective.

TOPICS FOR STUDY AND DISCUSSION

1. Consider some division or unit in a course you now teach or are preparing to teach. List and define the essential concepts to be learned by all students.
2. Take the same example as in Topic no. 1. Suggest one or more depth studies or potentially creative activities that might be profitable for (a) low achieving pupils, (b) average pupils, or (c) high achieving pupils.
3. Plan a learning resources center for your subject area indicating kinds of materials and their location.
4. Develop a set of guidelines to help instruction assistants supervise pupils in one or more of the places where independent study occurs.
5. Your visit to a learning resources center shows that almost all pupils are reading textbooks of encyclopedias or copying materials from them to complete reports. What steps do you take to make independent study more productive?

SELECTED REFERENCES

ALEXANDER, WILLIAM M., and HINES, VINCE A. *Independent Study in Seconday Schools.* Cooperative Research Project No. 2969. Gainesville, Florida: University of Florida, 1966. Multilithed.

This book reports on visits to thirty-six schools having innovative independent study programs. Purposes, curriculum areas, pupils served, types of studies, teacher activities, facilities, and evaluation are described.

BEGGS, DAVID W., III, and BUFFIE, EDWARD G., eds. *Independent Study.* Bloomington, Indiana: Indiana University Press, 1965.

Twelve authors describe junior and senior high school programs and procedures.

BERMAN, LOUISE M. *New Priorities in the Curriculum.* Columbus, Ohio: Charles E. Merrill Publishing Company, 1968.

The author's suggestions for curriculum development, especially, as summarized in hypotheses at the end of each chapter, are valuable guides to anyone developing materials for pupils to use in their independent study.

DAVIS, HAROLD S. *Independent Study—An Annotated Bibliography.* Cleveland: Educational Research Council of America, 1966.

This pamphlet lists 150 books and pamphlets relating to different aspects of the subject.

ELLSWORTH, RALPH E., and WAGNER, HOBERT D. *The School Library: Facilities for Study in the Secondary School.* New York: Educational Facilities Laboratories, Inc., 1963.

This book describes a variety of existing and proposed facilities designed to enhance the contributions of the library resource center for college and secondary school programs.

Libraries in Secondary Schools—A New Look. Bulletin of the National Association of Secondary School Principals, no. 306 (January 1966).

Sixteen writers redefine the library's role as a resource center.

McCLOSKY, MILDRED G., ed. "Students as Teachers—of Peers, of Younger Students, of Themselves." In *Teaching Strategies and Classroom Realities.* Englewood Cliffs, N.J.: Prentice-Hall, 1971, pp. 143–174.

Part IV in this book describes human resources for independent study that most schools utilize very little or ineffectively. Eight authors give examples in most curriculum areas.

POPHAM, W. JAMES, and BAKER, EVA J. *Establishing Instructional Goals* v-130 and *Planning an Instructional Sequence* v-k38. Englewood Cliffs, N.J.: Prentice-Hall, Inc., 1970.

These two self-instruction books will help one to understand and plan better programs of independent study.

TRUMP, J. LLOYD. "Independent Study: The Schools." *The Encyclopedia of Education,* vol. 4, pp. 557–562. New York: The Macmillan Company and The Free Press, 1971.

This article provides further details and includes additional bibliography.

CHAPTER 19

Motivational Experiences
in Larger Groups

Reading a book, magazine, or newspaper, watching television, going
to a movie, and attending a lecture are examples of participation
in large-group instruction. What a person hears and sees in these
activities frequently becomes the subject of discussions with other
persons (usually in groups of two to six) and often motivates him
to seek more understanding of the subject in independent study in
libraries, bookstores, museums, or elsewhere.

Every school has large-group instruction. The trouble is
that it is wastefully done in classes of twenty to thirty pupils, is
teacher-dominated, and often is not motivational. Typically,
teachers talk, show films, play records, give demonstrations, and
otherwise make presentations for about one-half the time that their
classes meet. The learner is physically passive, except for taking
notes. However, he can and should react mentally to what he sees
and hears, noting the matters he wishes to discuss with his colleagues or to study in an appropriate setting. Ideally, presentations
should be followed by specially planned independent study and by
student-centered discussions in groups of fifteen or fewer. Unfortunately, many conventional classes do not include either activity.
One other point to keep in mind is that when teachers talk or present materials, the size of the class or audience does not matter so
long as each pupil can see and hear well.

Motivational experiences in larger groups as a part of the
instructional system refers to presentations either provided by the

teacher himself or by the talking of some other person—pupil or someone from outside the school—or a film or recording.   Our experience is that variety heightens the motivational experience.   Although teachers have a basic role in planning the presentations, they should have about three-fourths of them done by persons outside the school, by pupils, and by audio-visual devices.   The key to success is whether the presentations actually provide a motivational experience that not only holds the interest of most students but also stimulates later discussions among them and more productive independent study.   There is nothing unique about this proposal.   These kinds of presentations occur regularly in all schools in all subjects and at all grade levels.

PURPOSES OF LARGE-GROUP INSTRUCTION

Ordinarily in conventional classrooms, teachers talk too much and they talk about the wrong things.   Three goals must guide large-group instruction.   First the presentation should be *motivational,* arousing student interest in learning more about the subject.   Second, it should be *informational,* providing facts, ideas, and points of view *not otherwise readily available* to students.   Third, it should be *directional,* suggesting activities for students to do following the presentation.   Failure to aim for these three goals—or adding materials that go beyond them—detracts from the effectiveness of the presentation.

Motivation

Determining who should teach the large group or whether to use a film are crucial matters in motivating pupils.   The basic criterion is to select the best teacher for a given topic to work with a specific group of students.   However, if someone in the community, or a film or television program, has more to offer than any local teacher, that person or the film or TV program should be used, with the best available local teacher complementing the presentation.   Remember, the basic purpose of large-group instruction is to place students in contact with the *best possible* teaching for the particular topic.

The presentation is like the appetizer that stimulates interest in, and prepares the body for, an excellent meal.   Unfortunately, teachers sometimes act as if it is the main course of the banquet— they overstuff their listeners, who then want no more of it or develop indigestion.   In contrast, the good teacher whets the pupil's appetite by providing only a part of the poem, problem, or experiment—then he tells the pupil how he can obtain more.

Other factors that influence motivation, discussed in Chapter 2, can highlight the importance of planning and preparing for large-group instruction.

Information

Some persons object to large-group instruction because it reminds them of experiences they had with certain college professors who failed to understand that large-group instruction should provide information *not* readily available elsewhere. For example, a professor may have lectured from the same notes that he used in preparing a textbook he had required his students to purchase.

If large-group instruction covers content similar to that which pupils are expected to acquire through independent study, students will be bored by the large-group presentation and develop various schemes to avoid listening, or they will be less interested in pursuing the subject in their independent study. On the other hand, if it is used creatively the large-group presentation can provide a more current interpretation of history or scientific data, develop an interpretation quite different from the conventional book or recordings, or cover materials not available to the pupils in the local independent study resource areas.

Teachers must avoid the tendency to cover the subject, topic by topic. Making that mistake causes all sorts of trouble. For example, teachers then believe that the progress of their pupils in independent study is locked into what is currently presented to the large group. That assumption is incorrect. The new information may relate to a topic some pupils studied previously—stressing the need to revise what they learned. The presentation may be current with or anticipate the independent study of other pupils. Remember, the teacher does not need to cover the course orally. His goal is for the pupils to cover the course requirements—and for them to enjoy the process as much as possible.

Direction

A presentation is incomplete without the third aspect of large-group instruction—the assignment. Students must be told what they need to know and how they may learn it. Such structuring does not inhibit creativity. Quite the contrary, it provides the foundation for new concepts and leaves open-ended a variety of directions in which students may go. These assignments are sometimes given orally but preferably are on printed or duplicated guidesheets and worksheets. A physically-present teacher thus supplements the instruction done by a film, a television program, or a community expert.

HOW TO PREPARE PRESENTATIONS

The preparation of a large-group presentation requires careful study and creativity, as well as considerable time and energy. The teacher must assess the pupils' past achievement and interest in the topic. Some teachers feel they can teach more efficiently by dividing students into groups based on the extent of their knowledge of the subject to be discussed. Of course, that procedure requires more teacher time, and there is no evidence to support the contention that pupils learn more that way. Pupils must be able to relate new material to what they already know. That reduces the necessity for pure memorization, enhancing interest and conceptualization.

Other important considerations when preparing presentations include use of simple explanations, use of clever illustrations, development of meaningful relationships, raising of thought-provoking issues that will encourage small-group discussion and suggest topics for independent study, and occasionally, use of questions which may be answered by group response. However, teachers should avoid asking factual questions of individuals, a practice commonly used in conventional classrooms. The teacher's goal is to find out whether all students understand the subject, not just one student. Moreover, the answers given by the individuals do not provide effective discussion.

A competent, experienced teacher may spend ten or more hours preparing a single presentation to be given for the first time. Later presentations on the same topic may require less time as materials are revised and updated.

Proper use of clerks and instruction assistants may reduce preparation time and facilitate presentations. Instruction assistants can check on needed data, prepare visual aids, and help to supervise students. Clerks can prepare mats and stencils, check attendance, distribute and collect supplies, and keep files and records.

LOGISTICAL ARRANGEMENTS

An overhead projector and sound system are essential in a large-group room, for each student must see and hear as perfectly as possible. Facilities for presenting films, slides, television, and recordings are also needed. The best rooms provide integrated media systems so the presenter can vary his performance by pushing buttons or signaling an operator. Ideally the rooms should be air-conditioned, for year-round control of temperature, humidity, and air circulation; windowless, for better light regulation; and carpeted, for better acoustical control. Electronic reaction buttons in front of student listeners have been used to indicate their failure to grasp new ideas; however, raising hands as a signal is less expensive.

The number of students included in a group depends on the size of the school, the enrollment in a given subject, the kinds of facilities available, and the personal opinion of the teacher-presenter. Millions of people simultaneously view a television presentation. Thousands of persons gather in a stadium to watch a game or listen to a lecture. Little research has been done on the effects of the size of the audience on the listener's comprehension, but it appears that the size of the audience does not matter so long as each person can see and hear well. Many teachers prefer to limit the size of groups to approximately 150 so the groups can be somewhat more homogeneous according to past achievement. However, the need for such homogeneity has not been demonstrated in research. Diverse populations read newspapers and watch television simultaneously, with each person getting his own degree of stimulation and content from the presentation. Obviously, large student groups produce greater economies in the use of teacher time and energy, outside community consultants, and building space.

The optimum length period for large-group instruction is unknown. Even small children, including those with relatively low ability, watch television hour after hour without losing interest and gain some understanding from the experience. The subject of the presentation, the audio-visual aids used, the effectiveness of the teacher, the opinion of the teacher, and the air-conditioning of the room are among the factors which must be considered when scheduling the period. Most junior and senior high school teachers prefer a period of approximately forty minutes for large-group instruction. If the school has no regularly scheduled intermissions, this means approximately thirty-five minutes for the presentation. On the other hand, many schools operate effectively with sixty-minute large-group instruction periods while others argue in favor of a twenty-five-minute presentation.

How many large-group presentations to schedule per week is another open question. The answer depends on an analysis of what the school hopes to accomplish in large groups, in small groups, and through independent study. The teachers in the teaching team must base decisions on their best professional judgment, and all discussions must be subject to change on the basis of personal preference and investigation. Most schools now schedule two large-group meetings per week. We believe one meeting per week is sufficient to accomplish the three functions of large groups.

Large-group instruction is being carried on effectively in all the subject areas. For example, physical education calls for the same teaching-learning analysis as history, mathematics, music, or agriculture. Obviously, in every subject, teachers need to talk or show films, and pupils need time to learn through personal experience and to discuss with each other what they have learned. The large group is an important ingredient in the process.

OTHER LARGE-GROUP ACTIVITIES

Students working on programed instruction devices (usually programed textbooks) can work in large groups under the supervision of instruction assistants with a professional teacher available for consultation when needed. This process saves teacher time and energy. Written examinations can also be administered effectively in large groups supervised by instruction assistants. Thus, testing procedures can be standardized more in the large-group than they could be when the tests were given in numerous small groups. Of course, other forms of evaluation (see chapters 26 and 27) require different arrangements.

TOPICS FOR STUDY AND DISCUSSION

1. Select a topic or unit in the subject you teach or plan to teach. Then plan a presentation that will motivate pupils, give information not readily available to them, and provide a diversified assignment as indicated in this chapter. Your plan should be a general outline, sufficiently detailed so you can discuss it with your colleagues.
2. Many teachers are not artists. Perhaps you also lack those skills. However, you need to communicate to an artist on your staff the ideas you have for a visual you will use on the overhead projector. Using the outline you developed in Topic no. 1, sketch one or more proposed visuals.
3. Using your plan for Topic no. 1, go to a visual aids catalogue and list possible films, filmstrips, slides, and recordings that you might use in your presentation. If possible, preview one or more of them with your colleagues.

4. Write a proposal for constructing a space, or remodeling an existing space, as a facility for large-group instruction. Consider such matters as size of room, seating arrangements, facilities for the instructor, and equipment.
5. Assume you are involved in a discussion with a colleague or have just finished an article in which the "lecture system" of instruction is deplored. Prepare an answer showing the differences between large-group instruction as described in this chapter and a lecture course you experienced in college.

SELECTED REFERENCES

BAIR, MEDILL, and WOODWARD, RICHARD G. "Large-Group Instruction." In *Team Teaching in Action.* Boston: Houghton Mifflin Company, 1964, pp. 122–153.

Although concerned with elementary school work, the basic principles and suggestions here relate to secondary teaching.

BEGGS, DAVID W., III. "Teacher-Centered Activity: Large Group Instruction." In *Decatur-Lakeview High School.* Englewood Cliffs, N.J.: Prentice-Hall, Inc., 1964, pp. 114–122.

This chapter emphasizes reasons, preparation, methods, and other aspects of large-group work.

DAVIS, HAROLD S. *Illuminate Your Lecture.* Cleveland: Educational Research Council of Greater Cleveland, 1964.

The basic principles for using the overhead projector in large-group instruction are presented in this pamphlet.

HOOVER, KENNETH H. "Informing Others: Large Group Instruction, Informal Lecture, Demonstration, and Reporting Procedures." In *Learning and Teaching in the Secondary School.* 3rd ed. Boston: Allyn and Bacon, Inc., 1972, pp. 451–477.

This chapter describes procedures for imparting knowledge and information.

PETERSON, CARL H. "Large Group Instruction Techniques." In *Effective Team Teaching.* West Nyack, N.Y.: Parker Publishing Co., 1966, pp. 75–100.

This chapter gives criteria for large-group instruction, techniques, and some specific examples.

SCHULTZ, MORTON J. *The Teacher and Overhead Projection.* Englewood Cliffs, N.J.: Prentice-Hall, Inc., 1965, pp. 1–30.

These two chapters offer practical suggestions for improving large-group instruction. The book's remaining 210 pages are divided into chapters for each of the curriculum content areas.

CHAPTER 20

Reaction and Interaction
in Smaller Groups

Life would be incomplete without the discussions that every individual holds with other persons in small groups. New acquaintances and friendships develop in such meetings, and the conversations help to clarify ideas, stimulate further inquiry, and persuade other persons to accept beliefs.

Specially planned educational programs involving small-group discussions are essential to a good school curriculum. The conventional class is too large for these learning experiences. Dividing the class into two or three subgroups, or holding buzz sessions, is not a good substitute for regular discussion groups of fifteen or fewer pupils because a teacher can assist only one of the groups at a time while the other groups lack teacher supervision. Moreover, the makeup of the groups tends to remain fairly constant, limited by the twenty-five to thirty persons assigned to the class. In contrast, the pupils in small-group discussion classes may be changed periodically to produce better results. And the teacher in those classes plays a role quite different from that performed in the conventional classroom.

Small-group discussions provide essential education for citizenship in a democracy. Pupils must learn to discuss controversial matters, to communicate effectively, to listen to and respect the opinions of others, and to deal with people whose backgrounds and interests differ from their own. The discussions use and reinforce some of the knowledge the pupils gain in large groups and in independent study—they help young people crystallize values and for attitudes.

These regularly scheduled reaction groups for systematic discussions differ from the various sized groups that the school creates or that develop out of independent study or those established for therapy or counseling purposes. These special reaction groups are scheduled as soon as possible after the motivational experiences that the school provides in larger than usual groups. The basic purpose is to permit interaction among pupils in relation to how they feel about the presentations. Such reactions not only may increase the motivation resulting from the larger experiences but also provide the staff with feedback about the effectiveness of the large-group presentations. Of course, teachers also are present to answer questions or clear up misunderstandings that the presentations stimulated. Teachers also may help pupils to improve their discussion skills and observe behavior that suggests the need for systematic instructions in the techniques of small-group discussion.

PREPARATION FOR SMALL-GROUP DISCUSSION

Few teachers and pupils have had adequate experience and training to achieve maximum benefit from small-group discussions. Most of them do not know how to discuss. The oral quizzing erroneously called "classroom discussion," that occupies much time in conventional classrooms must be forgotten if small-group discussion is to fulfill its purpose. Teachers must learn to handle the roles of listener, advisor, and co-participant. They must also be acquainted with sociometry and behavioral psychology. Once they themselves understand the processes involved in discussion, they can teach their pupils.

Before actually participating in discussions, students may learn the principles involved through large-group instruction and independent study. Large-group instruction may describe and illustrate the roles each member of a small-group discussion may play (leader, recorder, observer, or consultant) and the many functions of group members (initiates, questions, elaborates, argues for, opposes, challenges, blocks, harmonizes, ignores, keeps silent, entertains, summarizes, seeks consensus, and evaluates). Pamphlets describing small-group discussion may be placed in the independent study areas. Audio or video tape recordings of small-group discussion sessions illustrating good and bad procedures may also be placed in the resource centers so that pupils may listen to them and react.

Of course, the learning is best when the pupils themselves practice various roles in a small-group discussion which is evaluated afterwards by other young people and by their teacher. It is difficult to teach pupils to express ideas effectively, to listen, to point up issues, to seek consensus, to identify differences, and to respect each other in the process. Both pupils and instructors worry too much about the group's not covering a predetermined body of subject matter. Teachers constantly must seek a constructive balance between correcting too many pupil errors and letting mistakes go by, between too much control and too much permissiveness, too much structure and too much freedom of choice of topics, and so on. The middle-of-the-road approach with occasional deviations may be the best solution.

GROUP CONSTITUENCY AND MEETING ARRANGEMENTS

Experiences of schools with small groups, and research in group process, indicate that the maximum desirable size for a group is from twelve to fifteen pupils. That is the largest number that will have an opportunity to become actively involved in discussion during a reasonable period of time. A group of fewer than twelve to fifteen pupils is unnecessarily small and expensive to staff. Remember, the purpose here is to teach oral communications skills and improve relations among pupils, not to cover the subject or to provide group therapy.

One small-group discussion per week for each subject is sufficient in most cases. Most schools believe that from thirty to forty minutes is a desirable length for these group discussions. Schools often schedule more meetings than necessary because teachers tend to cover a given area of content rather than emphasizing the development of attitudes, values, and competencies in discussion and in group relationships.

Every school subject can profit from a discussion group. Physical education groups may meet to discuss health, physical fitness, and recreation. Mathematics groups may discuss the application of quantitative thinking to personal, community, and world problems. An English group may relate the content of reading to school issues. The world of work may be discussed by a vocational or practical arts group. A French group may discuss *in French* a political development in France that affects other countries. Imaginative teachers and pupils never lack content for discussions.

Teachers and counselors determine the makeup of groups, and they should change the composition as frequently as necessary. For example, if teachers observe that two or three students are dominating the discussion in a given group, they could transfer them to a group containing stronger student discussants. Both groups might benefit from this transfer, and the new group might have beneficial effects upon the transferred students.

Groups are composed on a variety of other bases, such as friendships, emotional maturity, sex, quality of past school work in the subject, special interests, and vocational or educational goals. Counseling records, interest inventories, teacher opinions, sociometry, school records, and other appropriate data are utilized in making original assignments of students to groups and in changing group composition. Teachers, counselors, and the principal meet frequently to exchange information and ideas about ameliorative arrangements for different individuals.

GROUP ORGANIZATION

Four persons with specialized roles facilitate small-group discussion. A *leader* helps to guide the discussion. A *recorder* keeps an account of what the group discusses. An *observer* constructively criticizes the discussion. A *consultant* provides information that the group needs.

The leader

One of the issues that divide teachers of small groups is whether students originally should be selected as leaders or whether the teacher should serve that role. The arguments pro and con are quite obvious. If a teacher is unwilling to relinquish the leadership role, it may be better never to assume it. On the other hand, much can be said for a teacher's assuming leadership for the first two or three meetings of the group to provide an excellent example of how a leader should relate to the group. Natural leadership can emerge from the group in that brief time, so that the teacher can relinquish leadership to a given pupil within two or three sessions. The teacher than alternates between the roles of group observer and consultant, sharing both roles with students.

The first task of the group leader, student or teacher, is to help the group decide on the issues it wishes to discuss, clarify the issues, and plan procedures. During the discussion, the leader tries to involve as many of the group members as possible. For example, noting that some members are not participating, he may raise a question regarding what the group is missing by not knowing what the others are thinking. He may even call on some of them for expressions or assistance.   If the group departs from the subject of the discussion, the leader tells them what is happening and asks the group to decide whether they want to turn to a new topic or continue discussion of the original one.   If the discussion is going badly, the leader calls on the group observer for reactions on why the discussion is not going well.   Periodically the leader calls on the recorder to summarize the discussion to date, or he may call on the consultant for clarification or for more adequate information.   The leader also helps the group to keep in mind the time limits on their meeting and to focus their discussion more sharply.   All in all, the leader aims to help individual members, and the group as a whole, to become more effective and efficient in their discussions.

The recorder

One member of the group is appointed *recorder*.   His job is to keep a record of the content of the discussion so that he can report back to the group on request.   Since the group is interested more in *what* was said than in *who* said it, it is unnecessary to record the names of persons making contributions.   The recorder notes the areas of agreement and disagreement, rather than everything that was said by each person making a contribution.   Usually the recorder provides a summary of the discussion at the close of the period, but he may be called upon anytime a report is needed.

The observer

One pupil, in addition to the teacher, is asked to serve as a group observer.   This person does not participate regularly in the discussion so that he can concentrate on what is happening.   He may keep a tally of who participates in the discussion so he can report whether some persons, perhaps including the leader, are monopolizing the group time or if some are not contributing.   The teacher may supplement this record by keeping a qualitative record for his own purposes.   A plus $(+)$ designates a helpful contribution, a negative $(-)$ marks a useless, incorrect, or interrupting comment, and a zero (0) indicates remarks that neither help nor hinder.   This scheme helps to evaluate individual and group progress in discussion skills.   The observer analyzes why the group is being particularly successful or is having difficulties in discussing a given issue.   When called upon by the group leader, he raises questions with the group on points of evaluation, trying to help the group grow in the quality of their discussion rather than serving as a conventional teacher scolding some people and praising others for what they say.

Pupils need the observer's report regularly. For example, assume that a discussion group in English has been talking about problems associated with *work*. They have been reading poems, essays, short stories, and novels about *work* as one unit in the course, but not one pupil in the discussion group has referred to anything he has read on the subject during the unit. In critiquing the discussion the observer might question the omission. Or the observer might have noted that at least three times during the discussion pupils said, "I have went." He might point out that while that expression communicates the idea, it is incorrect grammatically, and that society tends to lower its estimation of the person who fails to use the correct form, "I have gone."

Common sense keeps the observer from too many or too frequent criticisms that would make him appear to nag the pupils too much. On the other hand, failure to point out important shortcomings abrogates the teacher's role. The teacher observer typically reports near the end of the discussion but might do so anytime. The report usually raises questions for discussion rather than pontificates.

The consultant

The teacher, a pupil member of the group, or someone specially invited to meet with the group for a given discussion, may serve as a consultant. His purpose is to provide specific information and experience that other members of the group may not have, but he should not make a speech or monopolize the discussion. A teacher sometimes finds this role difficult because as consultant he must not set too high a level for the discussion or allow himself to dominate the group because of the status of his position. On the other hand, if a teacher or other consultant hears a group member making an error that could misdirect the discussion, the consultant is responsible for correcting that information. Deciding whether the error really matters is a difficult task that tests the consultant's ability to help students learn to discuss effectively.

Periodically, the teacher meets with the leader, recorder, and observer of a new group to help them grow in their various responsibilities. The teacher may suggest to the pupil-leader some provocative questions for discussion. However, too many such questions may become a crutch rather than a challenge to the creativity of the pupils. The teacher also talks to the members of the group, helping them to understand what they are doing as individuals and as a group. They must analyze the member who contributes little, who talks too much, who constantly gets the group off the subject, who asks irrelevant questions, or who irritates by being antagonistic constantly.   Conversely, the group should recognize especially helpful members who bring desirable information at the right time, summarize the discussion, help to clarify issues, and help noncooperative group members become cooperative.

RELATIONSHIPS TO LARGE GROUPS AND INDEPENDENT STUDY

When attending small-group meetings, the teacher must guard against the temptation to lecture, to quiz the pupils, or to feel the small group must cover everything presented in the large group or learned in independent study. He may, however, observe matters that need to be presented more effectively in large-group instruction, and listening to the discussion may help him to appraise the quality of independent study. The teacher may help to stimulate independent study through small-group discussions by scheduling occasional brief reports from students engaging in exciting projects. Thus the teacher ensures planned relationships among all three of the basic phases of the instructional system.

Our experience leads to the recommendation that the small groups should be scheduled as soon as possible after the large groups. The reactions that pupils bring from the large groups are more intense, thus contributing to the effectiveness of the discussion. Also, the teacher meeting with the small group can view the discussion as a sounding board to help him and his colleagues appraise and possibly change the content or the approaches used in other sections of the scheduled presentations to other large groups. Moreover, as pupils realize that they will have a regular opportunity to react to the large groups in the small-group discussions, they approach both experiences with a sharper focus.

TOPICS FOR STUDY AND DISCUSSION

1. Talk about some subject with your colleagues, recording the complete discussion on tape. Play back the recording several times to analyze various roles: member, leader, recorder, observer, consultant. Also, evaluate the quality of the different comments with a +, −, 0 scale.
2. Record a discussion involving pupils and a teacher. Analyze and evaluate it as you did for Topic no. 1.
3. Take a curriculum unit or segment in the subject you teach or are preparing to teach. List some topics which would provoke effective discussion.

4. Prepare one or more instruments to measure interpersonal relations among pupils or among a group of colleagues. Plot the relationships on a chart. Your question might be, If you had an opportunity to sit with three of your classmates [or of the faculty or of the department] around a table to discuss [list the topic], who would you prefer to have in the group?

SELECTED REFERENCES

BENNE, KENNETH D., and MUNTYAN, BOZIDAR. "Groups and Group Methods in Curriculum Change." In *Human Relations in Curriculum Change.* New York: Dryden Press, 1951, pp. 66–139 and 154–192.

These pages have many practical suggestions to help teachers and principals understand the roles of group members and help groups improve their operation.

BRADFORD, LELAND POWERS, ed. *Group Development.* Selected Reading Series One. Washington, D.C.: National Training Laboratories, 1961.

This book consists of an introduction to the field of group process, consisting of twelve articles by different authors on such topics as group dynamics and the individual, functional roles of group members, and feedback and group self-evaluation.

————. *T-Group Theory and Laboratory Method.* New York: John Wiley & Sons, Inc., 1964, pp. 336–394 and 452–486.

Robert Blake and Murray Horwitz show how to analyze and improve group action and to resolve conflicts. Mathew Miles relates the T-Group to the classroom. Leland Bradford and others look to the future.

GLATTHORN, ALLAN A. *Learning in the Small Group.* Melbourne, Florida: Institute for Development of Educational Activities, 1966.

This pamphlet includes descriptions of small-group discussion as well as special groups for independent study.

HOOVER, KENNETH H. "Promoting Interaction: Group Processes," "Simulating and/or Improving Reality," and "Utilizing the Microcosm: Small Group Techniques." In *Learning and Teaching in the Secondary School.* 3rd ed. Boston: Allyn and Bacon, Inc., 1972, pp. 273–313 and 478–509.

These chapters provide suggestions in the areas of group dynamics including teacher and pupil roles in groups, behavioral objectives, and methods of recording and evaluating participation.

CHAPTER 2

Technical Devices
in an Instructional System

Audio-visual aids have been available for educational use during much of the twentieth century. More than three decades ago there were heated discussions on the potential role of radio in education. Speeches were made and articles written on various sides of the subject. Some feared that the monster, radio, might replace the teacher in the classroom; others discussed dangers of introducing a technical device into the teacher-pupil relationship, making it less personal. School administrators worried about how difficult it was to schedule the broadcasts with existing classes. Certain educational philosophers warned against developing national networks for teaching all the classrooms of the country at the same time with resultant thought control. Others considered radio an opportunity to bring to all students of the country the best teaching that could be found. The arguments *for* radio approximated those given today in favor of television and other technical devices.

What happened as a result of all these discussions? Though students occasionally listened to radio broadcasts or produced some themselves, radio never became an integral part of the curriculum.

Most teachers today have only a few more instructional aids than teachers had three or more decades ago. The exhibits at educational conventions and advertisements in educational periodicals testify to the variety of available films, film strips, slides, projectors, recorders, radio and television receivers and transmitters, automated reading devices, programed texbooks and machines, books and other printed materials, pictures, flannel board, and numerous other audio-visual devices. A few places are experimenting with computer-assisted instruction.

Recently, cheaper and simpler recorders and listening devices using tapes in casettes have become more common in classrooms, resource centers, libraries, and other study and work areas. Learning packages may include recorded directions, explanations and tests to go along with, or in addition to, printed materials. Even small children use cassette recorders effectively. Older students increasingly are using video tape recorders to prepare programs. Film-making excites many students, providing wide variations in quality and creativity. There is no shortage of "hardware" (the machines) or "software" (the programs). However, technical devices still play a limited role in the total instructional system, for not enough people are trained to use them properly.

TEACHER AND PUPIL PREPARATION

Curriculum content and methodology that fail to include technical devices are sterile indeed. However, these technical aids require effective settings and trained personnel in order to accomplish the high purposes for which they have been devised.

Teacher education programs typically place little emphasis on the use of technical devices. Many new media become available constantly. Therefore, regularly scheduled clinics are necessary on the job to instruct teachers to prepare, use, and evaluate technical devices effectively.

The overhead projector currently is probably the most widely used of the newer technical aids to teaching. Teachers often write on the overhead visuals the same way they write on a blackboard—but that activity is not a very exciting adjunct to teaching. For example, they should avoid writing outlines, make more effective use of symbolic materials to stimulate creativity, use different colors to emphasize ideas, and develop other imaginative approaches to stimulate pupil interest and make better assignments.

Tape recorders are also used ineffectively. For example, a tape recording need not merely repeat instructions that students already have available in their textbooks, but rather may present information not readily available elsewhere. The list of suggestions for using technical devices could be extended, but such lists are available in numerous other publications.

Pupils also must learn to use technical devices to best advantage. They have been taught to read but have not been taught to view and to listen. For example, there is little evidence that they obtain maximum benefit from many excellent out-of-school radio and television programs. The three components of large-group instruction explained in Chapter 19 may be used to improve viewing and listening habits both in school and outside. Moreover, pupils need training in how to operate the various devices, how to know when they are not workng properly, and where to go for help.

TEACHER USE

Technical devices are used when they can provide a needed service better than a physically-present teacher can, when they complement a teacher's presentation, or when they save time and energy for teachers through adequate substitute performance. Therefore, teachers use technical devices in large-group instruction, to help them to motivate, to inform, and to make the assignment. The devices are also available to pupils for use in their independent study.

The need to use these devices in physical and instructional settings that are economical, effective, and feasible provides one of the more significant arguments against the conventional classroom with one teacher and thirty students. The classroom has to be darkened. If the school has only one projector, for instance, someone has to bring it to the classroom from a storage place—or if each classroom has one, it is unused much of the time. The school has to develop a variety of procedures for scheduling, delivering, picking up, and operating equipment in widely separated spaces.

Confronted by a number of technical devices, the creative teacher carefully studies the goals he has in mind for large-group instruction or independent study, then selects the mediums that will produce the optimum result. The qualities of simplicity, economy and effectiveness affect the decision. A film may be quite costly in comparison to slides, and the majority of materials in the subject to be covered may not require motion. Sound films are more expensive than silent films; in some instances, the sound track is not essential. A teacher may be able to get across a concept better with an overhead projector than with a fleeting television program. The immediacy of television may be superior to the film that, like a book, may have become dated. A recording without a picture may stimulate creativity more than a film or slide which relays a specific image to the mind. On another occasion, a picture is essential for understanding.

Technical devices help teachers to become more professional. Teaching is the only so-called profession that remains largely in the handwork era. The teacher's voice, printed materials, handwritten instructions, and a chalkboard are the usual tools of a teacher's trade.   The arguments about teachers versus machines are ridiculous.   The professional person constantly seeks ways in which technical devices can help him.   The professional teacher must work to determine what he must do himself and what the technical tool can do either for him or with his help.   He also teaches his pupils how to use the best technical aids to their learning.

PUPIL USE

In some respects the most promising development in recent times concerning technical devices is the degree to which pupils use them in resource centers, workrooms, and libraries.   A group of students gathered around a projector or a recorder, stopping the equipment at will in order to discuss an idea generated by the film or recording, presents a highly desirable image of curriculum in motion. Also desirable are the programed instruction devices that make individual pacing possible.   This technique represents a curriculum improvement over the uniform pace provided by the standard textbooks in which teacher assignments tend to keep the pupils all working together, pushing some and holding back others.

Pupils learn to use technical devices during large-group instruction and practice during independent study.   The instruction assistants help the students to locate materials, teach them to operate the equipment, and assist them in translating ideas and reports into audio or visual forms.

Some schools now provide relatively elaborate dial-access systems that enable pupils individually or in groups to call onto a screen and/or into a speaker a variety of films, video and audio tapes, and filmstrips that are stored in a materials center or library. A few schools have computer terminals for contacting distant sources of information.   Telephone systems are used to listen to lectures and for asking questions of authorities located at distant places.   All these technical devices add breadth and depth to the curriculum when integrated into the learning system.

Besides gaining information from technical devices, pupils also learn to express their own ideas through such devices—they are not limited to written or spoken reports.   For example, a set of slides or a film strip about safety in the school (developed as a result of a survey of school accidents and how they might have been prevented) is a good independent study project.   The product may be used later as part of a large-group presentation under the direction of a teacher.   Advanced pupils can be trained to prepare programed materials for beginners or for those having learning difficulties. Those preparing the materials will benefit as much as the pupils who will use them. At other times, students may prepare charts and graphs, some of which may be illuminated by overhead or slide projection, for a brief presentation to be followed by discussion in small groups.

THE INSTRUCTIONAL SYSTEM

Technical devices used as an adjunct to otherwise conventional instruction rather than as an integral part of a totally changed instructional system will produce disappointing results. The vast majority of experiments comparing educational television with conventional teaching reveal no statistically significant gains or losses in pupil learning as measured by standardized or typical teacher-made tests. The same findings often result in studies involving the use of language laboratories or programed instruction devices. Where there are significant differences, usually in one-fourth to one-third of the studies, the majority of cases report favorable results for programs using the new devices, probably a result of the typical Hawthorne, or halo, effect which favors experimental groups.

The television and programed learning proponents must recognize that their medium is merely one of numerous forms of large-group instruction, with all of the potential and the limitations of such presentations. (See Chapter 19.) They must also realize that their medium cannot fulfill its true potential if the administration does not change aspects of the program which constitute effective roadblocks to success. Failure to understand the purposes of large-group instruction and to change teaching and learning methods in independent study and small-group discussion, scheduling, and content, makes the resultant research on television and other devices no more meaningful than the large number of class-size studies conducted in numerous countries for many years.

All aspects of the curriculum system must be related if the results of the new devices are to be favorable. Consider, for example, the use of technical devices in foreign language instruction. In large groups, technical devices or someone who has been to the country may provide students with cultural backgrounds of the country whose language they are learning. The teacher or someone from the community who speaks the language can illustrate basic grammatical forms and vocabulary information. Grammar and vocabulary may then be studied by individual students using programed devices, slides, or film strips showing still pictures of the narrated motion pictures seen in the large groups. Work in the language laboratories with tape recorders may then improve pronunciation of the language and review vocabulary and grammar. Recorded lessons can also be made available for students to study at home with their own phonographs or tape recorders.

Small-group discussion provides the setting for practicing conversational ability in the foreign language. So do individual study groups of two to four pupils meeting around a table if at least one of the pupils is reasonably fluent in the language. All aspects of the system are related to each other through the instruction of teachers and by the sequence of the activities of students. Curriculum development requires that all of the persons involved plan how to use technical devices effectively.

MATERIALS PREPARATION

A study of catalogues reveals a tremendous quantity of commercially prepared audio-visual materials. Teachers must supplement those materials with a considerable number of visuals and recordings made locally, because a film or television program prepared for national use often needs to be complemented for maximum use in the local setting. The school must provide material and personnel to help teachers prepare these additional audio-visual aids.

The place where technical devices are prepared may be called an instructional materials center. Although a city or county system may provide a centralized center, each school needs its own center to complement the services of the centralized location. The teacher roughs out an idea; the personnel of the materials center translate the idea into an effective technical device to aid the teacher. Instruction assistants do the research needed to prepare a visual or recording, artists or technicians prepare the end product, and clerks store the materials and keep records.

THE SETTING

Technical devices lose their effectiveness when pupils cannot see and hear well. Yet, strange as it may seem, experience in visiting thousands of classrooms indicates that large numbers of teachers fail to appreciate the importance of the arrangements for seeing and hearing. Television sets are not adjusted properly; screens are placed incorrectly; sound address systems are inadequate; light control is not sufficient to ensure good visibility; sound fidelity is poor; distractions bother students working on programed material. These faults should be remedied.

Screens and television sets should be placed as near the ceiling as possible and tilted forward to minimize keystone effects and to provide better visibility for all students. That arrangement is especially important if the student seating is on a flat level floor. Remember also to place screens in partially lighted rooms with the screen's back to the light source in order to gain more visibility. To gain better sound distribution and quality, scatter a number of speakers throughout the room instead of using one or two speakers in the front of the room. Provide chest microphones so that teachers may move around while speaking. Pay attention to the importance of light control, ventilation, acoustical control, and the other features of good facilities described in Chapter 25.

TOPICS FOR STUDY AND DISCUSSION

1. Plan an overhead projector visual to go with some presentation that you might make in the course you teach or plan to teach.
2. Outline plans for a locally made filmstrip on a topic such as the following: how to avoid accidental injury in the school or on the grounds; gaining work experience in this community; local historical sites; architecture in our town.
3. Assume an annual school budget of ten dollars per pupil for audio-visual aids. Show how you would spend the money and defend your choices.
4. Considering a given subject, what audio-visual aids would you list as having highest priority for improving pupil learning?
5. Since technical devices provide optional learning strategies in addition to reading and writing, plan an experiment where different pupils learn by increased, or even total, use of viewing and listening programs.
6. Evolve some guidelines for incorporating the use of technical devices in a learning package.

SELECTED REFERENCES

BURKE, RICHARD C., ed. "The Television Teacher" by Bonnie Gilliom. In *Instructional Television*. Bloomington: Indiana University Press, 1971, pp. 57–85.

Chapter 5 describes techniques useful in large-group instruction.

BUSHNELL, DON D., and ALLEN, DWIGHT W., eds. *The Computer in American Education*. New York: John Wiley & Sons, 1967, pp. 59–107.

Don Bushnell discusses simulation and gaming, information retrieval, and the production and evaluation of curriculum materials. Karl Zim reviews systems and current projects involving computer-assisted instruction.

DAVIS, HAROLD S. *Instructional Media Center*. Bloomington: Indiana University Press, 1971, pp. vii–237.

Fourteen writers describe various centers for elementary, and junior and senior high schools for pupil and teacher use, giving theory, how to do it, successful operations, and further references.

ELY, DONALD P., and GERLOACH, VERNON S. *Teaching and Media: A Systematic Approach*. Englewood Cliffs, N.J.: Prentice-Hall, Inc., 1971.

This book relates classroom objectives to the selection and use of media.

GARNER, W. LEE. *Programed Instruction*. New York: The Center for Applied Research in Education, Inc., 1966.

After giving the reasons for programing, the author describes various types of programs, shows their applications in education, and explains how to train programers and how to make programs. The final chapters relate programed instruction to computers and look to future developments.

GORDON, GEORGE N. *Educational Television*. New York: The Center for Applied Research in Education, Inc., 1965.

This volume gives historical perspective along with reasons for, present status of, and effectiveness of instructional television. It speculates about the future of open-circuit and closed-circuit installations.

GREEN, ALLAN C., ed. "A Guide for Policy Makers." In *Educational Facilities with New Media*. Washington, D.C.: National Education Association, Department of Educational Technology, 1966, pp. A-1–A-42.

Report A presents a comprehensve account of new media as they relate to educational innovations.

KAIMANN, RICHARD A., and MARKER, ROBERT W., eds. *Educational Data Processing: New Dimensions and Prospects*. Boston: Houghton Mifflin Company, 1967.

This book presents statements from numerous experts on systems theory and analysis, information systems, computerized guidance and instruction, simulation in teaching and administration, and other aspects of data processing. It shows how this new and rapidly changing field will revolutionize curriculum development.

McCLOSKY, MILDRED G., ed. "Uses of Media and Technical Equipment." In *Teaching Strategies and Classroom Realities*. Englewood Cliffs, N.J.: Prentice-Hall, Inc., 1971, pp. 216–251.

Fourteen authors write on ways to use pictures, overhead projectors, recorders, music, advertisements, and student-produced films to liven up and improve teaching and learning.

McLUHAN, MARSHALL, and FIORE, QUENTIN. *The Medium Is the Massage.* New York: Bantam Books, Inc., 1967.

This volume states that technology is reshaping every aspect of life, calling for a new kind of education that "must shift from instruction . . . to discovery . . . to the recognition of the language of forms."

CHAPTER 22

The Nongraded, Continuous
Progress School

More than a century ago, many pupils in the United States did not attend school regularly. Someone learning to read, write, and compute could leave school to work (or for some other reason), then return and resume where he had left off. Administrators did not have to consider whether he should be put into the third grade or the sixth, because that classification was unknown. About a century ago, however, as schools became larger, a scheme for dividing pupils into different classes or rooms became necessary. A graded system was imported from Germany in the middle 1800's.

The system of grades like the Carnegie Unit and many other quantitative administrative procedures to simplify decision making were imported or developed locally by state departments of education and regional accrediting agencies. Colleges needed standards for determining who should be admitted to college and for evaluating secondary school courses. Secondary school administrators needed easily administered methods for determining when pupils should enter their schools, how much progress they were making, and when they should be permitted to graduate.

Needless to say, quantitative standards tend to bring rigidity to school administration and to teaching, making it difficult to treat the difference among pupils effectively. Content must be compressed or expanded into standard-length courses that meet a given number of minutes per week for one semester, one year, or some other specified period. Curriculum revision relates directly to the grade structure, or the lack of it, in any junior or senior high school.

The practice of ungrading schools, especially the primary grades, started to receive considerable attention in this country about a quarter of a century ago, when a number of studies revealed the ineffectiveness in many cases of making failing pupils repeat a grade. The use of ungraded primary classes proved successful in reducing failure, because many slow children, allowed to stay with their classmates, were able to increase the tempo of their achievement during subsequent years and catch up with the others. The ungrading of the 1930's and 1940's, however, failed to consider adequately such other potential improvements as curriculum reorganization, newer teaching and learning methods, changes in the organization of instruction, and the various extra-school influences that create differences among school pupils.

EXISTING PLANS

A number of plans are used today to permit students to progress at different rates of speed. In some places, secondary schools classify pupils on the basis of ability or achievement, tempered by teacher judgment, and select special content to fit the needs of each group. That procedure contrasts with the conventional program that arbitrarily organizes courses called English 8 or English 10, French 1 or French 2, or Sophomore Physical Education—and then tries to fit students into them.

Other schools have adopted a track system, so that low-ability students do not have to compete unsuccessfully with higher ability students, but may graduate with considerably less achievement in the lowest track. Different types of diplomas sometimes are given to students to show which track system they went through in high school. Such programs require basic changes in curriculum content, teaching methods, and evaluation. A disadvantage of this system is that pupils from less favored homes, or from some national or racial groups, tend to cluster in certain tracks. Also, teachers sometimes dislike working day after day with students in lower tracks.

Another issue relative to nongrading concerns horizontal or vertical enrichment of curriculum content. Some educators feel that students should be permitted to take advanced or additional courses so that they may graduate from high school in less time and go on to college. Those opposing that practice want all students to spend six years in the program between elementary and higher education. They believe higher-ability students can benefit simply by taking more courses and engaging in special projects in regular courses—projects not expected of less able students.   A compromise approach is the Advanced Placement Program, where students remain in the secondary school while taking college-level courses with the expectation that they will be given credit for those courses when they enroll in college.

Other nongrading procedures are being followed in some schools.   A small high school may cycle its required courses.   Instead of offering world history, U.S. history, and problems of democracy every year, one of the courses is offered each year to all pupils. Everyone in a given course, regardless of age, works in a group appropriate for him.   Correspondence courses supplement the curriculum when necessary for pupils who transfer into the school during the year and find that the course they need is not offered at the time they need it.

Other schools divide courses into segments designed for pupils of varied talents.   Teachers observe pupil progress in each segment to determine which subsequent materials are appropriate. The purpose is to place pupils in situations where they can succeed. Independent study time and the facilities for pupil activities are increased.   One school varies this pattern by organizing all courses into eight-week units.   Each junior high school pupil chooses the unit and study activities he wishes for the next eight weeks.   A teacher-counselor approves hs choice.

Although each of the foregoing proposals has some merit and is better than the conventional graded program, none of them represents the ultimate goal.   A truly nongraded school is one that has gone far beyond eliminating annual promotions, grouping students subject by subject on the basis of achievement, or making local curriculum revisions that contribute to a nongraded approach. Each of the foregoing may be the first step towards a nongraded program.   (Other first steps will be described in Chapter 30.)

For maximum curriculum improvement, the nongraded school must use team teaching, flexible scheduling, technical devices, and the teaching-learning methods described in earlier chapters that dealt with independent study, large-group instruction, and small-group discussion. It must also adapt to the socioeconomic, political, cultural, and other characteristics of the areas in which its students live.   Pupils in a large city are different from those in the rural midwest, and students in a community overwhelmed by poverty require a different curriculum than those in an affluent area.   The nongraded school negates student frustration because it lessens the pressures for conformity.   Students are comfortable with a peer group with whom success is a distinct possibility. The nongraded school enhances the possibility of individualized learning.

DETERMINING CONTENT

As indicated in Chapter 2, the basic task is to determine what content is *essential* for all persons who are educable. That content consists of the skills, knowledge, concepts, and attitudes in every area of human knowledge that are regarded as necessary for all persons in any particular society. Educators must also determine what additional material is *desirable* and what is *enriching*—desirable for the average students and enriching for the talented, the ones who are likely to be the leaders in the schools of today and the society of tomorrow. National experts may determine the content which is essential, desirable, and enriching for all persons regardless of where the school is located. The content is the *basic education* of all persons and may become, in fact, a national curriculum. State and regional agencies may supplement that curriculum to provide for particular local needs and interests. The faculty of the local school then will add to the state and regional curriculum content.

A second curriculum task is to arrange the required content logically and sequentially in relation to what is known about child growth and development. The schools group and regroup pupils on the basis of individual progress through this material. Each child should cover the entire content, starting when he first enters school and finishing near the end of the compulsory education age. Much of the content can be programed through texts and machines. Someday students will progress through it individually by means of computer-assisted instruction.

The third curriculum task requires the nongraded school to develop a program of *depth education* at all levels and for all subject areas. Whether a student completes the elementary school (including kindergarten and secondary school in fewer than thirteen years is a matter for professional decision. Making that decision wisely, however, assumes the availability of a broad program of depth education which aims to stimulate creativity on the part of all pupils, not merely the most able and the most creative. When a school administration considers it desirable for all students to remain in secondary school the same number of years, teachers and counselors can provide enrichment programs for the students who might otherwise complete the average program of depth education too early.

The charts on pages 332 to 335 illustrate how curriculum content for the nongraded school might be developed in the areas of social science and home economics. The charts are illustrative rather than definitive. The most able scholars in the subject dis-

Proposed Social Science Curriculum Model
(Recommended Pattern for All School Subject Areas)

	Present Grade Equiva-lent	Age	Subject Emphases	Basic Education for All — Topics	Depth Education for Some
Primary	K	5	All: Selected terms and concepts	Seasons, holidays, places and names in the news, value and use of money, families and neighborhood	Very little at this point. Students work briefly on special interest topics within their "home base" room or in a resource area
	1	6	from all seven social science subjects areas	People in selected lands (*e.g.* Japan, India, Nigeria, Australia, France, Brazil, and Canada)—how they live, their governments, their geography—in relation to ours	
	2	7		Effects of geography (environmental factors) on producers and consumers, transportation and communication, cultural patterns, social relations	
	3	8	History Geography	Local, state, and regional history and geography	
Middle	4	9	History	United States history and geography	
	5	10	Geography History Anthropology	Man's development from prehistoric to modern times showing intercultural influences, the flow of history, and general time relationships	
	6	11	History Political Science	Struggle for power and search for peace (contemporary scene with a perspective from experiences of the past)	From time to time, to explore personal talents and interests and to motivate others, some students make limited studies of selected aspects of
	7	12	Economics Sociology	Economic and social relations (*e.g.* food, clothing, shelter, exchange, urban and rural	

	Grade	Subject	Content	Level of Essential Knowledge	Level of Desirable Knowledge	Level of Enriching Knowledge	Level 1	Level 2	Level 3
	8	History, Political Science, History	life, social groups)—contemporary and in the past. Governmental institutions and services (local, state, national, international)—rights, responsibilities, and security for individuals and groups—contemporary and in the past				these subjects—usually in the social science laboratory		
	9	History, Philosophy, Psychology	Beauty in the arts, world religions, value patterns, personal and group adjustments (social psychology)—contemporary and in the past						
Secondary	10, 15					United States civilization up to 1900—review and reinforcement of historic, geographic, socioeconomic, political, anthropological, and scientific forces that have shaped this country with emphasis on the interplay of forces	*Level 1* Individual or 2–3 students spend 25–50 hours in a year on some topic or project	*Level 2* Individual or group works several hours per week for several months	*Level 3* Individual or group studies 10–25 hours per week
	11, 16	All				United States civilization to the present			
	12, 17					Problem solving and action—weekly presentations, discussions, and actions on topics of current significance			
Adult Education									

Note: During K-3 (Primary period), "home base" teachers do most of the teaching with social science teachers assisting and making some presentations in a team-teaching relationship. Programs for grade 4 and above are taught by social science teachers in teaching teams, using *large-group instruction* for presentations, films, television, and the like; *small-group discussion* for personal interaction, problem-solving, and communication skills; and *independent study* in social science laboratories. Schools are nongraded.

Proposed Home Economics Curriculum Model
(For Discussion Only)

PRESENT GRADE EQUIVA-LENT	AGE	BASIC EDUCATION FOR ALL	DEPTH EDUCATION FOR SOME
Primary K	5	Planned study, informal in treatment, of such topics as: relations with family and other persons, care of clothing, respect for others, consequences of acts, problem solving, group planning, personal responsibility for beauty in home and school	Very little at this point
1	6		
2	7		
3	8		
Middle 4	9	Personal and family health	
5	10	Food habits and practices	
6	11	Care and selection of clothing	
7	12	Care of home and surroundings	
8	13	Safety and sanitation, table manners, duties of family members	From time to time, some students make special, but limited, studies of selected phases of these subjects to explore their personal talents and interests and to motivate other students
9	14	Personal and family finances	
		The arts in the home, clothing, etc.	
		Food and nutrition	
		Clothing and textiles	
		Home management	
		Child study and family relations	

		Level of Essential Knowledge	Level of Desirable Knowledge	Level of Enriching Knowledge		
				Level 1	*Level 2*	*Level 3*
Secondary	10			Student spends 25–50 hours on some topic, e.g., survey of housing, or food habits in India	Group works for a semester; e.g., planning & furnishing a new home, or health and home nursing	Rigorous course; e.g., foods clothing, child study, principles of design, or consumer economics
	11	Review, reinforcement, and updating: special presentations, discussions and independent study				
	12					
Adult Educa-tion						

Note: During K-3 (Primary period), "home base" teachers do most of the teaching with home economics teachers assisting and making some presentations in a team-teaching relationship. Programs for grade 4 and above are taught by home economics teachers in teaching teams.

ciplines working with the most able scholars in child growth and in the behavioral sciences must develop the actual content, updating and revising it constantly on the basis of experience and research.

Some readers may object to the emphasis here on subject disciplines in contrast to what has been variously called *core, common learnings, life adjustment,* or *general education,* wherein subject matter is organized around general themes or purposes. However, the subject discipline approach helps pupils to understand the various subjects as such, in order to comprehend books and lectures better and to make advanced educational or vocational decisions. Teaching teams can cut across subject lines by pointing out areas where the subjects relate closely. Ultimately, the integration of subject content occurs in the minds of individuals as they discover relationships and develop generalizations.

ARRANGING CONTENT FOR CONTINUOUS PROGRESS

The curriculum goal is to arrange content so that each pupil can proceed at his own pace with learning strategies that are appropriate for him, a variety of options open, and emphasis on self-appraisal. The materials also need to provide for individual diagnosis and direction. Although teachers and assistants are available to help, the emphasis is on pupil responsibility.

Various arrangements can foster the foregoing goals. The contained classroom places responsibility for monitoring on one teacher. The future doubtless will see much of this monitoring done by computer-assisted instruction. In the meantime, teachers and other professionals are producing a variety of aids which bear such names as learning packages, UNIPAKS, Individually Prescribed Instruction (IPI), and guidesheets and worksheets.

The essential ingredients are:

The concept, skill, appreciation, etc., that the pupil is to acquire
The specific sub-concept, etc., in this particular segment
Definition in behavioral terms so the learner understands specifically what is to occur and how he will know that he has achieved the goals
Pre-test so the learner knows what he already has achieved and what remains to be accomplished
A variety of learning strategies that he may follow: read what, do what, listen to what, view what, take a field trip where, etc.
Self-test to enable the learner to know when he has accomplished the required learnings
Whom to see when he has difficulties

Arranges for a teacher (or instructional assistant) to administer evaluation and check results

Three alternatives when the learner finishes the required, prescribed program:

1. Go on to the next required segment
2. Go into greater depth: more of the same or similar
3. Create; "do your own thing"

The three options at the close of each segment are extremely important. Without those three alternatives, individualized learning does not occur. The departmental curriculum goal is to interest each pupil in the second or third choices. However, the department competes with all others in this regard. The pupil decides which course to follow with the help of teachers in all the departments and his personal teacher-adviser (see chapters 23 and 24).

THE YEAR-ROUND SCHOOL

A current interest is to utilize educational facilities more effectively by extending their use longer hours each day and for more days in the year, perhaps ultimately for every day including Saturdays and Sundays, all the months. Unless the continuous progress concept is incorporated in these plans, some unfortunate side effects may occur. For example, the school schedule might schedule different holidays for different children in the same family under some of the programs. One proposal is to have some pupils attend school for 45 days and then take a required 15-day vacation. This program simply divides the conventional school year into four 45-day segments instead of the conventional two 90-day semesters or one 180-day year with the usual three-months summer holiday. The curriculum task in such a program is ignored.

The individualized curriculum with self-directing, self-pacing, self-motivating (with a variety of learning strategies and options), and self-evaluating materials provides a more satisfactory solution to better utilization of educational facilities and human resources. The school regulation is that a pupil may drop in and out of school at times that are convenient for the entire family and that are good for each pupil personally. The only requirement is that he must attend school a minimum of 180 days per year. Incidentally, if the pupil is interested and his family and school counselors approve, a pupil may attend more days than 180 each year and complete the secondary school in fewer calendar years. If he wants to stay in the home community longer and take more subjects than the school requires for graduation, the school may decide to charge a special tuition for such an expanded program.

The continuous progress concept permits more extensive work experience and/or travel during the secondary school years than is possible in the conventional school, and at times when the pupil is especially interested or needs the experience as his family and school counselors approve.   The next chapter presents more alternatives in flexible scheduling.

TOPICS FOR STUDY AND DISCUSSION

1. Take a unit or segment of a course you now teach or plan to teach.   List the facts, concepts, skills, and other content that are essential, desirable, and enriching for pupils, as defined in this chapter.
2. Consider the subject area that interests you most.   Make a chart comparable to the one on pages 332–333.
3. After consulting the readings for this chapter, prepare to defend the concept of nongrading by listing all the potential advantages. Or, take the opposite point of view.
4. Analyze in greater detail than is provided in this chapter the other aspects of content, teaching methods, and school structure that need to change along with the development of a nongraded program.
5. What are the implications of the continuous progress concept for the year-round school, early graduation from high school, or work-study programs?

SELECTED REFERENCES

BEGGS, DAVID W., III, and BUFFIE, EDWARD G., eds.   *Nongraded Schools in Action*.   Bloomington: Indiana University Press, 1967.

Twenty-five authors write about elementary and secondary programs.   Part I includes the historical perspectives, basic organizational concepts, procedures for starting, methods of evaluation, and a look ahead.   Part II describes programs in specific schools; chapters 17, 18, and 19 concern high schools.   Selected, annotated bibliography suggests further readings.

BROWN, BARTLEY FRANK.   *The Appropriate Placement School: A Sophisticated Nongraded Curriculum*.   West Nyack, N.Y.: Parker Publishing Co., 1965.

Chapters Six and Seven, respectively, describe junior and senior high school multiphased programs. Two other chapters present a curriculum for dropouts and disadvantaged youth.

————. *The Nongraded High School.* Englewood Cliffs, N.J.: Prentice-Hall, Inc., 1963.

This author gives reasons for nongrading. He describes the flexibility it brings, and the concept-centered curriculum, the changes in evaluation, and the public relations program it requires. The author tells the story of Melbourne, Florida, High School, where he was principal.

JENKINS, JOHN M. "The Nongraded High School" and "The Curriculum in the Nongraded High School: Restoration of Curiosity." In *Curriculum Development in Nongraded Schools.* Bloomington: Indiana University Press, 1972, pp. 135–167.

An author with considerable leadership experience in nongraded schools explains an organizational pattern involving "phasing," proposes a Model, and describes in some detail the preparation, use and evaluation of learning packages.

MILLER, RICHARD I., ed. *The Nongraded School.* New York: Harper and Row, publishers, 1967, pp. 72–154.

C. Robert Blackmon and Richard I. Miller summarize the reasons for the nongraded school movement. Most of the material in these two chapters relates to intermediate and secondary schools.

CHAPTER 23

Individualized Scheduling
and Accountability

The schedule of classes or group meetings reflects the current educational philosophy of the school. The time arrangements specified in the schedule enhance or inhibit curriculum improvement. The schedule may encourage depth study or it may keep pupils from caring deeply about any subject. It may encourage a broad, general education including the fine and practical arts or it may keep those subjects away from most students in the upper secondary school years. It may give teachers variety and free them for curriculum planning and development, or it may keep them in a daily routine that saps their energy. Attention to the schedule has high priority in curriculum improvement.

New mechanical aids available to the schedule maker are stimulating a desirable interest in flexible scheduling. However, we must disassociate speed from the concept of flexible scheduling. Electronic data processing equipment may be used to do faster what should not be done at all; namely, facilitate and freeze a conventional school schedule. Doubtless, electronic aids can help pupils and teachers use their time better, but concentration on machines may well delay achieving the kind of flexibility that is needed. Since everyone has the same amount of time, the question is how to use it to best advantage.

The goal of the schedule is to give teachers and pupils as much freedom as is reasonable in the use of time, space, and numbers of persons, as well as content for instruction. The following are worthwhile objectives:

1. The class schedule may be changed daily, or at least frequently on the basis of teacher requests.
2. Each pupil, under competent direction and with appropriate controls, may make choices regarding his part in the established schedule.
3. Conflicts for pupils and teachers are reduced to a minimum.
4. Teacher loads and pupil loads permit both maximum professionalization of teaching and maximum individualization of learning opportunities.
5. The school knows what its pupils and teachers are doing and where they are.
6. The whole scheme is financially feasible and logistically operational.

STEPS TOWARD FLEXIBLE SCHEDULING

One of the basic reasons for changing schedules is to make possible a number of different institutional arrangements for education. For example, principals and teachers, understandably dissatisfied with the rigidity of today's schedules, may conclude that some courses need more time than others or that some classes need to meet less often, but for longer periods of time on certain days. Such considerations may lead to the "modular concept" of flexible scheduling. Instead of the conventional forty-five- or fifty-five-minute periods, the schools adopt a fifteen-, twenty-, or thirty-minute module, or period length, so that instead of six periods a day, the school schedule includes twelve, sixteen, or twenty-four periods in a day. The school then schedules various subjects for a different number of modules, sometimes the same number each day in the week. A degree of flexibility results, but once the change is made, the new schedule can become almost as rigid as the one it replaced. Examples of modular schedules are shown on page 342.

Some schools vary their schedule by rotating periods, sometimes of different lengths, or even by rotating special schedules on different days. This system is often chosen when a school which has been following conventional curricular organization patterns wishes to make it possible for a student to take six or seven subjects instead of the conventional five or six. The subjects are scheduled to meet four times a week instead of five; they are scheduled on a floating basis to fill out the five-day week, and some periods are made longer than others. Although this change is sometimes called flexible scheduling, the new program also can become quite rigid and actually contributes relatively little to the improved use of time by students and teachers.

Still another arrangement is represented by a variety of team teaching approaches. According to one form, six teachers are

15 Minute Modules—same schedule every day	
TIME	SUBJECT
8:00 8:15 8:30 8:45	Mathematics
9:00	Speech Correction
9:15 9:30 9:45 10:00 10:15	Science
10:30 10:45	Music
11:00 11:15 11:30	Spanish
11:45	Music Practice
12:00 etc.	Lunch

50 Minute Modules—two-hour classes, Monday through Thursday; one-hour classes, Friday

TIME	MONDAY	TUESDAY	WED.–THURS.	FRIDAY
8:00 9:00	Biology	Geometry	Same as Mon.–Tues.	Biology English
10:00 11:00	English	French	Same as Mon.–Tues.	French Geometry
12:00	Lunch and Activities			
1:00 2:00	Physical Ed.	Study or Elective	Same as Mon.–Tues.	Phys. Ed. Stu./Ele.

responsible for 180 students for a 2-hour block of time each day. Teachers and students may divide their time among large-group instruction, small-group discussion, and independent study.   All of the students may watch a film for 18 minutes, then separate into groups so that 90 students attend a supplementary presentation by one of the teachers. 4 groups of 15 each discuss with 4 other teachers, and the remaining 30 students go to a library or workroom for independent study under the supervision of the sixth teacher.   The new arrangements may last for 36 minutes, or any other specified time, so long as the total 2-hour block is maintained. Then the students are rearranged so that all have small-group work and independent study.   Obviously, this approach represents a more flexible use of time, space, and student groupings than is possible in a conventionally organized school.   But again, flexibility is limited, this time by the 2-hour block.

A few schools organize instruction almost completely on the team teaching basis, with large-group, small-group, and independent study arrangements.   Such schools achieve still more flexibility in scheduling by using a modular approach.   Large classes of 100 or more pupils in a given subject may be scheduled for two 20-minute modules (40 minutes) twice a week.   Seminar-size groups of 15 or fewer students in the same subject area are scheduled for two modules, twice a week, at different times in the day from the large group and possibly on different days in the week.   Independent study in each subject is scheduled for each student, depending on his interests and talents, for 3, 4, or more consecutive modules on different days in the week.

Rotation of Classes—Standard Periods

TIME	MONDAY	TUESDAY	WEDNES-DAY	THURSDAY	FRIDAY
8:00	1	1	1	1	2
9:00	2	2	2	3	3
10:00	3	3	4	4	4
11:00	4	5	5	5	5
12:00			LUNCH		
12:30	6	6	6	6	7
1:30	7	7	7	Special	Special

Note: Numbers indicate different subjects

Rotation of Classes—Periods Vary in Length

TIME	MONDAY	TUESDAY	WEDNES-DAY	THURSDAY	FRIDAY
8:55–10:26	1	2	4	5	6
10:30–11:26	2	4	5	6	1
11:30–12:26	3	3	3	3	3
12:26–1:04			LUNCH		
1:04–2:30	4	5	6	1	2
2:34–3:30	5	6	1	2	4

Note: Numbers indicate different subjects

Team Teaching—Block of Time

TIME	MONDAY THROUGH FRIDAY
8:00 9:00	3 U.S. History & 3 English teachers schedule 180 junior students as they deem desirable
10:00	Planning Period for Team
11:00	Conventional Classes
12:00	Lunch
12:30 1:30	Same as first period but with different students: e.g. sophomores
2:30	Planning Period for Team

Though schools using that approach usually change the independent study of their pupils at will they often hold quite systematically to the scheduled time for large-group instruction and small-group discussion.   The conventional idea (not based on research) that an English class must meet 5 days a week, 50 minutes per day, at the same hour of the day, with one teacher in charge, may merely be replaced by the equally unsubstantiated concept that English must meet twice a week, 40 minutes per time, in classes of 120, with the best teaching available and once a week, for 40 minutes, in classes of 15, with a teacher in charge of each class.   The new schedule says, in effect, that English requires 120 minutes of group instruction per week, plus whatever time (80 minutes or more) the staff determines is necessary for independent study by pupils in English resource centers or the library.   The staff becomes so enamored with these arrangements that the "flexible schedule" becomes rigidly established.   This is especially possible if the schedule is made with expensive data processing equipment. More research is needed to determine better the time requirements of different teaching and learning activities.

Team Teaching—Modular Approach

TIME	MONDAY	TUESDAY	WEDNESDAY
8:20 8:40	History LG	English LG	History LG
9:00 9:20	French Sem	French LG	French Lab
9:40 10:00	History Sem	Homemaking LG	English Sem
10:20 10:40 11:00 11:20	PE	Science Sem ——— Homemaking Lab	PE
11:40 12:00	Math LG		Math LG
12:20		LUNCH	
ETC	Humanities RC	Typing LG	Science RC

LG—Large-Group Instruction, Sem—Small-Group Discussion, Lab—Laboratory, RC—Resource Center—Independent Study

EXAMPLES OF SUCCESSFUL PROGRAMS

Several schools have initiated their own programs that successfully provide for flexible daily schedule changes by teachers and students.   Individual members of teaching teams determine three days in advance which pupils they need to teach, in what size groups, for what length of time, in what places, and with what technological aids.   Then they prepare job specification forms containing this information and turn them in to their team leaders.

The team leaders and a clerk assemble to make a master schedule that includes what students "must" follow for the day. The master schedule is then duplicated and made available to the pupils and their counselors.   In a daily twenty-minute meeting, with the advice and consent of his counselor, each pupil plans his own schedule, filling in his choices for the considerable amount of time open to him.   He may choose to spend his time in independent study in the art room, science laboratory, or the library.   The counselor either approves or rejects this decision.   The pupil then makes out his own schedule for the day in quadruplicate—one copy for himself, one for the office, one for the counselor, and one for his parents.   The schedule is developed mainly by hand. Doubtless, mechanical aids could simplify the process by helping to avoid conflicts and other problems that arise and by saving time for both students and teachers.   It should be noted, however, that the concepts of schedule-making come first and the machines that facilitate the process come second in their planning.

Another school constructed a new building without including a program clock or bell system.   Instead, teachers meet daily in grade-level teams to change the schedule at will.   This program and others like it in some ways represent an advancement over the block-of-time schedule described on page 344.   The larger the number of teachers, the larger the number of students, and the greater the amount of time they are brought together, the more flexible teachers and students can be in using the time.

The diagram on page 347 illustrates such a schedule, showing how various groups might be assigned during a given week. All of the 360 students involved are assembled in one place on Tuesday for a 35-minute mathematics test.   Science teachers have scheduled 3-hour field trips on Monday, Wednesday, Thursday, and Friday for 90 students each day.   Orchestra rehearsal for 90 students occupies 80 minutes Monday and Thursday.   A 24-student vocal ensemble practices for 40 minutes on three days.   The 360 students are divided in half for large-group presentations in history on Wednesday and Friday.   Small-group discussion ses-

PARTIAL SCHEDULE FOR ONE WEEK

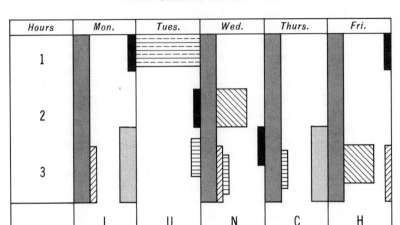

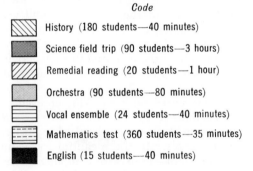

Code

History (180 students—40 minutes)

Science field trip (90 students—3 hours)

Remedial reading (20 students—1 hour)

Orchestra (90 students—80 minutes)

Vocal ensemble (24 students—40 minutes)

Mathematics test (360 students—35 minutes)

English (15 students—40 minutes)

The schedule also includes many groups not shown, and pupils spend much time in independent study in all subject areas.

sions, remedial reading groups, independent study, and other groups are similarly scheduled.

Still another school has devised a "Priority Period" to give teachers and pupils control over time. They have reduced the number of class periods per week from five to four to provide free periods for students and teachers. Each group uses these periods for what they regard as high priority activities. A teacher may take a group of students for remedial work. A student may spend time in the music room, shop, or science laboratory. Data processing cards avoid conflicts and provide class lists to check attendance during the priority periods. A next step might reduce class meetings to three times a week—one large group and two small groups or two large groups and one small group.

Will these persons and others following similar or even more imaginative practices fall back into a rigid schedule? Such a development is possible but certainly less probable than in the case of the approaches described earlier in this chapter. Further use of automated instruction devices (teaching textbooks and machines) and the development of computer-assisted instructional systems will encourage further individualization of instruction and consequently more individual scheduling.

Flexible scheduling ultimately depends on the reorganization of curriculum content into a nongraded sequence, an increase of time for independent study, and a decrease of group activities, both large and small. The flexible schedule that we envision provides one large-group motivational presentation and one small-group for a reaction discussion for each pupil once a week in each of the eight general areas of knowledge—nine in parochial schools.[1] All other time in the school week is for study and work experiences. These three activities were described in chapters 19, 20, and 18, respectively. Each school will make its own decision on the length and frequency of the large and small groups that we recommend. Our experience is that about thirty minutes per week in each activity in all the areas is preferred; however, much more needs to be known about the potential in such activities. The balance of the school week is for independent study under supervision.

The schedule presented on page 349 represents what we call, *individualized scheduling.*

These developments represent a level of sophistication not yet achieved in most schools. In the meantime, scheduling continues to be a knotty problem—even with computers to help. The stake that teachers have in the flexible schedule may be the force that pushes the balance in favor of pupil choices in the use of time. Both groups have much to gain.

HUMANISM AND ACCOUNTABILITY

Individualized scheduling aims to make a school more humane, more individualized for students and teachers, and to facilitate accountability of both groups. The goal is to provide students with a curriculum environment that facilitates self-ex-

[1] English, fine arts, health-fitness, recreation (physical education), mathematics, other cultures (foreign languages), practical arts (including vocational), religion, science, social studies.

MONDAY	TUESDAY	WEDNESDAY	THURSDAY	FRIDAY
A	DAILY MEETING WITH TEACHER-ADVISOR			
1 *				
2 **ENGLISH	PRACTICAL ARTS	SOCIAL SCIENCE	FINE ARTS	SCIENCE
3 *** English	Practical Arts	Social Science	Fine Arts	Science
4		MATHEMATICS		
5		Mathematics		
6 L	U	N	C	H
7				
8				
9				
10				HEALTH, FITNESS RECREATION
11				Health, Fitness Recreation
12				
13	OTHER CULTURES			
14	Other Cultures			

* Independent Study—supervised study/work
** Large-Group Instruction—motivational experience sessions
*** Small-Group Discussion—reaction groups

ploration, decision making, and learning in an environment best suited for each one of them.   Each pupil's teacher-adviser helps the pupil to accomplish that goal by varying the time, locale, and learning strategies available.   A school with the humane emphasis keeps the students in touch with all curriculum areas by means of motivational presentations and reaction discussions, as described in chapters 19 and 20.   Alternatives for study and in the use of time were outlined in chapters 18, 20, and 22.   The individualized schedule as described earlier in this chapter facilitates the process.

Accountability involves much more than how a school spends money and how those funds produce gains or losses on standardized tests.   Accountability also involves questions about how and where pupils spend time and what the alternatives in curriculum content and settings do to each pupil in the school. Accountability also involves different concepts of evaluation as we shall see in chapters 26 and 27.

The conventional school realizes accountability by placing each pupil in a class of about thirty, five or six periods a day, and assumes accountability by the classroom teacher as long as the pupil attends the class with some degree of regularity and conforms sufficiently to the curriculum provided there both in content and teaching-learning methods.

Individualized scheduling transfers basic accountability for each pupil to a teacher-adviser, although it holds the different departments responsible for a curriculum that provides options and for the monitoring of each pupil's progress, or lack of it, while the pupil is studying and working in the various resource centers inside and outside of the school. The teacher-adviser, unlike the classroom teachers in a conventional school, through the process of individualized scheduling and the reports received from all of the supervisors of study and work centers, now sees the pupil as a total human being *educationally speaking*. This central responsibility for each pupil, vis-à-vis the divided responsibility among a number of classroom teachers or with a professional counselor who makes out programs for 300 or more pupils (too many for individual monitoring), is the concept we urge.

The teacher-adviser exercises this curricular responsibility in the following manner. When a pupil first comes to the school, he is assigned to a teacher-adviser who works with him as long as he remains in the school unless a deliberate change is made. The adviser schedules the independent study time on the same day(s) that the office schedules the pupil's large and small groups in order to produce a reasonably balanced use of the school's facilities. The teacher-adviser's part-time secretary keeps tallies and informs the office. When a student wants to change his schedule, he first must determine the availability of space for him. He obtains from the supervisor of the area either a YES or NO form with the hours and place noted and properly signed. If the form is NO, that fact is noted by the teacher-adviser and the blank is sent to the Building Administrator in the school office so he can take action to provide more space when he receives a number of NO forms. Of course, if the student has a YES form and the teacher-adviser approves, the teacher-adviser's secretary changes the pupil's schedule.

Attendance is checked at irregular times in the various areas of the school and elsewhere where students are scheduled to be. Instruction assistants in the study and work areas periodically report progress or lack of it to the teacher-advisers who then discuss with pupils the possible need for further schedule changes affecting time and locations.

We cite the foregoing procedures to show the importance of developing accountability while permitting individualized scheduling. Too much permissiveness gets in the way of accountability just as too much structure gets in the way of humanensss; both extremes show that the school really does not care about the individuals in it.

TOPICS FOR STUDY AND DISCUSSION

1. Hold a brainstorming discussion on "the ideal secondary school schedule." What do you and your colleagues recommend in order to return the control over time to teachers and pupils?
2. Prepare a statement defending or objecting to a current regulation of your state education department or regional accrediting agency which specifies a given number of minutes per week for a selected course or subject.
3. As a teacher, what would you do if you had more time free from scheduled contacts with groups of pupils?
4. Is the individualized scheduling program described at the end of this chapter the ultimate goal in a humanized school?

SELECTED REFERENCES

BUSH, ROBERT N., and ALLEN, DWIGHT W. *A New Design for High School Education Assuming a Flexible Schedule.* New York: McGraw-Hill Book Company, 1964.

This book describes factors to consider in developing a flexible schedule.

MANLOVE, DONALD C., and BEGGS, DAVID W., III. *Flexible Scheduling Using the IndiFlexS Model.* Bloomington: Indiana University Press, 1965.

This volume relates quality education to flexible scheduling. It shows how staff and students are involved and explains how to make best use of facilities and equipment. It proposes a specific program for putting the data together and developing the schedule.

MURPHY, JUDITH, and SUTTER, ROBERT. *School Scheduling by Computer: The Story of GASP.* New York: Educational Facilities Laboratories, Inc., 1964.

This pamphlet describes one of the major projects using MIT

consultants and computers and tells how it operated in several schools.

Sciara, Frank J., and Jantz, Richard K. "Implication of Accountability for Educational Program Evaluation," by W. Stanley Kruger; "Accountability: Watchword for the 70's," by John W. Morris; "Accountability from a Humanist Point of View," by C. A. Bowers; "The Relevance of Accountability," by Don Davies. In *Accountability in American Education.* Boston: Allyn and Bacon, Inc., 1972, pp. 8–41.

This portion of the book emphasizes the significance of program changes for improved accountability.

Swenson, Gardner, and Keys, Donald. *Providing for Flexibility in Scheduling and Instruction.* Englewood Cliffs, N.J.: Prentice-Hall, Inc., 1966.

The mechanics for making different schedules each day instead of once a semester or year are discussed. Teachers and pupils have considerable control over their own time in a program involving large and small groups and independent study.

CHAPTER 24

Team Teaching and
Improved Staff Utilization

Helping teachers to find more time for curriculum improvement is a major concern of school administrators. Teacher organizations are more militant these days as they insist on smaller classes and higher salaries. The question is, What are the best ways for teachers to become more involved in improving teaching and learning?

The question may be phrased differently. What are the consequences for curriculum improvement if the only changes in teaching roles in schools are tied in with smaller classes and higher salaries? What other alternatives are there?

PROFESSIONAL TEACHERS

The further professionalization of teaching, an essential ingredient in curriculum improvement, requires more than higher salaries, smaller classes, and improved certification. What teachers do, how their competencies are utilized, the personnel and technical support they receive, and the educational setting in which they work determine not only the professional concepts held by teachers themselves, but also the understanding that others hold of teaching as a profession.

The professional concept requires that teachers have enough

time and the proper facilities for such activities as preparing for their professional tasks, keeping up-to-date, conferring frequently with colleagues, conducting research and innovations, and improving the evaluation of what they do and what their pupils accomplish. Specifying what professional teachers need to do themselves and what may be done by assistants and technical devices constitutes another ingredient of professional development. Certainly each professional person needs the opportunity to do what he is most interested in and able to do. Also, he should have the opportunity to improve his income on the basis of what he does rather than be inhibited by uniform standards applied indiscriminately to all teachers.

Team teaching aims to develop these requisites for the professionalization of teachers—as well as improved learning for individual students. Its goals are to recognize better the individual differences among teachers and to utilize better the special competences of each person.

WHAT TEAM TEACHING IS

The term "team teaching" applies to an arrangement in which two or more teachers and their assistants, taking advantage of their respective competencies, plan, instruct, and evaluate in one or more subject areas a group of elementary or secondary students equivalent in size to two or more conventional classes, using a variety of technical aids to teaching and learning though large-group instruction, small-group discussion, and independent study. If one of the foregoing ingredients is missing, the result is *not* team teaching. It may be "cooperative teaching," "rotation of teaching," "utilization of teacher aides," or something else—but it is not team teaching.

The members of a given team may come from one subject department or grade level in the school or from several subject or or grade areas. Although present research does not favor one kind of team over the other, we prefer teams that cut across subject lines. Such teams tend to plan instruction that recognizes better the interrelatedness of subject content. (In this regard, teaming has some of the same objectives as the core or common learnings curricular approaches.) Teachers still work primarily in their specialties, even with special interests within their subject fields, but they benefit from working in group activities with colleagues in other fields. Of course, we have seen excellent as well as ineffective teams of all types. The organization itself does not produce the goals of team teaching.

A team preferably includes older, more experienced teachers

as well as beginners and less experienced ones, each benefiting from contact with the others. The team should select a leader to preside at planning and evaluation sessions. However, formalizing this position too much, or paying extra salary to the leader, may inhibit achievement of team teaching goals. The position of team leader is not analogous to that of a department chairman.

WHAT TEAM TEACHING IS NOT

Early attempts to initiate team teaching may involve practices that do not harmonize with the definition in the preceding paragraphs. Though we do not wish to discourage persons who may find no other way to develop what they call team teaching, we must point out the shortcomings in such procedures.

Team teaching does not mean, for example, a procedure whereby three teachers and 90 students come together occasionally for a presentation to the total group and then return to their respective classes of 30. This simple variation of class size is not likely to produce any more gains for teachers or pupils than the hundreds of class size studies conducted in this country and in others for many years have demonstrated in their reports.

Team teaching does not mean rearranging standard-sized classes of 30 into independent study groups and classes of 15 or 120 without changing what teachers and students do. What teachers today call "class discussion" is inappropriate for large or small groups. Similarly, a small-group session is largely wasted if teachers continue to conduct oral quizzes or lecture. And productive independent study involves more for students than conventional homework or merely reading books and filling in blanks.

Team teaching is not limited to either secondary or elementary age students. Nor is it confined to the academically able or the highly motivated pupils. It is not a system that is appropriate only for some subjects, but rather works well in all of them since the principles of teaching and learning are similar.

Team teaching is not, in itself, an effort to solve the teacher shortage problem except as it identifies more stimulating and professional roles. It does not change teacher-pupil ratios merely for the sake of juggling numbers.

Above all, team teaching is not a fad to be engaged in simply because others are doing it, or as a temporary expedient to solve a building space problem or financial difficulties because a referendum did not pass. Team teaching is not a superficial arrangement for educators who have not thought deeply about how to improve educational quality.

The foregoing negations emphasize the essential need to plan team teaching carefully. It can and should be a basic, broad-scope educational reorganization to develop improved conditions for teaching and learning that are necessary for achieving better the major educational goals. If it is less than that, those who plan and direct the program should take another look and try again. Limited concepts of team teaching will produce limited gains. Compromises between ideal programs and what is realistically practicable may be made, but when those compromises are approved there should be an accompanying plan for reaching the necessary goals over a period of years.

PROVIDING ASSISTANCE TO PROFESSIONAL TEACHERS

A basic purpose of team teaching emphasizes the truly professional role of the teacher; therefore, a team needs the help of general aides, clerks, and instruction assistants. The term "auxiliary personnel in education" is sometimes applied to these assistants.

Actually, general aides are not usually assigned to specific teams, because their functions may be school wide. Unlike clerks or instruction assistants, they do not possess specific educational qualifications. They are employed to assist in such tasks as supervising playgrounds and cafeterias, taking tickets, storing materials, and supervising games, assemblies, or school dances.

Clerical assistants type and duplicate materials, keep records, assist in supervising large groups, take attendance, pass out materials, check objective tests, and so forth.

Instruction assistants are qualified in a given subject area, although they usually do not possess the certification requirements of professional teachers. Typically, the instruction assistant has at least a college minor in the subject area of the team to which he is attached. His tasks include helping to assemble materials, supervising independent study workrooms, and assisting with evaluation. There are three major sources of instruction assistants: housewives, advanced college students, and retired teachers. They are employed on an hourly basis—usually ten to twenty hours per week. Some of the work is done at home or in libraries or museums.

The number of such assistants was recommended in a 1959 publication.[1] The hours needed per week of the three kinds of assistants in relation to the number of teachers in a school is as

[1] J. Lloyd Trump, *Images of the Future—A New Approach to the Secondary School*, pp. 15–22 (Washington, D.C.: National Association of Secondary School Principals, 1959). Out-of-print.

follows: instruction assistants—twenty; clerical assistants—ten; general aides—five. These figures came from an analysis of the subprofessional activities that teachers perform in conventional schools. The curricular importance of these aides arises from the need for additional qualified adults to provide needed assistance for pupils engaged in independent study and to provide teachers with more time to produce instructional materials for pupil use.

Special consultants provide another type of assistance. Someone in the community who is better qualified than any member of the teaching team to make a presentation on a particular subject is invited to do so. Both a visual and a sound record should be made of the presentation so that the material is available for further use without asking the consultant to return repeatedly. The team should assemble a file of available consultants with appropriate notations regarding specialized competencies. The PTA, student council, or service club may take a census of the community to prepare the file.

The school selects all of the foregoing four types of assistants as carefully as teachers. Since they have essential tasks to do, they must be competent to do them. (Some assistants will become professional teachers.) They need to be paid employees rather than voluntary workers so the school has legal control over them. Also, that arrangement enables school officials to give the assistants legal responsibility for supervising pupils—as is done in the case of office clerks, custodians, bus drivers, and other school employees.

OTHER CHANGES THAT FACILITATE TEAM TEACHING

Team teaching requires a number of other provisions. Instructional reorganization, including changed teacher roles, and curricular organization affect team teaching. The teams must determine which purposes are served best by large-group instruction, small-group discussion, and independent study (see chapters 18, 19 and 20) and decide *who* will do *what* in the altered organizational program. The nongraded concept discussed in Chapter 22 enables the team to plan and supervise learning experiences more effectively than through the conventional approaches of track systems, homogeneous groupings, and similar developments that have accompanied the graded curricular organization.

Wide use of technical devices to aid teaching and learning is essential. (See Chapter 21.) Without technical aids, a large-group presentation may be no better than the lectures which teachers now give in conventional classes.   Independent study will resemble today's homework unless printed materials are supplemented with extensive projection and recording devices, programed materials, and the specialized tools of the subject that students can operate and use themselves.

Another requisite is a flexible schedule.   Team members will decide not only who does what with which groups of students, but also *when* and for *how long*.   Instead of rigid time arrangements in secondary schools fostered by the concept of the self-contained, or self-sufficient, classroom, time varies with the purposes of teaching and learning as described in Chapter 23.   Unless teachers and students control time for their respective purposes, new procedures are needlessly inhibited.

Evaluation methods different from those techniques now typical in conventional classrooms are also essential.   Chapter 27 will show how evaluation varies with instructional organizations and purposes.

The school administration and board of education policies respecting expenditures of school funds need to be altered for team teaching as described in Chapter 25.   The pre-service education of teachers should be reorganized and supervisory programs should be initiated to help teachers change and improve their teaching roles as will be discussed in Chapter 28.

HOW THE TEAM OPERATES

Teams operate in much the same manner whether their members come from one subject area or cut across two or more subject fields. Nor is the number of members important.   The three requirements for any team, whatever its organization, are that the members plan together, teach together, and evaluate together.

The team usually meets each day to discuss a variety of topics.   The following questions and answers illustrate subjects that may arise at such meetings and decisions that may be made.

What content will be presented to large groups of students, by whom, and in what manner?   Each member will teach the content he can handle best.   What visuals or records will be helpful? Ideas are "roughed-out" so the instruction assistant-artist can make or assemble the aids.   Who will observe the presentation?   There is no need for all team members to attend, but one person might. The school principal is a good selection.   That staff member may join the presenter in leading an evaluative discussion at the team meeting the next day.   How is the independent study program going? (Instruction assistants may join the team for this discussion.) Some team member should plan systematic observations in the study areas to obtain answers to questions raised in team discussions. What instructional purposes will we evaluate at this time? What data will we collect? What observations will we make? The team will assign responsibilities to different members and also involve appropriate colleagues outside the team. (More suggestions about evaluation and feedback will be provided in chapters 27 and 28.) Why are small-group discussions less effective than anticipated? What needs to be done? What distinctive overt pupil behavior has been observed—or should be studied? What remedial steps are needed? To get answers, the team uses its own resources and draws on consultants. The school principal and the assistant principal meet regularly with teaching teams. So do the school librarian, counselors, and other staff members who have something to contribute. Incidentally, principals, librarians, counselors, and others benefit from these regularly scheduled meetings, for they get out of their offices and become involved in the main stream of instruction.

The team focuses on the processes of teaching and learning, on instructional content, and on learning aids rather than on the performance of its members. They recognize that mistakes will be made. Criticisms are given freely, openly, honestly, tastefully, and professionally. Always there are constructive efforts to find solutions to problems. The old saying, "two minds are better than one," is the basis of team teaching.

Team personnel may change from time to time. The goal is to use the talents of each teacher to his best advantage and for the team's maximum success. Flexibility in team membership should be a staff commitment.

Continuous evaluation of team procedures as well as pupil gains is essential. Are the creative talents of teachers stimulated? Are staff interests utilized? Are better facilities being developed? Is instruction improving? Is curriculum content more effective? Many other comparable questions will be studied by the team. Failure to do so inevitably leads to frustration. Incidentally, taping team sessions is helpful.

The team must have time for the foregoing activities. The team member's *average* weekly schedule need include no more than one or two large-group presentations and a dozen small-group discussion sessions. Experience indicates that teachers need to spend more than one half of the conventional school week, fifteen to twenty hours, on preparation, team meetings, individual and special group pupil conferences, and evaluation.

A team that operates below the standards set here will be

less successful than it could be.   Therefore, the team must work constantly with school administrators to improve the conditions under which it functions.   Team teaching then will achieve its potential for curriculum improvement.

TOPICS FOR STUDY AND DISCUSSION

1.   Stage a mock team meeting. The topic might be planning a large-group presentation, evaluating the use of resource centers (or whatever you decide). Then ask your colleagues or members of your university class to criticize the session.
2.   List what you believe are the most important advantages in team teaching as compared with conventional teaching. Do the same for the most important difficulties.
3.   Take some instructional topic in the course you teach or plan to teach. Then plan how you would survey the community to discover adults who might contribute their time or materials to help students learn the topic. What forms would you use? How would you conduct the survey? What records would you keep?
4.   Read about one or more team projects as described in some educational periodical. (See "Team Teaching" in *Education Index*.) How might the project have been made more successful?
5.   Some persons argue that differentiated staffing including the use of a variety of assistants is the most important single ingredient in furthering the concepts of individualized learning and professionalized teaching. Argue for or against that statement.

SELECTED REFERENCES

ANDERSON, ROBERT H.   "Innovations in Organization: Theory and Practice in Team Teaching."   In *Teaching in a World of Change*. New York: Harcourt Brace & World, Inc., 1966, pp. 71–108.
      Concise statement of antecedents, rationale, types, practices, and evaluation of team teaching are included.
BEGGS, DAVID W., III, ed.   *Team Teaching—Bold New Venture*. Bloomington: Indiana University Press, 1965.
      Twelve experience teachers and administrators describe team teaching in various subjects and grades.
DAVIS, HAROLD S.   *How to Organize an Effective Team Teaching Program*.   Englewood Cliffs, N.J.: Prentice-Hall, Inc., 1966.
      This pamphlet describes team teaching in selected elemen-

tary and secondary schools and tells how to implement the new procedures.

————. *Team Teaching—A Selected Annotated Bibliography.* Cleveland: Educational Research Council of America, 1967.

This pamphlet provides general references for secondary and elementary schools plus articles under the major subject-matter headings.

HELLER, MELVIN P. *Team Teaching.* Dayton, Ohio: National Catholic Educational Association, 1967.

This pamphlet answers seventeen questions about team teaching and provides practical suggestions for planning, conducting, and evaluating a program.

————. "Team Teaching—Professionalism for Professionals." *Catholic High School Quarterly Bulletin* 23, no. 4 (January, 1966).

This pamphlet gives advantages, guidelines, and charts for evaluating team teaching.

HOOVER, KENNETH H. "Improving Flexibility: Team Teaching Techniques." In *Learning and Teaching in the Secondary School.* 2nd ed. Boston: Allyn and Bacon, Inc., 1968, pp. 328–348.

This chapter provides a further statement of ideas expressed in the chapter of this book.

LEWIS, JAMES, JR. *Differentiating the Teaching Staff.* West Nyack, N.Y.: Parker Publishing Co., 1972.

Using differentiated staffing as a central theme, the author also discusses teacher training, flexible scheduling, individualizing instruction, remodeling schools, accountability, and evaluating effectiveness.

OLIVERO, JAMES L., and BUFFIE, EDWARD G. "Educational Manpower in Perspective." In *Educational Manpower.* Bloomington: Indiana University Press, 1970, pp. vii–365.

The writers summarize a diversity of approaches to defining personnel roles in instruction along with attention to accountability.

NOAR, GERTRUDE. *Teacher Aides at Work.* Washington, D.C.: National Education Association Commission on Teacher Education and Professional Standards, 1967.

The author reports on-the-spot impressions from visiting teacher aides at work in various parts of the United States.

PETERSON, CARL H. *Effective Team Teaching: The Easton Area High School Program.* West Nyack, N.Y.: Parker Publishing Co., 1966, pp. 1–32, 121–161, and 177–197.

These six chapters describe one school's program to illustrate reasons for team teaching. They explain how to initiate and carry on a program and how to overcome "common team teaching problems." They suggest ways to use resource people, and methods for conducting accelerated projects.

SHAPLIN, JUDSON T., and OLDS, HENRY F. *Team Teaching*. New York: Harper and Row, Publishers, 1964, pp. 99–122 and 270–305.

These two chapters provide a taxonomy for team teaching and suggestions for long-range research. Both aspects are extremely important in planning and evaluating a new program.

CHAPTER 25

Humane Environments for
Teaching and Learning

Providing a more humane environment for learning constitutes a basic challenge in curriculum improvement. Whether the environment is humane has little to do with how new it is, how much it costs, how many machines it includes, how many acres of ground surround a school building, how large it is, or even where it is located. All these features can make the environment more or less humane, however, depending on how the program utilizes the environment as a vital part of the curriculum.

The term "educational facilities" refers to school monies available for educational purposes, to the school building and grounds, and to the supplies and equipment that the school uses in instruction. The allocation of school money enhances or inhibits curriculum improvement. That educational funds always are inadequate is axiomatic. Therefore, administrative decisions about allocating money are crucial to curriculum improvement. For example, better priorities are needed. The building shell contributes little to curriculum improvement; the critical aspect is found in the teaching tools and learning aids. Money saved on the former can be spent more advantageously on the latter. Teachers and school administrators must be more active in planning new buildings and remodeling existing ones in order to save money for curriculum improvement.

Today's school buildings are often unnecessarily costly, reflecting too much the residential architectural styles of the times. For example, because some people had fascinating views from their houses, architects fostered the concept of a picture window.   It became so popular that many houses without exciting views also were given picture windows.   Transferred to schools, the concept produced great glass walls.   The questions are, Do glass walls enhance or inhibit the educational programs they contain?   Are they more or less expensive to install and maintain than other, educationally more desirable walls?   What answers other than *yes* or *no* influence curriculum improvement?

Let us consider another illustration.   Many families resented the narrow lots that are associated with city living.   When they moved to suburbs, where land was cheaper, they sought new architectural forms to go with the land.   Architects brought them the concept of the ranch house, or the rambler, as it is sometimes called.   So their houses had fewer floor levels and spread out over the land.   This style was then transferred to suburban and city schools.   Since land was cheaper in the country, it became stylish to build suburban schools with twenty, forty, or even more acres of land surrounding them.   The question is: Do these sprawled-out buildings and the rolling hills surrounding them contribute to or get in the way of achieving educational goals?

Architects do not deserve all the blame for today's costly and often inefficient school buildings and grounds.   Often, they cannot obtain imaginative educational specifications from teachers and educational administrators, who may simply look at what other schools are building and then follow the current styles.   Some architects like this procedure, because they do not have to come up with as many new forms, new calculations, and new risks.   It is easier to follow the common mold than to be creative.

What is a school building for?   Dr. Harold Gores, of Educational Facilities Laboratories, reminds us that the building itself inherently serves two purposes: to maintain an inside climate that is better than the outside climate for comfort and maximum human efficiency, and to keep bugs, birds, and animals out of the way.   Beyond those minimum essentials, a school building takes its cues from what teachers and their pupils want to do inside the building —how they want to live educationally.   Too many buildings get in the way of curriculum improvement.   Even the best buildings provide little more than a neutral influence.   What can the building do positively to facilitate the teaching-learning process?

THE CURRICULUM AND THE BUILDING

This book presents two basic curricular emphases.   First, it supports the comprehensive middle school and junior and senior high school idea that requires a wide diversity of subject offerings available to all youth in one center.   Second, it says that students learn best through a combination of independent study, large-group instruction, and small-group discussion with sequentially arranged content designed to produce maximum development for each pupil no matter how he differs from the others.   The school building must provide places where students can carry on appropriate learning activities for all subject areas and places where teachers and their assistants can plan, prepare, conduct, and evaluate those activities.

Chapters 18, 19, and 20 described the five spaces necessary for independent study and the rooms suitable for large-group instruction and small-group discussion.   Here are some guidelines for including those spaces in new buildings or for remodeling old buildings to meet instruction needs.

Resource centers

Readers will recall that learning resource centers for students are needed in all subject areas.   Each of the resource centers has two parts: the place where pupils read, listen, view, think, and write and the place where pupils work with the specialized "tools of the trade" in that subject area.

Let us assume that facilities are being planned for 1,200 students who will spend 40 percent or more of their time in a variety of independent study activities.   The practical arts area, for example, needs a room in which boys and girls can read, listen, view, think, and write, plus specialized laboratories in food, clothing, electronics, machine shops, woodworking, agriculture, and whatever other areas seem appropriate in the local community. The equipment will be portable or easily moved to provide flexibility among the various curricular areas.   The fine arts area also will provide a room for reading, viewing, and the like, plus a variety of small rooms in which individuals and small groups may practice vocal and instrumental music; specialized workrooms for ceramics, metals, and the like; and larger rooms for orchestra, band, large vocal groups, and varied art activities, depending upon the nature of the local program.

Arrangements in the academic subjects will be comparable to those just described.   Regardless of the size of the school building, the independent study areas constitute its major floor area.

Some classrooms in conventional schools can be readily remodeled to provide the reading, listening, and viewing areas. Others can be remodeled to provide many of the laboratories and workrooms.   A first step is to remove student desks or, at least, take most of them out and place the rest around the perimeter of the room.   Substitute tables and chairs.   Carpeting helps acoustically and aesthetically.

Other areas for independent study

Chapter 18 described four other kinds of spaces for independent study. The library is one of them. In a school with 1,200 students, the central library should provide seating in carrels with quasi-privacy for reading, thinking, and writing. A new library should avoid tables in the reading room and older libraries should replace them with carrels as rapidly as possible. Adolescents are especially interested in each other and look around constantly as others walk by or as noises occur. Carrels with dividers that extend to the sides, beyond the desks and chairs, tend to minimize these distractions. Comfortable lounge-type chairs are needed for pupils who wish only to read. The library should also provide listening booths and a viewing area that will accommodate up to thirty pupils each. Dial access systems enable pupils to contact a variety of materials as needed for work in various subjects. The library also needs an informal area where students sit on the carpeted floor or on cushions to read and discuss.

The school cafeteria can provide most of the places for the three other kinds of independent study arrangements—conference work rooms, strictly supervised areas, and recreation rooms. An operable wall can divide the cafeteria into the recreation and work areas, each of which might accommodate forty students seated around tables in groups of two to six or seven. In an older school, the supervised area may be a conventional classroom that will house the fifteen to thirty students that will be assigned there.

A new school building should provide separate rooms for these three activities. One room is the student lounge with an automated snack service. A second room has various sizes of tables to seat two, four, or eight persons for conferences. The third room has tables and desks for pupils needing close supervision. Each of these three rooms should accommodate about forty pupils.

Older buildings can be carpeted, remodeled, painted (sometimes by students), and relighted to become cheerful, useful spaces. Sometimes pupils feel more ownership in an older building that they have helped to renew.

Area for large-group instruction and small-group discussion

All subject fields may use the same spaces for large-group instruction and small-group discussion. Assuming large-group instruction in all subjects, a building for 1,200 students can use six spaces, each accommodating up to 150 students, with operable walls that can be opened to create larger spaces as needed. Such an arrangement provides considerable flexibility in the use of spaces. Four spaces, for example, may be combined into an auditorium which will seat 600 for concerts, plays, community gatherings, and the like. The other two spaces may be combined for a "theater-in-the-round" arrangement to seat 300. In older school buildings, a wall may be removed between two conventional classrooms to provide a large-group instruction space that will easily handle 120 students.

Assuming small-group discussion classes in each subject, a school of 1,200 will need about 20 rooms for small-group discussion. Each room, about 250 square feet in area, should contain a table with 16 chairs ranged around it. Three such rooms can be made from a conventional classroom in an older building.

Precisely how many large and small rooms and how many independent study spaces a school needs depends upon the current decisions of the staff about teaching and learning. If only some of the staff are prepared to depart from conventional practices when the school moves into a new building, the building needs conventional classrooms plus enough large and small rooms and independent study areas to take care of the innovative teachers' needs. Requirements may be estimated easily. The important consideration in to provide walls that may be changed economically as teacher ideas change. A school can justify operable walls between classrooms *only* if those walls are as acoustically satisfactory as other walls and more economical. If they are not, the school should use the kind of walls that can be taken out later as needed. Most schools are likely to find that the three places for operable walls are the auditorium, cafeteria, and gymnasium.

A school building should never be finished. It must be constantly remodeled and improved so that it can best serve the ever changing educational needs of pupils and teachers.

Teachers' work spaces

An essential facility, and one that is often inadequate in today's schools, is a place for teachers to plan, to prepare materials, to evaluate, and to confer with colleagues, assistants, pupils, and visitors. Classroom space, often wastefully utilized for those purposes, is usually poorly equipped.

Curriculum improvement requires that each teacher has an office with some privacy. The area should also provide working space for instruction assistants and clerks as well as for artists, research assistants, and other specialized personnel that may be involved in preparing teaching aids. Soundproof recording studios are required in this area, as are photographic darkrooms and other places to prepare visuals and duplicated materials. Two or three small conference rooms, a lounge, and a dining room are also needed.

SOME SPECIAL CONSIDERATIONS

School buildings need to be compact to facilitate movement from one part to another, and elevators or escalators should be provided for those teachers and young people who should not climb stairs. Compact design also makes year-round air conditioning economical. Even in areas where the outside temperature is reasonably comfortable, the humidity control that air conditioning provides makes a school building a fresher and more stimulating teaching and learning environment, because it takes care of excess humidity and the stuffiness created by large numbers of people in one space.

Light and sound control both are important in planning new buildings or remodeling old ones. Glass should be used in a school building only when it enhances the educational program. It interferes with the effectiveness of light, sound, and temperature control in all large-group instruction and small-group discussion areas; therefore, no glass should be provided in those spaces. On the other hand independent study areas for pupils and work areas for teachers are enhanced by small windows so that persons can look outside, rest their eyes, and relax for a moment. Such "vision strips" are quite small and do not interfere greatly with light, sound, and temperature control. Incidentally, glass should not be used on inside spaces in a building, because the views distract students from work.

The amount of artificial light and the type of fixtures vary in different parts of the building. Standard regulations are obviously impossible for the task determines the requirements. Variable controls are needed in large-group areas. Less light is needed in small-group discussion spaces than in the work spaces of the independent study rooms. Some study areas need high intensity light and others more diffused light. The use of appropriate colors in walls and furnishings provides variety to visual experiences. Color dynamics suggests cool colors in sunny areas, warm colors in darker places, often a variety of colors in one room.

Sound control is essential. Carpeting quiets independent study areas used for reading, listening, viewing, thinking, and writing. It also helps acoustics in large-group instruction areas. Acoustical treatment of walls and ceilings is, of course, assumed.

Corridor and lobby spaces in schools are about as expensive as classroom space and contribute little to the educative process. Imaginative architects can and should produce school buildings that reduce this wasteful corridor space to a minimum; some buildings almost eliminate corridors. Flexible schedules can reduce concentrations of travel in corridors. In many instances, traffic from one independent study space to another can be incorporated into the rooms themselves.

School buildings should be beautiful places that reflect a concern for the artistic in everyday living. If there is a beautiful view outside the building, a strategically placed picture window can reveal and highlight that view while the opaque walls shut out undesirable scenes. Carefully placed fountains and gardens in inner courts can add beauty inexpensively. Strategic use of different building materials, color, and the like, may also create an atmosphere of beauty without adding greatly to construction costs. The creative ingenuity of architects is needed here. Today's schools in many cases are unnecessarily drab and ugly.

SUPPLIES AND EQUIPMENT

The typical industrial building today spends only 25 percent of the total capital outlay for the structure, while 75 percent of the outlay goes to the equipment and the tools of the trade inside the building. Strangely enough, school buildings reverse those figures. Three-fourths of the cost goes into the building shell, and only one-fourth into the all-important instructional tools and supplies. That ratio makes no sense when we recall that the building shell contributes little to the teaching-learning process other than temperature control and freedom from insects!

Chapter 21 emphasizes the wide variety of technical devices needed in schools. The future will see new aids to teaching and learning only dreamed about today. Efficient use of these devices, however, requires that they be placed in strategic locations in the school rather than being scattered about the classrooms as they are in most of today's buildings.

THE USE OF AVAILABLE MONEY

Money allocated to curriculum improvement may be used to produce change or it may be used as an excuse to maintain existing procedures and policies. Educational monies are valuable only to the extent that they produce better conditions for learning and teaching and better results.

How may a school use available money differently to produce a better educational product? Several ways to save money are obvious.   Teachers now spend about one-third of their time in activities that can be done as well, and in most cases better, by clerks and instruction assistants.   Clerks cost about half what teachers cost.   Part-time instruction assistants usually cost only slightly more per hour than clerks do.   It is also reasonable to estimate that another one-third of what teachers are doing now could be done by pupils themselves under the supervision of the less costly instruction assistants, and with the aid of technical devices.   Since instructional costs constitute the major portion of any educational operational budget, the savings may be considerable.

A school can also save money through more efficient use of technical devices.   For example, if teachers in conventional schools use overhead projectors frequently, they may want one of these devices for each classroom.   However, the use of projectors only in large-group instruction reduces the number required for a given school building.

Large-group instruction saves money while it saves teacher time and energy.   Obviously, it costs less to teach a lesson once to 120 students than it does to teach it four times to groups of 30.   Today's teachers spend almost one-half of their time in conventional classrooms with 25 to 30 students in activities that may be done just as effectively in large groups.

Earlier in this chapter reference was made to certain economies in school building construction.   Compact buildings with year-round air conditioning usually cost less per square foot to construct than do conventional school buildings without air conditioning.   A glass wall is more expensive to construct, to maintain, and to repair than masonry or wooden walls.   Making usable educational space out of corridors and lobbies, which occupy such a prominent place in today's schools, is another economy.   Broadly distributed decorative materials can be eliminated in order to provide selected beauty spots with more dramatic emphasis.

However, not all changes necessary for curriculum improvement will save money.   Some of the changes suggested in this book will cost more than the present practices.   For example, the proposal is made that about 20 percent of the students' school week should be spent in small-group discussion, in classes of fifteen as contrasted to today's conventional classes of twenty-five to thirty.   For that portion of the school week the instructional costs in teachers' salaries is doubled.   Also, the hours that teachers are scheduled with students must be reduced, the proposal being that that not more than fifteen hours per week should be spent with pupil groups.   Today's teachers have no more than five hours per week away from student groups, some even less than that.   This change in the teaching load costs more money.   Additional technical devices are required in independent study areas.

Experience to date is that the costs and the savings represented by the proposed changes just about balance each other.   Of course, other factors may enter the picture.   For example, holding school all year around may cost more because more pupils, than in today's schools, receive an expanded education.   Teacher salaries have increased markedly during recent years, but they still are not as high as they should be for the level of professional services demanded of teachers.

Today's schools spend something like .02 percent of the school budget on research and development—much less than business provides for the same purpose.   Raising that amount to one or two cents out of every dollar is not unreasonable.

The basic consideration in the use of available money is to relate financial input to educational output.   Chapter 27 discusses in detail what is meant by educational output.   Although it may never be possible to screen every educational dollar in relation to its impact on pupil learning, professional workers and board of education members must keep that goal uppermost in their minds. When a proposal for spending educational funds is made, a corresponding proposal should be made to evaluate, after a reasonable period of time (for example, one, two, or five years later), what effects the added funds or the reduced funds have on conditions of learning, the professionalization of teaching, and the individualization of learning, and the resultant quality of gains for each person. An analysis of this nature guarantees more consistent curriculum improvement than almost any other policy that the board of education might adopt, because it strikes at the very heart of the school's life.

The word *accountability* occurs frequently in current literature.   The term has many meanings: measuring and relating pupil and teacher output to changes in expenditures for schooling; testing the effects of different methods and material; analyzing various types of building structures; scheduling pupils into facilities for learning in addition to or in lieu of school buildings; utilizing facilities for more hours and months in the year; and analyzing many other input and output relationships.   Further discussion of this topic occurs in the final chapter of this book.   Certainly the more effective use of educational facilities can facilitate secondary school curriculum improvement.

TOPICS FOR STUDY AND DISCUSSION

1. Select some school building problem; for example, how to eliminate or greatly reduce corridor space, how to provide independent study space in your subject field, or how to remodel an existing school facility in your subject.   Prepare some *rough*

drawings (you are not an architect) and present these to your colleagues for discussion.

2. Locate in the library a plan of a proposed school building or one recently constructed. Criticize the facilities that relate to teaching and learning in your subject field or one that interests you.

3. Analyze a portion of the budget—your subject field, for example —or the total school budget of the place where you work or some place you know. How could some of the money be spent differently to produce curriculum improvement? Defend your proposal in a paper or oral discussion.

4. The proposal has been made to locate a senior high school in a densely populated location in the central area of the city. The first two floors would be leased for offices and small business operations—to provide both revenue for the school and work experience for pupils. Various surfaces, including plastic grass, on the roof and some upper story areas will provide physical fitness and recreation areas for pupils. Prepare arguments for or against this kind of school.

5. Develop a presentation to show how the use of the community rather than the school building as a setting for some aspects of the curriculum could save money and building facilities.

6. What are some consequences, based on functional analyses, of these three educational philosophies of curriculum: "open," "closed," "a combination of the two?"

SELECTED REFERENCES

Divisible Auditoriums. New York: Educational Facilities Laboratories, Inc., 1966.

This pamphlet illustrates several methods of dividing auditoriums to produce better utilization, with special emphasis on acoustics.

The Education Park: Report to the School District of Philadelphia. Wilton, Connecticut: Corde Corporation, 1967.

A multilithed report that gives reasons for and methods of combining primary, intermediate, and secondary schools in various locations to facilitate articulation, racial integration, and educational innovations.

GREEN, ALLAN C., ed. "A Technical Guide." In *Educational Facilities with New Media.* Washington, D.C.: National Education Association, Department of Educational Technology, 1966, pp. C-1–C-55.

This report provides data on lighting, climate, acoustics, furniture, and other equipment.

The High School Auditorium: Six Designs for Renewal.   New York: Educational Facilities Laboratories, Inc., 1967.

This book shows how to renovate little-used auditoriums in old and middle-aged schools to accommodate contemporary educational programs.

High School: The Process and the Place.   New York: Educational Facilities Laboratories, Inc., 1972.

This little book defines the concept of school facilities, special values in the school environment, and how to manage a "live" environment.   This beautifully written and illustrated document relates the humane and facilities factors unusually well.

New Life for Old Schools.   Chicago: Research Council of the Great Cities Program, 1965.

Several architects and educators from a dozen large cities discuss plans for updating school buildings.

New Schools for New Education.   New York: Educational Facilities Laboratories, Inc., 1961.

A report of a conference of architects and educators at the University of Michigan, where plans were proposed and discussed for schools to serve the "Trump Plan."

SCHNEIDER, RAYMOND C.   *Space for Teachers.*   New York: Educational Facilities Laboratories, Inc., 1961.

A pamphlet showing imaginative illustrations of places for teachers to plan and work.

Three High Schools Revisited: Andrews, McPherson, and Nova.   New York: Educational Facilities Laboratories, Inc., 1967.

This booklet, from the series "Profiles of Significant Schools," shows how innovative schools are using specially designed buildings.   Separate publications on the three schools were issued several years earlier when the buildings were first opened; this report shows their strengths and limitations.

PART V

Evaluation and Accountability

CHAPTER 26

Needed Stress and
Changes in Evaluation

Knowing whether a school is a good school, whether a teacher is a
good teacher, whether students are learning what they should be
learning, and whether a curricular change is better than what it
replaced are such fundamental factors in good curriculum development that no one may brush them aside lightly. Yet, finding
imaginative and comprehensive answers to those questions has
plagued curriculum planners for generations. This chapter explains why and provides some positive guidelines for moving ahead.

A SCHOOL'S EXCELLENCE

For years, those who would determine the educational quality of a
given school asked questions to get specific answers. The last turn
of the century brought some answers that stand in the way of much
curriculum improvement suggested in this volume. For example,
the answer to the question of whether a given subject or course was
acceptable ended up being, "if it meets 200 minutes per week."
That answer is called the Carnegie Unit. The answer to the question of how a school might limit the number of subjects taken by
pupils at one time and yet provide good curriculum with differentiation produced the "required-elective system."

The decades since the turn of the century have produced

many comparable questions and equally inhibiting answers enforced by state education departments and regional accrediting associations. Here are some illustrations: When has a student completed secondary education? The answer: when he has accumulated sixteen units of credit with two majors and two minors. What is the minimum time a student may spend in secondary education? Until the age of 16 [or whatever particular age is specified in a given state]. What is the optimum length of a school year? 178 days [or some other arbitrary figure]. What constitutes a good library? Spending "X" (the figure varies from time to time and in different places) dollars per pupil per year for new books, or having "X" number of books per pupil, or "X" square feet of space per pupil. What setting ensures quality instruction? A teacher-pupil ratio of 1:27 with no class larger than 35. How can one achieve excellent pupil personnel services? Provide one counselor for each 250 students. Of course, the list of questions and the expected quantitative answers could be extended. Provisions are made to rate a school on each of numerous criteria; then the ratings are averaged out to obtain the quantitative measures of school excellence. The question is, Do such techniques really answer the question of school excellence? Research does not support any of these measures as being better than minor modifications of the numbers one way or the other.

Earlier in this century educators in the United States placed much credence on the system of inspectorial visits to measure school excellence. A representative of the county, city, or state educational agency paid an unannounced visit to a school, roamed the classrooms with pencil and notebook in hand, and prepared an inspectorial report evaluating individual teachers and the school. That system remains highly regarded in some other countries. However, lacking confidence in the judgment of one person, school systems in this country have turned to cooperative evaluation, where a group of persons visits and appraises the school. But the question still remains, What criteria are used?

Periodically, someone proposes that we use national examinations to measure school excellence. Such examinations, externally prepared, long have been traditional in many other countries. Here again there are gnawing questions. Do the examinations measure the most important educational goals? Are they administered uniformly? Can school excellence be measured by the average rank of a school's students on the latest College Entrance Examination Board test, the average rank of students on some state or national achievement test, the number of scholarship winners in the school, or any other comparable achievement? Is it right to compare schools whose students come from different social, economic, or cultural backgrounds? Can these matters be equated to produce common measures of excellence?

The determination of school excellence is complex. Unfortunately, schools sometimes swear by certain techniques even though their value has not been proven by research. Questions that always need to be answered are, *Good* in comparison to *what?* or, On what basis? Standardized test scores alone do not indicate quality of teaching and learning; they should not be used to define excellence. Nor does a high ranking on some particular list of evaluative criteria demonstrate superiority. Following every regulation of some external agency does not guarantee quality.

One difficulty is that people sometimes accept simple answers in their efforts to accomplish specified goals. For example, a few years ago, one professional organization issued a statement titled, "Grading the Public Schools." With praise and blame they listed the top state in the union, the bottom state in the union, and the national average on such items as number of pupils per teacher, percent of enrolled pupils attending daily, percent of eighth grade enrollment that graduates from high school, per capita state expenditures for public education, and a number of other statistics.

An extremely useless practice, in terms of measuring school excellence, is to equate quality with per-pupil expenditures or median salaries paid to instructional personnel. Some recent court decisions and many writings have continued to fall into that trap. In one major city, for example, a court ruled that the per-pupil expenditure must be equalized in all of the city's schools in order to provide equality of learning for all pupils. Since some schools had more older teachers with higher salaries, the school system had to change teachers around quickly to meet the court order. No attention was paid to curriculum development, methods of teaching and learning, or related matters that bear on educational quality.

Comparative data such as those identified in the preceding paragraphs may be useful to school administrators in convincing the board of education and the public that more funds are needed for education, that a new course should be added to the curriculum, that the library should be remodeled, and the like. However, the items in isolation, or even in a statistically derived combination, do not measure the quality of teaching and learning in a school. Quantitative data are essential in high school evaluation, but should not be considered ends in themselves. If they are, they may stand in the way of needed curriculum improvements. Moreover, such practices contribute to the lack of faith in present accountability practices in schools, thus producing a creditability gap in the minds of taxpayers.

Evaluation of the total school program concerns the effectiveness of what the school *does*, rather than what the school *possesses*. Major emphasis should be on the degree to which the specific objectives of secondary education (derived from national experts and modified for the local setting) are being realized. The school must decide which objectives to measure and what evaluation techniques to use. How to make that decision is described in the next chapter. The effectiveness of various resources (financial, human, and material) which the school uses should be appraised in terms of their effects on pupil learning. The crucial matter in determining excellence is to examine the way the school develops optimum conditions for learning for its pupils.

TEACHER EFFECTIVENESS

Generations of educators have struggled with the problem of determining teacher excellence. Practically every conceivable scheme has been tried and all have been found inadequate in one way or another.

Some years ago, statewide evaluation schemes sometimes involved granting "success grades" to teachers on the basis of county testing programs. Each teacher was graded on the scores his pupils made on year-end tests compared with those of other pupils in the county. The "success grade" was even a factor in determining the teacher's salary for the next year. Ignored were such matters as socioeconomic and cultural differences from one community to another, variables in supplies and equipment for teaching in the different schools, the reliability and validity of the tests, and a variety of other factors. Teachers adapted to the system. For example, one of them raised his "success grade" seven points by teaching for the test.

Many schools have used teacher-rating schemes. Both the raters and the systems themselves have been proven ineffective. The human rater is subject to criticism on the basis of both reliability and validity of judgments. The rating scheme he uses may have the wrong priorities or teaching concepts. Moreover, since rating is done periodically, the times that the rater visits the classroom may be unusually good or unusually inopportune in terms of the total teaching-learning process.

Other schools measure teacher effectiveness by systematic observations of classroom behavior of teachers and pupils. Characteristic actions of so-called "good" and "poor" teachers are noted by trained observers, who spend considerable time in classrooms and then report their findings to the appropriate administrative and supervisory officials. Obviously, these tasks require a tremendous amount of time by highly trained observers with carefully defined plans for recording the right information.

Some school systems use examinations to evaluate pre-service and in-service teachers. State, regional, and national norms are set up as the basis for individual and group comparisons. The question is, Are superior teachers also superior test performers? Tests and scales are used to determine teacher attitudes, values, interests, adjustment, personality, and other characteristics. Still other instruments measure social interaction between teacher and pupils and among pupils in the classroom.

Through the years there has been no lack of interest and expenditure of energy and money on the evaluation of teachers. Today's techniques for measuring effectiveness are increasingly sophisticated. The problem is that all of the foregoing methods ignore the educational setting in which teachers are forced to work by local school policies. Working conditions and policies that ignore individual differences among teachers reward the conformist or the average person at the expense of the creative, especially talented teacher or the person with a peculiar weakness. One teacher may be stimulated by the opportunity to work with technical devices while another may be seriously frightened by them. A given teacher may be successful with small groups of students but quite ineffective with larger groups. This illustrative list might be extended. Before a school may evaluate teachers effectively, the conditions of work for each person must be optimal for him so that he may realize his maximum potentialities and conversely so that he does not reveal his weaknesses.

A first step that a school should take to improve teacher effectiveness is to develop behavioral objectives for the teaching staff and criteria for judging the various performances. A necessary adjunct is to recognize that all teachers are not expected to have the same tasks; therefore, they are not judged on a single set of behavioral goals. Criterion referenced items are applied to the particular performance that the system expects of a given individual.

PUPILS' GOALS

Schools measure pupil learning by a variety of standardized and local tests. The use of both types of tests has grown phenomenally in recent years.

Standardized tests

Most school officials actually know too little about their students. Typically, school records list attendance, grades, age, height, weight, family data, one or two group IQ scores, some achievement test scores, and an interest inventory. Such data provide incomplete and sometimes unreliable bases for deciding who shall go to what colleges, who is ready for what employment, and the like. Faced with student and parental pressures, the principal and counselors employ such measures as the *Scholastic Aptitude, Primary Mental Abilities, General Aptitude Test Battery*, and comparable instruments that yield scores. All of these tests have been criticized at one time or another for their failure to measure what the school is attempting to accomplish or for representing social, economic, and cultural biases over which the local school has little control.

Forward-looking admissions officers and employers quickly point out that they use criteria other than tests for selecting students. But they too are handicapped by not knowing the students well. Local school teachers and counselors know students much better, but they do not systematically record what they know. Pupil motivation, personal responsibility, sudden changes in goals, traumatic experiences, and other factors—alone or in combination—force new interpretations and change the predictive value of test scores. Until schools possess more information and communicate their data and recommendations meaningfully to colleges and employers, some very important mistakes are likely to be made because of too little information and too much reliance on the little that is available.

Standardized tests can help to determine the quality of pupil learning if they measure the right outcomes. Teachers state their instructional purposes quite easily, but they encounter difficulties in describing and evaluating objectives that involve changes in pupil behavior. For example, while English teachers attempt to teach literary appreciation, the absence of a reliable method for measuring student differences in the appreciation of "good" literature has forced them to use tests that mainly measure literary knowledge. Similar problems abound in all subject areas.

However, taking behavioral changes into consideration does not in itself solve the problem of better evaluation. For example, one of the major publishers acquired the rights to publish an excellent test that measured well the ability of students to interpret data—an objective in a number of courses. So few schools purchased the test that business economics required discontinuing the sale. Teachers either are more interested in whether students *know* some materials than in whether they *interpret* it wisely, or else they lack confidence in measuring devices.

Think, moreover, of how little interest schools have in evaluating such goals as the following: growth of individual student responsibility for learning, development of habits and skills of intellectual inquiry, acquisition of competence in critical thinking, ability to communicate accurately and persuasively with other persons, and growth in creativity. Yet the measurement of how well these goals are achieved is a more important indication of individual student progress and general school excellence than much data from conventional tests now in use.

Procedures for administering standardized tests vary greatly among schools. True, instructions for giving tests are specific, but frequently they are not followed accurately. Use of different days of the week, hours in the day, or times of the year can affect test scores. Increased use of television with video tape recordings could result in the application of more uniform standards for administration and thus help alleviate the problem of obtaining comparisons among students from a variety of schools. Until more television facilities are available, most schools could use audio tape recordings.

Doubtless there are advantages in the United States system of producing tests which compete on the open market with the aim of measuring similar educational outcomes. Not only is this system in harmony with the American free-enterprise scheme, but also in the opinion of some persons, it obviates the use of a single, all-powerful "national" examination. But there are defects in this system. Students are mobile; schools often have to compare a student's previous record in a former school with different tests given locally. Further development of equivalency tables for the various tests might save students from taking more tests than are necessary. The alternative is a national assessment of basic education objectives.

Tests are better today than ever before, but there are still too many poor questions or items. Test makers need to be even more concerned than they are now about constantly seeking better ways of doing things. The test business apparently is a good and profitable undertaking. New types of measuring instruments are needed to assist nongraded programs, independent study, stimulation of creativity, self-appraisal, and the like.

Locally prepared tests

Locally prepared tests constitute another measure of pupil learning. However, teachers often spend much time and energy in producing, giving, and marking *poor* tests. Too often the teacher-made tests represent a competitive guessing game between teachers and their pupils that frequently focuses on the less important educational goals. The tests typically fail to provide for immediate reinforcement of learning, do not direct learning toward logical next steps, and do not measure desirable behavioral changes. Moreover, such tests lack demonstrated reliability and validity for measuring what they purport to measure. The alternative has been to turn to standardized, commercially available achievement tests which either do not measure all of the teachers' objectives or else unduly influence what teachers include in their instructional programs.

Local, teacher-made tests seem to encourage student cheating. Teachers blame moral laxity, parental pressures for high grades, competition for college admission, and the like. The real difficulty is that the tests emphasize memory skills and isolated facts. A French teacher, for example, is more interested in "catching" student differences in memorizing vocabulary or the content of a story than in teaching facility in speaking and reading —so the test is a competitive exercise of doubtful value between pupils and teachers. The pupils are tempted to cheat in order to beat the system, and the teachers try to outguess the students. The resultant tests are poor, often based on outmoded goals of teaching and learning. They emphasize development of memorization rather than the higher mental processes.

Another problem related to the evaluation of pupil progress concerns the methods for reporting that progress to the pupils, their employers, or to the colleges they expect to attend. Teachers, principals, school counselors, and some college admissions officers like to reduce their descriptions of pupil learnings to single grade systems.

Principals and teachers question what grades to give students in advanced-placement or special-track programs. They worry because an *A* grade does not mean the same in Track 4 as in Track 2, or because class rank does not mean the same in a small school in Iowa as it does in suburban Oak Park. No wonder some parents in suburban Washington, D.C., recently demanded that the Board of Education remove their children from the school's gifted classes so they would receive higher grades in the poorer competition of average classes and stand a better chance of getting into the college of their choice. But the school officials did not change the system!

Evaluation needs to consider at least three general areas of pupil achievement: (1) what students *know* and *can* do; (2) the extent of change in carefully defined pupil behavior; and (3) the quality of what pupils do while engaged in independent study with a minimum of faculty supervision. Attempting to put all of the data that measure pupil accomplishments in all of these areas into one multipurpose grade is an educational crime. So is the calculation of a standard formula for college admission, or for promotion, for graduation, for admittance to kindergarten, for eligibility for athletics or the student council, or for a number of other similar practices now followed by educators who oversimplify professional evaluation and reporting.

INDIVIDUALIZING EVALUATION

Individualizing pupil learning requires that evaluation also be individualized. Three typical practices found in schools obstruct that goal: the oral quizzing of pupils, called recitation or, erroneously, class discussion; combining all aspects of pupil achievement into one grade; and constantly comparing the individual with the group to which he is presently assigned.

The oral questioning of pupils to discover their knowledge of essential facts is a waste of time for both teachers and pupils; moreover, it is not a good way to find out if the pupils know what they are supposed to know. The time that teachers and pupils spend in oral quizzing and answering varies from class to class, with the average being about twenty minutes per period. The teachers could use that time better for preparation, conferences, evaluation, and other professional activities. The pupils could use the time more advantageously in their own independent study.

The recitation plays into the hands of the academically able, verbal, extrovert pupils; other pupils are needlessly embarrassed. The small-group setting in which pupils are selected according to present ability to express ideas orally is a much better setting for teachers to appraise pupil progress, and programed materials and objective-type written quizzes are more efficient than an oral quiz for finding out what each pupil knows of the essential facts of a course.

The second practice to change in order to individualize evaluation is to move away from the multipurpose grade. Besides oversimplifying reports, making them less meaningful both to pupils and parents, the single letter grade fails to record individual differences in accomplishment. A pupil with less knowledge than others may be more creative; one with poor attitude, attendance, and self-control may have high achievement in knowledge; another may memorize well but be weak in applying what he knows to new situations. The school needs to appraise and report the various goals separately.

The third evaluation policy required is to emphasize the individual pupil's accomplishments in relation to his own past record, *not* in relation to the other pupils in his immediate group, for his group may not be typical. A high ranking pupil may develop laxity with mediocre competition and have difficulties when he moves to another situation where the general level is higher. Conversely, the pupil at the bottom of the group may work very hard and improve, but he still receives a D–, or unsatisfactory grade, because he is still low in comparison to the others. Effective competition with one's own past record is the best guarantee of effective competition with the group.

EVALUATING CHANGE

Someone has said that innovators are not evaluators. The converse of that statement also is true. In many cases, evaluators are not innovators. These two statements summarize the problems we face in evaluating educational changes. Basically, what is needed is to understand the relationships between the stated purposes of an educational change, such as team teaching, and how to evaluate or judge the extent to which the purposes are being realized.

Let us examine some purposes of team teaching—some more legitimate than others—that have implications for evaluation. For example, an article appeared some time ago in an educational journal in which a principal indicated that his school initiated team teaching because the plant was so overcrowded that they would have been forced to go on a double-session program if some other arrangements were not made. In order to avoid this development, which was opposed by both pupils and parents, they discovered a well-known fact; namely, that the combination of large-group instruction, small-group discussion, and independent study in a team situation could accommodate a considerably larger number of students than the conventional system could in the same building space. So they instituted that educational change. The principal reported that nearly every parent, teacher, and pupil approved. Since conservation of building space was the only reason for team teaching in that school, the evaluation was very simple. Team teaching succeeded because more students occupied the available space and they did not resort to a double session. Apparently they were not interested in other potential team teaching outcomes.

If team teaching is initiated to develop more personal responsibility for learning among pupils, evaluation needs to go beyond giving standardized or locally developed achievement tests. What the pupils do during their independent study inside and outside the school must be analyzed as will be suggested in Chapter 27. Or if team teaching aims to encourage more and better reading by pupils, the evaluation goes beyond giving standardized reading tests, to include records of *how much* reading and *what kind* of reading students did before and now do after team teaching.

The point is that evaluation must be related to the specific purposes of any change or innovation. Hazy purposes bring hazy evaluation.   Using wrong or inadequate measuring instruments to evaluate well defined purposes is equally out of focus.   Chapter 27 will illustrate the constructive action that is needed.   The emphasis is on stating the purposes of change in behavioral terms and developing criterion measures of the performance that ensues.

TOPICS FOR STUDY AND DISCUSSION

1. A newspaper article recently indicated that a neighboring school produced six finalists in the last national competition for Merit Scholarship winners. Your school produced none. One of your school patrons has just called to ask the question, "Why isn't our school as good as theirs?" What is your answer?
2. What do you believe is the best quantifiable criterion for judging curriculum excellence? Be prepare to defend your answer in a group discussion.
3. If the educational setting affects teacher excellence, what improvement in the setting should have highest priority in a school you know in order to achieve a better quality of teaching in it?
4. Taking the subject you teach, or one in which you are especially interested, list the goals you would use to evaluate pupils in your school in comparison with those in other schools of the city, county, state, or nation. Perhaps your answer is, none. In either case, defend your conclusion in a paper or discussion.
5. With your colleagues, discuss how to improve the system of reporting pupil progress to their parents.

SELECTED REFERENCES

FINDLEY, WARREN G., ed.   *The Impact and Improvement of School Testing Programs.*   Sixty-second NSSE Yearbook, Part 2.   Chicago: University of Chicago Press, 1963, pp. 163–210.

Max D. Engelhart and John M. Beck discuss how tests have developed over the years and present nine recommendations for improvment.   Ralph W. Tyler writes about the problems and effects of external testing and offers constructive suggestions for coping with pressures caused by the programs.

HOFFMAN, BANESH.   *The Tyranny of Testing.*   New York: The Crowell-Collier Press, 1962.

This book is a controversial classic in pointing out the evils in conventional testing programs.   It describes weaknesses in various testing procedures and in some tests.

Invitational Conference on Testing Problems.   Princeton, N.J.: Educational Testing Service, 1967.

The report of the 1966 conference, a program that has been sponsored annually for more than a quarter century. Pages 3–60 contain six lectures relating to educational innovations and evaluation.

MERRILL, M. DAVID, ed. "Proficiency Measurement: Assessing Human Performance," by Robert Glasser and David J. Klaus; "Instructional Variables and Learning Outcomes," by Robert M. Gagné. In *Instructional Design: Readings.* Englewood Cliffs, N.J.: Prentice-Hall, Inc., 1971, pp. 327–374.

Part V deals with the criterion referenced measurement plus conditions and criteria, thus providing the reader with both theoretical and practical bases for developing better evaluative techniques and instruments.

TYLER, RALPH W., ed. *Educational Evaluation: New Roles, New Means.* The Sixty-eighth Yearbook of the National Society for the Study of Education, Part 2. Chicago: The University of Chicago Press, 1969.

See especially Chapter VII on "The Evaluation of Group Instruction," Chapter VIII on "The Role of Evaluation in Programs for Individualized Instruction," and Chapter XII, "Appraising the Effects of Innovations in Local Schools."

WILHELMS, FRED T., ed. *Evaluation as Feedback and Guide.* 1967 Yearbook. Washington, D.C.: Association for Supervision and Curriculum Development, 1967, pp. 18–46 and 72–100.

Clifford F. S. Bebell discusses "The Evaluation We Have," emphasizing such factors as emotionality, grading system, tests and examinations, and the inertia that inhibits change. Doris May Lee writes about factors which inhibit realistic self-evaluation and urges important changes in teaching to improve evaluation.

CHAPTER 27

Appraising and Reporting
Pupil Growth

The preceding chapter presented the reasons for changes in evaluation. This chapter describes more specifically what a school may do to implement such a program. Since room for local uniqueness is required, no specific proposed program is described in total. The rate of change in curriculum improvement varies with local readiness and the commitment of local school personnel. Therefore, the degree to which evaluation departs from the conventional program is also bound to vary from one place to another. This chapter discusses pupil self-appraisal and how to measure what pupils know, what they do, and the quality of their independent study. The matter of reporting pupil progress is considered in addition.

PUPIL SELF-APPRAISAL

Pupil self-appraisal aims to enable each pupil to know continually what progress he is making. The test of the effectiveness of pupil self-appraisal is the degree to which test-taking on instruments prepared by teachers or external examiners ceases to become a traumatic experience for the pupils. If their self-appraisal is well done, the pupils know in advance how well they will do on tests prepared by others, assuming the tests are well devised.

Self-checking exercises

Every classroom or independent study area needs a series of exercises prepared by teachers that will enable a pupil to check his own progress. For example, in the field of English, exercises on capitalization, punctuation, number and tense, sentence structure, paragraph structure, and the like, are provided. These exercises are relatively brief with the answer sheets immediately available so a pupil may know how well he has done and, especially, the kinds of mistakes he makes that reveal need for further study on his part. Reading tests of various sorts are also available for his use at any time. Examples of comparable evaluative instruments in other subject fields are typing exercises, rating skills to judge productions in art and music, self-testing exercises in foreign languages, and a wide variety of factual tests related to the various topics being studied in history, mathematics, sciences, and, in fact, all of the school subjects. Pupils may work on these self-appraisal devices individually or with a partner. In any event, each pupil is encouraged to maintain his own personal records of what he has done.

Programed instruction

The school should provide each student with a textbook or technical device particularly planned to teach him a given subject area without the constant supervision of a teacher. That idea is not a new one, but it certainly has received increased emphasis in recent times. The *programed* materials may ask the students to fill in blanks, answer questions, select one of several multiple choice answers, solve a problem, find some new idea in science, or what not. Pupils engage in self-evaluation as they work through a programed textbook or teaching machine. The items are arranged in a sequential manner regardless of the type.

The program tells the pupil immediately whether his answer is right or wrong. He no longer needs to wait until he receives a grade on a test or answers a question in class to know whether he knows the right answer. The point emphasized here is that besides having tremendous implications for curriculum development per se, programed instruction also serves an effective function in reporting to pupils, to teachers, and to others what the student knows. That reporting is done constantly, hour by hour, rather than at the end of six weeks or the established grading period. However, in many instances schools fail to take advantage of this opportunity. The progress of each pupil through programed instruction materials should be recorded by the student and reported systematically to his teachers and to his parents.

Computer-assisted instruction

The programed instruction materials of today will doubtless constitute the museum pieces of tomorrow.   Already persons are suggesting that the first programed textbooks and "teaching boxes" belong in the Smithsonian Institution and other museums.   What teaching machines do today will be done more efficiently tomorrow by computer-assisted instruction.   Computer programs not only can monitor individualized instruction, determining progress for each student according to his talents and interests, but also may push the learner along more efficiently than most teachers and most programed instruction can today.   Moreover, in addition to mediating instruction, the computer will produce individualized records of progress, so each person will know much better than today how he is getting along.   In turn, his teachers, parents, and other interested persons also will know better than today what progress is being made.   The research and development programs of today will produce better and more economical computer-assisted instruction tomorrow.

Self-appraisal reports

The school should develop a system whereby each student can report what he hopes to do in relation to his own strengths and weaknesses.   The pupil will describe his plans for capitalizing on his strengths and overcoming or learning to live with his weaknesses—and his progress to date.   Such a program is essential for sound mental hygiene.   It is also important in any program of personal evaluation of progress.

Teachers in every subject field should develop the appropriate forms for self-appraisal and reporting.   One column can list the goals of the subject, defined in terms of what pupils are expected to do.   A second column, to be filled out by the learners, can indicate approximately how well each student believes he will be able to accomplish the goals.   A third column can indicate present progress as defined by each pupil with respect to the various goals.   To report to parents and to the students, the teacher can then check, in the fourth column, his agreement or disagreement with the self-appraisal made by the student.   A fifth column can be used for the pupil's final indication of agreement or disagreement with the teacher.   Such a scheme would be a tremendous move ahead in developing individual responsibility and understanding of the teaching-learning process.

The point emphasized here is that teachers must give pupils much more responsibility than is typically done today to assess their own progress in learning.   Teachers may waste much of their own time in grading pupil papers.   That time is spent better by teachers in improved planning and preparation.   What may be even more important, when teachers grade too many papers, they deprive their pupils of a significant learning activity and a sense of personal responsibility.   Teachers must constantly push their pupils to appraise their own productivity in the various curriculum areas.

WHAT PUPILS KNOW

The self-appraisal by students should be complemented by systematic programs whereby examiners verify to the best of their ability what the pupils actually know at given intervals during the year.   Standardized achievement tests and teacher-made tests provide this type of appraisal as a guide to pupils, parents, colleges, and employers.

Standardized achievement tests

A city, county, or state school system decides what people should know and employs experts to construct the most valid and reliable instruments possible to evaluate students' knowledge of that material.   Here is where the government, through its experts, tells what historical facts, what mathematical problems, what spelling and grammar, what information about typewriters, what French vocabulary, what health rules, what scientific facts, what beliefs about social issues—what knowledge and skills in all areas of human activity represented by the several subject disciplines—are considered essential, desirable, and enriching for students in this society.   The content that the state expects all persons to know should be measured by tests prepared at the state level and standardized within that level so that each student and each school can determine how well the pupils are learning.

This book recommended earlier that because of population mobility, such decisions should be national rather than local or regional.   Does it follow then that assessment of pupil knowledge also is national?   If curriculum experts determine, for example, the facts that everyone who is educable needs to know to be an effective, loyal citizen, then the assessment of pupil knowledge should be national in scope. Of course, regional and local differences in literacy, cultural goals, socioeconomic status, and the like, affect pupil scores on such tests, but the facts of such differences are known, and ameliorative steps can be taken.

Once more the fact should be emphasized that we are discussing here only that aspect of total schooling, called basic education, which is the same everywhere. The evaluation of depth education is not a matter for state and national assessment in the same way that basic education is. It is possible, of course, for curriculum and evaluation experts to construct standardized tests that will help students know the progress they are making beyond the requirements of basic education, but such tests are not necessarily given in every school.

Teacher-made tests

Because the curriculum of each school and of each class has certain elements which are uniquely necessary in the particular locale, teacher-made tests are needed to complement the standardized testing program. Moreover, standardized tests are given at major intervals of time whereas teacher-made tests are given much more frequently in order to provide guides for teachers and pupils to plan future instructional activities.

The local tests need to evaluate pupil knowledge not only of the subject disciplines but also of such matters as the library, the resource centers, and community learning opportunities. They also need to measure student knowledge of the availability and functions of various extraclass activities and the school's guidance services, which vary from one school to another.

The difficulties involved in teacher-made tests are well known. Many teachers have had little training for preparing tests that are valid, reliable, and useful. Even those teachers who know how to prepare such tests often lack the necessary time and facilities to construct them. Therefore, the resultant testing is in many instances less valuable than it should be.

The bibliography at the end of this chapter suggests books that teachers may study in their efforts to improve the tests they make. Teachers need not feel insecure in the construction of objective, performance, and essay tests. The school's supervisory program can help them to know how to score and grade such tests and to analyze the test data statistically to arrive at sound conclusions regarding the meaning of the results. Teachers realize how these tests help them to diagnose learning problems and suggest prescriptions to guide further assignments.

WHAT PUPILS DO

This area of evaluation may be the most important of all. A pupil may *know* something, but his inability to apply what he knows through constructive action may leave his education relatively incomplete. An old cliché says that what one does speaks louder than what one says. Yet schools typically ignore or treat lightly this aspect of evaluation and fail to report behavioral outcomes to parents and others in a systematic manner or cover them up in a multipurpose mark as described in the preceding chapter. Constructive steps should be taken.

Probably no one group has done more to evaluate behavioral outcomes than Dr. Ralph Tyler and his colleagues during the Eight-Year Study of the Progressive Education Association in the 1930's. They described the procedures and developed instruments for measuring behavioral outcomes.

The teacher's first step is to define what he expects pupils to accomplish in terms that can be measured. Every teacher aim is quantifiable if stated properly. For example, if one of the teacher's goals for students is to appreciate literature better after having completed a given course in English, the teacher describes what persons who *appreciate* literature do differently from persons who *do not appreciate* literature. Do they read more books of higher quality? (And what is meant by "higher quality?") Do they buy books to establish a personal library? Can they read a page from each of two stories and determine that one of the stories is better than the other? A similar procedure can be followed to determine behavioral outcomes in other subjects. In every case teachers must decide how to collect the data—through personal observation, through paper and pencil measuring instruments, through the application of scales, or by some other means.

Consider another illustration, this one from the area of small-group discussion as described in Chapter 20. Teachers hope that pupils in small-group discussion will express ideas clearly and persuasively, will listen effectively and understandingly to the oral statements of other members of the group, and will respect and appreciate each other in the process. Therefore, the teacher must keep an evaluative record of the discussion. For example, the teacher may record a tally each time a group member makes a substantive contribution, along with +, 0, or − to indicate the teacher's judgment of whether or not the statement was accurate, helpful, pertinent, or valuable according to whatever other criteria the teacher accepts for effective contributions.

Similarly, the teacher can appraise how good a listener

each pupil is by tallying an indication of whether he actually had listened to the contributions of other group members and how well he understood them.   The evaluation may also include an appraisal of the positive contributions of individual pupils: how constructive, how creative, how enlarging.   The teacher then combines tallies on quantity and quality of speaking and listening for a given grading period.   He compares what the pupil did during that grading period with his actions during a preceding one. To evaluate growth of the total group in discussion skills, the teacher may compare the average student scores for two different periods.

Sociometry may be utilized to determine changes in interpersonal relations among pupils and, therefore, whether a given individual is progressing in his relations with other students in the group.   Such measurements become an essential ingredient of the evaluation of pupil progress, or the lack of it, in programs of small-group discussion.

Another possible teacher goal is for pupils to read more books—and books of better quality.   Teachers may evaluate that objective by asking their pupils to fill out a three-by-five inch card each time they read a book or magazine.   They list the name of the author, the title, and the name of the magazine or publisher of the book, plus a sentence recommending or not recommending the book or article to other young people, then turn the signed card in to an assistant.   The measurement involves counting up the number of books read and evaluating the quality of each book on a predetermined scale.   Periodically, the teacher has a private conference with each pupil, going over the cards to verify whether or not he has in fact understood the books he has listed.   Having done this measurement, it is relatively simple for the professional teacher to evaluate the accomplishment of this reading objective for individuals or for a given group.

Some behavioral goals may be school-wide, cutting across subject lines.   For example, a faculty may wish to evaluate "ability to follow directions."   During a given grading period, without publicity, individual teachers may be asked to report occasions when specific pupils followed directions very well or, conversely, failed to follow directions.   Each example is recorded on a three-by-five inch card, which is then placed in an appropriate faculty box.   The school assigns each faculty member the responsibility for accumulating cards for a given group of the students for whom he has responsibility as teacher-counselor.   Thus the school evaluates each student on this particular objective, at the same time evaluating the total school.   The project may be repeated periodically to judge other all-school objectives, such as good citizenship, punctuality, or ability to think creatively.

The foregoing examples obviously represent only a few of hundreds that might be given. What we are saying is that the faculty, individually or as a group, needs to decide what behavioral goals are to be evaluated and then collect evidence to measure the extent to which the objectives are accomplished.

INDEPENDENT STUDY

Chapter 18 stressed independent study as the heart of the school program. We provide here a plan, developed by Dr. William M. Griffin of Boston College, for measuring the quality of independent study. Dr. Griffin used the following definitions and scale to evaluate special independent study projects in the Wayland, Massachusetts, High School.

A student performing effectively in independent study is one who—

Perceives things to do. *For example:* pursues instructional leads for further study, . . . compares various sources of information, . . . asks relationship-type questions, . . . integrates information from different subject-matter fields, . . . summarizes findings and places them in correct frame of reference.

Personalizes learning. *For example:* casts about for a project of real interest and value, . . . gives own unique reasons for doing what is done, . . . prepares a plan to structure the study, . . . distributes work schedule to allow for other commitments, . . . expresses satisfaction in a task of own selection and implementation.

Exercises self-discipline. *For example:* accepts limits of the school without denying self, . . . displays sustained and conscientious industry, . . . seeks procedural authority for own point of view and actions, . . . works in harmony with others in groups of two or three, . . . cooperates in maintaining climate for individual work.

Makes use of human resources. *For example:* initiates contacts with appropriate teachers and other persons, . . . shares interpretations, interests and ideas in good exchange, . . . comes prepared for conference discussions, . . . uses contacts to clarify thinking with pertinent and relevant questioning, . . . investigates suggestions which are offered.

Makes use of material resources. *For example:* broadens own knowledge through related readings, . . . makes use of tapes, records, and projectuals to expand knowledge, . . . displays deftness in locating library materials, . . . recognizes and uses the tools of the study area, . . . constructs special materials and devices for use in the work.

Produces results. *For example:* works at appropriate pace and follows through to completion, . . . plans projects which are subject to accomplishment, . . . states clear objectives, . . . displays habit of getting down to work, . . . finds applications for a creative idea.

Strives for improvement. *For example:* seeks advice from competent people, . . . corrects errors on one's own, . . . studies authoritative sources for best practices, . . . uses group sessions to test out ideas and clarify issues, . . . evaluates material in the light of personal experiences and first-hand knowledge.[1]

The independent study efforts of each student may be evaluated on a five-point scale. The school needs to decide which of the foregoing characteristics are to be judged. Although it is far better to evaluate a student on each characteristic, one generalized rating might be made to simplify the task for the teacher. In any event, the method of appraisal should be explained to students, parents, and others who may see the record. The scaled judgment should be accompanied by a sentence comment illustrating the basis of the evaluation.

The scale might look like this:

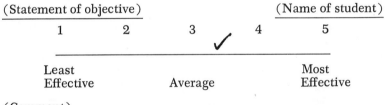

(Statement of objective)   (Name of student)

   1   2   3   4   5

Least
Effective   Average   Most
Effective

(Comment)

A check (✓) is placed at the point along the line that best describes a student in a given quality, judging his efforts in relation to the independent study efforts of all other students the teacher has ever known. The illustration shows a student who is somewhat better than average in effectiveness in the aspect of independent study being evaluated.

The important consideration is to accumulate a series of judgments and comments over a period of years so that changes in pupil performance may be evaluated. A qualified person then might summarize the changes for reports to colleges, prospective employers, and any other interested persons.

[1] William Maxwell Griffin, "A Study of the Relationship of Certain Characteristics of High School Seniors to Effectiveness in Independent Study" (doctoral dissertation, Syracuse University, 1964).

REPORTING PUPIL PROGRESS

The basic principle in reporting pupil progress to pupils, to parents, to colleges, and to employers is to report each type of educational goal separately, even though the report is in a consolidated form. What a student *knows* and what he *does* should be listed in different sections. A third section should be devoted to independent study, using the scales described in the preceding section.

The written report provides information each grading period regarding specific pupil achievements during that period. For example, it may include the percentage of right answers on teacher-made tests, standardized test scores, the number and quality of books read, the speed of typewriting—with the number of errors—and the like, listing comparable data for earlier marking periods.

The report to pupils and parents should not include the student's standing in relation to other students. If a parent wants to know such data, the school should reveal it to him in a personal conference. When a student applies for college admission or a specific job, the school can present median and range figures for each of the subjects being reported so that the reader may know how the student compares to other students in the schools.

What we are suggesting is a continuous progress reporting system instead of the production of letter grades every six weeks, twice a semester, final course-end mark, or other conventional procedures. Evaluation thus becomes a regular part of the teaching-learning system constantly rather than periodically. The report does not reflect a pass or fail situation. Some students simply progress faster than others.

Here is how such a program could work. The required portions of the curriculum areas are identified as segments, units, or portions distinctly separate from other parts which represent optional, additional creative or depth studies done by those pupils who develop different goals beyond the required sector. Each of the required segments has a name and a number, identified on the report card. When the pupil completes a segment, the teacher or instructional assistant punches or marks the card. A qualitative indicator, such as above average, may be provided for the segments when appropriate. Otherwise, the indicator means satisfactory completion. Periodically the school mails these reports home, once or twice a semester, with intervening reports only when requested or needed. The emphasis here is on the cognitive and skills areas of the taxonomy of educational objectives.

The required content in all subjects would be listed, evaluated, and reported the same as in English which is illustrated below:

1. COMPLETION OF LEARNING SEQUENCES AND COMPARATIVE TESTS

SUBJECT: English

No. of Sequence	1	2	3	4	5	6	7	8	9	10	11	12	13	14	15	16	17	18	19	20	21
Above Average						●							●								
Completed	●	●	●			●			●	●	●				●						

COMPARATIVE TESTS:

Reading – California CTB

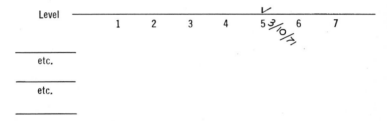

Level

  1   2   3   4   5   6   7

_____
etc.

_____
etc.

_____

See the reverse side for the names of the sequences
by number and the nature of the tests.

A second report form describes periodically what each pupil accomplishes beyond the required segments in each curriculum area. On each page of this report, the teacher in charge of a given project or activity records when a pupil reads more than is required, plays on the basketball team, produces an art work, develops a mathematics puzzle, or does any other special project. The report is simple: two or three descriptive phrases or sentences plus an indication of quality on such criteria as creativity, use of resources, self-discipline (staying with it), and the like, as selected by each curriculum department. The emphasis here is on the affective domain in the taxonomy.

The figure on page 400 illustrates how the form might be used for a special project in English.

2. SPECIAL PROJECTS COMPLETED

SUBJECT: English

DESCRIPTION	QUALITY		
	Superior	Average	Inferior
_____	Use Human Resources	L_____ I __✓_ I ____ I _____ I	
_____	Use Materials	L_____ I ___✓ I ____ I _____ I	
_____	Creativity	L_____ I ____ I ____ ✓ I _____ I	
_____	Self-Discipline	L _✓_ I ____ I _____ I ____ I	
_____	Value to Pupil	L _✓_ I ____ I _____ I ____ I	
_____	Worth Doing	L_____ I ____ I __✓_ I ____ I	
	Etc.		

This foregoing report emphasizes individual achievements with comparative judgments based upon all the pupils a teacher has ever worked with rather than on a particular class at a given time. Standardized instruments or district measures provide pupils, parents, and other interested persons with a basis for judging the relative quality of a pupil's performance in comparison with others.

Oral reports are also desirable. The point was made in Chapter 24, which concerned team teaching and staff utilization, that teachers should be scheduled with students fewer hours per week than is the case in the conventional school today. An important reason for freeing teachers from scheduled contacts with groups of students is to provide them with the time to confer with individual students and their parents regarding pupil progress. This pupil-teacher conference is used to amplify the written reports and to suggest remedial and progressive steps to improve pupil achievement. Variations in pupil needs prevent positive statements on the frequency of these teacher-pupil-parent conferences. However, school policies might reasonably suggest a minimum of one pupil-teacher conference during each six-week grading period and one teacher-parent conference during each semester.

At least one teacher in the school must know every student as a total human being; therefore, one teacher should have the responsibility of accumulating the reports from all the other teachers and of consolidating the data into a report card.   Such an arrangement is basic to the guidance functions of the school.   This teacher becomes a liaison person between the parent wanting a comprehensive appraisal of his child's progress and needs and the different teachers that the child has.   The arrangement saves both the parents and the teachers considerable time and systematizes the whole business of reporting pupil progress.   The teacher also provides information to colleges and to prospective employers. Obviously, the teacher needs time for these activities and he must have clerical help.

TOPICS FOR STUDY AND DISCUSSION

1.   Prepare for one topic in a subject you teach, or one you are preparing to teach, a self-checking test that will tell pupils what they already know and what they still need to study.
2.   A colleague says, "I will not be replaced by a machine (meaning a programed textbook, a teaching machine, or computer-assisted instruction)."   Develop a series of reasons to support or reject your colleague's opinion in a group discussion.
3.   What arguments will you use to defend or oppose a system of national assessment of pupil learning?   Include the relationships of such a system to curriculum planning and development.
4.   Think of some purpose in your teaching that you are not measuring reliably at the present time (or if you are a university student, that your teachers are not measuring).   Devise ways to quantify the objective.   What does a pupil do who has accomplished the goal as opposed to what others do who have not achieved the aim? Then prepare a plan for collecting and interpreting the data and for reporting your findings.
5.   Discuss with colleagues who teach other subjects some common purpose you share, such as developing more responsibility for learning on the part of pupils.   Plan and carry through for one or two weeks a school-wide system for collecting examples of situations in which students have or have not acted responsibly and for reporting them to pupils and parents.

SELECTED REFERENCES

BLOOM, BENJAMIN S., ed.   *Taxonomy of Educational Objectives, Handbook I: Cognitive Domain.*   New York: Longmans, Green and Company, 1956.

This book presents a system for classifying educational goals related to the recognition and recall of knowledge and the development of intellectual abilities and skills. It provides illustrative test items.

FRENCH, WILL, and ASSOCIATES. *Behavioral Goals of General Education in High School.* New York: Russell Sage Foundation, 1957, pp. 85–230.

Part III provides a basis for evaluation by listing a large number of performance outcomes under four general areas of competence: intellectual development, cultural orientation, health, and economic facility. It provides a table to help workers in any school develop evaluation priorities.

KRATHWOHL, DAVID R., et al. *Taxonomy of Educational Objectives, Handbook II: Affective Domain.* New York: David McKay Co., Inc., 1956.

Such affective goals as interests, attitudes, appreciations, values, and emotional sets are classified and illustrated under these categories: receiving (attending), responding, valuing, organizing, and internalizing.

LANGE, PHIL C., ed. *Programed Instruction.* Sixty-sixth Yearbook, National Society for the Study of Education, Part 2. Chicago: University of Chicago Press, 1967.

This is an up-to-date analysis by eleven authors of the bases, developments, issues and problems, and future possibilities in programed instruction. Chapters III, VI, and VIII are especially significant for curriculum development.

MAGER, ROBERT F. *Preparing Instructional Objectives.* Palo Alto, California: Fearon Publishers, Inc., 1962.

This booklet is a self-teaching primer for teachers or anyone else who needs to learn how to express educational goals in behavioral terms—the first step in improving evaluation.

POPHAM, W. JAMES, and BAKER, EVA L. *Systematic Instruction.* Englewood Cliffs, N.J.: Prentice-Hall, Inc., 1970.

This book provides a practical guide for goal-referenced instruction along with the techniques for evaluating the results and testing hypotheses.

SMITH, EUGENE R., and TYLER, RALPH W. *Appraising and Recording Student Progress.* New York: Harper and Brothers, 1942.

The story of evaluation in the Eight-Year Study presents the philosophy of appraisal that emphasized the development of performance objectives. Numerous examples of instruments and devices are included.

WILHELMS, FRED T., ed. *Evaluation as Feedback and Guide.* 1967 Yearbook. Washington: Association for Supervision and Curriculum Development, 1967, pp. 121–181.

Paul B. Diederich and Frances R. Link describe an innovative evaluation program that is generally conducted by groups of teachers rather than by individuals. The emphasis is on evaluating behavior goals. They also describe in detail a special project in English.

PART **VI**

Procedures for Improvement

CHAPTER 28

Organizing for Change

Many individuals and organizations are involved in curriculum change: principals, teachers, pupils, parents, taxpayers, government officials, university staff members, foundations, businesses and industries, labor organizations, and civic groups of various types. As leader of the school, the secondary school principal must exercise his responsibility with knowledge and vigor. He and the teachers in his school need to understand their own motivations as well as those of each of the foregoing groups.

THE PRINCIPLE OF ACCOUNTABILITY

Basic to change is an understanding of the consequences of alternative decisions for curriculum improvement. Requiring content that some pupils neither want nor need shows a lack of accountability. So does the failure of the program to schedule pupils into the best learning environments in the school or community that are appropriate for given tasks. Failure to analyze the consequences of any procedure in relation to expenditures and quality of learning violates the principle of accountability. So, in connection with the curriculum or any other aspect of schooling, the individuals involved need constantly to relate expenditures in effort, time, money (including all facilities), and personnel to productivity in terms of the stated purposes. That is the principle of accountability, a complex goal stated in simple terms.

Most teachers enter the profession because of a deepseated commitment toward helping young people become better persons. However, teachers are also persons, with the usual drives to succeed, to live well, to feel that their talents are utilized properly, to protect their security, and to avoid unnecessary hard work. Those who plan curricular changes must help teachers understand how the new program will affect each of the foregoing drives.

Pupils, more than any other group, have the largest personal stakes in curriculum change. The principal and other persons involved should provide pupils regularly with information that will assure them that they are learning as much as, and in most instances more than, they did under the former program. The pupils rightfully want assurances that they will be as able to get into the colleges to which they may reasonably aspire, that they will be better prepared for their chosen vocations, and that their present lives in school will be more stimulating and rewarding.

Parents want the same assurances for their children. When any alteration in the school program is being planned, they must be told how the changes will help pupils to achieve each of the appropriate pupil goals.

Taxpayers want to know if the changes are going to be expensive. If the costs go up, they need assurance that the new program is worth what it costs. School administrators sometimes ignore the relationship between financial input and educational output, but that is not a defensible business policy.

Civic groups are also concerned with curriculum improvement. They want to be proud of their schools when they write letters to their friends in other communities or when persons from other places come to visit them. Community pride cannot be ignored.

Employers in business and industry want assurances that the graduates of the new program will be better employees than the graduates of the program it replaced. Organized labor wants to be sure that the graduates of the new program will be more employable and that, other factors being equal, they will fare better if they graduate from the changed curriculum.

Representatives of governmental agencies also enter the picture. If the school is one of several in a city or county school system, the central administrative and supervisory staff will want to know how their services will be utilized in the new program. The system may exert pressures for uniformity among all schools. A given school must carefully describe the reasons for change, the methods of change, the manner of evaluation, and the financial implications.

Since state education agencies are responsible for maintaining standards throughout the state, they establish a number of quantitative measures of excellence that all schools are expected to achieve. The state officials check school reports carefully and on occasion visit schools to make certain that the quantitative aspects are obeyed. If the change proposed in a given school violates one or more of these quantitative standards, the school should report the change in advance and request permission to be released from existing standards. It should also specify how the program may be evaluated by state authorities.

If the school receives federal aid, there are bound to be certain restrictions on how that aid is used. A school planning a change that violates some existing federal standard must clarify the situation before putting the change into effect. Increasingly, governmental agencies and educational foundations are making funds available for curriculum innovations. If a school wishes to obtain a grant, it must plan a program that is in harmony with the grant's specifications. Of course, the availability of grants does not mean that schools should only practice innovations likely to be supported, but they should be aware of the types of fundable programs presently available and the procedures for applying to participate in them. A school planning to change should check various governmental and foundation interests if it wishes to obtain financial support for a given experiment or demonstration. Perhaps an existing school interest may be adapted to the programs which foundations or government agencies are promoting.

Universities and other higher educational institutions play specific roles in secondary school changes. Some innovations affect secondary school-university relationships—marking systems, course outlines, or procedures for reporting the school's estimate of students' ability to succeed in the university. School authorities should correspond or meet personally with admissions officers and other appropriate university representatives when planning revised programs for reporting and evaluating the competence of students who will go to the university. Administrators often invite university personnel to serve as consultants to the school in planning changes, reeducating teachers for the changes, collecting materials, and evaluating the results. The close working relationship that can develop between the schools and the universities from this practice is a major bonus factor in organizing for change, but it will not occur unless specific efforts are made by teachers and the school principal.

The first responsibility of the principal in organizing for change is to conceptualize an educational system that will serve individual students better and will raise the professional standards of teaching. These goals have been described in detail in earlier sections of this volume. Inconsistent or inadequate concepts of educational systems can plague schools and cause inefficient and ineffective instruction even in innovative programs. Language laboratories have been installed in some schools largely because government funds were available and other schools were doing it— with the result that the laboratories were only partially or uncertainly used. Some schools engage in team teaching because it is a prestigious or fashionable thing to do. Then they practice only large-group instruction, or fail to give teachers common time together to plan and to evaluate, or to do other things that show inadequate or incomplete understanding of the purposes of team teaching.

Before making an innovation, the principal and the staff involved in the change should prepare specific answers to such questions as the following: What do we believe? How do the various aspects of the new educational program relate to our concepts of the educational provisions necessary for individual students? Is this a carefully planned program of action that includes changes over several years? Are our educational specifications sharply drawn? What kinds of help do we need and from whom? How do we propose to evaluate the effects of the changes on students, teachers, and other concerned individuals? What will the changes cost?

The principal, his assistants, and the teachers in each school must bear prime responsibility for providing viable answers to the foregoing questions. They must analyze carefully in their plans and in progress reports what effects are anticipated and are happening. The principle of accountability with accurate and understandable reports must replace the glossy kinds of public relations releases that can produce creditability gaps. Everyone must understand that change does not come easily or quickly. Everyone must also have as much understanding and information as possible of what is occurring.

DEVELOPING READINESS FOR CHANGE

To effect a change, the principal and the central planning committee must have the cooperation of the various groups mentioned in the first section of this chapter; therefore, they should see to it that the groups are ready for change. They may develop such readiness through a variety of approaches. It is difficult to make specific suggestions that will work in every school; the recommendations that follow have been utilized in various places with success.

Principals often capitalize on events outside the school, using them as a psychological lever to encourage change. For example, there may be a group of critics who deplore the accomplishments of the students in the so-called "fundamentals" of reading, writing, spelling, computing, and the like. So the school undertakes a study of the need for changes in these areas and proposes a number of alterations that it believes will help the situation. Patriotic groups may complain that citizens do not know the nation's history, so the school takes a constructive approach to improve instruction in that subject. A successful space program by a competing nation may provide the lever to reassess science and mathematics programs. Problems in the economic world may stimulate work in the social sciences; so may political and social problems. A national program to combat poverty may lead to a reexamination of selected aspects of the school's programs.

Other procedures that may stimulate interest in curriculum improvement include studies to determine why dropouts leave school and what happens to them when they leave, and follow-up studies of graduates, analyzing their success or failure in colleges and in employment. Studies of attendance and disciplinary problems may point the way to increased guidance services, and they may also focus on needed changes in the curriculum.

Studies in each of the curriculum areas may be undertaken to ascertain what the teachers in that particular area believe their program should be like. In separate studies, pupils, parents, and employers may be asked the same question about goals. What people *think the program should be* may then be compared and contrasted with the program *as it actually exists* to reveal reasons for change. For example, What is the purpose of the health, physical education, and recreation program in the school? Is it to produce professional athletes, to serve as community entertainment, or to improve physical fitness of boys and girls? Are these purposes necessarily opposed to each other?

Another approach to developing readiness for change involves the principles of teaching and learning described earlier in this volume. The principal, or the teacher he thinks is best for the task, makes a large-group presentation at a meeting of faculty, PTA, a civic club, a women's organization or the like. (Occasionally, an entire oral presentation may be best; at other times a film may be more motivational than a live presentation. However, a combination of live and audio-visual presentations is usually best.) The school provides additional materials for individuals to read, view, or hear on their own. Small groups are then organized to discuss and clarify ideas and to make reports. In other words, the principal uses the same approach to teaching others that he expects his teachers to use effectively with their pupils.

Here is a specific illustration. Suppose the principal believes that team teaching would be a desirable change in the school.

For most of one school year he organizes faculty meetings to present various films and filmstrips on team teaching. He also invites outside speakers with team teaching experience to talk with the group. He puts a collection of books, pamphlets, and filmstrips on team teaching in the professional library and suggests that teachers examine these materials in their own independent study prior to discussions at grade or departmental levels. The small-group discussions produce questions which the principal answers in subsequent large-group meetings. Toward the end of the year, the principal finds out which teachers want to become involved in a demonstration-experiment on team teaching the following year. His next step then is to prepare the teachers for the changes they plan to undertake.

FURTHER EDUCATION OF TEACHERS INVOLVED IN CHANGE

The teachers who will be involved in a new team teaching system, along with their instruction assistants and clerks, should attend a summer workshop for two weeks or, preferably, one month. During the workshop, they prepare materials and practice large-group instruction with volunteer pupils who criticize and make suggestions. The teachers also produce assignments for productive independent study and organize small groups of pupils for discussion sessions. At discussions, one of the teachers acts as the teacher-leader and the others sit outside the circle as observers. Later, the groups meet for critique-sessions. The goal of those sessions is to produce plans and materials that teachers may use for at least the first month of the school year. Of course, the teachers benefit from the confidence they acquire in this "learning by doing" activity.

Incidentally, pupils usually volunteer their services happily for these summer sessions. They feel important when they help teachers in a new enterprise. The use of school facilities for swimming or hobbies plus some light refreshments are sufficient material rewards.

Before starting the new system, the principal makes all the appropriate administrative changes needed to give the innovation a chance to succeed. A different kind of schedule is necessary, for the teachers need adequate time to plan together, to prepare materials, to evaluate their work, and to consult with individual students. Changes in room arrangements are also needed, and a variety of materials for teacher use and for independent study must be provided. Before beginning the experiment, the school must prepare attractive, explanatory brochures and distribute them to all the groups mentioned in the opening of this chapter. The basic purpose of the publications is to acquaint all persons with the nature of the project under way. The brochures should not be burdened with too much statistical material, nor should they be overinvolved with historical backgrounds and quotations from authorities. The story should be told simply and directly. Line drawings and charts may be added to emphasize certain points.

Professional help in developing a brochure is usually necessary, since the training of most teachers and principals has not included preparing effective materials of this nature. Someone with journalistic training may take what others have written and remove excess or unclear verbiage. There is no magic length for brochures. They will usually be ten to twenty pages long if they are to be widely read. There should be a good deal of "open space" so that the casual reader is not overwhelmed by the printed material. He should be able to complete the booklet in fifteen to twenty minutes. Remember, the purpose of the brochure is not to tell the whole story, but rather to whet the interest of the reader and to provide a general understanding of what is taking place at the school.

ADMINISTRATIVE POLICIES DURING THE YEAR

The changes undertaken also need to be publicized throughout the year by competent writers and speakers. The experimentation to date should be described as effectively as possible in newspapers, on local radio and television, by means of slides and tapes, and if more funds are available, through professionally produced filmstrips and films.

Periodically the school should issue carefully written summaries of what is happening as a result of the changes that have been made. The reports should contain illustrations and data showing the effects of the changes, plus statements by students and teachers concerning their reactions to what is happening. The report should honestly describe unsolved problems as well as accomplishments.

Staff members not immediately involved in the experimentation may be suspicious and, in some cases, defensive about their failure to be involved in the studies. Psychologists call them the "out-group." They must be kept informed about what is going on and what is being accomplished, and must be encouraged and helped to plan studies for themselves. They may decide to join the "in-group" (persons immediately involved) next year. If so, they will be prepared at a summer workshop.

The most important matter of all during the first year of

change is close supervision of the teachers involved in the new program.   The principal must change his own priorities about how he spends his time and energy.   He needs to delegate responsibility for the cafeteria, the bus routes, routine discipline and attendance, conventional public relations, service club responsibilities, custodial care of the building, and comparable tasks to administrative assistants specially trained and employed for those tasks.   He has to concentrate on the improvement of instruction, working with the groups involved in change.   Teachers do not change their teaching methods easily, nor do students change their learning habits easily. To facilitate the process, the principal must ask many different questions, help to find answers, point out things that are being done incorrectly, and suggest how to improve procedures.   He must work continually at evaluation.

THE PRINCIPAL'S RESPONSIBILITY

The authors trust that this chapter has not destroyed the desire for change by making the task appear too complicated.   The barriers to curriculum improvement have been enunciated elsewhere in this volume.   Removing those barriers requires creative imagination, commitment, and hard work by the principal and his professional colleagues.   The principal in the final analysis bears the awesome responsibility of organizing for change to improve the curriculum. He works with all the persons mentioned earlier in this chapter, soliciting their suggestions and helping them to carry plans through to fruition—but in the long run, he alone is the responsible party. In too many instances, curriculum improvement projects have not reached their maximum potential—or have completely failed— because the changes were not well planned, conducted, and evaluated.   Effective results require broad involvement with strong leadership—and an open mind for new ideas and procedures.

We emphasize the central role of the principal in the change process because he is in the best position to see the total picture of the school—and he is *there* in charge.   The superintendent and his colleagues in the central office, or university consultants and state education department supervisors, may help mightily but they are not there in the school all the time.   They do not know the pupils, the teachers, and the community as well as the principal, if he does his job well.   A teacher in his classroom may innovate, but the principal's administrative restrictions will limit his effectiveness if he opposes the changes.   Conversely, the principal may stimulate curriculum improvement by changes he makes in scheduling, facilities, evaluation, and other instructional matters.   Organizing for change requires action by the school principal.

TOPICS FOR STUDY AND DISCUSSION

1. Consider some educational change which you believe is desirable.   Then analyze why teachers, pupils, parents, taxpayers, employers, representatives of governmental agencies or universities, and others that you may add, are likely to oppose the change. Why are they content with the situation that you want to change?
2. Either using your analysis under Topic 1, or taking a different educational change, plan a strategy to neutralize the opposition so they may be willing to accept constructive suggestions to individualize learning or professionalize teaching.
3. Select some change that you or others are advocating and analyze the potential effects of the change on teachers and pupils.
4. Select some local, state, national, or world development that currently is in the headlines or on TV or radio.   What, if anything, does the development require of schools?   Present a case for or against change in teaching or learning methods.
5. From ten current articles in one or two educational journals, select two articles that have the best and the worst style and presentation.   Prepare an analysis of your reasons for choosing the two articles.

SELECTED REFERENCES

ANDERSON, VERNON E.   *Curriculum Guidelines in an Era of Change.*   New York: The Ronald Press, 1969.
    This paperback provides practical suggestions for developing a rationale for curriculum changes.
FRYMIER, JACK R., and HAWN, HORACE C.   "Basis for Curriculum Change," "Establishing Relationships for Change," and "General Principles for Curriculum Improvement."   In *Curriculum Improvement for Better Schools.*   Worthington, Ohio: Charles A. Jones Publishing Co., 1970, pp. 19–49 and 237–251.
    These three chapters provide practical suggestions for planning and conducting curriculum improvement projects in schools.
GUBA, EGON G., et al.   *The Role of Educational Research in Educational Change in the United States.*   Bloomington, Indiana: The

National Institute for the Study of Educational Change, 1967. Multilithed.

Papers presented by seven authors at an international conference in Germany in 1967 describe the organization of research, how research relates to innovation, and how research findings are disseminated. An excellent bibliography is provided.

LESSINGER, LEON M. *Every Kid a Winner: Accountability in Education.* New York: Simon and Schuster, 1970.

See especially Chapters 1 and 2, pp. 3–37, that show the importance of linking learning to costs and suggest changing assumptions about education and improved management techniques.

MILLER, RICHARD I., ed. *Perspectives on Educational Change.* New York: Appleton-Century-Crofts, 1967.

Eighteen writers describe various forces and organizations that affect educational changes. Some chapters describe steps taken in given schools.

MORPHET, EDGAR L., and RYAN, CHARLES O. *Designing Education for the Future No. 3—Planning and Effecting Needed Changes in Education.* New York: Citation Press, 1967.

Twenty-eight authors discuss various aspects of changing schools. The materials describe programs in individual schools (chapters 8 and 9) in urban areas, and in states.

Rational Planning in Curriculum and Instruction. Washington, D.C.: National Education Association, Center for the Study of Instruction, 1967, pp. 111–154.

David Clark and Egon Guba present a schema that includes research, development, diffusion, and adoption—with recommendations for each process. Henry Brickell describes local inventions inside the school systems and local adoption of ideas generated outside.

TANNER, DANIEL. "Innovation and Curriculum Improvement." In *Secondary Curriculum.* New York: The Macmillan Company, 1971, pp. 403–35.

This chapter provides a model for curriculum change along with brief descriptions of some innovative proposals.

UNRUH, ADOLPH, and TURNER, HAROLD E. "Controlling and Directing Curriculum Change." In *Supervision for Change and Innovation.* New York: Houghton Mifflin Company, 1970, pp. 236–275.

The authors describe plans for building a rationale, developing a support system, and implementing a program.

VAN TIL, WILLIAM, ed. "Curriculum for the 1970's." In *Curriculum: Quest for Relevance.* Boston: Houghton Mifflin Company, 1971, pp. 123–218.

Fifteen writers, including Wilhelms, Havighurst, Robinson, Krutch, Doll, Crosby, and Shane write about new approaches, new subjects, priorities, relations between humanism and technology, and how to change.

WATSON, GOODWIN, ed. *Concepts for Social Change.* Washington, D.C.: National Education Association, National Training Laboratories, 1967.

The editor and nine other authors explore in depth factors that cause resistance to change and suggest remedial actions.

CHAPTER 29

Developing and Supporting
Experimentation

A good school system should have established procedures for studying curriculum to discover areas where changes are desirable. It is not advocated, however, that change must always be going on or that there should never be periods of stability.[1] Change for the sake of change is a foolish premise. Only after extensive study to determine need for change should it be contemplated. The improvement of the curriculum of any school should be a continuing process, and administrators must constantly evaluate its purpose, suitability, and effectiveness. Unfortunately, that is not always done; therefore curriculum movements have been developed to encourage necessary curriculum changes. These movements, under such labels as "curriculum revision" and "curriculum reform," are usually the result of changing social or technological conditions. Many of the new subject-matter programs are associated with curriculum reform movements.

Schools must establish guidelines for essential curriculum change. As suggested above, there should be a genuine need for change based on the relationship of the total educational function to community expectation and capabilities. Technical requirements, such as the information needed, schedules to be followed, and facilities for communication, must be considered, and boundaries must be defined.

[1] Galin J. Saylor, *Curriculum Planning for Modern Schools* (New York: Holt, Rinehart & Winston, Inc., 1966), pp. 462–465.

The involvement of professional personnel is an important consideration. At one time it was thought that all people in the school system should be included—administrators, supervisors, teachers, pupils, and lay citizens. It was contended that the success of any curriculum venture was dependent on total involvement. That point of view has been greatly modified, because it has become obvious that some of the school personnel are neither qualified nor interested in curriculum improvement. They would rather not be bothered and frequently resent the extra effort and time such demanding tasks involve.

Personnel for specialized curriculum study must be carefully selected according to capability, interest, and dedication. Provisions for released time or extra compensation are not only desirable but absolutely necessary. This is particularly true for classroom teachers.

Each person in the study should be assigned a function, for such questions as *who makes decisions* and *at what point* are very relevant to success. The cooperative involvement of teachers, administrators, and supervisors must be part of an over-all plan. The best procedures for curriculum study will have a carefully selected central committee with definite assignments and tacit understanding that all resources of the school system are available on call.

Changes in the curriculum can result from many causes, planned or unplanned. Most changes resulting from social or technological pressures are usually unplanned, but an alert school administrator will provide for more orderly processes by a continuing evaluation of the present program and frequent development of new curriculum guides. Important benefits can be achieved in situations where curriculum workers are encouraged to "brainstorm" or "go off into the blue." Provisions for the innovators and those possessing imaginative creativity are basic to curriculum improvement.

ESTABLISHING PRIORITIES

Deciding what problem to study first is difficult, because the contemporary curriculum relates to so many aspects of today's social and intellectual life. Each curriculum area holds numerous problems and unanswered questions. Polling of teachers, supervisors, or administrators does little to clarify the issue since their choice of significant problems is limited to the scope of their teaching level or operational area and to their personal strengths and weaknesses.

The establishment of priorities will depend on the objectives of the proposed studies, which in turn, depend on the social and cultural objectives of education and the behavioral objectives desired in pupils. Decisions will also result from an evaluation of the present curriculum design in comparison to the desired outcomes of new designs. It is a question, of course, whether curriculum leaders should constantly strive toward developing new curricula and teaching techniques or whether efforts should be directed toward evolution and refinement of the existing enterprise. It is deceptively simple to say that both should be continuous processes.

Another basis for establishing priorities in curriculum work is the availability of research. Experimentation may be necessary if applicable research is not readily available. Intelligent curriculum decisions require careful evaluation of possible consequences, awareness of available resources and personnel, and clear insight into avenues of appropriate action.

EXPERIMENTATION

The basis for scientific knowledge is established by observation. Sometimes an investigator merely records happenings as they are, but more often he creates conditions for a specific purpose. When he does that, the investigation can be called an experiment. How much real experimentation goes on in education is open to question. The testing of a hypothesis against an established practice requires patience and skill. Too often the educator falls back on opinion that is highly colored by established prejudices.

Much of the ferment in the subject-matter fields is said to be experimental. Thus, the new mathematics was often described as experimental, but the term was probably misapplied in this field. Changes in mathematics resulted for the most part from scholars and teachers coming together to discuss shortcomings in existent programs and to establish directions for change. New materials were prepared and various school systems were asked to try out the new materials and report on their usefulness. On the basis of reports, programs were revised, and the new mathematics curricula gradually developed. Rather than true experimentation the process was a trial and error process of implementing and refining an initial set of assumptions.

It is impossible to have true experimentation without alternatives. If an attempt is made to measure the value of new subject-matter procedures, alternatives must be created within the field, so that investigators, using comparable evaluation techniques, can experiment with different means to obtain similar ends. Comparing "old" and "new" subject-matter materials is difficult, because of the absence of comparable educational objectives and precise measuring instruments that are appropriate for both.

A barrier to experimental work within public schools is the fact that public school officials feel a reasonable responsibility to their conservative patrons, who get satisfaction out of a moderately stable curriculum that can be identified and defended. If experimentation suggests the attempting of new ventures, it must have built-in prestige and respectability. School officials are likely to take care that the risk of experimentation is not too great and that definite limitations are imposed.

Since local curriculum leaders are restrained from any widespread experimentation, most of that kind of activity is conducted by outside investigators who merely borrow pupils to test their theories. They promise a comprehensive report, and hopefully local leaders try to assess it in terms of local curriculum improvement. Even then, the board of education is sometimes reluctant to release pupils for enough time to do real experimentation.

Regardless of the problems involved, it behooves those responsible for improving the curriculum to place experimentation high on their list of objectives. Opinions, prejudices, or guesses will not suffice in keeping a school program abreast of constantly changing social and technological conditions. The answers must be found by carefully planned experimentation. The best types of experimentation will result when a fixed set of objectives has been established and basically different approaches are used to obtain these objectives.

Experimentation is needed in the development of curricular sequences from the bottom up instead of from the top down in order to explore the possibilities of relating longitudinal subject-matter sequences to the learning processes of pupils. It is also needed to compare patterns organized around single subjects with patterns combining several related subjects. There is constant need for the development of evaluating materials—especially materials that can be used with pupils from divergent cultural groups and disadvantaged environments.

Educators engaged in curriculum work can engage in specialized experimentation; many good documents on the subject are available with clear, concise directions. Study of these materials will reveal that planning for an experiment usually involves the following steps:

1. Statement of purpose
   (a) Question to be answered
   (b) Hypotheses to be listed

(c)   Estimated effects
(d)   Population to which conclusions will apply
2. Description of experiment
   (a)   Treatment to be followed
   (b)   Range of experiment and number of factors involved
   (c)   Type of measurement to be used and accuracy of measurement
   (d)   Experimental design to be used
3. Conclusions to be drawn
   (a)   Analysis of variance
   (b)   Tabular forms of results
   (c)   Control of errors and level of significance
   (d)   Possible outcomes
   (e)   Testing of hypothesis against results

EXAMPLES OF EXPERIMENTATION

Curriculum planners are frequently confronted with situations that require decisions concerning school organization and course arrangement. Examples that might be cited: whether to change the present school organization to include middle schools or whether to rearrange the curriculum of the high schools to include mini courses. At least three alternatives might be used in securing information as a basis for making decisions in such matters. First, the educational theorist could be consulted. Then there are the experiences of other school men who have made such moves. Finally, the wise school administrator may elect to have his curriculum people set up experimental situations for obtaining firsthand information.

Assume the school administrator is confronted with the problem of alienated youth. From observation he knows that the behavior of these youngsters will find expressions of discontent either in action and involvement or in withdrawal and failure. He hypothesizes that given a sufficient number of alternatives, most students elect involvement. He believes the middle school might offer involvement opportunities for younger children, and mini courses in the high school might bring a series of alternatives for older boys and girls. The prudent school administrator probably will elect to implement his ideas by controlled experimentation rather than take a chance on starting a great number of changes without reasonable assurance of success.

A brief assessment of the middle school idea might be cogent at this point. The real mission of the middle school is to meet the needs of children ready to cross over the threshold into early adolescence.[2] The physiological and psychological needs are sharply perceived at this time. Identified with this period is the stereotype adolescent boy, hyperactive and awkward, and the quickly maturing girl confused or ashamed of her rapidly developing physical characteristics. These youngsters are often in a state of confusion, conflict, and instability. Recognizing this, curriculum planners for the middle school provide those experiences that are particularly helpful to boys and girls in solving problems of this age. Such educational experiences are quite different from those sophisticated and frequently stilted experiences that follow in the later secondary years. Building the curriculum of the middle school offers opportunities for experimentation with open classrooms, ungraded sequences, and a wide variety of individualized learning experiences.

An assessment of the mini course concept also might be interesting. Mini courses, as the name implies, are compacted experiences in shorter periods of time. Mini courses enable secondary schools to offer a wider variety of prime interest, short-term courses that may be either within or without the available curricular structure. The possibilities of such courses are limitless in offering alternatives for frustrated youth. Regular members of the teaching faculty, students themselves, or members of the community may have special competencies that can be incorporated into the teaching of mini courses. Segments of regular curriculum courses may be subdivided at any point. Periods of three, six, and nine weeks are popular time arrangements. Integration of subject matter from various fields offers intriguing possibilities. Mini courses fit well into programs that are flexibly scheduled. Such schedules usually offer blocks of unstructured time, and students welcome the possibility of encompassing this time with interesting and often exciting experiences.

RESEARCH

Research will be treated here as the accumulation of experimental results that affects curriculum planning. The research process will be evaluated as it affects educational objectives.[3] There are many problems concerning the availability and use of educational research. Those who stress the need for more research in educa-

---

[2] Theodore C. Moss, *Middle School* (New York: Houghton Mifflin Company, 1969), pp. 1–48.
[3] Bernard Spodek, "Research and Curriculum Development: Same Issues," *Educational Leadership* (February 1966), pp. 417–426.

tion contend it is paper-thin in many areas, especially in areas involving the non-learner and the socially underprivileged.

The paradox in the above situation is that the educational leader feels he lacks time to keep up with the voluminous amount of research being completed, and he is constantly being chided for his failure to benefit from available research. The curriculum worker feels a certain insecurity because he cannot prevent the widening gap between completed research and its application to curriculum problems.

The use of research poses several problems. It is necessary to select those areas where good research has already been validated and decide how to use it in solving practical curriculum problems. Research must be applied in practice, not merely in theory. It is of little value to have a sophisticated, comprehensive curriculum plan in theory and continue to tolerate obsolete practices in the classroom. Another problem is the apparent lack of communication between the researcher and the curriculum worker. The last decade has brought a wealth of new ideas through experimentation and research, but the period has not been marked by extensive innovations in learning procedures. Much of this research deals with the disadvantaged pupil. For example, the knowledgeable researcher has had evidence for some time that pupils disadvantaged by their environment can be taught by methods that minimize differences in learning and motivation between them and the more advantaged; yet curriculum planners have not been using those methods.

There is a certain amount of honest doubt about the value of educational research. Many scholars take a dim view of the untested evidence-gathering techniques used by educational researchers. They are critical of the use of questionnaires, self-inventories, and methodologies of statistics. They also raise serious questions about the normative and the historic method of much of educational research. They point to the lack of reliable information in such crucial areas as learning rates and attitudes, motivations, quality of instruction, and evaluation of teacher competency. Criticism is further leveled at the efforts of educational researchers to apply scientific measuring techniques to human beings engaged in value-directed activities. This pinpoints the most baffling problem of educational research: how to get valid results despite the multiplicity of interdependent factors affecting human behavior.

The inability to control variables places limitations on educational research. It means the use of single factors, single instruments, and single dimensions. It makes necessary the labeling of certain variables as independent of other variables. It causes the researcher to find justification in the rules of theoretical systems.

Failure to control variables means that each system is governed by inherent laws and the assumptions that explain these laws. The concepts postulated and defined by the theory are the variables contained in the system. These variables behave according to the rules or laws of the system or according to the hypothesis proposed. Laws and hypotheses provide for conjecture about the regularities of the interrelationship of the variables. Thus, it may be deduced that if the concepts employed in a research design are part of the same theoretical system, they can be fruitfully manipulated in varying relationships to each other, and the conclusions or results will be generalizable to other situations in which the same or analogous systems of concepts or variables are to be found.

Despite the criticism leveled at educational research, there is ample proof of its value and justification for its use. It must be assumed that education has the properties of a rational enterprise that is anchored to a clearly comprehensive and objectively derived framework. The properties of good research are present if the research is based on the three accepted stages that characterize inquiry in any field. First, the problem is analyzed to discern basic elements. Second, a survey embracing observation, description, and classification is made. Third, a theory is deductively formulated. In the theory process, inferences are added to facts in order to obtain concepts and testable hypotheses. Research technology within the field of education is not yet comparable to the level of technology in the physical realm, but constant refinement has brought it much closer to that level. Using mathematical thinking, borrowing analytical techniques from the field of agriculture, and developing realistic applications, educational research is growing toward maturity.

It is true that education is a victim of unsubstantiated and conflicting theories as well as a host of unwarranted generalizations, but even the physical sciences are not entirely free from this egocentric tendency of mankind. It is not necessary for every educator to become a research worker; neither is it necessary for the research worker to oversimplify his results to make them palatable to the educator; but it is unfortunate if research methods and results are so esoteric they cannot be comprehended by professional people. Educational progress is dependent on the finding of intelligent and valid answers. It is the task of all concerned to harmonize their efforts to that end.

The concept of "research and development" may make experimentation more acceptable. The aim is to seek better ways of teaching and learning. If experimentation is carefully conceived and the results properly analyzed, curriculum development will improve.

RESPONSIBILITY FOR
CURRICULUM EXPERIMENTATION

The responsibility for directing curriculum experimentation will vary according to local conditions. The complexity of the task calls for well-trained people, and their availability will affect the amount of reputable experimenting that takes place. In the large school systems, curriculum directors are trained researchers. Where the curriculum director has adequate assistance, the sponsoring of experimentation will be one of his basic assignments. In smaller schools, where trained curriculum workers are not available, the responsibility will likely fall on the principals and teachers.

The principal of a school is the direct representative of the superintendent and the school board. He coordinates pupil-personnel services, student activities, and building maintenance, and is also responsible for requisitioning books and supplies, controlling facilities, providing transportation, budgeting funds allocated to his building, and fostering a high morale within his teaching corps and staff. In brief, he carries the direct responsibility for providing a good environment for learning. This includes, of course, the direct responsibility for curriculum improvement within his jurisdiction. If he cannot delegate the responsibility for experimentation, he must have time to handle it himself. There are inherent advantages in having the principal participate directly in curriculum processes: it keeps him close to his faculty and pupils and involves him in the things that are most important to them. That he be a good instructional leader is a basic characteristic of a good principal.

The classroom teacher is a pivotal person in educational experimentation. The teacher furnishes a practical approach to shaping of the research project and is frequently involved in the laboratory aspects of the situation. Care must be exercised in the involvement of classroom teachers. They tend to be conservative and frequently make decisions based on what has been successful for them rather than implementing the objectives of the experiment. Participation should never be forced. Some teachers are willing and capable but others have neither the desire nor the ability to participate.

Classroom teachers participating in experimentation must be given released time from classroom duties or extra compensation for hours beyond their regular assignment.[4] An overworked,

[4] Jack R. Frymier and Horace C. Hawn, *Curriculum Improvement for Better Schools* (Worthington, Ohio: Charles A. Jones Publishing Co., 1970), pp. 191–234.

tired teacher cannot maintain the fervent, optimistic attitude necessary for good experimentation. A project of any magnitude will require extensive in-service training of teachers involved.

The best type of curriculum experimentation germinates within the school curriculum process. Involvement may go beyond the school to include lay citizens, college personnel, and certain types of specialists, but the basic responsibility for inauguration and direction of the experiment should rest with the local school administration. When faced with that obligation, school administrators sometimes take extreme positions which disrupt the promotion of good educational research. Some see in it the opportunity for professional aggrandizement and jump on the bandwagon of every opportunity to experiment or innovate. They rush in to accept and promote new ideas even before they are tested. When these hastily adopted curriculum schemes fail to work out, the would-be innovators are disillusioned or they rush off to embrace another equally ambiguous innovation. In contrast to the opportunist is the reluctant conservative who resists change of any kind.

RESEARCH THROUGH FOUNDATION
AND FEDERAL GRANTS

Many schools throughout the nation are participating in research projects sponsored either by foundation grants or grants from the several federal education acts. Unfortunately, too few of these projects originate within the local school systems. The format of the research project is devised by investigators of an outside agency who have a hypothesis to test. They focus attention on a rather narrow area of a problem of interest to themselves, using the schools as their field testing laboratory. Although local school authorities may be furnished with the tabulated results of the experiment, it frequently is of no relevant value. Local school leaders should become involved in research projects of their own and seek foundation support. Patterns of research demonstrated by outside project agents may be emulated by local research designers.

The entrance of the federal government into extensive support of education has brought abundant opportunities for curriculum study and development. Through several congressional acts, grants are available for the building and evaluation of educational programs—including programs that are experimental and innovative. Efficient utilization of such grants calls for educational statesmanship from local school administrators.

Probably the most significant of the federal education acts is the Elementary and Secondary Education Act of 1965. This act not only offers broad support for many facets of education, it also opens whole new vistas for educational experimentation and research. Each of the titles under the act includes research provisions. Titles III, IV and V, in particular, have important research and development components. Title III authorizes local communities to establish supplementary educational services and facilities where exemplary programs developed through research may be displayed. Title V provides for the strengthening of the research and curriculum development capabilities of state departments of education.

The real impact of the Act on educational research is in Title IV. It provides for the coordination of a wide variety of agencies in a vast training program for research workers. Nowhere is the need for more and better trained research personnel so critical as in education, and now it is possible to support both graduate and undergraduate programs to train research-oriented curriculum developers and administrators.

There are two other good features in Title IV. One is the specific "dissemination" section, authorizing the exploration of effective ways for getting research results into the hands of potential users. The other is the provision of funds for building and operating a network of national and regional laboratories that concentrate educational, scientific, and cultural resources for the development of programs of quality education. This project calls for the coordinated efforts of universities, state departments, local school personnel, and other appropriate educational and research organizations. Curriculum development is an integral part of the work of the laboratories, and research results are tested and retested in the local school systems. Experimentation results in the development of new materials and techniques. The broad base of activities in the regional laboratory can augment the limited curriculum research and experimental facilities of local school systems.

EXPERIMENTAL ATTITUDE

Experimentation is a healthy activity in any enterprise. It may be true that research is not the cure-all for every problem faced by the practical educator, but it will provide many of the answers. The educator must be willing to test the results of research and to put into practice the best of tested innovations. It is his task to view the school's program of learning as an ever evolving and surely improvable situation.

An intelligent attitude toward experimentation ought to be basic in educational planning and policy. This means securing capable research people, providing them with facilities, authorizing them to proceed, and then maintaining a close working relationship between them and all concerned with curriculum decision making. Educational research must be utilized. If experimentation is an acceptable procedure in a school system, then every effort should be made to use the results to effect curriculum improvement. Progress is not made by those who stand by unwilling to go through the painful procedures of change. Nor is it made by those who resist change because of predetermined decisions that new ideas will not work. Satisfying rewards can come to those who dare to innovate. Real curriculum improvement can come from intelligent use of research, plus careful program planning and skillful implementation of creative ideas.

TOPICS FOR STUDY AND DISCUSSION

1. Analyze the relationship between stability and stagnation in curriculum development.
2. Weigh the values in curriculum changes originating in current processes and those suggested by "experts."
3. What responsibility does the secondary school principal hold for planning curriculum research activities?
4. Evaluate the vulnerability of educational research in relation to decision making in curriculum planning.
5. Many private agencies are engaged in educational experimentation and research. Develop a monologue on the feasibility of school systems employing such agencies to do their research.
6. A school system in a large metropolitan center has a curriculum research team. A small midwestern school system makes its principal and teachers responsible for research. Compare and evaluate the two policies.
7. Educational grants are being awarded by the federal government to school systems that show extensive innovations in curriculum planning. Analyze the soundness of this procedure.
8. Prepare a research paper that will substantiate the hypothesis: the purposes now being advocated for the middle school are the same as those advocated for the first junior high schools.
9. Postulate: mini-courses—viable or faddish?

SELECTED REFERENCES

Cook, David R. *A Guide to Educational Research.* Boston: Allyn and Bacon, Inc., 1965.
    This book examines research studies to illustrate scientific

methods, hypothesis formulation, and theory as the basis for research. It furnishes help for those engaged in curriculum experimentation.

DRUMHELLER, SIDNEY J. *Handbook for Curriculum Design for Individualized Instruction.* Englewood Cliffs, N.J.: Educational Technology Publishers, 1971.

A system approach: how to develop curriculum materials from rigorously defined behavioral objectives. The book lists a wide variety of examples for individualized instruction curriculum procedures.

FRYMIER, JACK R., and HAWN, HORACE C. *Curriculum Improvement for Better Schools.* Worthington, Ohio: Charles A. Jones Publishing Co., 1970.

This volume stresses the responsibility for curriculum development by local school officials. It urges that teachers, supervisors, administrators, and curriculum workers unite in providing more effective learning in the schools. Part II describes a series of research and evaluation approaches.

GROBMAN, HULDA. *Developmental Curriculum Projects.* Itasca, Illinois: F. E. Peacock Publishers, 1970.

Analyzed here are the processes and decision points of a large number of curriculum development projects. Reasons are suggested for successes and failures in curriculum procedures. Suggestions are offered for the next steps in curriculum projecting in this country.

HILL, JOSEPH E., and KERBER, AUGUST. *Models, Methods and Analytical Procedures in Education Research.* Detroit: Wayne State University Press, 1967.

This is a good resource book for educational research conducted by personnel within a school system. It clarifies the role of logic and philosophy in the establishment of research techniques. It includes a good chapter on statistical formations and model building.

JONES, JAMES J., et al. *Secondary School Administration.* New York: McGraw-Hill Book Company, 1969.

Emphasized here is the importance of the principal in curricular processes. Chapters 3, 4, and 5 evaluate the demands made on the secondary schools for change. Chapters 11 and 12 deal with curriculum construction and evaluation procedures. Chapter 22 is devoted to educational research.

PETREQUIN, GAYNOR. *Individualizing Learning Through Modular-Flexible Programming.* New York: McGraw-Hill Book Company, 1968.

This book tells the story of a team effort at one high school to pioneer a system of educational reform. Computerization, modular-flexible scheduling, team teaching, independent study, and all other phases of innovation are described and evaluated. This is a good reference for a principal and his staff.

TRUMP, J. LLOYD. "Experiments We Need." *North Central Association Quarterly* (Fall 1964), pp. 207–209.

This article points to the need for innovations and experimentation in all aspects of school organization. It identifies eight of the most important needs.

WOODRING, PAUL. *Investment in Innovation.* Boston: Little, Brown and Company, 1970.

The author presents a historical appraisal of the Fund for the Advancement of Education. He takes a look at new technologies, curricular updating and reform, and at the learning process itself. Educational assessment and other forms of accountability are discussed.

CHAPTER 30

Some First Steps in
Curriculum Improvement

Any person can do something to improve curriculum even though the final paragraphs of the preceding chapters emphasized the central role of the school principal in the process. Anyone—university student or professor, secondary school teacher, superintendent or central school office supervisor, state education agency staff member, architect, equipment manufacturer or salesman, PTA member or other lay person—may take positive action. This chapter describes how he can proceed in five areas: teaching methods, curriculum content, organizational matters, educational facilities, and local studies. The order in which he should consider each area is not fixed since any one may be the right starting point in improving a particular curriculum.

FOUR IMPERATIVES TO
IMPROVE TEACHING METHODS

Regardless of whether a given school is organized on the basis of one teacher per classroom with thirty students in it, more or less, or whether the school has already embarked on innovations such as team teaching, flexible scheduling, independent study, television instruction, or programed learning, the following four imperatives apply. Similarly, whether or not the school has revised its curriculum content recently, whether it has new mathematics or old mathematics, new science or old, vocational education, or special programs for the handicapped, the same four imperatives can improve teaching and learning in any school regardless of its location or the kind of pupils it serves.

A representative of a university or a state education agency can note the degree to which these four imperatives are being followed when he visits classrooms. A teacher can work in the direction of the suggested changes—starting immediately in any setting. A principal or other supervisor can use these four imperatives as guides on what to observe and the kinds of questions to ask teachers. Teaching teams or individual teachers can use these four areas for immediate self-appraisal.

The first imperative: to change the nature of teacher presentations

We refer here to what teachers do when they talk to groups of students. As indicated earlier in this book, the studies show that teachers spend almost one-half the time classes are in session talking to students. They talk personally or they talk via a film, recording, or television program. We remind you that there are only three reasons why teachers should talk to groups.

The first reason is to motivate. Motivation requires that the teacher talk with such commitment and in such an intriguing manner that the students will want to learn. The second reason is to present information that is not readily available elsewhere. A never-ending teaching task is to decide what information to talk about and what to leave for the students to find out for themselves. The third reason is to give an assignment. Elsewhere in this volume we have emphasized the necessity of telling students, orally and in writing, exactly what they are expected to know and how to go about learning it.

The talking done by teachers should occupy no more than 40 percent or two-fifths of the time that students devote to the subject. Actually, we would recommend reducing the amount to about 10 percent—or about one twenty-five-minute session a week. This figure is true whether teaching is done in conventional classes with thirty students or in large-group instruction.

The second imperative: to change the nature of independent study

The facilities for independent study in any classroom can be improved almost immediately by asking students to bring printed materials from home. The quality and quantity of the magazines, newspapers, mail order catalogues, etc., may vary, but there is something in every home that can be brought to school to help develop a reading resource area in every subject field. Professional and trade magazines are useful to suggest careers. Incidentally, that procedure is an important step in removing the gap between the *real* world outside the school and the *artificial* world which the school tends to create inside it. Breaking down that wall, figuratively speaking, is especially important for the so-called disadvantaged youth but it is also significant for everyone. Teachers and other persons may also donate items to the resource area, and the school may purchase a variety of paperbacks and other materials. The resource area should include study material related to all the interests and abilities represented in the student body. In addition to printed materials, classrooms need a variety of other items, such as slides, records, and programed materials, for students to view, to listen to, and to work with.

Whether the school uses a corner of each classroom for the materials or has elaborate resource centers and other independent study facilities (see Chapter 18), the students should be able to engage in independent study for at least 40 percent of the time they are scheduled in their classes. We would recommend increasing the proportion of time to 60 to 80 percent a week, with much more time spent in interaction among pupils and with the teacher, helping each other, and in self-evaluation.

The third imperative: to provide
for small-group discussion

If the class is a conventional one with thirty students or so, the teacher needs to divide the class into three subgroups for small-group discussion. The techniques for these discussions are described in Chapter 20. Even though the teacher cannot be with each group full time, he can go from one group to the other to observe how the discussion is progressing and to make suggestions for improving it. Moreover, he can train student assistants to perform the evaluations of small-group discussion described in Chapter 26. A teacher in a conventional class can regroup the students on the basis of evaluative records of discussion. He can also use sociometric techniques to guide them in improving interpersonal relations.

The important considerations are (1) that the teachers train the students for small-group discussion, give them the opportunity to engage in it, and make proper evaluation and (2) that students have 10 to 12 percent of class time per week for this activity. Pupils in every school subject should have time to react to teacher presentations, discuss the implications of their studies in that field —and to learn how to talk and to listen.

The fourth imperative: to change the methods of evaluation

A teacher in any classroom can stop almost immediately the three practices warned against in Chapter 26: oral quizzes, oversimplified reports with multipurpose grades, and constant comparisons between the individual and the group he is in at the moment. He can stop conducting oral quizzes (called classroom recitation). He can break down his reports to pupils and parents into what students actually know and can do, the quality of their independent study, and changes in what they do. He can divide the multipurpose grade into its component parts so that everyone may understand better what progress pupils are making. He can start an evaluation scheme that emphasizes changes for each pupil in relation to his own previous accomplishments, and he can define the purposes of the subjects he teaches in terms that he can quantify, measure, and report.

To make these changes, the teachers at each grade or department level should meet to discuss and agree on procedures that all will follow. Principals and other supervisors can help by joining these discussions and by making the necessary administrative changes. University students can observe the changes being made; their professors can work with schools to implement the changes; and representatives of city and state education departments can help to develop the public's understanding of the changes.

The foregoing four changes that we regard as imperatives may be made in any classroom. They are also required in connection with educational innovations as described in Part IV of this book. Thus teachers and principals may prepare for team teaching, educational television, independent study, and other innovations currently popular by immediately starting with the four imperatives in their present situations.

ANALYSIS OF CURRICULUM CONTENT

Here are some first steps that a staff may take in any school to improve curriculum content. After each teacher has read about the issues and developments in the particular subject area that concerns him (see parts II and III), he can decide which development he should consider first to improve his course. Or he can decide how to resolve for the time being the issues that are presented. Each teacher can do this work for his own teaching, or a group of teachers in a school or in a school system can do it for all subjects. The goal is to describe the purposes of the teaching and then to compare the present situation with what it should be.

A second analysis that can be done immediately in any school is to decide what content is *essential,* what is *desirable,* and what is *enriching,* for students in that particular school community. It is true that in the final analysis such decisions need to be made through careful study by curriculum experts in the various subject fields, but preliminary efforts may be made by any teacher or group of teachers in any school. The goal is to eliminate unnecessary curriculum content that takes so much time for pupils to learn that the pupils lack both time and energy to engage in what we have termed "depth education." For example, we believe that a careful answer to the question, What facts in United States history are essential for loyalty and good citizenship? might produce a reduction of one-third to one-half in required content. Not all pupils need to become professional historians. An analogous situation exists in all subject fields. With the time and effort saved, pupils would be able to follow their special interests and talents. Teachers would help by listing the required content and by suggesting topics for special projects by interested pupils.

A third kind of curriculum analysis that any school may begin with involves relating content to the activities of students and teachers. Three basic questions need to be answered: (1) what instructional content and purposes may pupils of different interests and talents learn and accomplish largely by themselves— if they have the time, the space, the desire, and special assistants and devices to help them? (2) What content and purposes require motivation, explanation, demonstration, or other types of presentations by a competent teacher who is physically present or by television, films, recordings, or programed instruction devices? (3) What content and purposes require personal interaction among pupils and between pupils and a teacher? Such an analysis of any unit or division of a course, as well as the total course, can lead to better understanding by teachers and others of the need for independent study arrangements, large-group instruction, and small-group discussion. The analysis will help improve curriculum in any class regardless of its organization.

Failure to conduct these analyses inevitably leads to disappointment in curriculum improvement. Human and financial resources largely are wasted when content is merely reshuffled or enlarged without questioning about necessity, relevancy, and methodology.

THE QUANTITY APPROACH—
SHIFTING PEOPLE AND THINGS

Not long ago a principal reported the following example of an immediate change that occurred in the school which he served. On the opening day of school, in spite of some earlier checks, the bell system was out of order. The principal announced that since teachers and students knew the time schedule of the school, they could simply watch the clocks and their personal watches. The situation was so relaxed in comparison with earlier days when the bells guided everyone, both teachers and students came to the office suggesting that the bells be turned off even after the repairs were made. A vote by the students and faculty confirmed that the overwhelming majority wished to eliminate the bell system. After several months, further evaluation revealed no desire to resume the bells. There was much less tardiness, and a more relaxed atmosphere existed. Whether comparable results would happen in other schools may only be determined through experimentation. The point is that any school, at any time, regardless of whether or not it has a flexible schedule, can experiment with turning off the bells.

The chapter on flexible scheduling described some other procedures that any school may undertake without extended preparation. A group of any number of teachers, a group of thirty or more students, and a quantity of time greater than forty minutes may be combined in new relationships. This arrangement is sometimes called, "block of time." Such a change permits a variety of innovations that may affect only a small proportion of the total faculty and students while the remaining part of the school is relatively undisturbed. As pointed out in Chapter 23, the greater the number of teachers, students, and minutes assembled in the new arrangements, the more flexible teachers and pupils may become in what they do. The point is that this change can be made almost immediately in almost any school without upsetting the rest of the school.

CHANGING HALLS AND WALLS

Lobby and corridor space is largely unused in most schools except for a few minutes at the beginning of each school day, during the intermissions between classes, and at the close of each day. It is economically wasteful to leave this space unused for so much of the time. After all, it costs as much to heat and clean this space as it does to maintain the classroom space that is being used all day long. The challenge is to find some use for it.

In some schools, large lobbies have been converted into areas for large-group instruction. The first group that uses the space in the morning arranges the portable chairs and lap boards in the appropriate locations. The last group in the afternoon moves the chairs back against the walls. A permanent screen has been installed for use with various types of projectors and the necessary sound equipment has been provided.

Corridors may be used for independent study by building carrels along the walls. If the corridors are particularly narrow, the carrel walls may be placed on hinges so that they can be folded back at the end of the period to facilitate pupil movement. However, most corridors in most schools are larger than they need to be. A study of pupil traffic may reveal corridor space that can be made into independent study areas without damaging pupil movement. More permanent wiring can then be installed to facilitate the use of listening and viewing devices as well as reading materials.

Cafeterias are often unused during much of the school day. A little remodeling can convert a cafeteria into a large-group instruction area, into places for small-group discussion, or into areas for independent study. Similarly, schools have remodeled spaces formerly used as study halls into areas for large-group instruction or independent study.

Many schools these days require additions because of increasing enrollments. Some schools build new additions just like the old buildings. More imaginative schools decide to make the new addition into resource centers for independent study. The major consideration is whether the remodeling or the new addition is to be "more of the same," or whether the alteration will facilitate curriculum improvement.

ARE YOU ASKING THE RIGHT QUESTIONS?

Critics of curriculum content, methods, and organization are found among all kinds of persons. There are those who would *add* to the curriculum. They ask, for example, why the school does not teach more American history, or place more emphasis on what they call the fundamentals of written expression, or give special emphasis to other matters that interest them or their particular group. Others would *subtract* from the curriculum. They urge the school to discontinue driver education, home economics, problems of democracy, or some other content they do not like. Other critics would make only *moderate alterations.* They propose a reduction of class size in all subjects, or a rearrangement of the topics in the world history course, or seven periods in the school day instead of six. The trouble with all three types of critics is that they are not asking the right questions. They need to consider more fundamental matters that get in the way of curriculum improvement as presented in Chapter 17.

What are the right questions? Since asking the right questions is an essential prelude to effective discussions and research studies, here are seventeen questions that should be raised:

1. *Does the school measure educational output (pupil gains) in relation to financial input (school expenditures)?* When teachers, administrators, or persons in state or federal agencies request extra funds, they should justify these funds by listing the anticipated improvement in learning outcomes for pupils. What pupil gains are expected to result from the expenditures and *specifically* how will these gains be measured? Remember, any educational goal can be quantified.

2. *What are the school's present financial situations; the levels of staff morale; the status of pupil achievements, abilities, and interests; and the records of school leavers (graduates and dropouts) at work and in further education?* Every school has an essential need for base line data for future comparisons with the effects of curriculum changes of one kind or another. Lacking those base line data, it is impossible to know precisely what effects the changes have produced.

3. *What portion of the local school budget is spent on research and development of new curriculum content, new teaching methods, changed organizations of instruction, and different evaluation techniques?* What should the proportion be? Commercial enterprises recognize that bankruptcy is avoided only by spending substantial amounts of money on research and development. Study the financial reports of outstandingly successful corporations and compare what they spend for research and development with what schools in the local community are spending in proportion to the total budgets. Should your school continue to be less concerned about research and development than successful industries?

4. *What portion of the local school budget is spent on new instruction materials—in comparison to allocations for higher salaries, improvements in the building, and other matters not immediately related to improved pupil learning?* This question does not imply that teachers should not be paid high enough salaries to permit them to live as well as professional workers in other fields. Nor does it imply that school buildings should not be attractive places in which teachers and pupils can work. The fact remains,

however, that many items in school budgets do not directly affect pupil learning. What priorities are needed for future expenditures in your community?

5. *How much money does the school spend on further education of the staff to use new curriculum methods? How much does it spend on supervision? and what techniques to improve teaching do school officials use?* Here again, comparisons with industrial procedures are relevant. Whenever an industry devises a new product or new procedures, pilot operations are established and workers are trained to operate effectively in the pilot situation. If the pilot operation succeeds, then the industry prepares all workers involved in the new process or product, using the best techniques known to industrial management. Unfortunately, in many instances, teachers are expected to learn new techniques on their own time, at the end of a long day or during holidays—often without the benefit of a pilot project.

6. *How does the school recognize individual differences in talents and interests among teachers in making assignments of what teachers are expected to do?* The special competencies of individual teachers should be utilized effectively. Schools that assign uniform workloads and salary schedules, that utilize standard certification requirements, that expect all teachers to supervise extraclass assignments, and the like, violate this principle.

7. *What steps are taken to provide teachers with more time during the school day to prepare better, to keep up-to-date, to confer with professional colleagues, to improve pupil evaluation techniques and reporting, and to work as needed with individual students?* Successful medical practitioners set aside time for these activities. So do practitioners in other professions. One way schools can give teachers more time for such tasks is to assign them fewer classes per day rather than fewer students per class. What is your local situation in this regard?

8. *Has the school applied the techniques of job analysis to the teaching staff in order to discover what teachers must do themselves and what may be done more economically and efficiently by machines?* In an age of technology, teachers still do most things by hand. Industries that do not keep up with the times go bankrupt. There is no question of replacing teachers, but rather of replacing some things that teachers now do that are unproductive and waste their time and energy.

9. *How much work are teachers doing now that could be done well by less costly clerks?* Clerks are trained to type, to duplicate materials, to file, to keep records, to prepare reports, and the like; most teachers are not prepared for these activities.

10. *How much work are teachers doing now that could be done by part-time instruction assistants; that is, persons with*

some preparation in the subject field or grade level of the teacher, but not as much as is required for certification as a teacher? As indicated in Chapter 24, instruction assistants are often housewives, advanced college students, or retired teachers. They may help teachers to prepare materials, to supervise independent study, and to evaluate some aspects of pupil progress.

11. *What are teachers doing now for pupils that pupils could do for themselves—if the pupils had the time, the places, and the materials they need for independent study?* As indicated elsewhere in this volume, independent study arrangements can save teacher time and energy for more essential tasks while giving students more experience in "learning by doing" and "responsibility for their own learning"—both desirable educational goals.

12. *How does the school principal spend his time?* What are his highest priorities? What should they be? What help does he need? School principals spend much time and energy on the schedule, the cafeteria, school bus routes, custodial chores, disciplinary actions, perfunctory telephone calls and visits, talks with salesmen, community activities, service clubs, and the like. All of these tasks have to be done, but do they have to be done by the principal, who in the final analysis is most responsible for curriculum improvement in the school?

13. *What other services does the school provide to help to improve, to support, and to administer local educational programs?* For example, what use does the school make of university consultants, specialists in the school system's central office, community experts, state department personnel, and other persons who could help? What special financial grants has the school applied for and received from foundations, state education agencies, industrial concerns, or the federal government?

14. *Have steps been taken in all subject fields to plan essential curriculum content and to arrange the content logically and sequentially from the kindergarten through the twelfth grade or through completion of general education?* There may be unnecessary or unplanned repetitiveness in curriculum content; for example, offering United States history several times during the thirteen years without changing the approaches or sequence of content.

15. *How do plans for new buildings or the remodeling of older buildings reflect current educational methods and proposed innovations?* Chapter 25 had much to say about new developments in existing educational facilities and how to plan for an uncertain future.

16. *Does the school have one-, two-, or five-year plans for the improvement of curriculum content, teaching, and learning?* Not everything can be accomplished at once, but a start is essen-

tial. Moreover, the school needs to think through some reasonable goals for future outcomes. A set of priorities is essential for planning.

17. *How effectively do the school personnel present their present program and their future needs to external decision-making bodies?* Schools may have to depend legally on other agencies for financial support. The board of education theoretically and practically represents current citizen thinking about education. State education agencies, regional accrediting bodies, federal education agencies, and university admissions officers present standards which must be adhered to by the school or else the school must make appeals for relaxation of those standards. Does the school plan its proposals well, explaining the need for the changes and describing how they will be effected and how they will be evaluated? Does the school utilize a variety of mass media in telling its story? Are the students and faculty sufficiently informed so that they can answer questions about curriculum improvements?

The fact that some schools are more innovative than others is no accident. Those schools always have dynamic leadership by a succession of able principals who work effectively with their staffs and the community. They analyze the barriers to curriculum improvement and find ways to overcome or move around the difficulties. Whatever the situation, some improvements can be made.

RELATING CURRICULUM IMPROVEMENT
TO OTHER CHANGES IN SCHOOLS

Deliberately we define curriculum broadly to include more than content. Also involved are the methods of learning and teaching, where they occur, how to evaluate pupil progress and the total program, changes in the personnel for instruction, guidance and supervision-administration, and such structural matters as time, numbers, spaces, money, and the provision of options or alternatives. The three major curricular aspects—program, people and structure—are so interrelated that none may be improved without affecting the others. Failure to recognize that basic fact has caused many potential improvements to fail or else be less effective than the proponents had hoped they would be.

Foundations and governments have expended large amounts of money to stimulate educational changes with frustrating results. Personnel likewise have expended time and energy with few more outcomes than the exhilaration that innovations produce. The remedy is three concepts of change: (1) recognition of interrelatedness, (2) application of consistent principles of teaching and learning to the change process, and (3) patience.

Interrelatedness

After the members of the staff decide to make a certain curriculum change, they need to analyze all the related alterations and then decide what portions of the student body and the staff are to be included. One alternative would be to involve a group of pupils, a group of teachers with a differentiated staff, a block of time, several subjects, and a system of evaluation. The rest of the school would operate in a conventional manner. Another alternative could be to involve all the pupils and all the teachers with a partially differentiated staff, operate with some simple form of flexible scheduling—e.g., twenty-five-minute periods instead of fifty—divide a semester into two nine-week terms with mini courses that would be completed in one-half a semester. Also by reducing the time spent and changing the methods in conventional classes, e.g., meeting two or three days a week instead of five, the program could provide pupils with more time for independent study. Conventional report cards could be augmented with some descriptions of pupil progress in behavioral and performance terms. Later and gradually, these changes would be expanded to produce the more comprehensive changes described in this book.

Change process

Application of sound principles of teaching and learning to the change process requires first the development of motivation. Presentations and reaction discussions that develop reasons for change may encourage the staff to study the possibilities of change. Interested persons then can use faculty resource centers to read, write, listen, and view in order to understand the concepts and procedures. The school and community become learning laboratories where teachers and pupils experience change through learning-by-doing.

The process includes diagnosing the needs for change, developing prescriptions, trying alternatives, and evaluating results to provide feedback for planning further improvements. Teachers and pupils then observe how the changes affect the conditions for teaching and learning and analyze the results. Consultants may help but the basic responsibilities are with the teachers and pupils as they learn the new techniques. The principal and support staffs help to organize, supervise and evaluate the whole process. A variety of meetings, discussions, and publications keep the public informed and solicit their active participation.

Patience

No knowledgeable person ever has said that it is easy to improve the curriculum in this broad context. The process is long and involved. Gains are measured yearly but significant productivity may require five or more years. In the meantime, during the period when significant differences may be difficult to achieve, patience is a virtue. At the same time, a reasonable amount of impatience helps to stimulate everyone to work at the tasks. Secondary school curriculum improvement is needed. Many schools have experienced the proposals and procedures described in this book.

TOPICS FOR STUDY AND DISCUSSION

1. This chapter presents many "first steps" towards curriculum improvement. Based on experiences in your present school—or one you know—select one or two of these steps that seem most realistic to you in that setting. Based on your study of this book and additional reading, propose a plan of action.
2. Take an approach similar to that described in Topic no. 1 and engage in some long-range planning. What steps seem appropriate for each of the next five years? List the steps and prepare a brief statement defending your selection.
3. Which steps in this chapter seem to you to be entirely inappropriate and why?

SELECTED REFERENCES

CAY, DONALD F. *Curriculum: Design for Learning.* Indianapolis: The Bobbs-Merrill Co., Inc., 1966, pp. 167–176.
The pages cited propose some immediate tasks for better curriculums.
CLARK, LEONARD H., et al. "New Developments." In *The American Secondary School Curriculum.* New York: The Macmillan Company, 1965, pp. 394–420.
Chapter 18 provides a brief, clear summary of current educational changes. The survey could help workers in a local school or community consider which changes deserve highest priority in their situation.

FALLON, BERLIE J., comp. and ed. *Fifty States Innovate to Improve Their Schools.* Bloomington, Indiana: Phi Delta Kappa, 1967.

The author catalogues and annotates 1,001 "innovations" in all fifty states. The index identifies schools, states, types of innovations, and bases of support. Although significant innovations and notable schools are omitted because of inadequate local and state reporting, what is given may broaden the perspectives of readers.

GORDON, EDMUND W., and WILKERSON, DOXEY A. *Compensatory Education for the Disadvantaged, Programs and Practices: Preschool through College.* New York: College Entrance Examination Board, 1966.

Chapters 1, 4, and 5 deal more especially with curriculum and secondary-age youth. Pages 198–299 include a directory of "Compensatory Practices" listed by states and grade level.

MILES, MATTHEW B., and SCHMUCK, RICHARD A. "Improving Schools Through Organization Development: An Overview." In *Organization Development in Schools.* Palo Alto, Calif.: National Press Books, 1971.

This chapter places emphasis on management, consultation, data collection, diagnosis, intervention, and related steps that are essential in changing schools.

TRUMP, J. LLOYD, and GEORGIADES, WILLIAM. "Doing Better with What You Have: NASSP Model Schools Project." *The Bulletin of the National Association of Secondary School Principals* vol. 54, no. 346 (May 1970), pp. 106–133.

The article outlines the Model which a group of schools are working towards in a five-year effort to individualize learning and professionalize teaching with increased accountability. Also included are a variety of transitional steps that any school might use in progressing towards the Model with a suggested bibliography of additional readings.

VERDUIN, JOHN R., JR. *Cooperative Curriculum Improvement.* Englewood Cliffs, N.J.: Prentice-Hall, Inc., 1967, pp. 72–137.

This section proposes methods and techniques for a cooperative approach to curriculum improvement and uses Cassopolis, Michigan, as a case study. Note the "Self-Evaluation Form for Public School Curriculum" in the *Appendix.*

WATSON, GOODWIN, ed. *Change in School Systems.* Washington, D.C.: National Education Association, National Training Laboratories, 1967.

The editor and six other authors present strategies for changing schools. The discussion on "change-agents" and "self-renewing schools" are especially important in relation to curriculum improvement.

CHAPTER 31

Acknowledging and Coping
with Some Obstacles

The status quo is the antithesis of change. While one may challenge the status quo, the burden of proof always rests more heavily on those persons who seek improvement. The final chapter of this book, *Secondary School Curriculum Improvement,* therefore, must deal with the forces that resist change and suggest some constructive alternatives.

FORCES, BELIEFS, AND PERSONS THAT
TEND TO OPPOSE CHANGE IN CURRICULUM

The list presented here certainly is not all-inclusive. Nor do we claim that all persons referred to oppose change or that all the forces and beliefs are universal. What we do believe is that every point is significant and those persons who would improve the curriculum must understand the potential in each item. Later in the chapter we present some suggestions for coping with the potential opposition. Obviously, each of the following items merits more explanation and discussion than our present space permits. We hope the following listing is adequate for creating the reader's awareness:

    1. Many university professors look upon all secondary school pupils as potential students in their classes, and even as

potential professional writers, speakers, historians, lovers of Elizabethan literature, scientists, engineers, musicians, athletes, and the like. Some of these professors write the textbooks that secondary school pupils are required to study so they have a personal financial interest. They oppose limiting the content, concepts, and skills to the relatively small minimum that is *essential* for all pupils to know in the subject as separate from the levels of hobbies and careers as described in chapters 2, 22, and elsewhere in this book.

2. Some high school teachers have the same kinds of beliefs and special interests as the subject-specialists and writers in the universities and, therefore, oppose curriculum changes.

3. Some secondary school principals and their assistants, as well as some subject supervisors in central offices of school systems, have developed a sense of security in present practices and/or enjoy the prestige in their present positions, the community limelight, the extracurricular activities, and other side-benefits of their present comfortable positions. At the same time, they feel insecure in attempting to work with teachers and the community in the areas of basic methods of teaching and learning, updating and refining curriculum content, individualizing evaluation with more emphasis on the affective domain, and other aspects of curriculum improvement.

4. The extreme "rightists" and other neo-believers of the same type regard change as Marxist or Communist inspired, using continuously, often out of context, such terms as *child centered, progressive education, permissive, undisciplined, free, watered down, ultra liberal,* and so on, without bothering to read, listen, or get the facts.

5. The extreme "leftists" and other disillusioned skeptics see no good in any proposal that they have not originated or that can be incorporated into an existing institution. They want to throw everything away as they oppose small or evolutionary changes. They are quite intolerant as they ridicule efforts to alter the system.

6. The smiling, agreeable "do gooders" who agree that most proposals to improve curriculum are appropriate—but not *now.* They present many reasons: the time is not quite ripe, there needs to be some more research done by others, there is currently a shortage of money (or something else), we need a foundation or government grant, we need a new school building, etc.

7. Teacher organizations, at least some of the leaders and/or influential persons in them, see the proposed curriculum changes as threats to the numbers of teachers required, the necessity of spending more time in training or continued education, a conflict between "men and machines," opposition to differentiated staffing which could change the role of the teacher, the question-

ing of longtime slogans that have held a positive relationship between quality of learning and higher salaries and smaller classes.

8.   Conformist-type students who have succeeded reasonably well in conventional schools that rewarded memorization, good attendance, and approved behavior but who are afraid of decision making, creativity, increased personal responsibility, application of what has been learned in new situations, and other additional outcomes that the improved curriculum requires.

9.   Closely related to the two preceding points are a number of conventional beliefs and practices in schools that constitute false pedagogy.   Years ago, research indicated that brief periods of rest among the times spent in learning skills and memorization were desirable; however, conventional schools schedule fifty-minute periods, five-minute intermissions, and rest only at noon and the end of the day.   Stimulus-response and memorization are low in the hierarchy of mental processes; yet those activities mainly make up the school's program and the highest part of the reward system for pupils.   The recitation methods commonly used by teachers result often in pupils' hearing *wrong* answers as well as right ones; some remember the wrong they hear, failing to distinguish between the two.   The foregoing malpractices illustrate only a few that might be cited.

10.   Teachers are reluctant to include current materials in the curriculum.   The daily newspapers, current magazines, and radio and TV programs deal with issues and materials that are relevant and important to many students not only for motivational purposes but to update science, statistics, music, writing, history, and so on.

11.   Persons inside the school and outside whose learning philosophy emphasizes memorization and conformity as opposed to the cultivation of the higher mental processes, creativity, and the like fail to recognize the importance of broad educational objectives in the cognitive, skill, and affective domains.

12.   Some adults in the community oppose all programs that they consider needlessly expensive and not universally necessary.   Illustrations of the latter include: high school; content beyond basic English, arithmetic, U.S. history (not social studies), and a little science—approving the 3 R's or basic education; fancy buildings; high salaries for professionally trained teachers and administrators; guidance counselors; and other developments that they consider frills.

13.   Certain persons are frustrated and mad at something in society and take out their feelings on the school programs.   Their aggressions involve such matters as school consolidation; high taxes (federal as well as local); rebellious youth; drugs; liberal politicians; dislike of some teacher, administrator, or board

member, someone who runs the PTA, or someone else in the local or national scene. Sometimes parents fight each other through their child or the school program. There are frustrated, paranoid, ambitious, lonely, rejected people who need a "cause" and find satisfaction in the company of others who attack curriculum improvement.

14. Some persons, inside the school and outside, vocally support curriculum improvement but fail to join the effort because they are sure the "state" will not permit the changes that are needed, neither will university requirements, regional accrediting associations, the superintendent and/or board of education, the taxpayers, nor a host of other "straw men" that they conjure up to help them rationalize their lack of aggressive participation.

15. Education as a profession is highly institutionalized. A prime purpose of institutions is to maintain the status quo, to prevent significant change, or at least to consider change as a threat. Learning, on the other hand, can never be institutionalized. Thus a major obstacle to the improvement of learning is the institution itself, the school.[1]

16. Most teachers tend to teach as they were taught. This trait of emulating behavior places a straitjacket on the learner whose excellence is judged on his ability to memorize, repeat, and replicate the behavior of the teacher. The whole institutionalized procedure becomes a closed circle.

17. Most evaluations of pupil progress and institutional excellence hold that content and methodology are constants, thus negating efforts to promote change. The paradox is that institutionalized education that professes an aim to change people itself is unwilling to change. Evaluations thus do little more than evaluate the instruments of measure and not the alleged purposes of the evaluation.

18. Teachers for the most part deal with minds, personalities and aspirations which in point of time are much younger than their own. Our culture, and most others, possibly all, place parents, priests, and teachers on pedestals and both expect and require the young to respect, obey, and believe this trilogy. Teachers come to accept this respect and obedience as a fair and accurate appraisal of their competence. The cult of infallibility mitigates against change.

We said earlier that the list of persons and forces that op-

---

[1] Lester W. Nelson contributed items 15 to 18 to this list. Dr. Nelson was for more than two decades principal of the Scarsdale, New York, High School and then prior to his retirement was associated with the Fund for the Advancement of Education and the Ford Foundation. He made these points in a recent discussion with one of the authors.

pose or inhibit curriculum improvement was large. Certainly this presentation does not encompass all the factors. It is nevertheless illustrative and imposing. The question is, What can be done?

CONSTRUCTIVE STEPS TO COPE WITH OBSTACLES

Here again, we must emphasize that the suggestions that follow are not the only possible ones that may serve to help a committed staff cope with the foregoing forces. Each group needs to analyze the obstacles in a given situation, make plans and decisions, take actions, evaluate the consequences, select alternatives, continue the evaluations, and work constructively along these lines in continuing efforts lasting over a number of years. Patience alone does not improve the curriculum, but it is a necessary part of the process. We enumerate a number of suggestions for your consideration and guidance.

1. Recognize that the presence of obstacles constitutes the basis of proposing improvements; we are happy because they exist. There will be neither change nor new ideas without the challenges of unhappy, discontented, frustrated, antagonistic people. The first step, therefore, is to understand the motives of the various individuals and groups. Thus in every school community, the staff who wish to promote changes need to analyze carefully the forces that operate, using the eighteen possibilities listed earlier in the chapter as a starting point.

2. The second step derives from what Kurt Lewin and others in the area of change analysis have referred to as neutralizing the forces that cause individuals or groups to take specified positions. So, we need to understand *why* people take certain positions. They will not move in the direction that we think is desirable unless what they regard as pressures are removed. Will people lose jobs, will the changes raise taxes, will youth protest more? If the answers are affirmative, what compensating factors can you devise that might offset these forces or others that propel people in one direction or another? The point is that until a state of instability is created in the proper direction, people will not move as you want them to do.

3. We emphasized in Chapter 26 the necessity of collecting more data and presenting more evaluative feedback to various individuals and groups in terms that they understand. In a sense, this requirement means that proponents of curriculum change must accept a responsibility that their opponents and skeptics often do not: to collect much more data and to express ideas more simply, directly, patiently, and honestly than usually is the case.

4. The foregoing techniques emphasize the need for accountability, a concept we have emphasized frequently in this volume, especially in chapters 23, 27, and 30. We need to show how we are spending funds more wisely, utilizing better the talents of teachers, providing better learning environments for students, developing a more relevant curriculum, and the like.

5. Take advantage of the current emphasis that politicians, educators, journalists, and other opinion-makers in our society are urging. At the time of this revision of our book, a current push is on "career education." There is nothing new in the concept of work experience, utilization of community resources, year-round schools, and so on. However, an alert person who wants to improve the curriculum can suggest how learning more English, mathematics, art, or anything else actually opens up more career opportunities. In the process, you can differentiate between *essential* content for everyday living, content for hobbies or special interest, and content for careers. What will be the emphases next year and the years after that? The alert curriculum worker accepts these slogans, old as they may be, and takes advantage of the situation. Thus he enlists the support of the opinion-makers in the interests of better curriculum.

6. Create options. When you want to change some program in a school, keep the old program as an available option for those students and their parents who oppose the change. There are different teaching and learning styles and also differences among students and teachers in the speed with which they adapt to changes. For example, when a school changes to a more comprehensive program for appraising and reporting pupil progress, as described in Chapter 27, we recommend keeping available the ABCDF system as an option for those students and parents who request that information. If the new system is better, the old will gradually disappear. Some students work better under close supervision while others work better in an open learning environment; the school should provide options as we recommended. The provision of options helps to facilitate the change process while reducing the effectiveness of the opposition to change.

7. Provide an environment where people can easily help each other. One example of how this goal may be achieved is when a school takes a classroom and makes it into an office space for teachers. Even though partitions may provide some privacy, the teachers talk together more and soon are working together to plan and evaluate programs. The principal who uses the faculty meeting as a forum for his lectures and announcements and seldom leaves his office to mingle and work with teachers violates this suggestion. As parents and other aides come to the school to

work with teachers and students, the school creates a better environment for creating community understanding than the typical PTA meeting develops. The foregoing few illustrations are a sample of the steps to create a more open environment that can lead to curriculum improvement.

LEST WE BE MISUNDERSTOOD

We would not imply that most, or even many, of the persons and situations listed in the first part of this chapter constitute the typical case. However, the ones that do are vocal, get into the mass media, write critical articles or are the subject of them, exert influence beyond their importance, and do, in fact, prevent the kinds of curriculum improvement that produce humane and accountable programs as described in this book. Those persons who would improve schools need to know about these forces, beliefs, and persons.

Also, we recognize that some readers will oppose the steps we suggest to cope with these obstacles. Some persons will view these proposals as opportunistic while others will object to the psychological methods of changing the opinions of people as we have described them. On the other hand, we reject with deep feelings the authoritarian methods that some persons use to maintain the status quo in curriculum. We reject also the tendency on the part of some persons to maintain the existing situation without adequate evidence to support that position.

Finally, we plead for the open mind, the scientific approach to curriculum improvement. That goal is what this book is all about. We ask you to join the search.

TOPICS FOR STUDY AND DISCUSSION

1. Select a topic that you would like to see emphasized more in curriculum improvement. Then write a paper or prepare a presentation to analyze the forces that would oppose the change.
2. Using a procedure similar to no. 1, make a presentation showing how you might neutralize the opposition and capitalize on positive, supportive forces.
3. Take any chapter in the book and devise a series of options or alternative practices that you might provide in a school during a period of curriculum improvement.

4. Indicate some illustrative evaluation techniques that could be used to measure the effectiveness of the optional programs described or developed under no. 3.
5. Read more widely in the literature on change either in the field of education or outside of it in order to suggest some techniques in addition to those listed in this chapter.

SELECTED REFERENCES

BENT, RUDYARD K., and UNRUH, ADOLPH. "Educational Values in a Changing World." In *Secondary School Curriculum.* Lexington, Mass.: D. C. Heath and Company, 1969, pp. 201–227.

Chapter 9 describes curriculum influences, needed changes, pressures and restrictions, and the influences of organizations, laws, textbooks, and foreign education. Traditional cultural values also are analyzed briefly.

CLARK, CHARLES H. *Brainstorming.* Garden City, N.Y.: Doubleday and Company, Inc., 1958.

This is a classic treatment, simply and practically written, on the techniques of stimulating creative discussion.

FOSTER, MARCUS A. *Making Schools Work.* Philadelphia: The Westminster Press, 1971.

This practical book, written in a popular style, is hard hitting on such topics as leadership style, what's happening, relevance, working with minorities, retooling, and the school as a social force.

ILLICH, IVAN. *Deschooling Society.* New York: Harper and Row, Publishers, 1971.

This controversial book may provide suggestions for coping with problems even though the author attacks vigorously the concept of organized schools as they exist and are controlled.

MARTIN, JOHN HENRY, and HARRISON, CHARLES H. *Free to Learn: Unlocking and Ungrading American Education.* Englewood Cliffs, N.J.: Prentice-Hall, Inc., 1972.

These authors present a Design for Community Education with a Family Health Center, a Community Arts Center, a Career Education Center, a Community Guidance and Education Center, and many other features, all developed and managed by an Education Assembly. These developments would get away from the school board, the graded school, and the other characteristics of present-day education that keep innovations from succeeding in both elementary and secondary schools.

MCCLURE, ROBERT M., ed. *The Curriculum: Retrospect and Prospect.* National Society for the Study of Education. Yearbook

LXX, Part 1, pp. 219–259. Chicago: University of Chicago Press, 1971.

Ole Sand in Chapter IX, "Curriculum Change," analyzes forces that support and restrain curriculum change, proposes strategies for change, and forecasts some developments in the decade of the 1970's. Frank J. Estvan in Chapter X emphasizes how self-discovery and realism influence how youth react and are involved in curriculum development. Both authors provide specific suggestions and illustrative programs.

TRUMP, J. LLOYD, and GEORGIADES, WILLIAM. "The NASSP Model Schools Action Program." NASSP Bulletin vol. 56, no. 364 (May 1972), pp. 116–126.

This article discusses some "myths of change," simple steps, widely publicized, that show how difficult it is to change curriculum and then describes how some schools are progressing in the task.

Index